Secrets to Success for
Professionals in the Autism Field

Secrets to Success for Professionals in the Autism Field

An Insider's Guide to Understanding the Autism Spectrum, the Environment and Your Role

Gunilla Gerland

Jessica Kingsley *Publishers*
London and Philadelphia

The checklist on page 39 is reproduced with kind permission from Kerstin Mahlberg and Maud Sjoblom (published by Mahlburg and Sjoblom, Stockholm).
Figure 5.2 on page 85 is reproduced from the book *Mellan Makt och hjälp (Between Power and Help)* by Greta Marie Skau with kind permission from the publisher Liber Utbildning.

First published in 2013
by Jessica Kingsley Publishers
116 Pentonville Road
London N1 9JB, UK
and
400 Market Street, Suite 400
Philadelphia, PA 19106, USA

www.jkp.com

Copyright © Gunilla Gerland 2013
Illustrations © Ossian Humble 2013

Library of Congress Cataloging in Publication Data
A CIP catalog record for this book is available from the Library of Congress

British Library Cataloguing in Publication Data
A CIP catalogue record for this book is available from the British Library

ISBN 978 1 84905 370 9
eISBN 978 0 85700 724 7

Printed and bound in Great Britain

Contents

1. Helping the Helper Help: A Preface of Sorts About Me, Why and for Whom   11

Part 1: The Professional Role... Interactions and Reflections on Professionalism

2. The Framework and Ideologies: A Chapter on How It Can Be A Constructive Action to Smash a Window   20

3. Same Same but Different: A Chapter for Everyone but Especially for Those Who Have Previously Worked in Psychosocial Treatment Settings   24

4. Just Doing Your Job or Being a True Professional? A Chapter with Some Thoughts About What Professionalism Could Mean   31
   4.1 Awareness, development and change   37
   4.2 Making it right when doing wrong   44
   4.3 Empathy, ethics and moral competence   45
   4.4 Some ideas   52
   4.5 Professionalism in exchanges with clients   57
   4.6 Conclusion   65

5. Remove the Cake Even If You Don't Think It's Ready – Common Pitfalls for Staff: A Chapter on Things You Would Rather Avoid   67
   5.1 Pitfall 1: Falling into another role (other than the professional) – parenting the person with autism   69
   5.2 Pitfall 2: Falling into another role (other than the professional) – being a buddy   73
   5.3 Pitfall 3: That's the way he wants it!   75
   5.4 Pitfall 4: Prohibit or allow – this is not the question!   76
   5.5 Pitfall 5: Steering the will of others   79
   5.6 Pitfall 6: Excessive empathy   80

5.7 Pitfall 7: Lack of empathy 82

5.8 Pitfall 8: Universal truths 86

5.9 Pitfall 9: 'We know this' 87

5.10 Pitfall 10: More normal than normal 89

5.11 Pitfall 11: The gender trap? 91

5.12 Pitfall 12: Good aids that no one uses 93

5.13 Pitfall 13: 'What if everybody...?' 94

5.14 Pitfall 14: Other children will never accept... 95

5.15 Pitfall 15: Normality produces quality of life 96

Part 2: Understanding the Impairments... The Symptoms We Often See and What May Cause Them

6. 'You never know if orange juice will taste like orange juice': A Chapter on Sensory Processing Issues 100

6.1 Visual perception 102

6.2 Tactile perception 109

6.3 Auditory perception 111

6.4 The olfactory sense 115

6.5 The sense of taste 115

6.6 Balance 116

6.7 Proprioception – muscle and joint sense 117

6.8 Interoceptive senses 118

6.9 Synaesthesia 119

6.10 Sensory integration problems 122

6.11 Desensitization (or habituation) 122

6.12 Different is not always a problem 124

6.13 How do we know, what do we do? 126

7. The Man with Two Left Feet: A Chapter on Motor Skills 129

7.1 Motor automatization 130

7.2 Other motor difficulties 136

7.3 Practical implications 137

8. One Person May Be of Many Ages: A Chapter on the Development Perspective 144

8.1 Mentalization in practice 147

9. Say What You Mean and Mean What You Say: A Chapter on Communication 152

9.1 Language comprehension being poorer than verbal expression 152

9.2 Echolalia 153

9.3 Truths, lies and subtext 155
9.4 Announcing your actions 164
9.5 Literal language comprehension 165
9.6 Lack of 'auto correction' 167
9.7 'Attitude' 168
9.8 Restorative communication 170
9.9 Repetitive communication 170

10. Living Without a Spare Petrol Can: A Chapter on Energy
and Stress 173
10.1 The drop excavates the stone (and the straw that broke the
camel's back) 173
10.2 Stress and stress management 176
10.3 Sleep 177
10.4 Time perception 178

11. I Don't Give a Damn About the Chores!
A Chapter on Cognition 180
11.1 Executive functions 180
11.2 Working memory 183
11.3 Categorization 184

12. The Short and Boring Chapter: A Chapter on Definitions,
Incidence and Other Things You May Want to Know, but
Which Are of Little Help in Practice 186
12.1 Definition 186
12.2 Incidence 187
12.3 Causes 188
12.4 Criteria 189
12.5 Work-up 189

Part 3: The Change Process…An Important Element of the Craftsmanship

13. Can We Make a Deaf Person Hear Better by Setting Limits?
A Chapter on Punishment of 'Violations', and Consequences
of Actions 192
13.1 Ch–ch–ch–ch–changes 192
13.2 Truth and consequences 194
13.3 Making the professional 'environmentally friendly' 198
13.4 Avoiding a financial crisis on the trust account 202
13.5 The development of mature strategies –
how does it come about? 204

14. CRAP: A Chapter with Thoughts on the Use of
Confirmations or Rewards, the Idea of Being Affirmative,
and Why Punishments Do Not Work   210
   14.1 Attribution   216
   14.2 Penalty marking is banned!   217
   14.3 A/C – Affirm and Confirm   219

15. Diving Lessons in the Ocean: A Chapter on How to Make
Assessments and Analyses   220
   15.1 Assessment   223
   15.2 Analysis and hypothesis   238
   15.3 Intervention plan   239
   15.4 Evaluation   246
   15.5 Documentation   246
   15.6 Troubleshooting or 'HELP – it does not work!'   247
   15.7 Finally, about assessments   249

16. An Underwater Guide: A Chapter on Common
Contributing Factors in Challenging Behaviours   251
   16.1 Self-esteem   253
   16.2 Ability to form mental images   255
   16.3 Developmental perspective and theory of mind (mentalization) 259
   16.4 Communication   264
   16.5 There and then, here and now: when someone fights or
      injures himself   266

17. The Danger of Focusing on the Behaviour Itself: A Chapter
About What Could Happen If You Do Not Learn to Dive   268

Part 4: Practical Intervention: The Things You May Need in Your Toolbox

18. The Toolbox: An Introduction to the Tools   276

19. Not Having to Learn to Be the Same as 'Others': A Chapter
on Adjustments   280

20. Inform More – and Well! A Chapter on How We Can Work
with Information as a Tool   283
   20.1 Surroundings   283
   20.2 The individual   284

21. Written, Drawn and Other Visual Aids: An Important
    Chapter on Aid That Too Many Get Too Little Of!   292
    21.1 Choices and ability to form mental images   292
    21.2 Informed choices   294
    21.3 Stress, overview and time   295
    21.4 TEACCH   299
    21.5 Social stories™ and comic strip conversations   300
    21.6 Nag-free information   310
    21.7 The time model   312
    21.8 Five-point scale   313
    21.9 Escape routes   314
    21.10 The clothes-by-temperature-thermometer   315

22. Talk and Babble, and a Little About How to Play: A Chapter
    on How to Use Conversation as a Tool   318
    22.1 Conversations for 'landing'   318
    22.2 Solution-focused conversations   320
    22.3 Furnishings   328
    22.4 Conversations in groups   329
    22.5 Younger children: play skills   333
    22.6 Rule play   335

23. Can You Be Yourself When You Do Not Know Who You
    Are? A Chapter on Working with Self-knowledge and
    Self-esteem   336
    23.1 Thought–feeling–action   337
    23.2 Getting your reality confirmed   340
    23.3 Positive feedback   341
    23.4 Balance of power   343
    23.5 Better communication skills break powerlessness   351

24. Methods and Approaches: A Short Chapter About Some
    Specific Techniques That May Be Useful   354
    24.1 Social stories and drawn conversations   355
    24.2 Solution-focused methods   357
    24.3 CAT-kit   357
    24.4 Cognitive behaviour therapy   357
    24.5 Motivational interviewing   358

25. Tips, Tricks and Gadgets: A Chapter on How Some
    Problems Have Been Solved   359
    25.1 Learning to shop   359
    25.2 Structure in the fridge   361
    25.3 Belt bag   361
    25.4 Smart phones and apps   361
    25.5 Brushing teeth and hygiene   362
    25.6 Other stuff   362

26. Finally: The Last Chapter   364

27. But Wait a Minute? Wasn't the Previous Chapter the Last
    Chapter?   365

    Appendix 1   366

    Appendix 2   369

    References   371

    Resources   374

    Index   378

1

Helping the Helper Help

*A Preface of Sorts About Me,
Why and for Whom*

More than 15 years ago, I wrote the book, *A Real Person*, an autobiographical book about growing up with Asperger syndrome, without diagnosis. Through the book I got in contact with people both with and without diagnoses. I became very interested in the field of autism and set out to learn as much as I could. I am still walking down that road. I have studied autism at university and college, and read a whole lot on my own. I have participated in numerous projects and networks and have met hundreds of people with autism of varying severity.My knowledge and experience eventually led to me being sought after, not only as an educator but also as an in-practice staff counsellor or supervisor. And nowadays I am most active in a professional role.

I meet many people with autism spectrum disorders who are doing well and leading a good life, some with the support they need, and some doing great without. This book is not about those people. It is about people with autism spectrum disorders who are high-functioning (i.e. have normal IQ, or above, and can communicate verbally), but who, despite that, have major difficulties, either because of the severity of their disorder or because a long period of incorrect treatment has worsened their situation and symptoms. This book is about people with autism spectrum disorders who need a great deal of highly qualified support but who, unfortunately, do not always receive it.

Many of the clients on the autism spectrum I encounter have received the diagnosis 'Asperger syndrome', a diagnosis which is likely to be eliminated from the diagnostic criteria in the near future. 'Autism spectrum disorders', or just 'autism', will then probably be the common term for this group, whether high-functioning or not (although, since people who received the diagnosis 'Asperger syndrome' will not be re-evaluated, the term will probably still be in use for quite some time). I will most often use the term 'autism' in this book, but when it comes to solutions and strategies, you will find that they might not be appropriate for the group with autism and severe learning disorders, although much of the understanding and thinking that I outline in this book will work for that group as well.

As I have mentioned, I have for more than 15 years been working as an educator and supervisor, and during this time met people with autism in various forms and degrees, and their helpers. It has been – and still is – extremely educative. When I supervise staff they also teach me, by sharing their thoughts, successes and mistakes, to help *them* better assist their users, patients, clients and students (or whatever the user of the services happens to be called in that particular service). When I meet with individuals with autism in services, I get lots of information about how they view their situation, which kind of support they want and how the environment can help them. To summarize what I have learned: for each of them, it's *different*.

If there is anything I have learned over these years, and continue to learn, it's *how different* it is. Whatever suits Shaun does not fit Alex and the right support for Mary is not the right one for Jane, and so on. But at the same time a lot of questions, problems – and solutions – are recurrent.

In practice, therefore, solutions often look very different for different people with autism, but there is still something that is common to all those which work well: the approach and the ideology, the craftsmanship.

The craft that I am talking about here is not a method; it can probably be best described as a filter of knowledge and experience which creates a framework for how to understand and work. If I compare it with other crafts, such as painting, a painter would have many methods at his disposal. He can be a decorative painter or specialized in window restoring, and so on. But basically he must have knowledge of painting and the tools he uses.

This is what I want to try to talk to you about in this book. And that is how I think of this book – as a conversation with you readers. This makes it the most chatty book I've written and it is full of sidetracks and footnotes. This book moves hither and thither (just as a conversation in real life tends to do). My hope is that when you read the last page you will have a greater knowledge, new perspectives for your thoughts and, not least, a lot of new ideas. My hope is that after reading this book you will see opportunities where you might previously have just felt exhausted or run out of ideas.

> If I were to wish for anything, I should not wish for wealth and power, but for the passionate sense of the potential, for the eye which, ever young and ardent, sees the possible. (Søren Kirkegaard, Danish philosopher)

The craftsmanship and the professionalism, thus, is found in a way to think and reason – which in turn leads to an approach, and sometimes to a certain problem-solving. This of course has to be linked to how we think about other things, how we understand the people in our private surroundings, to our *ethos*, our ideology.

This *difference*, of course, also goes for the staff; one particular way of working with autism does not necessarily appeal to everyone. This is why it is important to formulate and describe your way of working, as well as for you to know what you're doing: to make sure that those who are not comfortable with this approach may reflect over it (and perhaps choose differently).

The professions which have the greatest influence over the person with the disorder and therefore are most at risk for privacy violations – which also makes their jobs the most difficult! – are those that today in our society require little training and often have a high rate of turnover in staff. I am referring to such professions as residential home support staff and similar. Sometimes when I work with group homes, day centres, etc., I am appalled at how little the staff knows about autism, even when they are offering special services with a focus on autism. Furthermore, the staff often do not know who is responsible for the supervision of the services, or who makes important decisions affecting service users' lives.

Can we blame the staff for this? Certainly not.

Before I return to this problem, let me just say that I also found many service providers, such as day centre staff, residential supporters and many more who are great professionals and do fantastic work, based on true knowledge and experience. But I must unfortunately conclude, sad as it is, that the other services are in the majority. I would like to change that, although I know how difficult it will be since those who might be in the greatest need of certain areas of knowledge, may not be the ones who attend lectures or will be reading this book.

I would also say that we all fail in professionalism at times, me and you and all others working in this field. Therefore, we need all means, such as books, lectures and others which can provide us with new thoughts, even insights, and lead us into new paths. I myself have found much support and food for thought in books, and you will get acquainted with some of my 'household gods' in the field, later in this book. My guess is that some of you may find a lot of such support for your professional development in this book and others just a little – but everybody should find something!

Now back to the problem of certain services where staff lack sufficient knowledge, methodology, and experience to do a professional job. This 'fault' is not to be found within the people who work in these facilities, but is often in the structure. One of the problems could be that the head or director is often an administrative manager, who can do lots of the decision-making (the director hires staff, is in charge of money for staff education, takes charge of – or does not – staff counselling). At the same time this manager may not have a particularly strong influence on (or knowledge of) the service's practice, as in how the employees respond to help the client. In this case the staff cannot lean on the director for knowledge. Many heads of care have a stressed and pressured appearance and in some places, even this type of managerial role has a high staff turnover. Of course there are exceptions – I meet managers who are both dedicated and knowledgeable – but here I am trying to isolate the problem. You will find good examples later in this book, plenty of them.

Furthermore, there is a problem at the level below, in that we have not created clear enough guidance on how a good-quality help service should be designed – at least in relation to guidelines and regulations which reach right down to 'floor' level, that is, which affect those who work directly with the service users. General and comprehensive quality assurance to assess early on what support the helpers need to provide good quality care for the clients is also lacking in the services for people with autism spectrum disorders.

In spite of previous work on the Autism Act and ongoing revisions, there are still major difficulties in implementing it. Budget cuts are one factor affecting the quality of services. Furthermore, legislation tends not to be detailed enough, as well put by Dr Mitzi Waltz:

> Considering that adverts for direct adult care posts tend to include wording along the lines of 'previous experience is desirable but not necessary', the likelihood that autism expertise will suddenly appear seems remote. Unless the guidance sets clear standards for minimum and desirable training, this requirement may be met on paper rather

than in reality. Indeed, some adult care facilities and agencies that already claim a specialism in autism have nothing of the sort. (Waltz 2010)

Another problem is that when we who have a long experience of autism are talking about what we call autism-specific knowledge, it is hard to describe what it is. Also, we do not know if this is an actual requirement (i.e. if we can claim that all services should have autism-specific knowledge). But perhaps most problematic is that – since it is not clear what autism-specific knowledge really is – services and schools can believe they have it, although this is not so.

Real knowledge is to know the extent of one's ignorance. (Confucius, Chinese philosopher)

What I am getting at is that there is a crucial skill to being an autism professional (and no, it's not called either 'schedule' or 'structure', even though both those things *can* be part of the approach). This autism-specific knowledge that an 'autism professional' must have is, in my opinion, not something you can learn just by reading a book. A painter does not become a painter only by reading about how to paint. But this book is at least an attempt to identify what quality craftsmanship in our field means. What skills, what tools, what models does the professional autism worker have at his disposal? The answer to that question will follow in the next 400 or so pages.

Finally, on a cultural level there is a problem in the underestimation of work in care services. Supporting people in their daily lives is generally perceived as something that everybody 'should know' how to do, something that does not really acquire any skill. No one believes that anyone can be a musician or an economist, but many seem to think that everyone can give good care or support.

Of course, where the autism-specific knowledge is missing, staff often do a good job and give good care by compassion and intuition, but you also need professionalism. Merely to use your 'humanity' when working in a service, such as a residential service or day centre, is just as problematic as if you ceased to be human (as in a way sometimes happens when the use of a method is reduced to routine). Your professionalism must always walk hand in hand with your humanity. How easy it sounds – and how hard it is, if you are not given the right tools!

In the school world – this book also very much addresses teachers and teaching assistants – we can often find more distinct professional roles. But here you rarely have anything more than minimal knowledge about autism from your educational training; you do the best you can. Maybe you think this would be enough? Sometimes it is. But for students with autism who have bigger difficulties, a lack of autism-specific knowledge (i.e. good-quality craftsmanship) unfortunately will complicate their problems. Several examples of this can be found in this book, along with examples of better ways of thinking and working instead.

In my work as a staff trainer and supervisor, I meet with a lot of professionalism, but also quite often deficiencies in professionalism. I feel there are some pitfalls in common, though the types of services or schools are quite different. Perhaps the pitfalls could be avoided if we knew them in advance? Being a professional is really not the same as never falling into such a pit; instead to be professional is to identify when you have fallen down, crawl up and then work to avoid falling into the same pit again. You will understand what I mean later in this book. This book tells you 'do not do it like this' but also tells you 'this is how you can think, or do'. Now you may think that one shouldn't focus on the negative side of a problem. I know that. But there are exceptions. I truly believe that instructions on what to avoid can be very helpful.[1]

If you recognize anything in my bad examples that you, too, have said or done, please remember that you probably have not received the support you needed to have done differently. Do not feel guilty over it – guilt is not a particularly creative, inspiring and progressive feeling. Think rather that you can now choose to do differently in the future!

In this book I am turning to you who are working with people of all ages with autism. I think that whether you are a teacher, psychologist, rehabilitation assistant, doctor, nurse, teaching assistant, supervisor of care service, occupational therapist, social worker, or are in any other profession where you come into contact with people with autism spectrum disorders, this book will give you a greater understanding and quite a few more tools. The book is an attempt to give you as a helper various tools to become a *better helper* – tools to change yourself and your work.

What else do I want to achieve with this book? Well, I hope to give you the context, the framework, I talked about earlier, and I hope

---

1   As in the instructions I read the other day: 'Don't plug it in before you...' and I thought 'Wow, if I had not read that, I would have definitely put the plug in first.' It is even better when the manufacturer explains *why* one should not put the plug in first, as then I can also learn something I can benefit from in the future.

that you in turn can develop it further. Professionalism is both the content of the activity and how it is 'delivered', a job that never will be completed. I hope to give you a dynamic toolbox which you can continue to work with, and that this will ultimately provide better assistance to your students or clients with autism spectrum disorders, so improving the substance of the support as well as the quality of its delivery. Now I am starting to sweat. Can I really give you what I am proposing? It is up to you to decide. What I can promise you is that I have high demands on myself with regard to professionalism.

You may be wondering whether I am suggesting that all services should be alike and work in the same way. No, not at all, and not all pupils, clients and service users with autism spectrum disorders need the same kind of help. But there is a need for a common basis, a kind of positioning that allows quality of service and good professionalism of the staff. Part of this comes from thorough autism-specific knowledge. This book is thus, as I have mentioned, directed to all types of staff, from all kinds of settings, who meet and work with people with autism. But it especially turns to you who are 'standing on the floor' in the often local, sometimes private or county-run services. You often have minimal or no occupation-specific training, you have the hardest and most difficult job and also sometimes so little guidance and training that we should be ashamed as a society for how low we are valuing your work.

I am also, as I just said, turning to those who work in schools; you are also helpers but within another context. You must help your pupils with learning, but also often with their interaction with the environment. I have certainly met many wonderful and dedicated teachers, school psychologists and teaching assistants, evolving in their knowledge and in their professional role towards students with disabilities. But I have unfortunately also on several occasions met with pupils who have been treated unprofessionally and ignorantly (though sometimes with the best of intentions).

I refuse to simply divide the world into good and bad. Instead I believe that almost everyone wants to develop their expertise and professionalism, if only given the tools. Therefore, this is a book for all these professionals. And, even if you work in an operational environment and already have a good standard of professionalism, I hope this book will help you move forward.

Greta Marie Skau, a Norwegian social worker, has written a book on professionalism in her field. She says: 'It is not enough to just do more of what we did yesterday, we need qualitatively new approaches'.[2]

I use a mixed terminology in the book, mostly because it does not feel as if a particular terminology is the best one. Since I think that all of you who are professionals are 'helpers' in some sense I think of the individual with autism as a 'help receiver'. I will often refer to this help receiver as 'the client', 'the (service) user' or 'the pupil', when talking in general terms. But this help receiver may of course be called something else in your services. The disadvantage of general terms is that they make for generalizations. Therefore, I also try to provide a variety of clear examples where there are individuals with names. That is the reason for all the names in this book (plenty!) – as a means of avoiding generalizations.

You should read this book in the manner that suits you. The book has four main sections and you can read them in a different order than given, if you wish. There are numerous cross-references to various sections, mostly because I want to avoid repeating myself but also for you who read in a different order to know what I am referring to.

The chapters in this book that directly deal with the professional role are, I believe, transferable to working with (disabled) people in general. Thus, I hope, you will find the book useful whether you are working with people with 'only' learning disabilities, or with attention deficit hyperactivity disorder (ADHD), or any other disability. These sections are not specific to autism. However, the parts about the craftsmanship (such as the understanding, the approaches, and the tools) are very specifically about autism spectrum disorders.

Note

The examples used in this book are true, but I have, needless to say, changed the details so that they will not be recognized by others. I have also often mixed two real examples into one to avoid recognition. Of course, if for example you had me as a counsellor, you may come to recognize yourself somewhere. If you do, I hope you can understand how valuable it was for me to take part in this, and how I learnt from what happened, and that now your example may help others progress in their professionalism.

Welcome and please step inside!

---

2   My translation, from the book *Gode fagfolk vokser: personlig kompetanse i arbeid med mennesker* (Skau 2005).

PART 1

The Professional Role

...Interactions and Reflections on Professionalism

2

The Framework and Ideologies

A Chapter on How It Can Be A Constructive Action to Smash a Window

The outlook we have, the philosophy regarding people, will control how we interact with people not only in our everyday lives, but also in our work. You may have a private philosophy, an ideology (perhaps associated with a political ideology or a religious belief), and a professional philosophy (e.g. coupled with a treatment method). Ideally, these cannot be too far apart, or you will probably not feel satisfied at work. Some people know a lot about their ideology and reflect on it, but in others it is more unconscious. The unconscious ideology needs to be not less compassionate or less human or less good, but it can be a bit more problematic because it is harder to spot.

To consider your philosophy and ideology in relation to your work is a good start, for example by asking yourself questions like these:

- If I get angry with William because he is behaving violently when he is upset, how does this reflect on my view of William, how I am interpreting him? Can I understand him in a different way, and what would this mean?

- If I think that Sophie makes unreasonable demands, what does this say about how I am interpreting her, how does this reflect my understanding of her disability?

- In what ways do we commonly interpret the clients' or students' behaviours in our service? Am I interpreting in the same way as my colleagues?

- Through what filters do we see our services? If we try another, how would things look then?

I dare say that it is very common for professionals – often without even realizing it – to blame disabled people for their behaviours. This is reflected in mindsets which tell us that he or she must learn that 'you can't hit others'; must 'tell right from wrong'; must know that 'you should not be wasting your money', and similar. Or maybe you say that someone has destructive behaviours, is manipulative or 'seeks attention'.

As I see it, however, our pupils and clients with autism always do *their best*. Given their abilities this is the most constructive thing they can do at that moment (even if the result is destructive). If they broke a window and threw things around, it was the most constructive thing they could do. They didn't have the means to behave differently, and when the means are lacking, it is our responsibility to provide them. The *implication* of an action can be destructive (at worst, someone is injured) but the intention is not destructive and thus, as I see it, nor is the act in itself. This may seem like a construction of thought, since I deliberately choose to see it this way. It is, however, useful because it has a significant bearing on how I respond to people.

On ideologies when working with people with developmental disabilities, psychologist Herbert Lovett has written:

> There is no such thing as a value-free way of working with others. The challenge is to keep ourselves honest and to consider what values we actually use in our work and not just the values we say we use. One of the sad and painful ironies of psychology in the field of developmental disabilities is that we psychologists have judged (and often hurt) people on the basis of their observed behaviour. We, however, have overlooked, excused, and even congratulated one another on the basis of our intentions. (Lovett 1996)

Your ethos shapes your approach. Not only in a direct way, but also implicitly, and I shall shortly give you an example of this. First, let me just clarify that I do not think it works out quite as well to learn a way to relate to clients or pupils with autism as 'a technique'. It does not necessarily change your way of thinking, and means the staff has few possibilities to develop and modify their tools when necessary (and necessary it will be!). Unfortunately, this is the most common way of educating staff. 'Do such', the trainer says, but is not clear about why you should do this or what to avoid.

The art of teaching understanding and professional interchanges is much more about understanding how what I teach can be interpreted and misinterpreted, than it is about teaching what I know. People absorb information in different ways because the information is received within their personal framework, a framework which is modelled from their past experiences and their ideologies. Therefore, if I want to teach you something, I must build a foundation, as in an excellent recipe for a delicious chocolate cake which says: 'Bake at 175 degrees for 15 minutes. *Remove the cake even if you don't think it's ready!*' This is an author of a cookbook who has made mistakes and learned from them. Remarkably few recipes – be it food recipes or methods of interventions in the autism field – provide this kind of (necessary, in my opinion) instructions.

And yes, I promised to give an example of how a conscious ideology also implicitly affects the human interchange.

EXAMPLE

Once I visited a service providing pre-school, school and after-school recreation for children. The staff told me that some years earlier they had begun to listen to themselves and they reacted to what they heard. They heard that they were sitting in the staff room saying things like (you probably recognize this if you work with children):

'If only his mother would not…'

'She has such a demanding father.'

'If only John's parents could…'

'Hannah's mother doesn't listen to anything we say!'

'Chloe's parents let her stay up so late.'

'Samuel's parents don't set any boundaries.'

In this service it was decided to stop talking about the parents in this way. 'We decided to always assume that parents have good reason to do what they do even if we do not always understand it,' they told me.

Interestingly, what occurred was that they all felt they at once had a better climate of co-operation with the parents, even if they had not knowingly changed anything in their direct approach to the parents (these comments had obviously only been made when no parents were around). But it impacted on their way of responding to the parents. The ideology we have seeps over into our behaviour, whether we know it or not.

Finally, one more quote from the book *Learning to Listen: Positive Approaches and People with Difficult Behaviour*:

When someone using a service is described as attention seeking or manipulative, the service system itself is likely to be in need of significant behavioural change. I say this without any malice or judgement: just as people who use services adapt their behaviours to cope with a difficult world, so do the people providing services. And just as people who use services need acceptance, warmth, and understanding to change, so do the people providing that help. (Lovett 1996)

3

Same Same but Different

A Chapter for Everyone but Especially for Those Who Have Previously Worked in Psychosocial Treatment Settings

Many behaviours or difficulties we see in people with disorders within the autism spectrum may appear to be alike, and therefore you can easily be fooled into believing that they arise for the same reasons. This is true both when comparing individuals with autism among themselves, or comparing them with those without such disorders.

In 'standard development' there are a number of – sometimes problematic – behaviours that children and adolescents exhibit. Sometimes we also see these behaviours in people with autism. In standard development, we solve some of them by setting limits, while this often does not work at all in autism spectrum disorders. (You can read more about *why* this approach is not useful further on in this book. It has, among other things, to do with whether you have the ability to understand consequences in the same way as others).

It can be particularly hard for staff who previously worked in psychodynamically orientated or psychosocial services, which not only have a tradition of interpreting behaviours in a particular way (using concepts such as transference, resistance and splitting, etc.), but also often include a way to respond to children and adolescents which in neuropsychiatric disorders becomes counterproductive. In supervision of staff I have encountered many such cases: professionals who have worked with a psychodynamic approach, and brought this perspective into services for people with autism spectrum disorders.

I have to emphasize that it is not usually their fault that they have an inadequate 'gear' for the job; they were never given the correct tools when they were recruited. It is as if we employ them as firefighters when formerly they were carpenters, and now the employer sends them into the fire with only carpenters' trousers on and a hammer in their hands. The snag is that the carpenter in the burning house quickly realizes that he is wrongly equipped, although in our field it is not always that obvious. Here your equipment will often control the way you perceive the world. As in a quote often attributed to Mark Twain: 'If all you have is a hammer, everything will look like a nail.'

One example is Chris, a teacher in his forties, newly employed in a special school for pupils with high-functioning autism.

EXAMPLE

Chris arrives to supervision for the first time in his new workplace. A colleague mentions how many questions the pupils have about what is 'right', and about the motives behind other people's actions. Chris quickly points out how important it is to be just a 'present adult' and argues that it is not so important to actually respond to young people's questions about how 'to be', 'why people do this or that' or what 'normal' really means.

Chris previously worked in a treatment centre and he feels that the adolescents there (who did not have autism) frequently asked such questions too. He perceives this as a searching for and construction of identity during the teenage years. With adults present as good role models it will work out just fine, according to him.

Chris looks around in the meeting room and expects to get 'gold stars' from the supervisor, as this was the right answer in supervision at his old job. My job is to explain to Chris (without embarrassing him, preferably) that he is wrong. The questions may sound alike but here they are asked for other reasons. Our pupils ask questions about what is normal rather from a (painful) recognition that they are actually on the other side of that border.

In standard development young people often struggle with the question of what actually is normal and if they really belong there. Resolving this conflict then often means, in one way or another, coming to (or 'landing' at) the conclusion 'Yes, I'm normal but what normal is can be very different.'

But pupils at this school do actually have a disability – one which certainly does not make them 'abnormal'– but which means they really, genuinely, find themselves on the other side of that invisible border between being diagnosed and non-diagnosed. They also need to reach a conclusion, but when the runway looks different, the landing also will. This is the first thing.

The second is that young people with autism often lack the ability to deduce answers to questions arising from a situation. They cannot comprehend the implicit because the disorder means deficits in mental imagery (difficulty in inventing general internal images). This is typically so in things that others just 'know'. As in how to show someone that you are interested in him or her; in why people react differently if you are seated equally close in a sauna as you do on the bus; or in what someone really is expressing with their body language.

And the third is that the very basis of Chris' reasoning does not apply since we know that in autism imitation is not a primary learning strategy. It means that using adults as role models will not work.

Now your question might be: what should we do, then? I will not answer that question here since there is never one simple answer to an example problem. You always have to dive into and poke about in all the individual factors. We will do this further on in this book; at that point we will look at the many symptoms and many ways to support development which are at hand when working in the autism field.

EXAMPLE

Another example is Sheri, who for 15 years worked in an environmental-therapeutic setting. She has a great deal of experience with girls acting out, and with problematic sexual behaviours. Now Sheri meets young girls with autism spectrum disorders; these girls are, however, adults, in terms of the law. The girls with autism that Sheri now encounters have a sexually risky behaviour which raises concerns.

Sheri has seen young girls behave like this before but she feels it is an even bigger problem with these girls since they – due to their disorder – are even more vulnerable. They cannot see others' intentions and thus risk getting into more difficult and even dangerous situations.

These girls are making contact with men through the internet, whom they then meet with; they go into town and get picked up by men, in many cases more than twice as old as themselves. Sheri interprets this as a question of adults needing to put their foot down – someone needs to talk to them about what is right and wrong, about 'acceptable behaviour'. In Sheri's mind the girls are seeking limits.

Sure, the young girl with this behaviour, but *without* an autistic disorder, can often display unacceptable behaviours in a limit-seeking way, subconsciously wanting adults to be clear about what is acceptable, and thus show that they really care. So it may be a relief: 'Whew, I cannot do just anything, adults will see and react to what I do.' In the girls with autism whom Sheri is now supporting, the behaviour *may look the same* but there may be completely different reasons for it. They may have been bullied throughout school, always the ones who were never even noticed by the guys. Now suddenly, for the first time, they find themselves attractive to older men. For the first time they feel that they are attractive. We cannot respond to this as a testing of limits, rather we must be clear about what the issue is. This does not mean that we will easily solve the problem. But the first step to a solution lies in acknowledging and clarifying this fact – putting it on the table. Maybe we can open up a conversation with: 'Hey, I understand that it feels pretty good when a guy comes up and is interested in you...' But if you do as Sheri did and say, 'It is my job as an adult to tell you that it is not acceptable that you do this' you will perhaps, as Sheri did, get the response 'Shut up, bitch, I will never talk to you again' and then complete silence.[1]

Often, phenomena that look the same in people with autism spectrum disorders occur for a variety of reasons. Let us for example talk about lack of hygiene, a fairly common problem. It is easy to believe that the lack of hygiene is a common symptom in autism that can be corrected in a certain way. But there may be completely different reasons for such a problem even within the group.

EXAMPLE

Adnan, an adult male with autism, argued strongly that he would take a shower when he needed, and change his clothes when they were dirty, and that he could manage on his own without help from residential staff. He was not disapproving of the staff, it was just that he was actually quite sure that he did not need assistance with this. The staff felt that forcing him into support he did not think he needed and did not want, would be a violation of his privacy.

Around the same time staff called from the day centre and pointed out that Adnan smelled so bad that the other clients there would not go near him. The residential staff felt caught between their desire to help Adnan and to respect him. (In addition, they felt that they as professionals would look bad in the eyes of the day service, when 'their client' was not clean; they felt Adnan's lack of hygiene suggested that they did not do their job well.)

From me as a supervisor they wanted the answer to whether they should force help on Adnan, or leave him (see Pitfall 4). I could not of course advise them to do either one until we had investigated the situation further. Why did Adnan think that he did this so well? Did he actually shower, but not well enough? Did he not understand the consequences of smelling or looking dirty? Did he just say that he took a shower, though he did not do it? Was it a question of integrity, and so on?

---

1   Since perseverance also can be part of the autism spectrum symptoms, as well as actually meaning what you are saying, the girls also stood by their words. They never spoke to Sheri again, ever. Which made it, to say the least, hard for her to support them in any way.

It finally turned out that the crux for Adnan was that he had a visually very concrete conception of the word 'dirty'. To him, being dirty meant that you could see the dirt in the form of a stain, for example. And of course we can all understand that you can start smelling pretty badly, long before you actually see the dirt on your body. He also washed his clothes only if they were stained. How we understand a problem will influence the intervention and in this case it means, of course, to help Adnan understand the concept of *dirt* in a broader sense.

EXAMPLE

Jessica was a young girl with autism, who also had problems with hygiene. Jessica went to a college for students with special needs, that housed residents. The staff in the student accommodation did not really know how to handle Jessica. They found it incomprehensible that she smelled bad, since every morning she went into the shower and stayed there quite a long time. And she looked wet when she came out.

It turned out to be a question of motor skills. Jessica had, as do many with autism, significant motor deficiencies. She would stand for a long time in the shower with the water running, but she was only able to lather a small spot on her stomach. She did not have enough motor co-ordination to get the soap all over her body, and maybe she had not really understood what it was that others meant by 'taking a shower'. Due to her motor problems, Jessica needed hands-on help in the shower and eventually it turned out she also wanted help to wear make-up (she had always wanted to but could not use mascara and lipstick because of her poor motor skills).

Again, it is interesting to bring forth the development perspective. I will go on about the importance of such perspective in several places in this book, and then devote the whole of Chapter 8, 'One Person May Be of Many Ages', to this. If one puts a three-year-old in the shower, puts soap on his hand and asks him to wash himself, he will do exactly as Jessica did: lather a small spot, often on his tummy.

EXAMPLE

Mark, who lived in a group home, told his staff that he understood very well that you should keep yourself clean, and that it smelled bad when he did not, but that he actually did not care about it. We found that in Mark the problem was a combination of deficits in mental imagery, and difficulty in understanding the outcome (that no one wanted to sit next to Mark in the lunch restaurant, and that people would withdraw when he wanted to ask something).

How we understand the problem, and who the individual is, will influence how we respond to it. We must find not only the cause but also the approach that suits this particular individual.

I will not give you more examples here, but for the sake of clarity I want to mention that a lack of hygiene can have a variety of additional causes as well as those I mentioned (sensory processing issues, for example) and that this reasoning – that a behaviour may seem similar but can have many different origins – is valid in every imaginable symptom and behaviour you may encounter when dealing with people with autism, in all types of services and settings.

But can't what looks the same actually be the same? As in the very common question 'How do we know what are "normal teenage symptoms" and what is autism?' Well, of course we cannot know this in a general way, but if we understand the problem, we can also understand how we can reason about it.

Table 3.1 Teenager behaviour

'Normal' teenager	Teenager with autism
Does not clean his room	Does not clean his room
Sleeps half the day	Sleeps half the day

Look at Table 3.1. We can imagine that the 'normal' teen behaviour is due to several things: changed priorities (other things than cleaning his or her room or spending time with family are more important), the physical and hormonal changes of puberty, and an increased need for self-determination being demonstrated, to mention just a few examples. In autism theoretically these things could be valid too; the teenager with autism is also a teenager, of course. But we also know that autism spectrum disorders may mean that it is difficult to organize and plan things, or to get started with an activity such as cleaning up your room.

So if the teenager with autism sleeps half the day it could be because he or she has is using up too much energy and needs more recovery time and needs more, or problems with their circadian rhythm, and if so, we need to help the individual with that. But it can also be normal teenage behaviour. The more information we acquire about the individual and the situation the easier it becomes to guess what is what.

So we try to make sure that the young person with autism has the tools to clean up (and I am not just referring to a mop and a bucket); we create the conditions that make it possible. If then the individual does not clean his room, even though we supported him, and we now conclude that there is actually a demonstration of teenage priority change, protest and demand for autonomy going on, we can choose to applaud it (not literally), since this actually means progress, considering the disability. What? Progress – how is that? My point is that if we now see these normal teenage patterns of demonstrating autonomy, and keep in mind that many with autism do not liberate themselves from their parents as easily[2], or in the same way, as their peers do, it's a good thing.

Figure 3.1: 'I refuse to clean up in here!'

If you are working and making an effort to avoid the pitfalls (which will be described in detail in Chapter 5), such as Pitfall 10 'More normal than normal', you will find a tool for the assessment of 'What is autism spectrum; what is just teenage behaviour?' It may also be true that the reason for the apparently similar problem *actually is* the same in two individuals, but that it still must be resolved or addressed in different ways. The reason for this is that each individual has their own personality and unique situation. What suits one may not suit the other. The example of Andrew, Scott, Dawn and Tracy on p.97 gives more insight into this.

---

2   Sure, if you are a parent of a teenager, or have ever been a teenager yourself, the word 'easy' may not be the first that comes to mind. I mean 'easy' as in automatically, and as in compared to those with autism. Not 'easy' as in 'painless'.

4

Just Doing Your Job or Being a True Professional?

A Chapter with Some Thoughts About What Professionalism Could Mean

In the workplace a group can have very different ambitions, and also different views on what professionalism really means. I do not believe it to be possible to establish in any definitive way what professionalism actually is. Merely by talking about how we look at our work and about the professional role, we can catch sight of new things, make it clear to ourselves what we think and become more conscious. Perhaps it might be a definition of professionalism, to be conscious? No, I would rather put it that *the quest for consciousness* is one definition, among others. But there are of course many ways of defining professionalism and soon you'll see some examples.

First, let me quote Emilie Kinge (1999), a Norwegian pedagogue who wrote a book titled *Empathy in Adults Who Meet Children with Special Needs*.[1] Much of her book is relevant to other professionals who work with people (at any age) with special needs.

> I am convinced that the only real possibility of helping others lies in expanding and developing our own understanding of them and – just as importantly – showing our understanding in ways that expand their own awareness and understanding of themselves so that they can accept and respect themselves as they are.[2]

Working with our own understanding of the individual is thus a part of our professionalism, I would say – and this work is continuously ongoing. But others of course may define professionalism differently.

---

1   My translation of the Swedish title *Empati hos vuxna som möter barn med särskilda behov* (Kinge 1999).
2   My translation of the Swedish text.

I asked participants at a lecture I gave what they thought professionalism meant, and the answers were as diverse as these:

Carer:

- Being empathetic
- Being open-minded.

Head of a residential service:

- Making use of knowledge and experience and having a genuine interest in doing the best for the client
- Constantly developing and challenging yourself
- Evaluation of services in a salutogenic, holistic perspective.

Nurse:

- Knowledge
- The right [adequate] education [training]
- Suitable for the job
- Ethical thinking
- Human thinking.

Psychologist:

- Knowledge
- Engagement/attendance [presence]
- Method/approach.

Occupational therapist:

- Knowing the disabilities and understanding how to work, and then also actually working according to this in all daily interchanges
- Seeing the perspective of the disabled person
- Acting on knowledge.

Residential assistant:

- Being one step ahead and anticipating situations.

Residential assistant, short-term residential service:

- Being respectful
- Knowledge
- Common sense
- Trust/confidence
- Being empathic
- Structured
- Understanding.

Teacher:

- Having a good knowledge of the disability
- Meeting and treating everyone equally
- Not taking things personally (e.g. when challenging behaviour occurs).

Employee at day centre:

- Sensitivity
- Humility
- Positive attitude
- Being able to ask for help if problems arise.

Teacher:

- Seeing the individual in his own personal history and context and not just reacting to what is occurring.

Team leader/pedagogue:

- Working in an evidence-based way, and using knowledge that you actually have

- Focusing on for who or for what am I here?
- Respecting and doing the job on the basis of joint decisions.

Psychologist:

- Knowledge
- Respect for the individual and family
- Listening.

Carer, social support service:

- Meeting people with empathy and interest, and having the courage to be yourself and yet leave outside certain feelings and values.

Not stated occupation:

- Seeing details
- Being responsive
- Translating theory into practice.

Co-ordinator of young people with disabilities:

- Uniformity
- Rule of law/security of life and property
- Efficiency.

Supported living assistant:

- Knowledge of disability
- The staff working as a team
- Assuming a professional role when coming to work
- Being clear and explicit.

These were just a few examples, and there is something in all these thoughts about professionalism.

One reflection when reading my participants' descriptions of what professionalism means, is that perhaps we can sort out some things that are *prerequisites for professionalism*, but are not professionalism in itself. Knowledge, for example, I would say is a necessary condition for professionalism. But there are people who have knowledge, and still are not professional (we probably all have, unfortunately, at some time encountered one of those). Having an open mind might be more of a part of professionalism, which is what I am getting at here.

Similarly, one might argue that although experience (which many participants also wrote in their notes) is a prerequisite for professionalism, the professionalism lies in how you make use of your experience. Is the experience used as the basis for arguments like 'I have always done this, and it definitely works', or as a ground for reflection? I would like to see experience as a chest of drawers, where there is much information to retrieve, but there is also an awareness that each 'now' is a new drawer, and is never exactly the same as the previous one. Or maybe we should see it as a dynamic trampoline where what I encounter at work today can bounce off my old experiences, and old knowledge, and then grow into something new. Could it be that professionalism is not what you know – although as I said, knowledge is a necessary condition – but *how to use what you know?*

I feel it has been interesting to reflect on the concept of professionalism as it is obviously something you want to pursue. This applies both to the occupational role: *to be professional*, and to the service or school as a whole: *to run a professional service*. It's not measurable, though. And as you have just seen, professionalism can be wisely, but differently, defined by professionals, even within the same profession. Could it be that reflecting upon the concept – that quest for consciousness which I mentioned earlier – is an essential part of professionalism?

How would I myself describe professionalism if I spontaneously threw down a few words? Something like this:

- Reflection

- Being in a process of growth and progress

- Being confident in your knowledge as a basis for your work

- Always trying to see several sides of an issue

- Being able to live with doing the 'wrong' thing sometimes (including apologizing when necessary)

- Actively trying to be non-prestigious

- Respecting the majority decisions but also daring to stand up for something I really believe in.

I think that some things as mentioned by my participants, such as 'showing respect', 'being sensitive', 'seeing details' and many other great things they wrote, are not really professionalism in itself. Being disrespectful is certainly unprofessional, but showing respect is an obvious minimum requirement for people to even say they are doing their job. 'Being curious' is perhaps more a personality trait (which facilitates the emergence of professionalism), but is it professionalism per se? Could professionalism be seen as a set of stairs?

High level of professionalism

Professionalism

Doing the job, but nothing more

Unengaged/Not suitable for the job

Figure 4.1: The stairs of professionalism

Think about your approach to your job and ask yourself the following questions: Where do I find myself on the stairs? How would I like it to be? How do I know when it is the way I want it to be (that is, how do I recognize my goal when I get there, how do I feel when I've reached it, and what would it look like when I've reached the goal?). How could I take half a step towards what I want? If you find yourself on the first step (you probably won't, since people on the first step rarely read books like this) – there is nothing to be ashamed of. Almost everyone has at one time or another found themselves in a job they weren't suitable for. Your responsibility, however, is to realize that it is time to move on to another job. People with disabilities are in many ways vulnerable, and they deserve staff who are committed.

I once asked a group of staff to anonymously choose how they wanted the service to be; they could choose from a five-point scale which went from 'I'm not sure I want to be working here right now' and 'I am satisfied if I have a nice day when I'm at work', to the top of the scale 'I want to work in a service that is leading the field'. In the process of getting the group to pull in the same direction (as was my assignment), it was important to point out how differently co-workers actually looked at their job and the service.

As an employer, colleague or supervisor, you can neither require nor assume that everyone has the same level of ambition. And if there is tension in a group which leads to joint decisions not being followed, it might help to clarify this. Reflecting together over the different levels of ambition can also be helpful to those who are actually not cut out for the job; it may help them to catch sight of this. I have seen this happen more than once.

If you work in such a group, you can suggest to the group that you anonymously complete a questionnaire describing different levels of ambition. You all have the same pens so that everyone can answer honestly, and no one is allowed to talk about how they have responded. Then count the results, and discuss such things as 'What could motivate those who currently have a low level of ambition?' Here it is good to use solution-focused techniques for the discussion (described later in this book – see p.63 and p.320). You may also like to do a brainstorming, when everyone is allowed to bring up ideas without censoring or thinking too much. Someone takes notes and afterwards you sort the ideas together and look at what may be reasonable and possible.

If it is a group of staff who are 'pulling in different directions' or often decide things that are never implemented, it may be helpful to seriously discuss such matters as:

- What is our minimum level for it to be all right to work in this group (for example, to follow the mutual decisions)?

- What procedures do we need to follow up on what we have decided?

- How can we ensure that everyone speaks up? (Otherwise it is often the same people who speak, and the same who are always silent in staff meetings and planning meetings.)

4.1 Awareness, development and change

If professionalism in some sense is consciousness, or the quest for consciousness (about the state of affairs, of what we do, how we do it and why), then of course the truth about the group of staff is also part of this awareness. It is a fact of life, and will always be so, that we are good at different things. Often we know very well ourselves, and so do our colleagues, where our strengths and weaknesses lie, but it is, in our culture, a taboo to talk about it. Although Maryam and Steve are uncertain, and therefore quite unskilled, in establishing contact with the pupils' or clients' families, they have just as many (and sometimes difficult!) relatives in their caseload to deal with because…yes, why? Because this is 'how we do it'.

But OK, let us accept this – this justice that says that responsibility for contact with the clients' families should be equally distributed among staff. This means that just because Annie and Amir always make good contact with the families of their clients, they should not have to have more families to deal with than others.

Let us now assume that this is a reasonable argument (though it might not be). What can we do about it then? Will Maryam and Steve always have to be nervous about meetings with families? And do the parents of their clients (or pupils or patients, be it a school or a psychiatric service) have to feel offended or not listened to (or whatever is the effect of the unskilled response)? Please note that I think that both Maryam and Steve are very skilled in their work *in other areas*. Maryam may be the only teacher ever who got this pupil to open her maths books and Steve might have built a solid and trustful relationship with one of the most difficult clients, which means this client makes serious progress in several areas.

Well, what can we do? If we acknowledge that this is the state of affairs, we can begin by letting Maryam and Steve attend when Annie and Amir are meeting with families. They can be instructed to spot what Amir does that works. They can practise in role play to increase their skills. And furthermore, we can create pronounced routines of how we conduct dialogues with families, that is, a checklist to help everyone carry out these interchanges as well as possible. For sure, Maryam and Steve may perhaps never be as skilled as Amir and Annie in this particular area, but could we not, at least (for the families' sake) give them the best chance possible?

Creating policies and documentation to help the employees to be as professional as possible and to follow its operational objectives, ideology and ethos are part of good craftsmanship in any profession.

This checklist is from a school for adolescents with special needs:

DIALOGUES WITH PARENTS[3]

We assume that they want to:

- have a good relationship with their child
- be proud
- feel that they are a resource
- have a positive impact on their child
- hear good news about the child
- receive information about the child's strengths
- receive information about everything that happens.

If we have to call home about something:

- We say we have a problem/a concern that we do not know how to solve.
- We provide factual information devoid of value judgement about what happened.
- We ask for help. We want to find a joint project with families.
- If a parent cannot come up with ideas, we present several proposals, and the parent chooses.
- We repeat what we have come up with, and who should do what and what the first small step is.
- We make an appointment for follow-up.
- We always end by THANKING (e.g. for taking the time to talk to us, for their ideas and views, for caring, for letting us call).

But how many checklists are possible in a service, you may wonder. It would be absurd to write down *everything*, one might object. Well, sure, maybe you cannot have a written policy document and explicit procedures for each element of work – but you can probably have many, many more than currently exist in most services and schools I come across.

I would like us to, for a moment, focus on what I mentioned a while ago: that professionalism could mean *development* or *being in progress*. This is something addressed by the Norwegian social worker Greta Marie Skau, mentioned in Chapter 1. She writes, among other things, that nowadays being a professional in social, health or educational professions is, to a great degree, to be in a process of *change*.

---

3   Thanks to Kerstin Måhlberg and Maud Sjöblom for letting me publish their checklist.

Responsibility can no longer mean defending the permanent. It should rather mean the endeavour to develop something which is qualitatively better than what we have today. [...] Where shall we start? The tasks may seem so overwhelming, the areas so many. But whichever the field of action each of us chooses as his primary field of accomplishment, we cannot pass what is closest to us: the quality we ourselves represent, both in relation to ourselves and in relation to others. (Skau 2005)[4]

This is difficult, according to Skau, since employees in social and health care have not learned enough about leading and participating in processes of change. In these areas the progress or development of the employees is not prioritized, and therefore we see that the whole sector is lagging behind in relation to the tasks it faces, with constant improvisations and emergency solutions as a result.

The staff therefore needs to be taught how to lead the process of change themselves, and Skau wisely wonders how it could be possible for staff to support and guide pupils, patients and clients through processes of change, without any experience or knowledge of such processes among themselves.

When dealing with autism the work is so multidisciplinary that sometimes it is unimportant whether you are an occupational therapist, special education teacher, psychologist, residential supporter or otherwise. I am not saying that the training and experience you have is insignificant; rather that everyone, regardless of their background, must be what the Division TEACCH (see p.299) names a generalist. Therefore, there is also a lot that is said and written for a certain occupational group, which also applies to other professions.

One example of this is Professor Max van Manen's (1991) definition of what makes a good teacher; the points he makes are equally valid for a nurse in psychiatry or a residential or day centre supporter, or a social worker. Van Manen questions whether pedagogy can be taught at all, under a heading which gives food for thought: 'Can teaching be taught – or are real teachers found or made?' He points out that one can train teachers (and again, this applies to all professions where you care for or support human beings), but that not everyone with the same training becomes a good teacher.

One thing van Manen highlights is that there is always a degree of irrationality when it comes to working with people, therefore it is not

---

4   From the Norwegian book *Gode fagfolk vokser: personlig kompetanse i arbeid med mennesker* (Skau 2005). My translation. (The title translates: *Good Professionals are Growing: Personal Expertise in Working with People.*)

enough to know your subject and be well prepared. He argues that the real teacher has a good sense of *timing*, similar to the timing a stand-up comedian must have. Additionally, van Manen speaks of *reflection*, and suggests that it is good to reflect before and after, but that being a real teacher calls for a 'reflective decision-making' here and now; thus we need to reflect on what is happening as it happens. Van Manen calls this *reflection in action*.

Personally, I would say that the talent for this varies among people, just as our musical or artistic talents vary. But likewise, just as with playing an instrument or making a painting, you can train your ability to do this. As an external supervisor and counsellor of staff I have worked a lot with practising reflection. I usually start by allowing the group to reflect a little each day (in their own notebooks), and later give them assignments where they practise simultaneous reflection at work. Reflection in action is about dividing your attention, so that a part of you can interact, while another part of you analyses what is happening.

Professional progress and personal maturity often come hand in hand. And that's great, in my opinion, that you can use your job to mature personally. Maturity is as hard to define as is professionalism, but I would say that at least to some degree, it too is about awareness. Once made aware of certain things, it is difficult (or at least more difficult) to opt out of the development opportunity that lies in the perception and understanding of what is going on.

Margareta Normell is a Swedish pedagogue and psychotherapist who writes about the need for emotional maturity in the teaching profession. Again, this goes for many other professions. Normell argues that we left behind the obeying culture (with fear of the authorities) and today have a responsibility culture, with much freedom, and many possibilities. But this is not always easy. Hence the need for emotional maturity.

> I believe many agree that today it is harder to hide behind a professional role than it ever was before. Now the human meeting is often emphasized in a completely different way, and this puts greater demands on personal maturity than at the time when you could, so to speak, leave part of your person outside of work. (Normell 2007)[5]

---

5 From the Swedish book *Pedagogens inre rum – om betydelsen av känslomässig mognad* (Normell 2007). My Translation: (The title translates: *The Inner Rooms of the Teacher – The Importance of Emotional Maturity*.)

To be emotionally mature, according to Normell, is to be aware of, to be able to express and to tolerate your emotions. Additionally it means to make use of your feelings. Feelings are always a source of information, they tell us how to act. If you shut off what you feel, you become 'remote-controlled', which is why you need to practise listening within.

Man is basically quite lazy. This may sound negative but is not necessarily so. Idleness has probably had a survival value; to preserve energy has been important during evolution. And since many of us are at least a bit lazy (I certainly am), change means hard work, whether it means changing everyday patterns (e.g. eating more healthily or exercising more) or professional patterns (embracing new ways of working). So the first step perhaps is to realize and accept that it will not be easy. Change requires work.

Some, such as Björn Lenke (Lenke and Wennberg 1999)[6], have argued that we all have some personal instinct traps, sort of knee-jerk reactions, which often keep us from reaching our goals, or doing things we set out to do. Recognizing that trap, being aware of what it is that makes us do certain things, even though we decided to do otherwise, gives us at least a choice. Again, it is about being conscious. The trap can, for example, consist of ingrained thought patterns and emotions: 'I might as well do it tomorrow'; 'Liz isn't doing what we decided, so why should I?' Or feeling sorry for yourself as in: 'Poor me, I really deserve a break'; 'I'm so tired today so I can allow myself this'. Or something else. Only you can learn to recognize your personal trap, and when you spot it, it will be at least somewhat easier to avoid being trapped by it.

To create the conditions for professionalism to emerge or grow is, I think, to ensure that tools are available to those who work in the service or school (preferably tools which are so good that they make impossible the choice of 'Doing the job, but nothing more' and lacking any degree of professionalism). My point is to build routines, methods and policies into practice. They should be there because we know we can all lose our professionalism from time to time. I do not believe that the procedures and policies are the same as professionalism; absolutely not. But I do think that they can help to facilitate professionalism

---

6   The Swedish book *Instinktsfällan: om människoskap, ledarskap, gruppens dynamic* (Lenke and Wennberg 1999) translates as *The Instinct Trap* (my translation).

being kept alive. What I see is that the staff need *aids* to maintain their professionalism. They also need *visual clarity, structure and continuity.*[7]

Haven't we all at some point worked in a group where we agree on something at a meeting, but some, or even everyone, then refuses to do what was agreed? To attend staff meeting after staff meeting, to discuss and decide to adopt new ways of working, and then not pursue what was decided does not come across as an effective way to work, and yet it frequently occurs. Why is it so often like this in the care professions?

Let us compare this with a company that produces something, some merchandise. Say the management and staff jointly (or just the management) decide that as of Monday they will have a new routine, be it on the shop floor or in the office – I would say that the probability is higher that the new routine actually will be implemented in the shop or office than in social services, mental health professions and schools. Why is that?

It's probably a matter of culture and leadership as well as measurable results. Often the management of commercial businesses are more present and may see or receive signals if some of the employees do not follow the new routine. If this happens the head will have a talk with this employee individually, to find out what is going on. One problem with our care services is that we often do not have a leader or manager who is close enough to the service for her to know who follows the new routine and who does not (or perhaps even which decisions about new routines are made).

We also often have a culture of consensus within schools, social services and similar, which makes us want everyone to agree, and it feels wrong to steamroller someone. We are not sure who should tell Alison or Tony that it is not OK to disregard the new routine, and to tell on them to the head feels like too big a step.

I believe this is due to a culture which is characterized so much by the idea that I cannot criticize someone without being absolutely sure that I myself in all respects am spotless. What easily happens is that since I am not flawless, I can never criticize or question anyone.

Moreover, if Curt wants to question the fact that Alison does not follow the mutual agreement or routine, he could be afraid that Alison will respond 'But what about you, you always leave five minutes early' or 'But what about you, you never do the dishes in the lunch room'.

---

7   Oops, that's exactly what they say that people with autism spectrum disorder need. Imagine it being so universal!

Being able to respectfully give and take criticisms is definitely a part of emotional maturity and this ability can be learnt.

We therefore need pronounced leadership, and pronounced policies with routines and follow-ups, as well as a workplace which allows us to respectfully question one another, and people who are mature enough to truly receive criticism (which I shall return to shortly).

It is interesting that some of the participants who wrote about what professionalism means, raised the issue 'not to mix one's own values and personal opinions into the job'. Is this avoidable?

Perhaps they meant that you should work from the perspective of the client's values and opinions, and that sounds sensible. But if we are to help someone, working closely with him, perhaps in his home, can we ever eliminate our personal values? I do not think so. However, I believe we can train ourselves to be aware of them, and see when and how they come into play at work. If we perceive and understand – yes, are aware of – when and how our values affect us, we will automatically recognize that others have different values and that there are several ways of being 'right'. At that point our own values become a tool at work.

You will find an example of how unconscious values can be negative in the example about expensive food in Pitfall 8 'Universal truths' in the next chapter. But, on other occasions, personal values can be a useful tool at work, as when I met with a teenager with autism who thought he was possibly gay, and whose own values, at the time, told him that this was wrong. Here I can use my personal values (which say that homosexuality is OK, of course) to reason with him and broaden his view. Again, as with much else, it helps to be aware that this is a value I may encounter, whether it be my own or someone else's.

4.2 Making it right when doing wrong

Being a human being has enormous complexity, and working with human beings is a complex task. It is quite a natural desire that there should be 'one right answer' per issue. Many of us are affected by a school that taught us to think in terms of rights and wrongs (marked with a red pen by a teacher). Many people who come to my training want to know 'how to do' things when working with people with autism spectrum disorders. These are questions that have not just one answer, or even a couple of answers, but require reasoning and reflection.

So, yes, it *is* challenging to work with people, it *is* challenging to pursue professionalism and emotional maturity. But if you embrace the idea of how complex it really is, you can also find a sense of security. Not a security found in guidelines like 'if I do it like this I will not make a mistake', but a new one: 'because it *is complex*, I *will* make mistakes sometimes, everyone does it, but when (not if) it happens, I have the tools to deal with it'.

What do I mean by making mistakes? I am thinking of things such as accidentally hurting a pupil or client; or having too high (or low) demands, which lead to a meltdown; or falling into any of the pitfalls described in the next chapter; or making a decision that proves to be wrong or rash. One could say that professionalism also means having a back-up system. When things go wrong you cannot just stand there helpless, but you (and your organization) need to have the communication skills necessary to sort out the situation. An apology is always a good start. But then what? Well, frankly I am surprised sometimes at how big a difficulty people have communicating, and how little we train our children in communication skills (may there be a connection?). For many people it seems incredibly difficult, if they make a mistake, not to fall into a giant crater of guilt, and immediately feel overwhelmingly bad about it. And for many too, it seems unfortunately difficult to question something, bring forward some criticism or raise an issue that they were hurt by something, without at the same time sending strong signals that the person responsible really ought to *feel guilty*.

To be able to take responsibility for what went wrong without guilt is a very good skill to have – to be able to say 'You're right' and 'I should have done this differently'. And if you want to have this skill – to be able to receive criticism without being defensive or feeling bad – well, just start exercising.

4.3 Empathy, ethics and moral competence

According to the Danish philosopher Knud Ejler Løgstrup (2007), it is a part of the human condition to find yourself in ethically problematic situations, when you are relating to others. He believes that the relationship between individuals is crucial. Løgstrup attaches great importance to trust in a relationship, such as that between carer and patient (or student and teacher), and therefore sincerity and clarity are part of ethics.

The Swedish psychologist Kjell Ekstam (2003) writes about the concept of *moral competence* in a book titled *Vardagens etik* (which translates as *Everyday Ethics*), and he believes that this competence has three components: reason, empathy and conscience. Ekstam is also aware of the importance of clarity as he says that you can develop your moral competences by clearly expressing your will, your values and the reasons behind your actions. Another part of this development is to find out the conditions of others, and take responsibility for the decisions you make that affect other people.

I believe that this responsibility is incredibly beneficial to our pupils and clients. We have the power (we get paid), we can affect the life of the individual, we can decide what support is needed, the conditions of the support and so on, so then – for goodness sake – we should be able to say 'This is my responsibility' and 'I apologize' when something goes wrong.

Taking responsibility is also about seeing (and admitting) your own part in what is going on.

EXAMPLE

Teacher: On Friday I'll be at a seminar, Maggie is coming in and will be with you in the morning.

Pupil: Maggie's always so grumpy.

Teacher: No, no, it will be fine.

Or:

Teacher: On Friday I'll be at a seminar, Maggie is coming in and will be with you in the morning.

Pupil: Maggie's always so grumpy.

Teacher: You may have a point.

EXAMPLE

Client: You shouldn't say that!

Carer: It wasn't that bad.

Or:

Client: You shouldn't say that!

Carer: You're right, I should have realized that you wouldn't like it.

Question: 'What message do we give if we continue to apply strategies that aren't working?'

Answer: 'We don't understand you and we can't help you.'

[...]

Question: 'Why do many schools continue to apply reactive, back-end interventions that aren't working for their inflexible-explosive students?'

Answer: 'They aren't sure what else to do.'

Question: 'What happens to students to whom these interventions are counterproductively applied for many years?'

Answer: 'They become more alienated and fall further outside the social fabric of the school.'

(Greene 2001)

Some professionals talk about a 'fighter relationship' which can arise between children and adults. The book *Fighter Relationships: Children's Battles with Adults*[9] is exclusively about preschool children. But much of the reasoning in the book transfers excellently to the teacher–pupil, carer–user or nurse–patient relationship. A fighter relationship is characterized by the emergence of a vicious circle in which both the child's and the adult's way of interacting is mutually reinforcing the problem-creating issues. It may be the ultimatums ('boundaries') from adults breeding new demands from the child, and harsh reprimands leading to the child acting out even more.

The authors, the Danish psychologists Margot Jørgensen and Peter Schreiner, write:

> It is the child's vulnerability, *its vitality*, and the adult's vulnerabilities which in combination create the critical conditions for a fighter relationship to be established, and maintained.[10]

The italics, emphasizing vitality, are mine. I think that the great vitality of people with autism spectrum disorders who happen to be in a fighter relationship (with staff or teachers) is obvious. I believe that in the vitality there is enormous potential for development. But the key

---

9   My translation of the title *Fighter-relationen. Barns kamp med vuxna* (Jørgensen and Schreiner 1985).

10   My translation from the Swedish book.

is to put yourself in the pupil's or client's inner reality. In the words of Jørgensen and Schreiner:

> The adults' understanding of the child's personality is crucial to how they are tackling the child's actions. The consequences of the fact that they (naturally) will experience and understand the problematic situations as a result of the child's characteristics or personal qualities, are that they react to the child as if it is aggressive, destructive, and so on. If the adults cannot see the problematic situations in their entirety, they cannot see their own potential to influence them. (Jørgensen and Schreiner 1985)[11]

The authors attach great importance to adults' ability to understand how *the child* perceives the problem, and this form of empathy is in my opinion also crucial for many with autism spectrum disorders. The *wanting* to understand, the empathy is needed, but to really understand also requires knowledge specific to autism, because it is so complex that only a caring personality and emotional maturity is not enough (although it helps).

According to Professor Max van Manen, whom I mentioned earlier (see p.40), a true teacher possesses a number of qualities. Most of these are transferable to work with people in support services and health care:

- A sense of vocational animating: periodically we all must get in touch with why it is that we got into education in the first place.

- A love or liking for children – I do not think you can truly understand children if you do not like them.

- A reliable personality – a teacher must be a person that young people can count on.

- A deep sense of responsibility for children – an educator must feel responsive to the needs and vulnerabilities of children.

- A belief in children – there is nothing more powerful in a child's world than the motivating trust that your teacher thinks the world of you and believes in you.

---

11   Again, my translation.

- Openness – a good teacher should be constantly prepared to see things from different perspectives; good teachers are experts on perspectives.

- A thoughtful maturity – a thoughtful maturity includes a certain understanding or wisdom of what goes on in the world.

- A sensitivity toward the child's subjectivity – we must always ask ourselves what the child's experience is like.

- A selfless sense of generativity – this involves giving of oneself; unfortunately sacrifice is an unpopular and neglected notion nowadays.[12]

Figre 4.2: A true professional?

Some of this is about personality and some about maturity, therefore not things you usually learn in vocational training. But in a service you can build in things that promote professionalism (and maturity) and contribute to the growing of this in the staff group. Here's some of what I have found useful.

---

12 These are 9 out of the 15 qualities enumerated by Professor Max van Manen in the paper *Can teaching be taught or are real teachers found or made?* published by the University of Alberta in 1991.

4.4 Some ideas

Practice reflection

There are various traditions in different occupations, and in several of the group homes and supported living where I have supervised, the staff had no practice of using reflection in a conscious way. An easy way to exercise your ability to reflect is to have a notebook, and spend five to ten minutes each day before you go home writing down a few words under the headings: 'This is something I did well today' and 'This I could have done better'.

Every staff member does this and then you bring your notebooks to the staff meetings where you all take a few moments to jointly reflect on some of the situations. The point is not to report everything, but to practise how to reflect consciously. Eventually you will become quicker and more present in your reflections. The aim is to achieve 'reflection in action'. As a positive side-effect you will also, as you share your successes and your shortcomings, be confident with each other in the working group.

Another idea is to just take a piece of paper (as my participants did, if you remember) and throw down an answer to the question 'What is my view on professionalism right now?' Date the paper and tape it into your calendar six months from now. When you look at it six months later, consider whether you would add, reword or delete anything. If you make yourself aware of your own process towards increasing professionalism, you will get there faster. You will get there faster, because the awareness creates a focus that allows you to see more opportunities to improve your professionalism in your everyday work.

Another tip is to find good quotes from books (why not take some from this book?) or lectures, photocopy them and pin them to the wall in your meeting or lunch room. Change them often – you get immune quickly – and you can put the old ones in a binder and from time to time use them as topics for discussion at staff conferences.

Questioning respectfully

In a group where there is a sense of basic trust, you can also create a formula for questioning each other. The aim is to be able and to have the courage to express things that concern you, as well as – above all – to learn from each other. The formula is: 'I wonder how you were thinking when…' If I work together with someone and my colleague does something which seems strange to me (or says something I think a client or pupil does not understand, or becomes upset about, etc.), then I will later (at an appropriate time) say: 'I wonder how you were thinking when you said that to Mary?'

This form of questioning something someone did is friendly and respectful, and my experience is that it makes the person being asked think it over. They may then say that perhaps it was foolish or recklessly done. Before asking my colleague how she was thinking, I cannot know what her reasons were. It sometimes turns out that the colleague can explain exactly why she did what she did – and then *I* realize that it in fact made sense.

Ideally, you agree to use this 'method' in the group, and then all should feel free to question the others, and appreciate being questioned (since it will give you an opportunity to reflect and explain your motives).

It is great to combine this with the tools available in the solution-focused work.[13] In the solution-focused work the importance of praise and positive feedback is stressed. You can practise to become a 'positive feedback detective' which will allow you to quickly and instantly provide feedback, such as 'What a good meeting you arranged' or 'It was really smart of you to do that'. In such a climate it also becomes much easier to question and challenge each other. Furthermore, if we within the staff are really good at giving positive feedback, we also become better at giving it to our clients and pupils.

In one of the services I supervise we take turns in meetings to be 'detectives'. This means someone has the assignment of noting strengths and skills among colleagues during the meeting, and then briefly, at the end of the meeting, gives positive feedback to everyone about what he or she contributed.

Receiving and giving criticism (constructive criticism)

A few pages ago, I mentioned that the ability to receive criticism in a mature way is important. Actually, in all kinds of occupations where you are working with people, you should receive training in giving and receiving criticism. Not only because this is necessary between

---

13   Solution-focused methods appear in various places in this book, for example p.63 and p.320.

colleagues, but also because your pupils or clients and their families may criticize your work and your service.

If you are among those who let criticism get you non-plussed, and find it difficult to deal with, it is a good idea to practise a technique to handle criticisms. You might say 'OK, I hear what you say, you think that... I need to digest this for a while and sort it out. I will get back to you this afternoon.' What you do with a response like that is that you receive the criticism, you show the person who complains that you have understood it by reflecting it back to them, and then you give yourself space to reflect before answering.

Not everyone needs such space; some people, often the more emotionally mature and non-judgemental ones, can respond constructively to criticism immediately. They may say 'You're right, I apologize' or if they think the criticism is unfounded, they may explain the reason behind their position in a factual way, and try to take note of why the other person perceived it differently.

The questions you want to ask yourself when someone criticizes you, are:

- Is there anything in the criticism?

- Do I agree?

- What can I or should I change?

- If I agree, how do I take responsibility in a mature way?

- If I think the criticism is unfounded, how can I express it in a mature way?

- If I think the criticism is unfounded, how can I understand it from the giver's perspective?

- Are there questions I should ask in order to understand better?

If you can distinguish between *actions* and *persons* it will make giving and receiving criticism easier. If I am criticized for how I handled a situation at work, or for a system in our service, it does not mean that someone says I'm a bad person. All services and all people have their shortcomings, and criticism is an opportunity for development.

But what if you get unfair or unjustified criticism, and the person who delivers it cannot distinguish between action and person? Well, of course, it is hard to be 'attacked' by someone who seems to imply that you do not understand one iota, and that you don't know your job. The good news is that if there are no reasonable grounds for the criticism, you do not have to initiate a process towards change.

Still, you have to have the ability to truly be a good and mature receiver of criticism; it is a part of your job. Your reply can be something that sends the message that you hear what the other person says (it's a good idea to repeat what the person said and ask if that is what he or she meant). Then you can say you disagree with this, and explain your perspective. Be factual, not emotional. You can also say that you are sorry that the person perceives it like this, even if you do not agree with it. And, finally, thank the person for having the confidence in you to express his views.

Try it – it's not as difficult as it may seem. And remember, practice makes perfect!

Documentation of approaches and tools

I believe the way you work, not just what you do, but how you do it, should be documented. This goes for working on your own competence, as well as the pedagogy, support or care you deliver. This (i.e. how we think, our ethos, and what tools we use to achieve this) can be written down in a folder called 'This is how we work'. This will help you to maintain a high degree of professionalism in the service. Of course, the direct work with the pupils or clients also needs to be documented.

It is good to be explicit; for example, you can break it down into *Objectives/goals, Resources* and *Concrete tools.* One can also have four categories: *Vision, Objectives/goals, Resources* and *Concrete tools.* There is no razor-sharp line between the categories; there is not always a difference between a resource and a tool, for example. But a structure helps us to think about what we do. You can see examples of how it might look in a moment.

Twice a year you can have 'Are we working like this?' meetings, where you go through the descriptions and see if they correspond, or require modification. Not only will the document help you become more aware (professional) in your occupational role, it also helps new employees and temps to quickly get into the service. There is less risk that we lose skills when we have staff turnover if our work is properly documented.

In the services I've worked with, it is common to have a document showing goals or objectives for the service, commonly looking something like this:

Objective/Goals[14]

- To improve the quality of life of those the service supports.
- To provide a safe service which is responsive to the needs of each individual resident.
- To offer care to residents in a sensitive way which affords dignity, privacy and respect towards each individual.

You could express it something like this instead:

Vision

- All service users receive encouragement and a personalized support for daily living and developing skills in a respectful and safe environment.

Overall objectives
(Not measurable but permeate the service)

- We work to improve the quality of life of those the service supports.
- We are responsive to the needs of each individual resident.
- We offer care to residents in a sensitive way which affords dignity, privacy and respect towards each individual.
- We are curious and willing to learn.
- We strive for clarity in all parts of the service.
- We offer support to increase awareness of the disability.
- We are actively working to establish good relations and trust.

Specific (measurable) objectives
During the coming year we will:

- offer group activities for users with the aim of increasing their understanding of their own difficulties and strengths, and to allow them to practise social interactions

---

14   I've downloaded these example goals from some websites belonging to residential services; they are fairly typical of the many services I've worked with. In essence they are not goals, since they are not measurable; they rather express a vision.

- make an inventory of users' hobbies and interests
- provide more aids than previously
- measure users' trust in the service through a survey
- increase staff knowledge of autism spectrum disorders and of assistive aids.

Means

- We gather users to start a users' council. Responsible staff are_____. First follow-up _____ (date).
- We make five educational visits or field trips to other services for people with autism spectrum disorders. Responsible staff are _____. First follow-up _____ (date).
- We have a training plan for staff (recorded separately).
- We will make observations in the service on six occasions, and then draw conclusions on how we can improve communication and increase clarity. Responsible staff are _____. Observations shall be made before the conference days of autumn _____ (date).
- All members of staff choose one book each about autism spectrum disorders, reads it and then shares the content at staff meetings (follow-up: each staff-meeting).
- We have supervision once a month, with regard to autism-specific approaches.
- We work on interviewing our users to learn as much as possible about their needs and wishes.
- We consult an occupational therapist for more ideas on aids.

4.5 Professionalism in exchanges with clients

Being able to take the other's perspective was one of the Max van Manen criteria of a good pedagogue (see p.50), and I am inclined to agree. But how can we do this when we do not have the same experience as the student or the user? The autism-specific knowledge is a prerequisite. If you do not know what difficulties a person with an autism spectrum disorder may have, it will be hard to take her perspective.

On another level, one can say that we should open ourselves up to the other perspective, which also means to be open to our own shortcomings. Greta Marie Skau did a survey in Norway in 1998 where she collected experiences from clients of social services. Skau travelled around her country and interviewed clients about how they experienced their encounters with professionals.

The results revealed, among other things, that clients had met many different people in different posts, over the years and that many after a meeting had had a lingering feeling of having been used, 'used by someone who maybe wanted to feel strong, and professional'. Quite thought-provoking, in my opinion. Do we use our users, clients and pupils for our own purposes? We probably all do, from time to time; true altruism is rare. And there can be something quite good in the fact that there is something in it for me too, when working as a helper, supporter or facilitator of some kind. The key is awareness, and making sure we do not only take the perspective of the client, but also put that perspective at the top of the agenda.

What we can do is to consciously and with an open mind try to learn as much as we can about clients' (or students', etc.) perceptions of the support we offer. In my experience, using more structured forms is very helpful (you can read more about documentation in Chapter 15).

Sometimes when I have tutored or supervised in a school or service for people with autism, there has been a pupil or client who some of the staff felt provoked by or afraid of. This is problematic, as we often do not make well-founded decisions when we are provoked or afraid. Sometimes we have had a conference with the aim of discussing things that will affect both the life here and now and the future of this client (sometimes the topic is as serious as 'can we have this client/pupil here?').

I usually first designate one or two people to 'be the client' in a fictitious meeting. We do a small role play about, for example, a meeting discussing how a school should deal with Samuel, who has autism and is behaving in a threatening way. Teachers Rachel and Jian (who both find Samuel particularly difficult, and frequently say that he should not be allowed in this school) will now both try to be Samuel's voice at the meeting. So for each argument on possible support and interventions that the team leaders, teachers and remedial teachers make, Rachel and Jian will make a comment from Samuel's perspective. Such sessions usually start out being quite tentative and stiff but end up giving some new insights about how the situation is perceived by the student (in this example, Samuel).

Time is sometimes in short supply, and then we might not do a role play, but just let someone be Samuel's voice at the actual conference (if this is not a conference where Samuel and/or his parents are present themselves, of course). This is in general a good technique in services where we have conferences about users/patients/students who are not present: to always appoint someone to be the subject's voice during the meeting. You can take turns so that all members of staff can play the 'advocate role'.

You might find it helpful to use the exercises regarding solution-focused questions (see p.63). If you come to a standstill with a client, a solution-focused conversation, with what we call creative process questions, can bring new opportunities. In this conversation you focus *only* on what is working.

Zooming in on the solutions

Let us say that Margaret (who works in a supported living service) needs advice on a client, Beth, whom she is seriously concerned for. Margaret has listed all of Beth's problems and difficulties, everything Beth *cannot* do, and now starts to talk about Beth (saying that Beth has major learning difficulties, that she is acting out). Here she is interrupted by the supervisor:

Supervisor: I understand your concern for Beth and that all of you in the service are worried that she might not be able to stay in your service.

Margaret: Yes, all the time when we…

Supervisor: I am interrupting you again now, because I have an idea that we could try to talk about Beth in a different way today.

Margaret: OK.

Supervisor: Can you tell me when it works out well with Beth. Are there some occasions when it works out at least a bit better than otherwise?

Margaret: Yes, that would be when we go shopping. But it is probably just about the only thing that works out with Beth. And that's only once a week.

Supervisor: So it works out when you go shopping?

Margaret: Yes.

Supervisor: Does the shopping work out just about tolerably or really well?

Margaret: Well, actually really well.

Supervisor: OK, so once a week, there is an activity where Beth functions really well!

Margaret: Yes.

Supervisor: How wonderful that you have been able to arrange such a good activity for her every week! Can you tell me something about what it is that makes that particular activity work so well?

Margaret: Well, I guess…that she is motivated…she likes to shop… and she has a task, to look after her wallet and the money. That's it, I think.

Supervisor: Is there anything else? Anything else that makes this work so well?

Margaret: Well…OK, she likes to go by car, and she likes to read road signs.

Supervisor: OK, we already have, in a couple of minutes, identified several factors that make things work for Beth: she has something to focus on, an assignment that is clear to her, and she is motivated by the goal of the activity. In addition, we described two things she likes, going by car and reading the road signs! Is there anything more about the shopping activity that may be of assistance to Beth, another factor that makes it work so well?

Margaret: Yes, it is perhaps that it is always one of the three staff members she likes best that goes with her, since they are the ones who drive.

Supervisor: So knowing beforehand who is going with her, and that it is someone she really likes, are also success factors for Beth?

Margaret: Yes, that's true.

Supervisor: Can you think of any way that you could use these factors, for Beth to have success with other activities as well?

Margaret: You know what, just as you have asked these questions, I have come to think of several things we could do differently, or new things we could try.

Supervisor: That's great! Let's now talk about the situations where Beth has had major difficulties, and perhaps been acting out aggressively as you described earlier. Is there some point where you have been able to end this, or helped her to calm down in a good way?

Margaret: Yes, there was once when she started screaming and kicking...

Supervisor: OK, right now, it is not so important what Beth did, but I want to hear what resources *you* used on this occasion; what was it that made the difference this time?

Margaret: I get it. The difference was that we backed off, I think. We backed off and I lowered my voice. I think it calmed her.

Supervisor: Was there anything else you did?

Margaret: Yes, I guess, after that, when she went inside her apartment, we stood in the doorway. She knew she could close the door and be alone.

Supervisor: OK, so having an escape route is important for Beth? And how great of you to think of lowering your voice with Beth!

Margaret: Yes, and you know, now I feel so much more hopeful about Beth than I did just 15 minutes ago!

Supervisor: That sounds good. I just thought we would round off by looking at Beth's good qualities. What are the good aspects of her personality? And how are they expressed when you meet her?

Margaret: Good aspects... um... she doesn't even let us in that often, so it's not so easy to know about her good sides.

Supervisor: I understand that, but if we look at the shopping, for example. What good aspects of Beth's personality can you see there?

Margaret: Well, her motivation to shop, I guess that's a good side?

Supervisor: What else?

Margaret: Well, she is generous! She always wants to buy gifts for others when we shop!

Supervisor: What else?

Margaret: Um... Well, perhaps that she is patient when we shop? She really is, you can see that it is taking a lot of energy out of her, when we have to queue for example, but she really makes an effort.

Supervisor: OK, here we have two things, both that she is patient, and the fact that Beth is good at really making an effort sometimes. If we look at other situations, what can we find?

Margaret: Well, *when* she lets us in, it sometimes happens, she always offers us a glass of juice. So she is caring then.

Supervisor: Yes, caring, and trusting as well – the times when she actually lets you in, she shows her confidence in you, right?

Margaret: Yeah.

Supervisor: What else?

Margaret: Well, I can't think of anything more now. And she is quite new to us, so when I know her better, maybe I can think of more things.

Supervisor: OK, then I would like to hear if it feels possible for you to convey all those good points you see in Beth to her?

Margaret: How do you mean?

Supervisor: I am thinking of positive feedback. In these situations you mentioned, could you start giving her compliments and comments about her patience, kindness, effort, trust and so on?

Margaret: Sure, I could do that.

Supervisor: OK, when can you do it? When is the first opportunity you have?

Margaret: Well, Thursday when we go shopping…and yes, next time she lets me in.

Supervisor: Fine! Good luck with your new ideas.[15]

Maybe you want to take a moment to reflect on what the supervisor is doing here? Some points: 1. She is not leaving space for the negative. 2. She reinforces the positive and feeds it back to Margaret. 3. She does not give up when Margaret doesn't seem to be able to think of anything positive. Sounds easy? In fact, it is not so easy. As a supervisor, I often notice how easy it is to slip into only focusing on what is difficult, things that seem impossible or insurmountable. We human beings are like this, and it is perhaps not surprising; it has probably served human survival to be observant of what is problematic. But today it is a cognitive style that often serves neither ourselves, nor the students, patients and users we are there to support.

Now you might object that you do not have a supervisor who works in the solution-focused area, but if you just understand the principles of this method, you can easily coach each other in being solution focused. You could even just take a pen and paper, and guide yourself by writing down what works, the pupil's good traits, when you can give feedback, and so on. Questions for this kind of exercise

---

15   You can read more about solutions based conversations in Chapter 22.

are found, for example, in the book *Becoming a Solution Detective* by John Sharry and his colleagues.

The solution-focused strategies originated in therapeutic settings, where there have been great results with Solution-Focused Brief Therapy (SFBT), but have recently moved into other areas, such as solution-focused leadership, and lately to the school world. If you are a teacher or teaching assistant in a school, you may find lots of helpful hints in books about therapy, since the principles and ideas are the same whether you work with clients or pupils. However, you can find some school-specific documents at the Department for Education – National Strategies website (Department for Education 2011), as well as in other sites on the web.

EXERCISE 4.1

Solution-focused questions

If you work in care or support services, here is an exercise for you. Read this case and try to find as many solution-focused clues and questions as possible. Take time to think, then you can read my 'key' which follows.

> Bob has high-functioning autism and schizophrenia, and is on anti-psychotic medication. He has a daughter who is seven years old, whom he gets to see once a month, in a park, under the supervision of social services. Bob studies maths in adult education. Since Bob was discharged from a lengthy stay in institutional care at the hospital a year ago, he has had increasing problems with hygiene. Bob usually does not open the door when his supported living team call. The team members who have been inside his apartment notice that it is often in terrible disorder, and are worried about it.[16]

---

16   Some ideas for solution-focused questions:

This is my 'key' (i.e. my suggestions). You might come up with more!

- Bob takes his medication. This means he has a routine working for him.
- What is it that makes this routine work?
- Can we use this strength in other contexts?
- He has a daughter whom he sees regularly, and they meet outdoors. Would it be easier for Bob to meet outdoors?
- Could his support workers begin to meet him somewhere other than in his apartment to start building trust?
- If the problems with hygiene have got worse, they have therefore been better in the past! What was it that made it work when he was an in-patient. What kind of support did he receive while in care?
- Bob lets the support workers in at times. Who does he let in? When? Under what circumstances?

You can also use these questions as an exercise, either as a group discussion with your colleagues, or by yourself with pen and paper (everything you put into words is reinforced!).

EXERCISE 4.2

Strengths

1. What are your strengths as a professional/as a group?
2. In what way/in which situations are these strengths useful?
3. How/when do the students/clients see these strengths?
4. How could you use your strengths as a professional/as a group even more? In what situations?

Perhaps you now believe that what I am saying is that you should *never* focus on what is difficult or problematic, but no, that is absolutely not so. Let us, in contrast to the solution-focused approach, talk about problem-focused work – this is essential too. By focusing on the causes of the problem (though not so much on the problem itself), we often find clues to interventions, and how to create aids (see Chapter 15 'Diving Lessons in the Ocean'). For me, problem-oriented and solution-focused approaches work just fine, side by side, and are complementary. Each in its time and place.

EXERCISE 4.3

Empathy

This is a different exercise, more problem-oriented; I call this one an empathy exercise. This can be used when there is a client or pupil for whom significant problems are perceived. First you list all the known difficulties this individual has. So it may be a list like this:

- difficulty understanding the context/seeing entireties
- motor co-ordination problems/clumsiness
- sleeping problems
- difficulty understanding the social context
- concrete and literal understanding of language
- sensitivity to sounds and touch.

When you have listed the known difficulties, you hand them out to the group of staff. You work in pairs and each couple gets assigned two or three of the difficulties. Then you get 15–20 minutes to discuss in your pairs how an ordinary day in your life would be if you had these difficulties:

- How would I feel?
- Where would there be problems in the course of the day?

After this discussion you all give an account to the group and without doubt you will become aware that though the pupil/client has *all* these difficulties and you were only assigned two or three of them, you still imagined that life would be that difficult.

4.6 Conclusion

There is of course much more one could say about the topic of professionalism, and what being a true professional could mean, and in several places in this book, thoughts about professionalism and the occupational role will be interspersed. I hope, by writing this chapter, to encourage you and your colleagues to work jointly on your increasing professionalism.

In summary you could say (with a message to your boss, unless you yourself happen to be the head) that many of us working in the autism field learned decades ago that we need time for planning and preparation in order to meet the basic needs of individuals in our service. Now, some 20 years later, we have to put forward that we need time for planning and reflection *for staff* if they are to establish and maintain professionalism in their occupational role. It is time well spent. But this time should obviously be effectively and constructively spent (to use the first 15 minutes of a staff meeting for people to get coffee and go to the bathroom is not my idea of efficiency). Neither do I believe in meetings where the staff spend time 'venting', or 'giving tongue to' or 'letting off steam', such as:

- How disgusting it is that Stacy (who has autism) always puts her hands in her pants and then smells them.

- That you are so annoyed or provoked by the fact that Garth is intimidating or that Melissa is so 'unreasonable'.

If we want to help Stacy, Garth and Melissa, it is often more important what *they* feel and live through, than what the staff feels. I never supervise assignments where the request includes a notion that staff need to let off steam. On the contrary, I believe that if you dwell on these kinds of feelings and perceptions, they become increasingly cemented. (Remember that everything you put into words is reinforced? What do we want to reinforce here?)

Working for change is what I believe in. A clear and effective plan with an agenda for staff meetings, supervision and other meetings.

Documentation and updating and clear areas of responsibilities, a follow-up of decisions – constant work to increase professionalism, your personal professionalism as well as the professionalism of the group as a whole. And – of course – the actual content of support, which the rest of this book is all about.

I close this chapter with a quote from the Danish philosopher Løgstrup (1956):

> A person never has anything to do with another person without holding a bit of the other's life in his hands – it may be very little, a passing feeling, or a zeal that you get to wither or to raise, a tediousness which you deepen or revoke. But it can also be of terrifying importance in that the other's fate is at stake.[17]

---

17   My translation.

5

Remove the Cake Even If You Don't Think It's Ready – Common Pitfalls for Staff

A Chapter on Things You Would Rather Avoid

The cake? Wasn't that in Chapter 2, you might ask? Yes, but now my analogies. This chapter is all about the pitfalls which you so easily can fall into as a professional. Sure, I can come as an advisor and help you up. But it is easier for you, and better for your clients and pupils, if you do not fall at all. Therefore, I list here point by point examples of occasions where staff can lose their professionalism, either because it happens so easily (because we humans are made that way), or because no one told you that you should or could do things differently. With awareness of the pitfalls I hope to prevent some 'broken bones'.

First, a little something about the professional role. For those who, for example, work in residential support, a big part of your job is being in the users' everyday lives, in their leisure time. Part of the job may even be something as vague as 'hanging out', that is giving social support. It can mean going to the city, to the library, having a coffee or any other activity with a user. In this case it is not always easy or clear to know what a professional role really means. Having a professional role is more difficult, but still very important, when you do not have things that help make visible the role (such as a desk or a waiting room). Such paraphernalia are of course no guarantee of professionalism, but they help to create the distance from the private self that needs to be there.[1]

There are risks if you have deficiencies in your professional role. This role is, as I suggested, easier to maintain in occupations such as psychologist or physician. I mentioned having a desk or a waiting

---

1   Remember the last chapter and the discussion on the need for greater emotional maturity in our professions today.

room as helpful in these occupations. But other reasons are that the role also comes with the training, and psychologists and physicians furthermore meet with their patient for a very short time, usually at most an hour, and very rarely come into his or her home and everyday life.

There are, of course, obvious risks if being a professional means that staff try to discharge their private selves altogether. When you work with people this is not (or shouldn't be) possible. I have heard frightening examples of when this has happened, as when a train manager threw a child off the train because she couldn't show her ticket (the older sister was in the lavatory with the tickets), and the child had to spend the night alone in a city where she had never been before.

Or an extreme example: the Winterbourne View scandal uncovered by the BBC Panorama team in June 2011 where residents with autism and learning disorders were being tortured by staff (pinned down, slapped, dragged into showers while fully clothed and taunted). This is rare of course, and most staff would never dream of treating vulnerable people like this, but unfortunately I think it is safe to say that it is not as rare as we would wish.

This is frightening. The task of being human can never be detached. One must always act as a human within the framework you have, and if you perceive the framework as inhuman you must try to change it.

Greta Marie Skau, whom I have mentioned already, is also the author of an excellent book on power relations between clients and staff in the social field.

She writes:

> Even if there is an important distinction between the private and the professional, it is inconceivable to develop a sustainable ethical professionalism at an advanced professional occupation level, without including the personal element of the professional.
>
> This concerns the personal element in the context of a professional goal, a deliberate activation of the helper's overall human resources in meeting with the client.[2] (Skau 1998)

The art is thus to pair the personal with the professional in a fruitful way. Easier said than done, sure – but not impossible.

Now to my examples of pitfalls.

---

2   My translation of the text in the Swedish book *Mellan makt och hjälp* (Skau 1998).

5.1 Pitfall 1: Falling into another role (other than the professional) – parenting the person with autism

One sign of losing professionalism is having slipped *into another role*. The reason why this happens can be lack of clarity in what the professional role should imply, but it can also happen because the service user or student, in their acting or appearance, generates something within you, something which will make you take the role of a parent (or a buddy, to be discussed in Pitfall 2).

Since the person you are supporting has, and sometimes also radiates, a need for care, she can pull out the parental instincts in you. These are not always good – as parents we (of course) want to take care of our children, but we can also be incredibly annoyed with them, or think they are rude or ungrateful. The staff whom I have met, who slipped into this role, are often very good-hearted. But is benevolence always that good? Could benevolence even perhaps do damage? I think so.

Let's just stop for a while now, and point out that it is human (in the sense that we are all fallible) and quite common to fall into these pitfalls. If you do, or have done, this, it does not mean you are a bad person or a lousy professional. It means you do not (yet) have all the tools you need to develop your professional role. The first step to change is to raise an awareness about the mistakes you made, and put them behind you; this is when you make room for something new.

Back to these parenting roles. You might work in the user's home and help him or her with all sorts of things, such things one often helps children with. And then it's certainly not surprising if you imperceptibly glide into a parental role. But besides the fact that you are not a parent to this person, that role provides a variety of problems. In this role we more easily fall into the trap of nagging ('You must understand that you cannot sleep in your clothes'; 'But I told you yesterday that you cannot sleep if you drink coffee at night', and so on). It is also easy to believe that we know best. We want the best for the person we are supporting, and sometimes we mix things up as to thinking we *know* what is best for him or her. When we have this notion it can lead to us controlling the person – often unconsciously, on our part – in a way that is not really compatible with good practice and being professional. I will return to this aspect in Pitfall 5 'Steering the will of others'.

When I am hired to counsel staff who are stuck in a parental role, they are often quite convinced that, with regard to this particular situation (whatever it may be), they actually know what is best for the person with autism. It can be things like feeling that Luke should not be taken advantage of by his girlfriend, or that Jessica should not spend all her money on beer. This is very similar to how we as parents think we know what is best for our children.

'But,' I often ask staff in these situations, 'do you really think *your* parents always know what is best for you?'(They usually do not.) It is not necessary to have a malfunctioning relationship with your parents to feel that you haven't made the same life choices your parents would have made for you, if they had had the opportunity.

This is perfectly fine in a real parent–child relationship. It may be that parents sometimes tell their adult children that they should not wear that sweater, or should not drop out of education, or travel abroad, or whatever it may be. It is OK because if you are a parent and a child, you have a long history and a lifelong relationship in front of you. You are also aware that many emotions such as concern, consideration and likewise can be expressed in different ways; in relation to your real parents you have learned to read between the lines.[3] It works, also because you once (in your teens probably) freed yourself from your parents and thus you now know that you can stand on your own two feet. It does *not* work in a caring or supporting relationship which should be characterized by a humane professionalism.

When you at your job happen to fall in the parenting pit you can also lose even more of your professionalism, as you are blinded and it can become a downward spiral.

EXAMPLE

I am asked to advise a group of staff in residential support. They are concerned about a user. They feel the user's girlfriend is taking advantage of him. She eats his food, and empties his fridge, she gets him to buy expensive things for her although he has very little money, and she is (in the staff's eyes) not 'nice' to him. They take his side, he's 'their user' and they care a lot about him.

Of course it is good that they care about their users, but the situation has gone so far that his girlfriend knows that staff dislike her, and she is

---

3   Of course, this does not mean that one cannot be annoyed with one's parents if they think they always know what is best, but it is a relationship where you for natural reasons are ready to make more sacrifices than you would in other relationships.

sometimes, therefore, rude to the staff (which of course does not make them feel better about her).

The user in question is a bit ambivalent: on the one hand, he is partially aware that he is 'exploited' and he vents this with the staff when he feels the girlfriend has not been nice to him; on the other hand, he wants to continue his relationship with her.

The staff ask me what to do about the relationship. 'Absolutely nothing,' I say. They have already gone too far into something that is not their territory.

Now you may wonder if I am saying that you should not bother about the user's well-being. Of course you should. The question is how to do it – and what is productive to do. In this case, staff had asked the user why he continued the relationship despite the fact that he did not think she was being nice. The reason he gave was 'good sex'. Interestingly, when staff passed this on to me it was with a wry smile that clearly said that in their world sex was not the meaning of a relationship (not meaning enough anyway). But it is nevertheless the case that several adults without autism spectrum disorders have had at least one more or less 'dysfunctional' relationship. Many also at some point have stayed in a relationship for reasons such as 'good sex', or for the sake of economy, or the children – how could one say that one reason has more or less value than the other? All relationships are package deals where you will take the advantages with the disadvantages of being with the other person and of the relationship in general.

People with autism have a right to autonomy, which also in fact means a right to make choices in life that others characterize as destructive. As long as you do not harm yourself or someone else, I might add. But what does 'harming' really mean, you may wonder? Well, we have laws governing this. This means that we as staff of course have to act if we think for example that someone is abused in a serious way, or harming themselves in such a way that their life is at risk. But it does not mean you should make your own assessments (like 'it is bad for him to be taken advantage of'). But what *should* we do, then? Did I not just say 'nothing'? What I meant was that we should not intervene in the relationship, and not take sides (and the truth is that we know nothing about how the girlfriend's staff – this woman was also a user of disability services, but in another council – or how she herself views this situation). Intervening and taking sides like this, is also an example of focusing on the wrong side of an issue, or shooting past the target.

What we must do is analyse and ask ourselves questions. The key word is *why* (and it is a word that you will notice permeates this book). *Why* has he chosen this relationship? Well, the good sex part we know already, but *why*, we imagine, is it that he seems to believe he cannot have a relationship which holds both good sex and a greater equality in other respects?

The staff are guessing:

• It is his first girlfriend, he has no other experiences.

• He has low self-esteem.

• He has not ever had friends before, without having to 'pay' for them.

• He was severely bullied when he was younger, and having a girlfriend gives him a higher status.

• He meets no other girls, as he rarely goes out in public.

These explanations for his present choice sound reasonable as well as probable. And in our professional role and attitude it therefore seems sensible that our focus is on helping this man to develop a better self-esteem (which we can do in a variety of ways), and giving him more opportunities to meet others, that is, helping him to expand his social life. This is also consistent with our aims as support workers.

We can hope that working in this direction will give him insights, and perhaps eventually the power to change his role in the current relationship, or to end it, if that's what he wants. But it is not our place to choose for him. We create the best conditions possible, but he chooses, and lives, his life. We can also use the tool 'informed choices' described in more detail in Chapter 21 'Written, Drawn and Other Visual Aids'.

It is quite common for staff in the social field (group homes, supported living, day care) not to be so used to this line of work. A small survey in 2002, measuring quality in Swedish group homes found:

> A general observation was that the quality of the care was rated especially high when it comes to 'hard' facts that are easier to make concrete or develop routines for, e.g. the housing, organization, basic safety and daily routines. When it comes to 'soft' values, there was more often a shortage of quality. An exception to this is in the area of respect and integrity, that was rated high, which probably is

explained by the fact that the personnel have a very positive attitude and a great commitment to the people with learning disabilities. (Anderberg 2002)

What I am talking about here most certainly concerns the 'soft values'. We, as a society, are working on rights, choice, independence and inclusion for people with disabilities. We need to bring this work down to the floor, to the actual service we are giving to an individual user or student.

In a small booklet, written many years ago by a group of people with learning disabilities, they expressed their views on these issues. It is well worth considering the following points:

> We must be given support to make our own decisions, without regard to the degree of our disability, or the risks that may follow the decisions.
>
> We have to be able to take risks when we understand what can go wrong. (ILSMH 1994)

Honestly, I believe we grow as human beings by making mistakes. Would you be the person you are today, if you hadn't made mistakes? Is it not in fact *because* of your mistakes, rather than in spite of them, that you have reached a certain level of maturity and understanding?

5.2 Pitfall 2: Falling into another role (other than the professional) – being a buddy

You may not have fallen into the parenting-role trap, but another aspect of this pitfall is slipping into the role of a 'friend'. However, it is completely incompatible to be staff and friend at the same time. In the staff–user relationship there are several built-in inequalities (one is paid, one has more power over such things as how much and what kind of support you may receive); this makes it impossible to classify it as friendship. Nonetheless, one sometimes encounters staff calling themselves friends, or, more typically, they slip into the role of a friend.

We certainly have a social assignment; when we provide residential support we also make a social intervention. We will chat and interact socially with the user as part of our job, and since we're not machines we may talk about our own lives. If this – that is, the supporter's relationships, children, gardening or whatever it may be – comes to fill a very large part of the time spent together with the user we have fallen out of our professionalism.

It may even go so far as with (in a hypothetical example) the support worker Louise, who even longs to go to the user Jenny, since at Jenny's Louise can talk about what she herself was doing over the weekend, whereas at Evan's she knows she will have to talk about his (boring) interest in trains. This can easily happen, especially if the user has poor communication skills. But my gosh, what should I be talking about with the users? Am I not supposed to talk about myself at all? Relax, you can certainly talk about yourself but you need to distinguish between being personal and being private, and to be careful with how much of the space you are occupying in the social interaction. With a user who has poor communication skills you can try to, instead of filling the entire contents of the social interaction yourself, help the user to develop better conversational skills.

You and your user could perhaps together write notes of what you could talk about. You could make up and sketch out topics for conversation in advance that would be of interest to the user. You can also 'rig' a situation where you and the user have something to talk about; suggest that he or she watches a television programme, which you yourself also will be seeing, so you can talk about this later. And last but not least, it is not dangerous to be silent, either. Sometimes the staff's need for chatting (read: fear of silence) takes over to the degree that it prevents the user from being as well-functioning as he could.

How do we avoid slipping into the role of a parent or a friend? Sometimes even the user pushes us into the role he expects, or even 'wants', us to have! I wrote 'wants' in quotation marks, because I feel that it is difficult to talk about wanting when we are dealing with a person who has a limited world experience and great difficulties in imagining something he has never experienced. I shall return to this shortly.

There is no such thing as a vaccine to make us totally immune to the risk of ending up in a parent or buddy role, but the more you are aware of how easy it is to fall into these roles, that this is a hazard to everyone in this occupation, the more likely you are to discover when it is about to happen, and begin to correct yourself.

If you frequently and clearly formulate how you want the contact in general and the specific encounters with your user (or patient, etc.) to be, for example that the user can practise conversational skills with you, you will begin to prepare for it, and it will happen. The more you discuss with your colleagues and try to find examples of when you (sometimes collectively) find yourselves in a parental role towards users, the easier it is to avoid it. Awareness and ongoing discussions are keys, and preparation and planning is often preventive.

5.3 Pitfall 3: That's the way he wants it!

Another common pitfall (and a sort of paradoxical contrast to the example of the potentially destructive relationships above) is where staff regard a person's right to independence as a reason to limit his or her life. Perhaps the most striking example I have is from consulting with psychiatric care, where I occasionally hear that the person himself *would like* to be strapped, belted or otherwise restrained physically.[4] The argument is used by staff to convince themselves that physical restraint is the correct response: that's the way he wants it. From care services, such as group homes, I sometimes get to hear comments like: 'She wants us to hold her down' or 'He really wants to be wrestled down'. In care settings restraints tend to be physical rather than mechanical (i.e. using bodily strength rather than restraining equipment), which is actually not more 'humane' since there are a higher number of risk factors in physical restraining.[5] Be assured that this does not mean I am recommending mechanical restraint. I am recommending no restraint at all.

A person with limited ability to envision things he has never experienced, and who does not have any experience of another way to be stopped, can of course express that he wants to be restrained. This

---

4   If you are a teacher or an assistant in a school, you may think this pitfall doesn't apply to you. Well, actually I see quite a lot (too much) of physical restraint of pupils with special needs in schools too. Here not so much because professionals think the pupil wants or needs it, but rather because, as they say, 'He will run away and lock himself into the bathroom' or 'She will run out into the school yard'. Even if holding a child tight may not be all that physically risky (for the pupil), the teacher doing the holding often ends up with some scratches or bruises. And the pupil ends up with mixed, unfruitful, feelings; on the one hand feeling bad about hurting his teacher, and on the other being hurt and offended by the holding. In a pupil's choice of fight or flee, I believe fleeing is a good choice! In fact, I think an excellent strategy is: 'If a situation is overwhelming you, remove yourself from the situation', thus running out to the schoolyard or the toilet makes good sense. However, we can work with improving the pupil's skills to handle overwhelming situations. Read more about this in Part 4.

5   In fact there have been many deaths of people with learning disabilities and psychiatric illness worldwide in care settings; see for example the article: 'Deaths associated with restraint use in health and social care in the UK: the results of a preliminary survey' (Paterson *et al.* 2003).

can also apply to other kinds of punishments[6] and restrictions, where staff justify them with the person asking for it himself. But it is in such cases our job to clearly (literally) show him the alternatives, making his archive of experiences grow, and providing him with more options to choose from. If we believe that a person with challenging behaviour can only be stopped by us holding him down in his bed or on the floor, we must remember that every time (over years and years) we held him down when he had a meltdown, we were *teaching him* that this is the way he can be stopped. No wonder then if he believes this himself and does not 'call it a day' until his goal is reached. Consistently and clearly, we must 're-teach' him, and this will inevitably take some time (you can read more about how to do this in the section 'There and then, here and now: when someone fights or injures himself' on how to handle challenging behaviour, p.266).

5.4 Pitfall 4: Prohibit or allow – this is not the question!

It is often the case that staff groups I meet tend to end up in extreme positions of either allowing or prohibiting something. This could also involve using restrictions versus doing nothing. We see no middle way, although there often is one.

Occasionally I encounter environments that on the one hand are very rigid, restrictive and full of prohibitions, rules, and 'nots', but *simultaneously* on the other hand, are leaving the person with the autism spectrum disorder adrift in many situations. I assume that it is difficult to spontaneously see the middle ways, since so many staff groups end up in extreme positions. I guess this means you have to look for them intentionally. Professionalism in the occupational role is, among other things, to be aware of what you need to be aware of!

Thus we should, as staff, if we are facing the question 'Should we allow this?', always ask ourselves 'Where is the middle way?' Of course, we have no map with this middle way plotted; we rather have to search for this path. How do you find your way without a map? By asking. Here you ask, 'Why? Really why?' And like a six-year-old you don't give up until the final why is asked.

---

6   I know, we don't like to think we punish people in care services. But what is a reward system where you lose points (and benefits) for 'bad behaviour', if not a punishment?

Let us take the example of a school for children with autism which is considering whether to ban the playing of computer games in breaks because there is so much conflict when the children are asked to finish, and get back to lessons. We must consider the folllowing:

- Why is there so much conflict around playing computer games?

- Because they do not want to stop.

- But why do they not want to stop?

- Maybe because they like playing games.

- Will they never stop doing something that is fun?

- Yes. But not this.

- Why – what do they say about it themselves?

- They say, 'I have only just begun.'

- But why do they think that they have only just begun?

- Because their disability means they have problems with time perception, and because it takes more time for them to begin (and end) doing things.

All right! Now we can start thinking about solutions in the form of middle ways. And I'm sure you can think of them yourself when you understand what the problem is, so I will not spell them out for you.

Another example is the man with autism who drinks lots of coffee all evening, is unable to sleep and then is late to his day service (and is very tired during the day). 'Should we take away his coffee in the evening?' the staff are asking. The most important answer to that question is 'No'. Simply because it is not permissible to take coffee away from a man who is legally of age.[7] But since this is also a problem which we want to work with, we must ask why he drinks coffee. Is it because he cannot sleep? Or does he not sleep because he drinks coffee? If it is the first maybe he needs another type of day service (one where he doesn't have to get up that early), or medical help

---

7   In fact, many people with disabilities on the autistic spectrum, as well as with learning disabilities, are unaware of their rights as people who are legally of age. They do not know when and how they can complain about support workers prohibiting or withdrawing something they have a legal right to access. As a side note one can reflect over the research by United Response showing that only 16 per cent of people with learning disabilities who were registered to vote in England used their vote in the election in 2005 (see Sayer 2010). How, if at all, are we supporting people with disabilities to use their legal rights?

with his sleeping problems. If it is the second you might want to try working with informed choices (which I write about later in this book – see p.294). The question is always *why*.

Along the same line as bans, are locks. Putting locks on things is in my opinion never a solution. I have come to group homes with locks on user's closets and fridges, and lockable gates between rooms, and it frightens me that we have not come further now, entering the second decade of the twenty-first century. The knowledge of how to work with clients with such difficulties exists, but how do we bring this knowledge down to the floor of the services? Well, this book is my best shot at it.

Recently I came into contact with a woman with obsessive compulsive disorder (OCD)[8] and a washing hands obsession, which in her service is managed by staff locking her toilet. This resulted in her, a women of normal IQ with autism and OCD, needing nappies! Not being able to go to the bathroom (or open the refrigerator or closet) when you want is, in addition to being a huge reduction of personal freedom, *not* a solution.

Solutions must be built long term. But when you are finding yourself powerless in a situation, and do not have the craftsmanship of working with people with autism spectrum disorders, it may unfortunately be the case that a padlock is all that is rattling at the bottom of your otherwise empty toolbox. What to do instead? There is no universal solution, but you will find many ideas in this book and, most important, you will find that you often need to *understand* the problem from the perspective of the person with autism. And above all, that restrictive 'solutions' such as bans and locks are never ever used until several other strategies are tested thoroughly (and evaluated) by the model in Chapter 15.

---

8   Sure, not everything can be understood. We need not, and probably cannot, understand *why* a person with severe OCD washes their hands a hundred times a day. But we may need to find out more about where obsession lies: Is it that each finger had to be washed a certain number of times? Is it the stress response that makes you sweat and feel sticky all the time right after you washed? Is it that she must feel she has 'finished' and that it is difficult to find that feeling? Is it that she is not sure whether she really has washed her hands or not? Or something else? The more we know, the easier it is for us to find the options that can be aids for her (and which do not include limiting her life and liberty). And just for the sake of clarity, when we speak of OCD, medical and therapeutic treatment may be needed also. But unless you are a doctor or a cognitive behavioural therapist, you are not the one providing that sort of help.

5.5 Pitfall 5: Steering the will of others

How, seemingly imperceptibly, are we influencing others to want what we want, in all types of interpersonal relations? In the way I suggest something, ask or give a specific answer, I can influence you to want what I want. Some people are better than others at this, and some people are easier to influence than others. Children are an obvious example. Say to a three-year-old: 'Now I am going to brush your teeth, open your mouth.' He may or may not do what you demand. Now try saying: 'Look, I have this magic brush. Let's see if there are any scary leftovers beeping in your mouth? Maybe they are striped? Do you think I can do some magic with this brush and make them run away? Don't open your mouth just yet. We need to be ready for magic. First say abracadabra! And now open your mouth.' Different strategies like these two give different results. Well, my example may have been a bit exaggerated, but I hope you understand what I am getting at.

When we believe we know what is best for others (which we seem to easily believe when it comes to children and people with disabilities) we often steer them to want what we want. Let me give an example:

EXAMPLE

Jonathan, a 22-year-old man with learning disability, is living in a group home. One day he comes up with the idea that it would be really cool to have one of those red punk hairstyles, a mohican. He is obviously very happy with his new idea and presents it to one of the staff. Annie, the support person (who is probably thinking of all the possible consequences of such a choice) answers him 'Nah, I don't think you would look so good in that'.

Jonathan, however, is not discouraged by Annie's response, and continues with unremitting enthusiasm to speak about his idea for a couple of weeks. But through a continuous and, in this context, deadening response from the staff saying that he would not look good in a mohican, in addition to a strategy of showing him other (very traditional) hairstyles he can choose from, he gives up his idea and finally goes (with Annie by his side) to a hairdresser and gets an ordinary haircut.

The haircut is one he now believes is his own choice, and he is now also happy with it. The idea of the mohican evaporated. Everybody is happy, the staff as well as Jonathan himself. Happy ending.

Figure 5.1: 'Normal' is usually defined by majority

Or is it? Is it right to manipulate people into choosing something that we have chosen for them? And furthermore, to make them believe that they have chosen this themselves? Is the fact that someone is content indeed a proof that we as professionals have done the right thing? How often do we do this, really?

Now you probably wonder how I think you should respond instead. Should you just say 'Gee, what a great idea!' and buy red hair dye and hair gel? No, that is not what I am saying (remember what I have said about extremes?). In order to avoid pitfalls like this and be a true professional you need some tools: you will read about these tools in Part 4, 'Practical Interventions'.

5.6 Pitfall 6: Excessive empathy

Now what? Empathy must be something good! Sure, but you can have too much of a good thing, and it may be coming from the wrong direction. I have a friend who becomes sad (really sad) when she sees a restaurant with no guests, and she begins to worry about what will happen to the poor owner, and so on. This is not beneficial for her nor for anyone else. On the other hand, one can obviously argue that she has a right to feel whatever she likes in her spare time.

In a professional occupational role excessive empathy does not belong. First, it can blind you so that you see a 'poor thing' with deficits, in circumstances where the individual would benefit more from you seeing her assets and strengths. Some clients or students with autism spectrum disorders additionally have an appearance which we as preprogrammed robots may react to with feelings of pity; they raise our compassion. This appearance need not reflect the person's true personality and resources. We are probably biologically programmed to react to certain looks and ways of being, for the reason that we need to take care of children and vulnerable people in a society. But it is important to be aware of our automatic reactions because, as I just mentioned, they do not always match reality.

Sometimes also the knowledge of someone being disabled can make us pity them in advance. Several people with disabilities, such as physical disabilities and visual impairment, have met these reactions.

Our attitude is reflected in how we talk to and about these persons. Here is an example of a situation I once witnessed:

EXAMPLE

A woman is about to present two employees in a new project to a large group of people at a seminar. Laura (in a clear, distinct voice) says: 'This is Tim Phillips, he is a registered social worker and he is responsible for the parts of this project I just mentioned. Laura strikes out with her arm in Tim's direction, to show the audience who is Tim, but without touching him.

Laura now lowers her voice and changes her way of speaking to a 'cuter' manner, she turns to the second man. Laura puts one hand on his shoulder: '...and this is Simon. Simon has autism and he helps us with the computers.'

Not many (and perhaps least of all Laura herself) thought that the presentation of the two men differed, and if someone noticed, they probably accepted it because 'it's how things are'. The facts that Simon had a more extensive university education than Tim (Simon had a PhD in Computer Science), and that he as much as Tim was employed in this project because of his skills were lost. Furthermore, Simon lost his last name, and his professional title and the presentation of his job in the project was reduced to 'helping with computers'.

Another risk with empathy is to read yourself too much into the other person. As in 'If I were Lisa I would want...' This of course originates from the Bible and is usually regarded as a genuine expression of goodness: 'Ye shall do unto others as ye would that others should do unto you. One example is the mother of a 19-year-old boy with autism who called me to ask how her son could get himself a girlfriend.

> 'He's both stylish and nice,' she said. 'You probably have some good advice.'
>
> The problem-solver in me went off, and I began to suggest things like maybe he should get out in surroundings where he could meet girls his age, maybe go to a camp for young people with autism, put an ad on a dating site, practise his relationship skills, etc.
>
> Until I realized I had to ask the question: 'Does *he* want a girlfriend?'
>
> 'Uh, no, not really,' she replied.

It easily happens that we read our own dreams, desires and needs into others, not only as parents, but as staff too. Perhaps we believe that client, pupil or user would like or need something when in reality it is we, ourselves, who *think that we would want it if we were them*. But we're not.

There is a lovely Zen Buddhist anecdote about this:

> 'What are you doing?' I asked the monkey who was retrieving fish from the sea and putting them in a tree.
>
> 'I am saving them from drowning,' answered the monkey.

5.7 Pitfall 7: Lack of empathy

On the other hand, it is obviously not good if you lack empathy. Sometimes I consult professionals, teachers and support staff, who are provoked by the behaviour that people with disabilities exhibit, or, at the other extreme, want to add some pink shimmering clouds around the disability.

A teacher whom I counselled a couple of years ago comes to mind. Let's call her Marge. The reason for my counselling with the teachers, who worked in a special education class where all pupils had autism spectrum disorders, was that they wanted to be more skilled in talking to the pupils about their diagnosis. At the moment they were tiptoeing around the subject, and they felt they wanted some support in how to give the pupils better information about what autism is. However, Marge didn't exactly trot along. Marge told me, in a very upset tone of voice, that she had previously worked with people with cerebral palsy and how they, as she put it, pretended they were learning disabled (which they were not). She went on to say that they did this, taking advantage of their disability, to get benefits in the form of gifts and other things. And, Marge now wondered whether, if we gave the pupils with autism information about their diagnosis, was there not a risk that they would take advantage of it in some circumstances? 'I think they could use their disorder as an excuse, or to get benefits', she said.

Here I believe you can make use of your ability to put yourself in someone else's shoes. I think: what could the reason be for an urge to grab what I could in all kinds of situations, or to feel a need to blame my diagnosis or use it as an excuse to escape demands, or even to pretend to be more disabled than I was? What state would I be in, for such a scenario to occur? My answer is that I would have to feel run over, invisible, powerless to exhibit this behaviour.

Now, this does not mean that I *know* this is so, but if I use my empathy, combined with the constructive ideology described in Chapter 13, my conclusion will be as follows:

> If the pupil (or client) exhibits a behaviour in which he is constantly taking advantage of or exaggerating his disability and is trying to get favours because of this, it is a sign that he is not feeling good about himself, and that the support we are giving is probably not well adjusted to him.

I would respond by giving this person *more possibilities* to affect his life, *more opportunities* to make use of his resources, and to show off his skills, and *more power* over me as a professional, over my interaction and the design of the support, that is, I would provide him with the tools to tell me how he perceives me as staff.

A fear of doing this is often based on an idea of what is expressed in the dreadful saying, that if you give someone an inch they will take a mile. Remember that you don't really set limits for others, you rather set limits for yourself. For a professional who knows where her own limits are, there is no need to be so afraid of having them invaded that it is necessary to put up a barbed wire around them, way before the limit is reached. Unfortunately ever so often the pupils, patients and users with autism spectrum disorders who show all signs of what I call a chronic powerlessness, are met with 'barbed wire' by staff. This, I believe, will only lead to a behaviour that may not be so desirable being established in a rock-solid way. You can read more about this chronic state of powerlessness in the section on working with challenging behaviours, (see Chapter 17).

Sometimes people wrap up their lack of empathy a bit more neatly, but as I see it, it is still the same thing. I am referring to the 'it-was-all-better-in-the-old-days-erians' that I occasionally come across.

> 'Yes, imagine how much better life was in the old days. Back then we did not have a lot of diagnoses. People helped each other. In the town where I grew up we had some real originals. But they were just eccentrics, and nobody questioned that. Everyone knew who they were.'
>
> 'We had a guy, Donald, in my town, he could not cross streets, he was always just standing at intersections, but then someone came by and helped him over. Nowadays there is not such a concern.'

I am thinking: how much was Donald *really* part of the community? To be known by all, is this always that great? (There is a saying: more know Tom Fool, than Tom Fool knows.) And if Donald could have chosen, would he not rather have had a diagnosis and a support person to help him cross the streets when he wanted, instead of standing there waiting until someone happened to come by?

I am not saying that everything is better now, but certainly everything was not better 'back then'.

Another way to wrap up a lack of empathy and make it look like an act of love, is when people say things like 'People with development disabilities are put on this earth for us to learn from them' or 'Autistic people are sent here as angels', which I have heard quite a few times. Or 'All people with Down's syndrome are happy and cuddly', a stereotyped picture which many people still like to believe in.

Perhaps you are thinking this is kind. But the question is, would you yourself like to be in the cuddly angel category? If so, do you think you would feel like you were seen and met as a complete (and complex, as we all are) human being? Would you perhaps rather feel like an object (for others to project *their* need for caring and prattling upon) rather than as a subject who is seen and met as a unique individual?

But, how can we find a balance in this, a kind of humane professionalism, where we neither lose our capacity for empathy, nor drown our clients or students in it. Herbert Lovett, whom I mentioned earlier, has put it like this: 'Without the engagement of both head and heart, we see dangerous practices heartlessly unleashed or people loved blindly without their whole selves taken into account' (Lovett 1996).

Again, the first step is that we raise our awareness, and then recognize that we too – yes, you and I – can be guilty of this sometimes. Then we create a framework to help ourselves remember this, which gives us less room to fall into the pitfalls. The Norwegian social worker Greta Marie Skau has made a model of the relationship between the client and the helper in the system. The meeting between clients and helpers takes place in one of four 'rooms' (see Figure 5.1).

Figure 5.2: A model of the relationship between client and helper
Source: Skau 1998[9]

The vertical line (P) stands for the personal level and the horizontal (S) for the structural level.

Skau points out that assessments of where an encounter is taking place would probably be very different depending on whether the helper, the client, or an observer made it. In the first room we find a good helper who works in a power-oriented organization. In the second room there is an ideal situation for our modern society, where both services and individual helpers are aware of the balance of power in the situation and endeavour to build trust and show respect (but, says Skau, ideals can often be quite far from reality).

Nobody would want to believe that their encounters occur in the third and fourth room, but unfortunately I see quite a few examples

---

9   The figure is reproduced with the permission of the Swedish publisher Liber Utbildning.

of services (it might be schools, group homes, psychiatric wards or day services) where meetings are taking place in these rooms. (You will read about some of these examples further on in this book.) It often occurs on a hidden level. Externally, for themselves and others, the service has ideals in line with the 'greenhouse', but due to lack of knowledge of autism, and lack of effective tools the services will unconsciously interact with clients or pupils exercising a high degree of power use.

One could also say that when the structure (the organization) betrays their employees by not providing them with the right training, tools and directives, the organization becomes the 'constraint cell', no matter what is said about their goals in the document on the directors' shelves.

5.8 Pitfall 8: Universal truths

A pitfall in the interaction and assessment of how support should be designed lies in the idea that there are universal truths. A staff group wanted support from me in how to make a young man with autism understand that he needed to learn to cook. He did not want to learn to cook. He thought he could just as easily buy ready-made food and heat it in his microwave, or order a pizza or buy fast food.

'Well, why can't he do just that?' I asked.

'It's so expensive to buy fast food,' a woman said.

'Is it that he cannot afford it?' I asked, 'Is he short of money?'

'No, he can afford it all right,' another staff member replied.

'But it's so expensive,' insisted the first woman.

'If you think it is expensive, I suppose this is based on how *you* make priorities in your economy? Could it be that you may choose to spend money on things that this man would never spend a single penny on?' I objected.

'Ready-made food *is* expensive, everyone knows that,' she said.

Perhaps you think I am arguing that you should just follow the path of least resistance, and say to the young man 'Oh well, you want to have ready-made food, OK then'. No, we should absolutely look into the state of his culinary interest. We would of course, if possible, try to awaken an interest by creating the right conditions (maybe we do field trips with him, or find fun cookbooks on the right level). We, of course, have to find out more about *why* he does not want to cook – if it's just lack of interest or if it is really about some difficulty that we could help him with. But having investigated this and tried some interventions, if the person still does not want to cook, then we must be able to let go.

EXAMPLE

Jackie is 16 years old and has autism. She is placed in a residential treatment centre because of her family situation. At the centre, it was decided that Jackie could have 'phone time' of 30 minutes daily.

Most ordinary girls in their teens I know, are on the phone significantly more than this (see also Pitfall 10 'More normal than normal'). And Jackie both had managed to make new friends in the village where the centre was, and also wanted to speak with her mother and sisters on the phone (since she could not live with the family). In fact, Jackie should have had *more* time to talk on the phone than other adolescents.

5.9 Pitfall 9: 'We know this'

Believing yourself to be fully skilled is another pitfall. I occasionally encounter groups of staff who want counselling in methodology for a client or student who has challenging behaviours, perhaps is verbally or physically abusive, and staff say to me 'We know autism, so that is not the problem.'

But who 'knows autism'? I have spent many years in the autism field; I have both studied autism and have had lots of practical experience and I cannot say that I *know* autism. There is always something (often much) left to learn.

The solution to the challenging behaviour is *always* partly about knowledge of the disorder, the autism-specific knowledge. And there is always more such knowledge to acquire. Of course you also need knowledge about that particular individual you are there to support. But when you say 'We know autism', you are also saying 'It's not our fault' and 'We have already tried everything.'

Nevertheless, it is often this conscious approach, a framework for their understanding of autism, and of their work, which is missing. Greta Marie Skau (as you will by now have understood, I am a great fan of hers) writes:

> Big changes are forcing their way through at a rapid pace, at the same time as most employees have not learned enough about how to lead or how to participate in change processes. In this situation you would

think that the development of such skills would be high up on the agenda in the various professional fields, but it seems still not to be the fact. Too often, the social and caring sectors are falling behind in relation to the tasks they face, with constant improvisations as a result. (Skau 2005)[10]

The employees may have been at a number of conferences and lectures on autism, read a couple of books, but not been able to make whole their knowledge, the whole which is necessary to understand – and thus treat – the challenging behaviours.

Change is of course not always easy, but as Skau wrote (see p.40): 'Responsibility can no longer mean defending the permanent.' 'We know autism' is thus in fact a statement which in itself shows that you do *not*. However, it may be, of course, that you do know the basics of autism in theory (without a connection to actual practice) and have had them repeated so many times that you neither want nor need to hear them again.

Being able to recite the triad of impairments and the diagnostic criteria in your sleep is rarely helpful when working with a person with challenging behaviours. (What really does help? You can read more about that later in this book.)

Another variant of 'We know this' comes from those representing another – often older – approach and who are convinced that they do not have to learn something new (or something different). I have met this attitude among some teachers, carers in psychiatric hospitals, and residential supporters at group homes, who fold their arms and yawn during counselling, and will make it clear that they have worked like this for 30 years, and it sure as hell has worked for them. It is not so unusual that they also think that 'common sense' is enough. It is not. If you work with people with autism spectrum disorders, you need to have autism-specific knowledge.

Sometimes I hear that ignorance is a problem, but I would say that lack of awareness of one's ignorance is a far worse problem. Knowing what you do not know, that is, what knowledge you are lacking, is one measure (among others) of professionalism, in my opinion.

---

10   My translation.

5.10 Pitfall 10: More normal than normal

There is a risk that people who are different are expected to be 'more normal than normal'. It may be that everything they do is interpreted as a symptom, or that the staff thinks that the individual's behaviour reflects upon staff, and therefore feel an obligation to stop or to promote certain behaviours. It may feel awkward to be around town with a user who is sloppily dressed or who has an odd behaviour; you may have a fear of being judged, or feel that people who see you will think you are not doing your job as you should.

One example is two members of staff who were on the subway with three 16-year-old girls with Down's syndrome. The girls whispered to each other, giggled and became increasingly loud, after which the staff tried to hush them down as if they were babies.

But the loud giggling on the subway is a perfectly normal behaviour for a teenage girl, and why should we deny this just because they have Down's syndrome and happen to have staff around them everywhere they go?

It's about learning to stand back sometimes, and staff need to have a discussion about when we intervene, and how to act when we are out in public. Do we sometimes feel ashamed of behaviours that we believe bystanders feel we should 'fix', for example?

Another example is when staff put a lock on Kate's closet, because otherwise she 'would change clothes all the time'. Why can't she change clothes when she feels like it, I wondered? The answers I received were: 'Then she will have some favourite clothes that she wants to wear all the time' and 'She could change clothes three or four times a day'. When I asked why this would be so problematic, I was told, 'There will be so much laundry!'

Figure 5.3: Is it really a problem that Kate is doing her laundry more than twice as often as everyone else?

There are quite a few people who change clothes several times a day, for various reasons. And you too, have favourite clothes, I guess? I certainly do. And before you start thinking about the environmental aspects of doing your laundry ever so often, let me point out that Kate does not drive a car, and she hardly ever throws away food so I don't think she will have to buy emission allowance credits for doing her laundry more than twice as often as others.

More normal than normal can also be expressed as an expectation that people with autism spectrum disorders should never become upset or have a meltdown. As if being even-tempered (having a happy or docile mood) is a normality, when the truth is that most people have a life that goes up and down.

In addition, people with autism spectrum disorders often have more reason than others to become bored or angry. This does not mean that one should not work to help someone who shows violent behaviour when becoming upset (and this will become obvious as you read the rest of this book). It just means that basically you must have an understanding of the fact that having autism often means having many more frustrations and exhaustion factors in your daily life.

A good example of 'more normal than normal' is found in the book *Autism and Learning: A Guide to Good Practice* (Powell and Jordan 1997). The teacher Margaret M. Golding describes in the chapter 'Beyond Compliance: The Importance of Group Work in the Education of Children and Young People with Autism' how she and her colleagues first happily took credit for 'their' young students with autism being so well behaved, but then began questioning whether it was particularly good that they were so compliant. Golding and her colleagues developed groups with assertiveness training for their students. In her commentary on this chapter Professor Rita Jordan argues that compliance can create as many barriers to a working life as resistance.

5.11 Pitfall 11: The gender trap?

I am writing this with a question mark because I do not know how much unconscious gender beliefs affect those of us who work with people with disabilities. Gender is not really the biological sex, but rather the social sex, that is, the gender roles we create in our culture. Having an awareness that gender is relevant to the expectations we have of people, does not mean we have to deny that there is a biological sex, which implies differences. Looking with a bit of hindsight we can see that men and women because of their gender differences were thought to be suitable for different jobs, and it is often with reference to alleged as well as factual differences that women have been seen as 'the weaker sex'. Pioneers have fought for such things as women's suffrage and the opportunity to practise certain professions. Of course we have not yet reached the goal; we can see that just by looking at the over-representation of women and men in certain occupations, wage differentials and so on.[11]

To my knowledge, there has been no study of how support is distributed to people with autism according to their gender. We speak a lot about equality in society today: equality in race, gender and disability. But these concepts are rarely blended, and what if you are an immigrant disabled woman? Will you receive the same support from the social system as if you were a British disabled man?

We who work in social services or care do not want to believe we may be biased. And just recently, at a two-day training in working with autism which I held with a colleague, we had three upset social workers marching out of the room with the words 'We make equal decisions for all our clients, regardless of gender!' on the second day

11   Anyone who thinks that we do not transfer ideas about gender to our children can make a visit to a store for children's clothes and take a look at how boys' clothes, always in drab colours, are decorated with action/aggressive tones and shapes, and how the girls' clothes in bright colours are strewn with flowers, butterflies and lace. Or when you are in a toy shop look at which toys have a baby boy on the package and which have a girl, and think about which professions they represent.

when we were trying to discuss this. But the thing is, if (or should I say when) we make unequal decisions, this is not (of course!) a conscious process. We are all (more or less) coloured by prejudice concerning gender. And we do know from reports and research (Ayanian 1999; Hilliard and Liben 2010), even if employees have difficulties seeing it themselves, that boys and girls are treated differently in kindergarden, and that women have not been receiving as good treatment as men do for diabetes and heart diseases.

As far as autism goes, Svenny Kopp PhD, a child psychiatrist at a university hospital in Sweden, found in her research that boys with suspected ADHD or autism spectrum disorders were examined more thoroughly in the clinic and therefore more frequently actually received a diagnosis (this led to a change of routines at the clinic).

Svenny Kopp also made an interesting remark at a conference I attended. She pointed out that although the symptoms of ADHD and autism spectrum disorders may be different in boys and girls, these differences can also be a matter of different expectations. If girls with autism spectrum disorders are said to have more traits of demand avoidance[12] this may reflect that there are actually other (higher) demands on girls.

My own impression – as I get to see many services for people with autism – is that men as a group may receive a lot more support, and to a greater extent than do women, even when their need for support is very similar. I believe that men with high-functioning autism in general receive more support with household tasks, and if they have residential support they are given more hours of support time. Perhaps we subconsciously perceive it as more obvious that a man with autism will need help in cleaning the dishes, doing the laundry, vacuuming the floors, than a woman?

Do our perceptions of gender (social sex) also affect how support and interaction is given in the direct encounter with the user? If so, then perhaps it is not just always in favour of men. I have a feeling that women with disabilities are expected to like to have their homes more neat and nicely decorated, and to care more about their appearance, and thus may receive more support in that.

---

12   Pathological demand avoidance (PDA) is a term coined by child psychologist Elizabeth Newson, who believes it is a part of the autism spectrum. The National Autistic Society says that people with PDA 'will avoid demands made by others, due to their high anxiety levels when they feel that they are not in control' and that they are 'obsessively resisting ordinary demands' (NAS, 2012).

I believe that among those who work with autism teenagers acting out, girls with autism raise far less of the staff's sympathy and nursing instinct, than do boys with similar behaviour. Staff tend to respond with stronger limits and more consequences for the girls. In some ways a girl's acting out is more provocative than the corresponding behaviour of a boy.

These structural differences do not mean that each single man receives more support than each single woman. At the individual level this may vary. But at the structural level, I am convinced that there is a problem, which is why I also believe that gender awareness is wise to have when working with people.

5.12 Pitfall 12: Good aids that no one uses

Sometimes I come to an ambitious service where staff have had lots of education in autism and theoretically understand the importance of aids, but have not really got to grips on how or why they should be used. They have made neat schedules, fine binders with pictures of leisure activities and similar things. But the clients or pupils never use them.

Staff may then be thinking that visual aids seem to be just a new 'fashion' in autism, and that they're not working. The reason that aids aren't in use is often because staff never learned to implement them. This means that you must teach the person with autism spectrum disorder to use them, and doing this also requires that you both understand your own role and what the aid is compensating for. The very purpose of an aid is typically to compensate for the reduced function and increase independence. If the client or pupil still gets help from you (rather than from the aid) there is no immediate reason for the client to use the aid.

So if you have created a leisure map with suggestions of activities[13] you must also teach the person to use it. Or another example:

EXAMPLE

In the day service some users had verbalized that they wanted a clearer overview of the day. In counselling the staff, I proposed an outline

---

13   For those who find it difficult to engage themselves in activities (often according to deficits in mental imagery) a binder or folder with photos of suggested activities to choose from when you do not know what to do can be a good aid. You will find a lot more about aids in Part 4 of this book, 'Practical Intervention'.

schedule of the content of the day.' We have one,' staff said, 'but nobody ever looks at it.'

The reason for this was that the schedule was pinned to a wall in a room that no one really passed, and if a user, arriving in the morning, asked one of the staff 'What happens today?', staff responded orally to the question (instead of referring them to the schedule, preferably located in a strategic place).

How do you teach the person to use the aid? Well, by referring to it. In the example of the leisure map, the user/pupil says (or shows by his behaviour) that she doesn't know what to do. You say 'Look at the map' or you may follow the person and get the map and help her to look something up. How you do this depends on what the person needs. The important thing is that you fade out your support so that the person gradually learns to do this independently.

Working with aids contains several components: assessment of needs; assessment of what type of aid will meet the need; acquisition or production of the aid; implementation; and then, over time, new assessments (since aids must always grow and develop with the individual). Too often, I see that the only part of all of this work which is done is the acquisition.

5.13 Pitfall 13: 'What if everybody...?'

This is an approach that you may come across in various places, but perhaps especially in schools: 'What would it look like if everyone ...' This posture is often rooted in a fear of doing different things for different students, and a fear of the consequences of making an exception for someone – and it is almost always a totally irrelevant argument.

Let us, for example, look at Libby with autism who does not want to go out on breaks, she wants to stay in the classroom. But this is not possible because 'What would happen if every pupil wanted to be indoors at break time?' But first, there is no question of *everybody* staying inside, and second, there are relevant reasons why we would make an exception for Libby. Perhaps this child has great difficulty handling their sensory input, which means that a break outdoors together with many other children may not mean the rest and recovery that is its purpose. But please do not forget that this was just an example: all children with autism spectrum disorder need not be indoors at break, and among those who do want and need it, there may be several reasons for this, not only the one I just mentioned.

This pitfall is also seen among professionals who work with adults with disabilities, unfortunately. 'What if all of our users...' you can hear staff say. 'If they did what?' you are wondering. Well, I've heard about all kinds of things:

What if everyone who lives here had a car in the garden? (This was about a resident in a group home who liked to repair cars.)

How would it look if all of our clients in the day service would have to squeal every time someone says a certain word?

It is one thing to try to anticipate problems that may arise in the future, another to predict them.

Worry is interest paid on trouble before it comes due. (W. R. Inge)

5.14 Pitfall 14: Other children will never accept...

This pitfall is very much connected with the previous one. It may sound like this:

- We cannot let Judith have macaroni every day for lunch, it would make the other pupils envious.

- We cannot let Ali be indoors at recess, because then all the children will want that.

- If we make exceptions for Jorge, the whole class will oppose them.

- It won't make any difference if we stop nagging at Marcela, because her classmates also nag at her.

I feel that these arguments reflect a lack in the pedagogue's own confidence, that is, a lack of confidence in their own ability to explain things, lack in their confidence as a teacher, as well as in other children's ability to understand and accept. Perhaps children cannot develop more acceptance and understanding than we expect of them? And if we expect so little, then what?

I think that if we as adults just explain in a straightforward and honest manner why we do what we do, and what is the purpose, children can absolutely both understand and accept it. 'But we are not allowed to tell the classmates about Judith's diagnosis,' you might object. Relax, I am not saying that you have to involve the other students in the details of Judith's difficulties. The psychologist Ross Greene puts it like this: 'Children are actually pretty good at understanding the "fair does not mean equal" concept and at making exceptions for children who need help; it's much more common that adults are the ones struggling with the principle' (Greene 2001). So you can explain that while other pupils may receive help with what they need (tying shoe laces, studying maths or other things), Judith will get the help *she* needs, which among other things, happens to be not having to go out at break time.

On the whole it's a good idea to point out the differences between pupils to them as often as you can, to really *celebrate* differences. The school is supposed to teach tolerance, and thus create a basis for the pupils to accept that there are different rules for different people. Another good idea is to take this opportunity to tell pupils that everyone needs help with something and this is why it is so good that we are different; we can help each other. I also find it very useful to offer children examples of things I myself need help with (as they often tend to think adults can handle everything). I am sure you as well have things you need help with, like reading the manual for the DVD player, remembering to water your plants, fixing something with your car, or whatever it may be.

If the children feel confident with your assessments and you make sure all individuals get the help and support *they* need, they will accept exceptions.

5.15 Pitfall 15: Normality produces quality of life

If you do not have to be 'more normal than normal', as I mentioned earlier, as a pitfall, you should probably at least be as 'normal' as everyone else, shouldn't you? I encounter quite often a belief that normality and quality of life are linked with each other; indeed that the first is a prerequisite for the second. This can be manifested in the idea that it is best to make the person with autism as normal as possible (in the sense of 'like others'), perhaps by training him to stop odd behaviour, making him behave 'as people do' (e.g. give eye contact, say hello, etc.). 'It's best for him – if he behaves like others he will be better perceived by others' is often given as an argument and, by extension, professionals (or parents) think that person also may lead a better life.

There are a lot of very different people, with odd behaviours who actually lead very good lives, who have a good quality of life, although anyone can see that they are different. There are also a lot of so-called 'normal people' (or neurotypical[14] if you want to call them that) who actually have miserable lives. They may be unhappy with their marriages, jobs, housing, or their life situation in general, and in fact do not in any sense have a particularly good quality of life, despite their normality.

But what will determine if someone is to achieve good quality of life? I doubt it has anything to do with your level of 'normality', or that you have as little need for support as possible. Quality of life, I believe, has much more to do with having good self-esteem and being self-confident. Trying to 'normalize' someone who does not himself have a desire for it can unfortunately have negative effects on self-esteem.[15]

Every now and then I meet young people with autism who say that they sense that people around them think that they should be somebody else. What they are saying is that the wishes and expectations surrounding them are so essentially different from the person they actually are, that they think that others are not only trying to change them, but even turn them into *someone else*. What will this do to their self-confidence?

Now, this does not mean that I believe that a person with an autism spectrum disorder should never learn to greet others, or to be taught some other 'normal' behaviours. What I want to do is to challenge the general notion that it is always better to act like 'everyone else', and (again) point out how different people with a disability are. The latter means that if Andrew, Scott, Dawn and Tracy all have autism and none of them give eye contact or say hello to other people, then what is right for Dawn could be completely wrong for Scott, and so on. Andrew might avoid eye contact because he feels that it is difficult to decide how long you should look into someone's eyes when talking to them. And let's say Dawn avoids eye contact for the same reason. Scott, however, is perhaps very sensitive to light and has a cap pulled down

---

14   'Neurotypical' is an expression that came about in the autistic community when a word was needed to describe people who do not have autism.

15   You can read about factors that can affect self-esteem in a positive direction in Chapter 23 'Can You be Yourself When You Do Not Know Who You Are?'

more or less covering his eyes because of this, which then also means that he does not give eye contact. While Tracy on the other hand finds it difficult to both listen and look in the eyes simultaneously, and thus has problems doing things simultaneously.

They also have different personalities. While Dawn feels it is OK to declare to people, 'I have autism' as an explanation for her behaviour, perhaps Andrew instead has a strong incentive to 'fit in', and therefore is keen to practise his eye contact skills.[16] On the other hand, for Scott the cap is perhaps a good strategy to avoid the disturbing light, which is working so well for him that people around him must learn to live with not receiving any eye contact. Tracy may have yet another strategy.

Figure 5.4: There is no one size fits all in autism

If it actually *is* a problem, always considering the person's own experience (i.e. is it a problem for him or her?), both the reason and the individual's personality must guide the intervention, that is, how we 'fix' the problem.

Of course, there are more common pitfalls. There are (at least) two more; I could call them 'Over-estimating comprehension of language' and 'Too much focus on behaviour'. But these subjects will be covered later in this book – in Chapter 9, 'Say What You Mean and Mean What You Say', and in Chapter 17, 'The Danger of Focusing on the Behaviour Itself'.

---

16   This does not have to mean actually looking into their eyes. A guy I know trained himself to look at people's earlobes when they talked, so they would feel as if he looked at them.

PART 2

Understanding the Impairments

...The Symptoms We Often See and What May Cause Them

6

'You never know if orange juice will taste like orange juice'

A Chapter on Sensory Processing Issues

Sensory processing is about how sensations are processed in the brain. When we speak of sensory processing problems we mean that there is a difficulty in organizing and coordinating the sensory input. It has little to do with the sensory organ (e.g. the ear or the eye) itself but rather with how the brain deals with the impressions.

Having sensory processing problems is not a criterion for autism spectrum disorders, but is the rule rather than the exception. For individuals with sensory processing problems, it may be that there are worse in childhood and then improve over the years. Others, however, continue having significant problems with sensory processing in adulthood. While some have several sensory problems involving more than one sense, others have only one. And a few individuals have none at all, but those are, as I mentioned, the exceptions.

Are sensory processing problems unique to autism? No, but they are not all that common outside the neuropsychiatric field. There are descriptions of how sensory processing becomes a problem for people who have suffered a neck injury (like whiplash), and people with hemiplegia (a form of cerebral palsy)[1] often have sensory processing problems. There are of course some people who have a single sensory processing problem without any disability in general. A friend of mine who is very sensitive to sounds (and she does not have autism or any other disability) describes it as having 'glass ears'. I have another friend who cannot stand touching some materials (cotton-wool pads for example).

Sensory processing problems are not entirely uncommon in the population, but within the autism spectrum people often have

---

1   See, for example, Children's Hemiplegia and Stroke Association (www.chasa.org), and research by Michele Sterling on whiplash injury (Sterling *et al.* 2003).

more intense problems, involving multiple senses. In addition, they already have a disability that affects, among other things, their energy consumption. Therefore, sensory problems are often more difficult for those with autism.

What is the cause of sensory processing problems in autism? There may be several possible ways to understand this, but the most basic is, in my opinion, that if you look at the development of children in general, you will notice that sensory processing is a developmental skill – the infant is not born with fully functioning sensory processing. When the foetus is protected in the mother's womb, there is no need for mature circuits in the brain to deal with sensory input, and we can only imagine the sudden meeting with the world outside the womb. Now the sensory processing (together and in interaction with motor skills) must develop. It's as if the infant is 'preprogrammed' for this, even if the individual variations are large – that is, sensory processing does not develop at exactly the same pace and in the same order in all small children – but still 'all roads lead to Rome'. The brain will eventually have a mature sensory processing system, meaning the brain can filter, sort, distinguish between important and unimportant, and manage and respond adequately to sensory input.

If we look at 'standard development' we can see that many small children during various periods have small 'problems' with sensory processing. But what happens is that as these pass, we as parents tend to forget them very quickly. It could be things like:

- a three-month-old baby who suddenly cannot tolerate the sound of the vacuum cleaner or dishwasher

- a newborn who reacts by screaming or crying when location change occurs (when lifted up, laid down, dressed, etc.)

- a two-year-old who cries and covers his ears when a moped drives by

- a four-year-old who suddenly is unable to tolerate a certain taste or texture of food

- a five-year-old who suddenly finds that some clothes he liked before are now 'prickly'.

Since these phases pass, we do not attach much importance to them. Maybe such 'states' occur when sensory processing develops, when immature structures of the brain retract and the more mature structures emerge? As I see it, autism spectrum disorders are very much *developmental* disorders, which means that many of the symptoms found in autism, are also found in 'standard development' but are then – as I mentioned – of a temporary nature. I often put this as 'one person may be of many ages' (you can read more about this later).

What are the consequences of sensory processing problems? Well, apart from often affecting the person's life in a negative way, it is easy to imagine that a brain that is over-stimulated by sensory input does not have the opportunity to develop other skills at the expected pace. Of course, a different sensory processing may also be enjoyable. I will return to this at the end of this chapter (see 'Different is not always a problem' on p.124).

Let us look more closely at the sensory processing ability. I'll try to be a bit systematic and go about it sense by sense, but I want to emphasize that this is easier said than done. Sensory function often develops in interaction, and one sense affects the other (typically as in smell and taste, but this also applies to other senses). In addition, the senses are in interaction with motor skills, as I mentioned before.

I am trying to describe the problems with sensory processing that I have come across in people with autism spectrum disorders, and of course no one has *all* these problems. Some have several, others hardly any, and they can also vary over time. Of course, there may be varieties which I have not yet encountered, and perhaps you know someone who has a problem with sensory processing that is not mentioned here.

6.1 Visual perception

Since visual stimuli are not processed by the most complex parts of the brain (such as those using language), it is easy for most people to quickly interpret visual stimuli in the form of images. This is why we have visual instructions with pictures and symbols in the form of road signs and other important information which we need to be able to interpret rapidly. Information about escape routes and how to act during a fire are always accompanied by pictures. During high levels of stress we all find it easier to 'read' a series of pictures, than to read, process and understand a text.

In autism spectrum disorders, this is even more significant. Whether it is due to the fact that people with autism often in everyday life experience stress, or to deficits in mental imagery (difficulty in 'inventing' general internal images), or to language comprehension problems, is hard to say. My guess is that all these factors interact.

As you probably already know, this is why we build a lot of aids on visual perception[2] (even written text is often easier to process than the spoken word). Despite the strength of visual perception, there may be some who have problems in this area.

EXAMPLES

Lynne has difficulties estimating speed and distance. She cannot catch a ball, or anything else, thrown to her. It is too difficult for her to determine whether it is safe to cross a street. Lynne is an impulsive girl and often just runs straight into the road.

Kenneth, however, who has similar difficulties, is often just standing, seemingly paralysed, at the crossing point, even if there is no car in sight. Because of his difficulty, he doesn't feel confident a car will not turn up and run him over before he reaches the other side of the street. Thus, the same difficulty can be expressed very differently in behaviour.

Jane perceives things moving towards her as very unpleasant. If someone leans forward slightly, she often jerks backwards. She says it scares her, it feels as if the other person could fall on her.

Speed and distance assessment of course interacts with motor function; this may have implications for physical education (see also Chapter 7 on motor skills) for a pupil who has autism.

Depth perception is linked to distance estimation, and there are people with autism who perceive this as difficult. This may have implications for spatial understanding, for example understanding that things can be located behind, under or in other things. If you have problems with this it can be difficult to look for something.

EXAMPLE

Marc is the father of Susan, a nine-year-old girl with high-functioning autism. Marc asks Susan to go and look in her room for her homework. Susan comes back to Marc saying that the homework is not in her room. When Marc goes into Susan's room he need only lift her sketchbook on the desktop to see that the homework is right there. Marc previously thought that Susan was just lazy but now he has understood that she does not understand that one thing can be underneath another thing.

A person may also be enormously fond of (or dislike) a particular visual stimulus. Many people with autism like things that spin or glitter.

---

2   You will find examples of such tools in Part 4 of this book.

EXAMPLES

- Shameela, who has autism, loves green, and wants everything in green. Shameela has green walls and floors (!) in her flat. She is always dressed in green, and when she recently saw a green portable CD player, she obviously had to buy it.

- Joshua, in contrast, cannot look at decorated things and says that patterns on wallpapers and fabrics are 'moving'. It makes him feel sick and dizzy, and new staff in the residential support have to be instructed not to wear patterned clothes, because it is difficult to create a good relationship with Joshua otherwise.

- Liam, who has high-functioning autism, has a 'foggy' visual perception. Some days he says it's hard to see anything at all; it is as if there is a coloured fog over everything he looks at. Liam also has problems with recurring headaches and it is possible that this is linked to a migraine phenomenon in his case.[3]

Sense of direction

There are a lot of people with autism who have difficulty with their sense of direction. Some children I've met also have difficulty understanding that a room that has two doors is the same room, when you come into it from different directions.

EXAMPLES

- Jenny often takes the wrong route home, even when she is in her own neighbourhood. Jenny hates to be lost, so she stays at home, which means that she becomes very isolated.

- Charles often opens the wrong door when he is going to his classroom. When he comes into the wrong classroom he feels very stupid, and that is why he's started to skip school.

- Elinor always goes to the same shop for groceries, but although she has shopped there for several years she never seems to learn to find her way around. This means that the shopping is very time- and energy-consuming for her.

Spatial relationships

Spatial relationships are about perceiving how things relate to each other, and how they relate to the room. Some people with autism

---

3   Visual warnings in the form of bright spots or lines, blurred vision and so on are common in migraine.

spectrum disorders have difficulties with organizing something on paper, for example, a calculation. It can also be difficult to get the address, sender and stamp in the right place when writing and sending a letter. (It is sometimes called dysgraphia when you have real difficulty with this, but anyone who has dysgraphia also tends to confuse the words, mix capital and lowercase letters and can have difficulty expressing themselves.)

Light sensitivity

It seems reasonable to mention light sensitivity when talking about visual perception. Although it has nothing directly to do with visual perception, it is through our eyes that we take in and perceive light. To be sensitive to light is relatively common in autism spectrum disorders. Several of the people I have met who are sensitive to light also have sleep disorders, and I wonder if maybe there is a connection since light intake through the eyes also controls sleep hormones.

I sometimes meet people who themselves come up with strategies for this (though they cannot always explain why), and they may have a cap pulled far down over their forehead, or always wear sunglasses to avoid the light.

EXAMPLE

Hollie is very sensitive to light and always has the blinds closed in her apartment. She has problems with her sleep–wake cycle, and will stay up all night and sleep all day. She avoids going outside when it is sunny. In the group home where she lived previously, the staff thought it was 'depressing' to have the blinds down and used to pull them up, creating much extra trouble for Hollie.

EXAMPLE

Ruben, a 15-year-old with autism, always had his cap pulled down over his eyes. In fact, he pulled it down so far that he could not see more than a few inches of the floor in front of him. Both school staff and student housing staff had been nagging him for more than a year to take off his hat. Of course, without success, as he really needed protection from the light that bothered him so much.

We changed tactics, and now the staff were given the task of celebrating his ingenuity and creativity in order to solve his problem. They were also tasked to review all possible positive things about the cap, and to give him positive feedback. It could sound like this:

- 'What a great colour your hat is!'
- 'It's just amazing that you never stumble even though you see so little when you have that hat on!'
- 'It is good to wear a cap as then you don't need to fix your hair!'
- 'We are so glad you've come up with your own aid for your light sensitivity.'

Some time later, when this response had had a positive effect on the staff's relationship with Ruben, we could suggest that he might like to try other means for the same problem, such as sunglasses. And see – the cap went up, but not off, and sunglasses on.

We could not have introduced the sunglasses before we had built the relationship (with him as well as with his cap) with the help of our first response. It is simple in theory but difficult in practice: if we devalue what is useful or essential for someone else we will not win his confidence, and without his confidence, we will not be allowed to help him. This applies to you and me and everyone.

Figure 6.1: If we want changes to occur we must build a positive relationship

Unfortunately, it is entirely reasonable to imagine that a light sensitivity may have further negative consequences for the person, such as the already mentioned disturbed sleep, but also perhaps in the form of a lack of Vitamin D (which is produced when we are exposed to sunlight). I do not have any suggestions for solutions to this. The most natural way to work with sensory issues is of course with understanding and adapting the environment. But this will not, unfortunately, help with any negative secondary effects arising from the avoidance of light. This is why one would wish there was more research on sensory processing problems – and preferably research founded on the real problems that people with disabilities experience.

Detail orientation

The distinctive orientation towards details seen in persons within the autism spectrum is often obvious in their visual perception. For example, students with autism may have difficulty understanding the purpose of an illustration in a school book. Illustrations, meant to be a support for the text, can for the visual-detail-oriented person be very confusing.

EXAMPLES

- Toby is doing his homework. In the illustration he sees a small line that does not match; it is a bit too long. He is unsure if this has any meaning or is just an error made by the person making the illustration. Toby will be thinking for hours about this, not getting anywhere with his homework.

- Alice is doing her homework. In the illustration she sees a small line that does not match; it is a bit too long. The line not fitting into the picture annoys her, and Alice shreds the page into pieces and throws the book across the room. Again, the same difficulty but different behaviour!

Olga Bogdashina who has written several books on the sensory issues in autism has suggested that this phenomenon may be attributed to what she calls *gestalt perception* (see Bogdashina 2003). She offers the example of artists with autism such as Steven Wiltshire[4], who takes in the whole picture when he draws a building, and also relates that several children with autism can do a jigsaw puzzle without even looking at the pieces. Bogdashina's idea is that if what you see is a unit, the entire picture falls apart if you change one detail.

Prosopagnosia

Face recognition is a complex mechanism involving more than just visual perception. If you have a significantly impaired ability to recognize faces, this is called prosopagnosia. It is known that people

---

4   www.stephenwiltshire.com.

with acquired brain injuries can suffer from this. But several individuals with autism spectrum disorders also seem to have difficulty with face recognition.

EXAMPLES

- Ian was furious if someone on the staff in his residential or daily service had a haircut, dyed their hair, shaved off a beard or something like that. He simply couldn't recognize them anymore. (At first the staff thought – erroneously – that this was about Ian wanting to 'control everything'.) To help Ian they now will put up a picture of themselves with the new hairstyle and write their name underneath. This helps Ian to memorize their new look more quickly.

- John has great difficulty recognizing his classmates in the schoolyard. He tried to recognize them by hair colour, and consequently, he believed that any kid with short brown hair was his friend Max. Other children thought that John was funny when he mistook people like this.

A person who has problems with facial recognition will also often find it difficult to recognize so-called celebrities and have a hard time keeping up with movies and television shows, as many actors may be similar in external attributes. One trick that has helped some individuals is a conscious training to recognize voices. One theory put forward by researchers is that the reason for the difficulty could be that people with autism spectrum disorders look more at people's mouths than at their eyes. One study (Rutherford *et al.* 2007) found that the group with autism spectrum disorders could be clearly divided in two: one subgroup in no way differed from the control group in regards to the focus on the eyes, and one subgroup had impaired ability to focus on the eyes. In this study they did not, however, find that those with the impaired ability to focus on the eyes were more focused on the mouth.

Another study (Barton *et al.* 2004) investigated facial recognition in people with what they call 'social developmental disorders' (in which they include autism spectrum disorders) and compared them with both a normal control group and a group of people with clinical prosopagnosia. This study also found that the subjects with 'social developmental disorders' could be divided into two groups: two-thirds had problems with face recognition (though not such great difficulties as in the group with prosopagnosia) and one-third had no difficulty.

6.2 Tactile perception

Having problems with tactile perception is one of the most common problems in autism spectrum disorders, but can be expressed in several ways. Perhaps most common is that it is hard to handle touch[5] and especially light touch. If someone grabs you thoroughly or even hard, it may feel better.

EXAMPLES

- Awela, who was 14 years old and had autism, refused to shower. She could not explain why herself (and perhaps no one really asked about how she experienced the shower). The family thought this was obstinacy, and maybe a difficulty understanding how others perceived her lack of hygiene. But when moving to a new apartment which was equipped with a bath tub it was discovered that Awela actually had nothing against keeping clean, as long as she didn't have to use a shower.

- Karim was 'hysterical' about clothes; he shouted that they hurt him and was very sensitive to every detail of the clothes (such as zippers, buttons and laundry labels). He had to wear soft, big clothes that were not tight anywhere. Karim would also exclaim 'He hit me!' when someone just touched him lightly.[6]

Accordingly, the individuals who have these sensory issues can have difficulty with showering (tiny water droplets on the skin that hurt), while it is nice to swim (which gives an even pressure of the water around), and find it difficult to endure the small details of the garment. Light touch can hurt.

---

5   A while ago I was riding on the underground. It was already packed when it stopped and a number of passengers squeezed themselves in. At the next stop a man entered the already crowded car, and when the doors closed, he started pushing those of us of who stood near him, swearing and shouting, 'Get away from me, you morons! Move!' Where most people heard aggression, I heard the desperation. While those standing near sighed, hissed and glared, I actually smiled compassionately and thought that here is a man with autism and tactile hypersensitivity. 'Are you allowed to behave badly just because you have autism?' you might want to ask. Uninteresting question, I'd say. I see a man with a real problem with flexibility (i.e. to change his plan when the first plan does not work), with tactile perception, and with social adaptability. Why should I be angry with him for it? Even if he pushes me? If you or I are repressed, desperate and overwhelmed by a situation we cannot handle, do we want people to be angry with us or to be compassionate?

6   It is extremely important that in our response we do not rob Karim of his perception of reality by saying things like 'That couldn't hurt'. In Chapter 23 on building self-esteem, you can learn more about why.

Therefore, one can guess that this is about 'foreground–background perception' or discrimination in the sense of touch, a function in sensory processing that distinguishes the important and unimportant, and places the unimportant stimuli in the background. If this works as it should, one does not register the sensations that are irrelevant (background impression) and they do not reach consciousness. But here seems to be the problem for some people with autism – too much information reaches the brain. It seems that when there are too many details they become unbearable and overwhelming.

EXAMPLES

Harry, who has high-functioning autism was screaming 'Ouch, ouch' when his parents tried to cut his hair and nails. At first they did not understand it really hurt (but guessed that he was afraid of the scissors). But Harry indeed has, as do some other people with autism spectrum disorders, a pain sensitivity in his hair and fingernails. Today we have no good explanation of how this is possible (but this makes the pain no less real).

So, it does happen that people with autism spectrum disorders feel pain from the 'wrong things', that is to say you can have sensation in nails and hair. As I said, there is to my knowledge no explanation for this, but one can imagine that the nervous system 'misplaces' pain signals somehow.[7]

Speaking of pain, you can sometimes read in the professional literature that people with autism have a high pain threshold. This is a bit misleading in my opinion – indeed some do not react that strongly to ordinary pain. But first, we do not always know if this is about an inability to feel or to communicate it, and secondly some obviously have painful sensations of things that others do not react to (such as water droplets or touch). This is why I consider it more correct to speak of a different kind of pain perception.

In the outer tactile sense, we can also include temperature perception (and regulation). If you have worked for some time in the autism field you probably recognize examples like these:

---

7   As a parenthesis it may be interesting to know that I've met two people with neck injuries (but without autism spectrum disorders) who also have experienced this. One had fallen off a horse and the other had a whiplash injury.

- Samantha, who has autism, happily run outdoors in winter without a coat or even a sweater, whatever the weather. And she does not seem to be cold.

- Owen, who has autism, undresses all the time. Outdoors he takes off his outdoor clothes and indoors he takes off everything. He seems to be most comfortable when he is naked or just in his underwear.

There are several examples of people with diagnoses within the autism spectrum who have an over- or under-sensitivity to temperature. Among those who have problems with this, it seems to be most common to have a weakened perception of cold and hypersensitivity to heat. These are people who are happy to be thinly dressed outdoors in winter, and who want it really cool inside. They often suffer from the heat and function less well, for example, during hot summers.

I have encountered the opposite occasionally, that is, a person with autism who puts on lots of clothing even when it is hot, takes extremely hot showers, and drinks almost boiling liquid without perceiving it as too warm.

6.3 Auditory perception

Auditory perception is perhaps the sense that causes most suffering for people with autism spectrum disorders. Some have 'acute' hearing, and cannot 'turn down' the volume of background noise.

EXAMPLES

- Nicole is the mother of Joe, a 12-year-old with autism. Nicole tells me it has happened that Joe heard what they talked about in another room, even when he slept (and Nicole says that she is quite sure he was asleep).

- Frederick, aged 17, thinks that the sounds of the day are so disturbing that he turns the day around and sleeps during the day, since it is quieter at night.

- Amelia is suffering tremendously from all the sounds that don't 'add up': a false note or sound that has a little dissonance that others do not perceive.

- Mohammed could not sleep because the staff's room in his group home (which has night staff) is located next door to his apartment.

- Grace does not want to go out to a restaurant or coffee shop because she cannot filter out background noise and thus becomes awfully tired from trying to keep up with what her company is talking about.

- Christopher cannot pay attention at school in class, because other students talk about their projects. Christopher does not have attention deficit, but his sound sensitivity negatively affects his ability to concentrate and be attentive.

As mentioned, many individuals with sensitive hearing suffer as a result and it can interfere with both sleep and concentration. They can become very tired and get headaches from sounds that others do not seem to react to at all. There may be both sustained and abrupt background noise, such as (sustained) traffic noise, fan buzz, watches ticking, and (abrupt) coughing, talking, scratching with a chair or a ringtone. For those who have difficulty with the 'volume control' in sensory processing (to automatically turn down the 'volume' of the unimportant and turn up the important) a wall of sound is formed where they have to use their conscious attention to isolate the important, (e.g. when listening to someone talking). It obviously can be very tiring and thereby affects what to other people seems to be their motivation.

It is interesting that there seem to be many sensations that are actually recorded by the brain but that do not reach consciousness. You've probably also at some point experienced 'after-hearing' something. I am referring to those moments when someone says something, but since I do not think it is me they are talking to I don't 'hear' them. After a while I get that it was addressed to me and *then* suddenly I hear what the person said, but retrospectively, so to speak. What the person said made an imprint but reached consciousness only when I realized that it was important. The brain obviously had received the sensations, processed them 'halfway' but not really brought meaning to them, not let them reach consciousness. Still the sensations remained there, and when meaning was added I could become aware of what was said. This suggests that there are probably many sounds that are recorded but most of us still do not hear them on a conscious level, and therefore are not disturbed.

'But he cannot be sensitive to sounds, he makes so much noise himself' is a fairly typical comment. But the one thing is not necessarily connected with the other. Some people with autism spectrum disorders makes lots of noise, and sometimes actually the reason seems to be to create their own wall of sound, to avoid being disturbed by the noise of others (the noise a person himself produces is both well-known and predictable). Making noise could of course also be about vocal tics, such as in Tourette's syndrome.[8]

EXAMPLE

Charlie has an autism spectrum disorder and likes raves. He has become a highly sought-after and popular DJ at free parties. Charlie's residential staff and parents find it somewhat difficult to understand how Charlie, who is so sensitive to sounds, can be a DJ. But in addition to his musical interest and skill that gives him status in the free party culture, the rave environment has several other positive effects for him. Among other things, it makes Charlie's difficulties with social interaction less obvious – with all the dancing and the loud music it is not required that you make small talk. Charlie says that the loud music is a pleasant background (he also has loud music in his earphones at home and claims it helps him concentrate).

The brain probably handles different kinds of sounds in different kinds of ways. There is a difference between sustained and sudden sound, a difference between the well-known and expected noise and unknown and unexpected noise, and so on. Göran Söderlund is a Swedish researcher who found that cognitive abilities in children with ADHD improved by listening to stochastic noise (Söderlund, Sikström and Smart 2007). This white noise is, for instance, such a noise as a TV makes when there is no programme on. This is entirely in line with the experience of that noise, and vibration during a drive is also reassuring for many with autistic and attention disorders. In the residential care I run outside Stockholm, we have also found that our clients with severe self-mutilation, autism and anxiety find using a vibration exercising machine very calming.

'Auditory allergies'

Some people with autism spectrum disorders seem to have a 'sound allergy', that is, a sensitivity to a particular frequency and pitch.

---

8   Tourette's syndrome is a psychiatric disorder. Having Tourette's means having repetitive reflex-like movements and so-called vocal tics. Vocal tics may come in the form of sounds, words or whole sentences.

EXAMPLES

- Lucy is 16 years old and cannot tolerate the sound of road works, mopeds or motorcycles. Lucy told me how much energy it takes just to get to school. She must be on the lookout for everything that is painful to her ears, and sometimes she has taken a long detour (making her late for school) because she thought she saw someone with a helmet in his hand close to a moped.

- Michael cannot ride the bus because he can't bear the hissing sound that occurs when the doors open.

- Shahid's parents thought he was afraid of dogs, but he was not so much afraid of dogs as of the noise that could suddenly come from a dog. He also couldn't stand whistles and other high-pitched sounds.

An auditory allergy has a direct impact on the person, of course. You may not want to go out, or if you go out, you have to be vigilant of all hazards.

Hearing voices

Hearing voices can of course also seem to be connected to auditory perception. As some, Professor Christopher Gillberg among others, have rightly pointed out, of course everyone hears voices. So if a psychiatrist asks a person with autism if he hears voices and the person replies 'Yes', it may simply be a question of a literal understanding and concrete thinking.

The phenomenon of hearing voices (i.e. inside your head, voices which are not heard by others) are otherwise considered a psychotic symptom. Many probably have the idea that such voices force the person to various actions, sometimes violent. This idea probably comes from the many thrillers with this theme, and the fact that people with voice-hearing sometimes commit crimes that we read about in the newspaper. Voice-hearing may indeed have this character, but most people with psychiatric illnesses and delusions are not at all violent, and these days there is a movement towards learning to live with voices instead of working against them or medicating them.

I have encountered a few people with autism (both children and adults) who hear voices but are very aware of their voice-hearing, and have an intact sense of reality and no delusions or psychotic disorders. They do indeed think the voices are real, very real (since they hear them!), but they also know that others do not hear them and do not suffer from other delusions such as that they (or others) would be controlled by something; they are not paranoid. These voices are not controlling or demanding, not depreciatory, but have more of a commentating nature. The people I come across who have autism spectrum disorders and hear voices have not had psychoses, nor have they been in a state of extreme stress. I believe this phenomenon might be better understood as a form of synaesthesia, which you can read about later in this chapter.

6.4 The olfactory sense

It's not very common to have problems with smells, but it happens. For those who have a hypersensitive sense of smell it can be a nuisance. One boy with autism I met vomited straight out at any kind of smell from food, and several others have described the smell of food as particularly intrusive and unbearable.

EXAMPLES

- Victor who is nine years old and has autism cannot stand the smell of cheese. He does not want to go home to classmates' houses because he is afraid that someone will suddenly put cheese on the table.

- Harold, who has autism and learning disability, used to vomit in the food while he ate. When he was allowed to eat only odour-free food (which according to Harold was mostly cold food) the vomiting stopped.[9]

- Ellie does not want to use some of her school books because they smell. Ellie's teacher, who does not understand that Ellie's processing of smell is different, reacted in quite an insensitive way. The teacher took the book and smelled it, and firmly declared 'It does not smell,' as if her nose would be a universal measure. Ella has also come into conflict with other adults because she thinks that they smell bad, and does not want to be near them.

6.5 The sense of taste

Taste is of course as everyone knows, closely related to smell, and a different sense of taste can sometimes be the reason why people with

---

9   In a group home where I supervise, one of the staff told me that years ago she had worked with a man with autism who always threw up the food while eating. They had worked with behavioural training. It meant teaching him to eat without throwing up by means of rewards. 'Imagine,' she said, 'if all we had needed to do was to help him cover his nose!'

autism spectrum disorders do not want to eat certain things. Many are very choosy in their diet.[10]

Also in the sense of taste there seems to be this foreground and background perception, that I described earlier, and one can guess that if the 'filter' function is working well, one does not perceive all details of taste when one eats or drinks something. A man with autism said, for example, that he could never be sure that orange juice really tasted like orange juice. Perhaps he perceives only details with his sense of taste, details that others do not perceive at all? Orange juice can probably taste quite different depending on which manufacturer it is, what kind of oranges, what time of year it is made, if the bottle has been already opened, if it is cold or at room temperature, and so on. These are all details that most of us do not register; instead we experience the overall taste of orange juice.

So if Oliver does not want to eat more than just a certain brand of chicken nuggets (or another food), he may not just be a 'picky eater'. He may actually perceive it as if we serve a whole different dish if we serve a different brand. And Nadia who buries all her food under a thick layer of lemon pepper seasoning may need to do it, because as she says, otherwise it does not taste of anything at all.

6.6 Balance

The sense of balance is obviously connected with vision and also with motor skills. Some people with autism also have problems with balance. Those I've met with balance problems had, for example, difficulties climbing stairs, riding an escalator and also doing things while walking (for example, carrying something in one hand).

Some also have what you may call a balance uncertainty, that is, standing on a step may feel like standing on a cliff. Having difficulty walking on uneven surfaces is also found in some cases.

EXAMPLE

Alex, who was eight years old and had autism, insisted on not taking part in forest excursions. School staff speculated that maybe he was afraid of the woods or something like that. It turned out that the uneven surface was simply too difficult for Alex to walk on. His school aide made paths in

---

10 Being choosy about food can also have several other causes (e.g. problems with sensory perception inside the mouth that makes you sensitive to the texture of food; reduced feelings of hunger; or a minimum need for variety).

the schoolyard where he could practise balancing on an uneven surface in the breaks (with an adult on hand at the beginning) and one semester later, the forest was no major problem for Alex.

6.7 Proprioception – muscle and joint sense

This is a sense concerning receptors in the muscles and joints. Proprioception gives you the ability to determine your own body position without the help of sight, as well as where the various parts of the body are located in relation to each other. If you have problems with proprioception, you can have difficulty with co-ordination (as Christopher with autism tends to put it: 'I have two left feet'); with regulating muscle strength; and with moving around in the dark. It is with the help of proprioceptors – receptors located in muscles and joints – that we know, even though we close our eyes, how we have bent an arm or a leg. (By the way, the proprioceptors are affected by alcohol and that is why a drunk person makes so many miscalculations and wobbles.)

Occasionally you meet people with autism spectrum disorders who have difficulty here. You can see this when the person always does things with force – perhaps always slams the door, puts down the glass so that the contents spill out, shakes hands so hard it hurts the other person and so on.

You can probably recognize this yourself – everyone misjudges the muscle strength needed for a task from time to time – for example, you may have lifted an item you thought was heavier than it actually was. If this has ever happened to you, you also know that how much muscle power you use is not a conscious decision, but an estimation that your brain makes entirely in silence for you. The person with difficulties in this area often tries to compensate by thinking about how much force to use, which is both attention- and energy-consuming.

Even if the person, so to speak, detours through consciousness as compensation, it is important that professionals understand that the person is not really helped, and the problem is not facilitated, by someone telling him that he should not slam the door, or making remarks such as 'Set the glass down carefully'. It is not possible to remove a real problem with the regulation of muscle strength by asking (or nagging) the person to do something differently.

Problems with proprioception can also make it hard to determine body position without the help of sight. Some people describe it as feeling totally lost in the dark, not being able to feel where or how their body is positioned. It may also affect the perception of 'rear'.

EXAMPLE

Lauren is 13 years old and has autism. Lauren gets very scared (which is expressed by screaming and swearing) as soon as someone or something comes into her line of sight from the rear. It is as if only what she sees exists. In PE classes, it happens that someone throws a ball to Lauren from the side, but she does not catch it because she has no idea that something might be coming from an area she does not see. If the ball is not in front of her, in her visual field, there is no ball. If someone comes from behind and puts a hand on her shoulder, she is startled and may attack the person. She has no perception whatsoever about what may be behind her.

Now, what might this 'perception of rear' be? My guess is that a newborn child has no idea of his rear, of what may be behind him, out of his visual field. The development of this perception probably occurs gradually and may start when the child is 9–13 months of age, typically throwing things out of sight and seeing them reappear. This will teach the child that even if you don't see something, it can exist.[11]

To define what we call body perception is not easy, but I would say a normal body perception is based on a well-adjusted interaction between sensory integration and motor function during childhood.

To have a functioning body perception is important in social interaction with people and therefore it can also help build self-confidence.

6.8 Interoceptive senses

Hunger, thirst and the feeling of fullness are not quite part of perception, but are controlled by such things as hormones and innervation. They are probably also linked to perception in a way as whether the signals are interpreted correctly (or even 'let in') or not depends on how the 'filter' or 'volume control' I mentioned earlier, works. For instance, it is not difficult to imagine that a brain that is fully occupied with 'manually' dealing with too much input does not 'have time' or space

---

11   During a period in 'standard development' the favourite game is often 'peekaboo', which also deals with the perception of what is seen and what exists. I have met children with autism in the last years of primary school who love peekaboo games, and I believe that in terms of body perception they are only just 'getting there', so to speak.

to perceive hunger. Some people with autism spectrum disorder do not seem to really perceive these signals. Some find it difficult to perceive them at all, while others may perceive them only when there is a very urgent situation.[12]

Reduced hunger is perhaps the most common example of not perceiving signals from within found in autism, and some individuals are capable of eating very little (to the family's concern) and at times forget to eat at all. But there are also those who instead relate entirely to the clock and the amount on the plate, a different approach to the same problem. They eat 'by the clock' and those who don't perceive fullness will eat everything on the plate even if it is too much.

In the case of bladder and bowel signals we also know that human beings are not born with good perception of these signals; this is something you learn to perceive. In addition, you develop the ability to perceive signals and control the bladder before you learn to perceive and control bowel function. Therefore, it is entirely possible that some people with autism spectrum condition have a developmental delay here.[13]

6.9 Synaesthesia

Synaesthesia[14] means that the senses are blended together. It is a neurological phenomenon that has been known for quite some time. It is relatively rare in the general population, but seems to be slightly more common in people on the autism spectrum. This does not mean however that even within this spectrum it is common.

The most common form – of this in itself unusual phenomenon – is to have coloured 'concepts' and coloured hearing. This means that sounds and concepts such as characters, numbers and weekdays produce an immediate colour for those who have synaesthesia. Some 'feel' or perceive the colour within, others describe that they see the colours around them.

---

12 You can read more about how to understand (and work) with this in the examples of Matthew and Gemma on pp.262–263.

13 It *always* makes sense to look at the symptoms in autism from the perspective of delayed development, rather than as odd behaviours. More about this later.

14 The word comes from the Greek *syn* and *aisthesis*. *Syn* means 'with' or 'together' and aisthesis means 'senses', 'feeling' or 'sensations'. If you want to read more about this I recommend the book *Wednesday Is Indigo Blue: Discovering the Brain of Synaesthesia* by Richard E. Cytowic (2009).

To be recognized as synaesthesia, this experience must be constant over time; it is not just about associating a colour to, for example, a weekday or a letter.[15] If you have genuine synaesthesia it means that if you as a child experience, say, the letter A as yellow, it will *always* be yellow, for the rest of your life.

One wonders if those who have colour synaesthesia agree on colours, if everyone feels that the letter A is yellow? No, among those with coloured conceptual understanding and hearing, they all have their own colour for a sound, a tone, a voice, a letter, a number or a day of the week.

There are other forms of synaesthesia, and there may be even more variations than have been described in the literature up to this day. For example, I have encountered in people with autism spectrum disorders a tactile-auditory synaesthesia, and a shape-auditory synaesthesia.

EXAMPLES

- To Roseanna every tactile sensation produced a sound. If someone touched her or if she touched an object, it could – depending on the type of touch and materials – produce different internal sounds. Since some sounds are very unpleasant (and other sounds are pleasant) she is very reluctant to touch some things and very keen to touch others.

- Anthony perceived that logos and other types of shapes, sometimes also architecture, had a sound, that he wanted to listen to. The M for McDonald's he particularly liked, and he would often want to stop and 'listen to the M'.

So Zachary who wants to listen to buildings is not necessarily suffering from a lack of perception of reality. And Melissa, yelling 'Ouch!' when she touches a pillow might not have a tactile sensory problem but could hear a distressing sound. However, it is understandable that people with autism and synaesthesia can be perceived as psychotic when they talk about and act according to their synaesthesia in an environment that does not have any knowledge of this.

In the literature there are also descriptions of taste-shape synaesthesia. Neurologist Richard Cytowic (2003) tells in his book *The Man Who Tasted Shapes* of a man who cannot serve the chicken until

---

15   For instance, if you perceive Sunday as red (which is often the colour used on calendars), it does not mean you have synaesthesia – it rather means you are imprinted with the colour of the calendar in our culture.

the taste has enough 'dots'. For this man this is (as for most people with synaesthesia) such an obvious sense that he believes that everybody perceives taste like this. If there is no shape, there is no taste, according to him. In addition to these forms of synaesthesia, other even more rare variants have been described, such as for example, audio-posture synaesthesia (where sounds produce different body postures).

Common to people with synaesthesia is the feeling that their perception is very natural, and they are often surprised to realize that others do not perceive things in the same manner. There are various theories about what synaesthesia is, but there is a fairly widespread perception that it is about a separation of the senses, which for some reason does not occur in some individuals. The idea is that all infants have sensations that 'leak' into each other, but that when senses are developed and integrated the sensations are separated; this occurs so early in development that normally you do not remember that you as an infant experienced the world in a 'synaesthetic way'. The theory is that for some reason this separation does not occur completely in some individuals, and thus they have synaesthesia in adulthood.

And yes, about hearing voices, as I said earlier, it is possible that voice-hearing in people with autism (who do not have a psychosis) could be a form of synaesthesia.

EXAMPLE

Jordan, who has autism and is hearing voices, has a description of this, which is easy to recognize from a synaesthetic point of view. He says that the voices have always been there, and they are very natural to him. 'My earliest memories are my voices,' he says. He also says, as do many with synaesthesia, that life must be a bit meagre for those who do not hear voices.

What are these voices? Jordan says it can be described as if his thoughts and his instincts simply have a voice.

In Jordan's description his voices do not seem more remarkable than just being voices. What he hears is, in his description, such thoughts as most people have. There are thus commenting thoughts following what he does, as in, 'What now, the dishes first and then...'; questioning thoughts: 'Where did I put that book?'; and invectives like 'Damn, I've missed my appointment with the dentist!'

In other words, these are things we all think, with the difference that for Jordan these thoughts have different, distinct voices. Perhaps thought-voice is just another form of synaesthesia?

6.10 Sensory integration problems

Among those interested in sensory issues in autism, there is no consensus on what the real problem is, behind the difficulties we see. Some, for example Wendy Lawson (2001), argue that people with autism spectrum disorders are 'mono-channelled' and have difficulty processing input from several senses simultaneously. I have encountered this. An example is Brandon, who often seem hopelessly clumsy. But Brandon has discovered that if he closes his eyes he performs better in motor tasks. It is fascinating to see him hit a nail with a hammer perfectly with his eyes closed!

Olga Bogdashina, whom I mentioned earlier (see p.107), has pointed out numerous problems that may exist; she speaks among other things of *distorted perception, fragmented perception* and *delayed perception*. She has also pointed out, as several others have, that an individual can be both over- and under-sensitive to certain types of stimuli (or have inconsistent perception that varies between hypo-and hypersensitive). For people who have sensory problems it is a good idea to make a sensory profile. By that I mean a mapping, assessment and documentation of the sensitivities and strengths in the sensory area. You can then decide what adjustments, aids and tools are appropriate.

6.11 Desensitization (or habituation)

Habituation means gradually becoming accustomed to something, and is something that occurs spontaneously in the nervous system. There are people with autism spectrum disorders, who appear to have substantial problems with habituation.[16] This means, for example, that when the nervous system turns on the alarm function, it will take a long time to shut off. Picture this: you are standing at an intersection, waiting for the lights to change so you can cross the street. Now the light turns green for pedestrians and you take the first steps to cross. Now an ambulance with sirens on comes at high speed just in front of you. You manage to step back in time, but the entire physical alarm system in your body turns on, your heart rate increases, you feel your heart pounding and your breathing becomes different. If you habituate

---

16   There are researchers (e.g. Rogers and Ozonoff) who suggest otherwise, arguing that people with autism are hyporesponsive and don't have a problem with habituation. But honestly I think the everyday experience of those working and/or living with, or near, autism clearly shows the contrary, and above all, that the variation is extensive.

normally the system will turn off after a while, your breathing and heart rate go back to normal, and it is just as if it never happened. There are people with autism spectrum disorders who have great difficulty here. Some have described it as a process that takes a whole day, or even longer, before their alarm system turns off after an incident like this.

So if Ashley, who has autism, is very anxious about being startled, it needs not be about anxiety in its general sense, but might be on the basis of her experiences. If Brian, who has high-functioning autism, for weeks dwells upon every startling incident (a fire drill in school, an ambulance on the street outside the school), he may be neither 'repetitive' nor 'compulsive', but have found it was just so difficult, so demanding and took so long to calm himself down that he needed a lot of support afterwards.

Desensitization is one way of working with progressive habituation. It is used when working, among other things, with phobias and certain forms of tinnitus where you have become anxious about what creates discomfort. In desensitization you gradually discover that it might not be that bad, and learn to accept your reactions (and live with them). It is unclear how well this works with sensory dysfunction, as the fear here is not irrational (as in a phobia); in a person with sensory problems a sound can mean actual and pure pain.

EXAMPLE

Dawn has a daughter, Phoebe, who is five years old. Phoebe has been diagnosed with pervasive developmental disorder not otherwise specified (PDD-NOS) and ADHD, and has very extensive auditory sensory problems. As soon as Dawn turned on the dishwasher, the washing machine or other household appliances (food processors are unthinkable!), Phoebe would cry, scream and throw a fit. Dawn could not even vacuum when Phoebe was asleep.

Dawn tried recording the sound from the various household appliances and then let Phoebe listen once a day, beginning at very low volume, which she then gradually increased. Now, a month later, Dawn thinks that something has changed: Phoebe is still sensitive to sounds, but does not have as strong reactions anymore.

About ten years ago the researchers Geraldine Waters and Renee Watling went through the few studies that exist in the area of 'sensory integration training'[17] and concluded that the studies are so small that you cannot say that there is a scientific basis for suggesting that the treatment works (Waters and Watling 2000). But since the area is yet to be researched, you cannot come to such conclusions on an individual level, and I certainly think that for those who have serious problems with sensory dysfunction, who want the training and can afford it, it may be worth a try. I have found people who said they were greatly helped by such training, as well as those who thought it did not help at all.

6.12 Different is not always a problem

A subject I touched on at the beginning of this chapter is that having a different sensory system could also be something positive. As a woman with autism said to me, 'I do not need drugs, I can get high on my own nervous system.'

In cases of severe autism, occurring together with learning disabilities, we often see that people can love one particular sensory stimulus: listening to a sound over and over again; touching a certain material; or looking at anything that spins or glitters. Sometimes these behaviours will be named as obsessions or fixations.[18] As I see it, it is rather an expression of what we in autism call *special interests*. If the person does not have the intellectual capacity to collect facts about something, or the ability to collect certain items, the special interest may have a sensory expression instead.

This means that I also think it is presumptuous of the outside world to claim to be able to determine what is meaningful to another person. Luke, a young boy I know with autism and severe learning disability, enjoys, or even loves, watching the washing machine. How would anyone be able to determine that this is not a meaningful activity for him? Who can decide what makes sense for someone else? If you think about it – have you not yourself (maybe even several times?) watched programmes on TV that are actually of

---

17   Sensory integration is considered to be the neurological process that organizes sensations from one's own body and the surroundings, in order for the body to function efficiently. The American occupational therapist Jean Ayres coined the term and developed sensory integration training, a method for treating sensory and motor difficulties. You can read more in the book *Sensory Integration and the Child: 25th Anniversary Edition* (Ayres 2005).

18   Funnily enough, the professionals themselves who speak of 'obsessions' and 'fixations' seem to be obsessed with impeding obsessions. Perhaps they should start with themselves?

poorer quality than a 40 degrees colour wash programme in the washing machine...?[19]

Of course if you, like Luke, have autism and learning disability, you will need help organizing your life to make sure that you do not sit 24/7 watching at the washing machine. But to say you could not do it at all because it is not meaningful or 'an obsession' – I think that's disrespect.

EXAMPLE

Callum had high-functioning autism and was 12 years old. Twice a month he stayed at a short-term residential service for children with autism. There Callum would get stuck into poking everything that he found into the space behind a chest of drawers in his room. This was called a 'fixation' and it was decided to 'address it'. Next time Callum came to the service the chest of drawers had been glued to the wall so there was no space to shove stuff down there!

I do not of course believe that this was malice on behalf of the staff, but things like this can happen when care providers do not have sufficient understanding and knowledge of an individual and his disability.

If Callum, or anyone else, has a narrow repertoire of behaviours, and if they seem to be repetitively doing the same thing over and over again, we can try the following:

- See what function it has for the individual. (Could it be that Callum likes the sound when things fall, or maybe he likes small things that fit right into other things?) Can we offer more and new things that serve the same function?

- See if it is a sign of stress, a need for relaxation or difficulty with imagination, and offer other activities that may give more variation or be more suitable.

- Try to expand the activity from within. We do this by participating in it, doing it together with the person, and trying to introduce new elements or variations.

- Give the activity a clear time and place (e.g. on a schedule).

---

19   You should try it! I promise, it will be more satisfying than the last episode of whatever junk-TV you usually watch. And, if you think about it again, how often do you yourself engage in 'pointless' repetitive (obsessive) behaviour as when playing games on your computer or mobile phone?

6.13 How do we know, what do we do?

In a child or a person with a sensory dysfunction who does not understand their own problems, and maybe is unaware of them, there can be direct consequences on behaviour. The person perhaps hides, takes cover or has a meltdown, when over-stimulated.

EXAMPLES

- Niki, an eight-year-old with pervasive developmental disorder (PDD), often sat under her seat and covered her ears. Niki's teachers thought it was some sort of protest, until they realized she had a sensory problem.

- Nadif, a ten-year-old boy with autism, often had meltdowns, shouting and throwing things around him. When we mapped the situations in which it occurred, it was almost always in PE lessons, in the dining room and at break time – situations which all placed great demands on his sensory system.

What we could see with terrifying clarity was that if Nadif was *about* to erupt (exhibiting signs of stress, in his case he began muttering curses to himself) and someone then started talking with him, which meant both an additional sensory stimulus and also demanded his language comprehension (the latter was reduced from the start because of his disorder but was even more reduced during stress[20]), then he would *certainly* have a meltdown. We saw that what others said or did was of crucial importance for the outcome of the situation.

When the problem can be seen in the behaviour, it can be in the form of an active as well as a passive expression. While some become hyperactive or disruptive when their senses are overloaded, others become passive and introverted, and 'shut down'.

Perhaps the most important consequence of having knowledge of a person's sensory problem is that you can avoid making things more difficult for him or her. Simply understanding will often get you a long way. Sometimes, of course, aids (such as noise protection, earplugs, sunglasses) are also needed.

While some individuals with autism spectrum disorders can very clearly and properly put words to their problems if someone asks, there

---

20   We all lose some of our language comprehension skills during stress; the more severe the stress, the greater the loss. Maybe you yourself have an experience of, for example, having someone tell you something really distressing, and finding that you couldn't make sense of what they were saying.

are others who may not be aware themselves, let alone put into words, what is stressful. Some speak spontaneously about their problems but because of the way they do it, the people around them might not listen.

EXAMPLE

Eric, aged 15, who has autism, would yell every time he came into the dining room 'Shit, what smell! I hate this fucking place!' No one in Eric's surroundings got the message of what he said, because they were all so busy responding to his 'nasty' tone and language ('Eric, don't use that language!').

To really learn to *listen* to what your pupil or user says (and ignore how it is said) will help you to help him or her better.

But what can you actually do about sensory problems? There are never any standard solutions, but some good things to start with are first that individuals often need to learn to recognize and put words to their problems (it helps them knowing when it occurs and explaining it to others) and then adjustments in the environment and aids could be needed. Now remember that adjustments and aids must be specific, not general. It's *not* that people with disabilities in the autism spectrum generally require a monotonous environment with little stimulus! If you have a service where many people with autism spectrum disorders are residing you should not strip off everything 'just in case', because it actually can be too boring and monotonous for those who are not subject to sensory processing problems. This is one of the most common mistakes I see in services, that staff instead of individualizing aids and adjustments, make them general. There are other ways forward.

Nadif for example would have a daily chat at the end of the day with his pupil assistant who would help him reflect on how he felt inside when he had too much input, and practical assistance to avoid these situations. When Nadif seemed to be stressed out adults would show him a picture of a pair of headphones, and point in the direction where his MP3-player was. Nadif could with this help move away and listen to music for a while. Eventually he did not need to be reminded, but did it himself. It is important that the information follows Nadif so that adults in new environments will know that this is his 'medicine' and not begin discussing whether he should really listen to music now. In Sweden it is becoming more common that adults with autism who are extremely sensitive to sounds receive municipal financial support to soundproof their apartments. But this kind of support is not available everywhere, and not possible for all sensitivities. That is why it is so important to think creatively.

EXAMPLE

Megan, who has autism, is very sensitive to light. In winter, when her residential support is at her place to help her with cleaning, they must turn on the light. Megan turns it off, and the staff turn it on again. The interaction becomes slightly repetitive: 'Megan, you must understand that we need to have the lights on to be able to see anything.' But Megan has, because of her disability, difficulties mentalizing, and cannot see it from the staff's perspective. The new strategy was to find a time of day for her cleaning when there was usually enough daylight, and (when it was necessary to turn on the lights) to get Megan her cap and sunglasses. Less nagging, and a nicer atmosphere!

What about this desensitization – are there more examples of how to desensitize? Well, it seems that some sensory problems can be managed by training. For example, exercises that involve feeling and describing various types of touch; physical activities involving balance and co-ordination including various spinning and rocking movements; and carefully exploring tastes or sounds. With children, much of such sensory training can be done in play. You should not have too high expectations; it doesn't work for everyone, and above all, the person himself must want to do it, and not find it too unpleasant.

Finally a question I am often asked: 'My son likes to hug – does this mean he does not have autism?' Answer: no one has all of these sensory problems, everyone is different. Many have some sensory deficits, some have many. Some have none at all. The type and extent thus varies.

7

The Man with Two Left Feet

A Chapter on Motor Skills

Having difficulties with motor skills is not currently in the diagnostic criteria for autism spectrum disorders, but Hans Asperger[1] included physical clumsiness in his description of children with Asperger syndrome. One does therefore not have to have motor difficulties to be diagnosed with autism, but nevertheless a relatively large number of people with this diagnosis have such problems. As with the sensory problems, it can be expressed in a variety of ways.

Motor skills are not just a single function but several, and you can have one single problem or many. Motor skills are developed in close interaction with the sensory system you read about in the previous chapter. Motor skills are also development skills. That is to say the baby did not come into the world with motor skills already developed. And that in turn means that we can understand the motor problems in autism spectrum disorders from a development perspective, which helps us to show understanding. We would not scold or nag the baby because she cannot do certain things, so let us avoid doing it to the teenager or adult with autism, too.

Most people are familiar with the distinction between gross and fine motor skills, and know that some children have greater difficulty with fine motor skills even if gross motor skills are functioning well. In autism the opposite is sometimes seen to be true – that it seems easier to manage the fine motor skills, and a person with autism may really like to work or play with very small things, while having a clumsiness in the gross motor area.

There is a diagnosis known as developmental co-ordination disorder (DCD). My experience is that there is an under-diagnosis of DCD. I believe that motor problems are often neglected in autism spectrum disorders, and that people of all ages on the spectrum often

---

1   Hans Asperger is the Austrian doctor who gave the syndrome its name. He was active in the 1940s, but his work was translated and distributed only in the 1980s.

do not receive support and training to develop optimally in the motor area.

In addition to an overall retardation of motor skills leading to general clumsiness, and difficulties with jumping and running, or holding a pen, writing neatly, and so on, there are several other features of motor function that may be affected. I will not (and cannot) provide an exhaustive list of the difficulties that may occur, but rather describe the ones I usually encounter. Thus, if you have met someone with autism and a motor difficulty that is not listed here, you shouldn't be surprised.

7.1 Motor automatization

Motor automatization – what is this? I'll try to explain. We have expressions like 'He's got it in his bones', or 'It's like second nature to her', which states that the ability is 'sitting in the spinal cord'. Frequently, in fact, we talk about automatization. When learning a new skill everyone has to put some effort in, often by using concentration and conscious thought. But when the skill is learned, automatization kicks in.

People in the general population probably have varying degrees of automation skills, as this goes for most human abilities – that is, they exist in varying degrees. Thus, for some, it is surprisingly easy to automatize a new motor skill, such as swimming or cycling, while for others it takes longer.

Please note that I am not talking about *having* the skill, being able to ride a bike or to swim – but about how fast it is possible to acquire the skill to the point that it no longer requires full mental attention. When riding a bike is automatized you can think about lots of things while doing it, while before automatization you may be able to pedal and keep your balance but still have to have your conscious focus on the task.

Although someone has a lack of automatization they can certainly learn to perform skills; the problem is that without automatizion, they will have a higher energy output than others. Perhaps it has been a long time since you learned to swim and ride a bike but if you have a driving licence, you can think of what learning to drive demanded of you during your first few lessons, for example.

If a task requires all (or most) of your energy, you will obviously not have the energy to go on with this (this can be walking, sitting, standing, cleaning, cycling…) as long as others (who have intact automatization functions). In addition, it will – of course – affect simultaneous capacity, that is, doing several things at once.

Let us return to the example of getting a driving licence. If you now have a driving licence, I'd like you to think about how likely it felt during the first lesson, that you would be freely talking to people in the car about this and that, while driving? Not so likely? And yet you probably do this now. When you no longer needed to follow what you did with your conscious thoughts, this released energy and attention could be directed towards other things than the actual driving.[2]

For those with a lack of automatization this stage simply does not occur, or it takes them an extremely long time to reach it. Therefore, you can meet people with autism for whom walking, standing and sitting is still not automatized. You can recognize them as their favourite position is to be lying or half-lying everywhere; they often complain that they are tired or simply say 'I don't have the energy to' when you ask them to do things, and they try to avoid things that require automatization.[3]

It is difficult to say how common automatization problems are in autism spectrum disorders, but I see it quite often. In each autism-specific activity I supervise – for example, a special education class, a daily service, a group home – there are usually at least one or two clients or pupils with such difficulty. Frequently they are perceived as lazy and unmotivated. This is really quite unfair because they have to work harder for things that others 'get for free' from their nervous system. Some of the children who are perceived as lazy are in fact children who are ever so creative and talented! They are very creative in inventing arguments – their mental energy is not affected as much as their physical energy! – against why they should do certain things

---

2   When it comes to driving, a person who drives often and has good automatization can get into her car, drive several miles and then 'wake up' when she gets to her destination, without really knowing how she got there (and still have driven completely safely!).

3   Even more demanding are often things like doing chores and other activities that require repetitive motor movements. What could it be that a person with poor automatization functions refuses to do or tries to escape?

   1. Cleaning
   2. Going for a walk
   3. Brushing their teeth.

   Correct answer: All three.

(and they of course cannot explain why they don't have the energy to do them).[4]

The environment attributing negative characteristics to the person with the difficulties is unfortunately quite common. This often happens when the difficulty is not visible, and is only – as is the case with many other things mentioned in this book – manifested in behaviour.

If you are a teacher you might recognize these pupils; I think of them as 'sliders' or 'slippers'. This is a pupil who sits down to work independently in an exercise book, and at first is properly seated on the chair (the first three to ten minutes maybe). Then the pupil begins slipping. Some slide over the bench and soon have their exercise book underneath them while lying across the table. Others might slip down on the chair until they are more or less on the floor beneath the table. It is obviously hard to get much work done in this position. And, every so often, an adult comes and prompts the pupil – perhaps in a very friendly way – to sit properly on the chair. But, as we have seen already, you can't help a person by requesting a skill that he or she does not possess.

The great risk with being perceived as lazy is that you eventually internalize others' image of yourself to the degree that you become convinced that you are lazy. The environment's picture of the pupil, who is himself not aware of the difficulties he has, can offer an explanation. It may, oddly enough, be a relief for a pupil to understand himself as 'lazy and unmotivated' when the alternative is to not understand himself at all. Unfortunately, this is not so good for the pupil's progress; it would be much better to really understand, and receive support for, their automatization problems.

EXAMPLE

Henry was in a special education middle class for students with autism. His main characteristic was that he would always lie down, if he could. He would lie on the table, on the floor, across the chairs and so on. At break time, he might be hanging over a swing (not in order to swing on it) or lying on a wooden bench outside.

Henry was considered very difficult to motivate. He had never done more than what was required of him. If he was to work independently to

---

4   You would not expect little Jenny to raise her hand in the classroom and state 'Ms Johnson, I can't do this because of my poor automatization skills!' (But wouldn't it be great if Jenny could do just that?). Instead she may come up with 'I feel sick', or just yell 'I can't do this!' or even do something naughty in order to deflect the teacher's attention to something else.

page three of the exercise book, he never did anything more than what he was asked, even if he happened to complete the task ahead of time.

He would also argue and protest, much to his teacher's frustration, before he did any schoolwork at all. Henry was a gifted child, and had no problems with learning, so why did he spend so much time arguing to escape tasks in school? Henry had at the age of 11 read all the books about autism he could get his hands on (all of Tony Attwood's books, among others), and he was very verbal. He could seemingly tirelessly argue why he should not have to do certain tasks in school. In addition, he knew more than his teachers about his disability, which meant that adults sometimes found it hard to win the debate.

And, yes, Henry was also a 'slider'. I recognized him as a person with suspected automatization problems. My first suggestion was that he should get a good chair. An office chair with good back support and arm rests, a chair that would give very good support for his sitting posture.[5] Funnily enough, there was already such a chair in the classroom. It belonged to the teacher (although she rarely had time to sit on it).

The first day with the new chair, he suddenly did more pages than he had to in the exercise book, which had never happened before. I would be lying if I said that he never again argued to avoid doing things. But the fact is that he did not argue to the same extent as before, and it was obvious that his new chair influenced 'motivation'.

As you will see from more examples later in this book, getting the right support is not only about finding an aid which compensates for the deficit (in this case a chair compensating for lack of automatization), but also about the *attitude* that comes with the aid and support. When we offer an aid and support we are giving the message: 'We understand that you have a problem, and that you need help. We do not blame you for your difficulties.'

Now, you might object 'We don't have the means for buying expensive chairs in our school!' Well, you should know that it is actually seldom a question of resources. It is rather a matter of knowledge and doing careful 'detective work'. By having understood the problem we will often find a solution, and it can be costly or cheap.

If one understands that this is about a difficulty with motor automatization one can obtain an old mattress, or at worst only a pillow, and let the pupil in question lie on the floor and work. Often an unconventional way of thinking is what is required. It sounds easy, but can be ever so difficult in an environment (such as schools) that sometimes has so little room for the unusual. But, you might be

---

5   By the way, why do children in school often have to sit in chairs that we adults would never accept to sit in for the entire day?

thinking, should we really have all the pupils lying around on the floor, what would it look like? And if we let Ellen do this, won't Charles, Simon and Noah also demand to lie on the floor? If this is the case, go back to Pitfall 14: 'Other children will never accept...'[6] on p.95.

'What if he never learns how to sit properly?' is an objection I get sometimes from staff. Now here is something important which I will come back to later in this book: if a person has a genuine difficulty in a particular area, we cannot demand that this difficulty should be addressed at the same time as the person is to accomplish something (e.g. intellectually).[7] If we are to teach the ability – and that is not a bad idea – we need to put the training on the proper level for the individual, and without requiring intellectual performance and simultaneous capacity!

To return to a previous example: if you take your first driving lesson, you do not start with skid pan driving or driving at night, while you are still learning to read the road signs, and practise getting the clutch control right.

OK, you might not be a teacher, and so you are probably thinking that this does not apply to you. So let me take an example from another type of service, a residential support or a group home. It can be, for example, a situation where the user is to wash up the dishes together with the staff. The staff's assignment is not to perform chores for the user, but rather to help the disabled person get started and get it done, which usually means that they do it together. Well, now that the sink is filled, detergent added and the user Frederick has begun scrubbing with a washing-brush, the residential supporter gets started: 'Did you see the film on Channel Four yesterday?'; 'How hot it is today'; 'Did you talk to your sister?' If (I say *if*) Frederick has poor motor automatization functions and motor difficulties in general, and therefore a difficulty with doing things simultaneously, he might pause, stop washing the dishes and respond politely. The support worker may then come to a staff meeting stating: 'It feels as if Frederick does not want to do the chores, but rather wants us to do them for him' or 'I feel Frederick is difficult to motivate'.

Am I now saying that you should never talk while washing the dishes with a user? No, I am not. But if the user or pupil does not

---

6   As you may know, justice does not mean that everybody should get the same things, but that each one should get what he or she needs.

7   What if I forced you to practise something that you find difficult, while at the same time you have to describe the content in this book that you are now reading?

seem to do what we expect of them, we must ask ourselves why, and whether something we say or do is the reason.

Let me also add that when it comes to activities such as cleaning and cooking, you have to do a reasonable assessment. Autonomy and participation are obvious basic ideas that permeate our work as helpers. But if the cost is too high for the individual, and it means a lot of negative interaction over a task, one must assess whether it is not reasonable that we would rather do it for the person. Naturally we always try to have the user participating in cleaning, washing and laundry as much as possible and with aids, if needed – but if the user still cannot do it…then you maybe have to rethink. Sometimes you need to consider the circumstances.

EXAMPLE

Robert, who has autism, had lived at home with his mother until he was 57 years old. He received his diagnosis when his mother passed away at the age of 93. Robert's mother had managed everything for him. Now Robert was moved to a group home. Is it reasonable that he should start doing all these chores himself if he finds it too difficult and he doesn't want to? We try, of course, but when Robert always says 'Mother used to do that' we have to realize that a 57-year-long habit may not be easy to break.

Speaking about motor functions I also want to mention speech motor functions. In problems with speech motor control, professionals tend to primarily think about such things as difficulties articulating and pronouncing certain sounds. But automatization problems also seem to affect speech in some cases. It could be that a person – even if he clearly articulates and speaks well – has great difficulty with automating the speech.

EXAMPLE

Alex has a problem with being interrupted. Every time someone interrupts him he starts all over again from the beginning, repeating the whole sentence. Alex is also very slow, not in the actual speaking, but when you ask him a question, he will pause for a long time before responding. In a group it is very difficult for Alex to obtain the time needed for him to say what he wants to.

Alex says he needs to make the entire sentence complete in his mind first, and then consciously 'send' the words to his voice to speak it. He must, therefore, in an energy- and attention-consuming way 'create the speech' for it to happen. No wonder he is not fast and flexible when he gets interrupted!

It may be that this automatization is a major problem in autism spectrum disorders, not only in the motor area, but in other areas as well. I am thinking about a difficulty with automating social behaviours, that many with autism seem to have. Perhaps automatization is a superior function that, if it is not working properly, can create problems in many areas.

7.2 Other motor difficulties

You sometimes see people with autism spectrum disorders who have difficulties knowing what to do if they have both hands busy, and need to put a hand to something (such as when putting on a jacket or opening a door).

EXAMPLE

Adam, who was 13 years old, a gifted guy with autism, was going on a skating outing with his class. Adam walked a bit ahead of the group and was the first one to reach the train station. He stopped at the doors.

The others, who were behind him, saw how Adam suddenly had a meltdown: he started yelling and cursing and kicking a waste bin. The teacher and the teacher's assistant could not see any reason for his behaviour. They tried to calm him down but he was frantic.

The assistant took Adam back to school. Only after a long moment, could he explain what had happened. It turned out that when he came to the doors of the train station, he had his school bag in one hand and his skates in the other hand – and then he did not know how to open the door.[8]

Many with autism spectrum disorders appear to have significant difficultly with copying a movement if it is reversed (i.e. motor imitation). This can be to do with spatial relationships (see p.104) which are part of visual perception. There are also theories that this may be connected with attention as well as with mirror neurons.[9]

8　That it is extremely stressful not to understand your own difficulties when you are 13 years old and in a situation like this, and therefore not strange at all to have a breakdown, is obvious, I hope.

9　Mirror neurons are a kind of neuron that are activated when we, for example, see a movement carried out, and which then helps us to do the movement ourselves, to copy it. There is a discussion of the role of mirror neurons in autism (such as what role they play in order to take others' perspectives on a mental level) but there is still insufficient research to draw any conclusions about this relationship.

Figure 7.1: Difficulties with motor automatization affects simultaneous capacity

EXAMPLES

- Mia, who has autism, needs help in woodwork class, but if Anna, who is the woodwork teacher, stands facing Mia, on the opposite side of the bench, then Mia cannot copy what the teacher is showing her.

- Braden, who has high-functioning autism, does not know how to turn on the washing machine. The support worker Sam stands in front of the washing machine and shows what buttons to press, but since Braden is facing Sam, he still cannot perform the task.

'I have shown him/her hundreds of times,' Sam and Anna sigh when speaking to colleagues. But if they had seen to it that Mia and Braden were *beside* them in these situations, Mia and Braden would have perhaps had a better chance to learn.

There are several reasons to choose the beside-interaction instead of opposite-interaction and this is one of them. Another reason is that for many people with autism spectrum disorders social interaction (i.e. reading others and participating in exchange of non-verbal communication) is easier when people are sitting beside each other and there is less expectation of non-verbal communication.

7.3 Practical implications

But what does it mean in practice to have problems with motor skills and body perception? Some consequences are of course obvious, as in the pupil having difficulties coping with PE lessons. Sometimes pupils receive 'adapted physical education' with reference to their difficulties. In my experience this can be great or it can be a catastrophe. In some schools this means a teacher's assistant will take the child with autism for a walk, or go bowling. Although there are many great assistants, and as much as the child may (or may not) love bowling and walks, a teacher's assistant is not trained to work on physical education for children with special needs. And bowling and walks may be good in that you actually move rather than being still, but they are not activities that specifically promote development in the physical and motor skills area.

If a child has difficulties learning how to read and write, we don't say that this child should sit with a teacher's assistant reading comic books, right? No, we say that this child needs special education with a skilled teacher. The same should go for PE. So having motor difficulties means you need physical education even *more* than others, but perhaps individually or in small groups – and on the right level. It requires a trained person to be able to find the right level, and to create the best learning situation for the child to actually develop their motor skills.

Speaking of walks: in many services children, adolescents and adults are offered walks as their main motor activity.[10] Should we not instead offer cool, fun, and status-enhancing activities that they can 'brag about'? (Having gone for a walk isn't really much to brag about to your classmates.) And of course, they should be offered an activity that also helps them to make progress with motor skills.

What would it be? Well, for example, climbing on a boulder wall (and outdoors) is something that suits some people. It offers training in motor planning and co-ordination, and it is helpful in that there is no rush; you can stop and think about your next step when needed. When climbing outdoors with others you also will get practice in trust and co-operation. In the case of climbing, there is also a clear and concrete objective which is beneficial for many with autism spectrum disorders – first up and then down.

Sports like Tai Chi, Aikido and Taekwondo have also been helpful for several young people with autism. Ron Rubio, who has a black belt in Aikido and runs the Aikiki and BodyKi Centre in New York, is working with children and young adults with autism spectrum disorders. He believes that many of his students have difficulty turning

---

10   Frankly, if we want to encourage young people with autism to exercise, should we really offer walking? I have a feeling that the age when you usually start to think it's nice to take a walk in the park or in town, is often beyond your thirties. Very few children and young people I know, with or without autism spectrum disorders, like walking.

on and off the energy of a movement (and perhaps turning on and off in other areas too), and that the movements in martial arts are excellent for training this ability (see Rubio 2009). Also balance, co-ordination and body awareness are trained in martial arts.

Why some sports and activities fit better than others for this group can be discussed. Having a clear objective is one, as mentioned before. Martial arts can be trained individually, and for some it is helpful to have the slowness in movements, as in Tai Chi. Being able to train step by step is also often helpful.

Swimming as an activity also has the co-ordination and clear objective advantage, as well as that of being able to do it at your own pace, and being in water also invites several other playful activities. Counting lengths in the pool can give the person a clear sense of the beginning and end of the activity.

A friend of mine who is a PE teacher with a special education degree, and specialized in small groups for children with ADHD and/or autism spectrum disorders, creates adventure trails in the PE classroom. This type of exercise has the advantage of being very clear (one station at a time, and after the last station you are finished), and each station can help the child develop in different areas (e.g. motor planning, co-ordination, muscle strength, muscle tone, fitness, ball-handling, etc.). This type of activity also invites playfulness, where the teacher (or children in turns) may be a crocodile chasing the child through a tunnel or something similar. Having fun is an extremely important (but sometimes overlooked) component of learning and making progress! And throwing in play in the exercise furthermore gives the child the possibility of practising turn-taking and other crucial ingredients of social interaction.

Since people with autism spectrum disorders are individuals, you have to find out what is fun and on the right level for your pupil, client or user. The important thing is to give people the opportunity to develop to their full potential, whatever that might be.

One thing that is obvious is that team sports are difficult for many people with autism spectrum disorders – football, handball, basketball, etc. have lots of complicated rules.[11] Team play is often based on automating a variety of movements and interpreting the rules flexibly, an obvious difficulty for many with autism spectrum disorders. As a team player you also have to be able to take your teammates'

---

11   No rule is without exceptions, however. I know some young people with autism who enjoy playing football. But important for their success is that they have been playing in special teams for people with disabilities.

perspective and your opponents' perspective, and also be able to do what you think the opponents do not think you will do.

EXAMPLE

An adult man with autism told me that when he was a child, he saw the other children playing football in the yard and wanted to participate. At first he did not quite understand how the game worked, but then thinking and using logic, he figured out that since football players have numbers on the shirts (as he had seen on TV) one rule must be that you take turns having the ball, based on which number you have on your shirt. And a penalty must mean that you have to forfeit your turn, he reasoned.

When he felt he had it all sorted out he went out to play with the other children. It was a bit difficult because they had no numbers on the shirts. But he reasoned logically that without numbers it must be that he would get the ball last, since he had been the last one to join; so when the others had had the ball once each it must be his turn. But it seemed to never be his turn and he felt that the others played with such contempt for the rules!

When it comes to adults, it is of course not a question of PE lessons in school. But since many adults do have difficulties in the motor area, and most of them did not receive any of the support they needed in terms of motor skills in their childhood, one would hope that they too would be helped to find personalized ways to exercise.

My view is that body awareness helps to regulate and control behaviour. This is a developmental skill. If you look at a toddler you will see they react to frustration with their whole body. This will not have serious consequences since a two- or three-year-old is not that big. But at the age of 17 you can unfortunately cause a lot of damage with the same natural, but immature, response to frustration. Therefore, it is apparent to me, since I often have the opportunity to help people with challenging behaviours, that I also have to create many (and fun!) opportunities where they can develop better body awareness.

It is also important to remember that something that might take the form of, for example, a problem with hygiene may actually be about a motor difficulty (or about something else). Again, it is necessary to use the question 'Why?' If Justin does not keep himself clean, we do not need to immediately ask ourselves 'How do we get Justin to shower and change his clothes?' but rather 'Why doesn't Justin keep himself clean?' If the answer is not obvious we should use the assessment method described in Chapter 15 'Diving Lesson in the Ocean'.

But since it is motor skills that are on the agenda in this chapter, I would like to point out that it may be that Justin actually does shower daily but cannot handle his hygiene for motor skills reasons.[12] It can be about things like clumsiness, difficulty with motor planning and motor automatization. But, remember, problems with hygiene may be due to a variety of things: organization and planning difficulties, problems with time perception, delay in development of theory of mind (see p.144), and tactile over-sensitivity to name a few.

We see a number of behaviours or symptoms – the causes can be many and quite different from individual to individual!

What do motor difficulties mean for the individual, then?

- Christian is the guy who says he has two left feet, as a way to describe how hard it is to co-ordinate his movements.

- Travis says he hates PE because he is the worst of all at everything.

- Nicole refuses to participate in PE when it is team games, because it hurts her to feel that her motor difficulties 'will ruin it for the team'.

- Olivia, who has a balance uncertainty, says that escalators scare her. She also says that she can carry things, but not *while* she walks up or down the stairs, which others may find difficult to understand. Olivia feels that many think she is just lazy.

- Spencer has problems every morning when he is getting dressed; it takes a long time and is difficult for him as it requires motor skills. That he also has a difficulty with planning and organizing does not make it better. Spencer says that it often happens that he discovers that he has put his jeans on, and forgotten his underwear, and then he has to take off his jeans, put on his underwear and then put on his jeans again. Which means that it takes even longer.

- Emma often says 'I can't' in school, but adults tell her (encouragingly, they believe) 'Sure, you can!' and praise Emma

---

12   See also the example of Jessica in Chapter 3, p.28.

when she joins the excursion. But Emma almost vomits from the effort, though she doesn't let on about this in school. She wants to be good.

- There is a tendency to put motor skills in 'another room' when talking about symptoms in autism spectrum disorders, as if the motor skills are separate from the rest of the person's abilities. But my view is that motor skills affect many aspects of life, especially self-esteem. If you are unsure of managing things physically, and feel you can't rely on your strength and balance, it may be that you'd rather avoid everything. It can be difficult for others to understand that you do not have the energy or skills necessary to do things which come so easy to them.

With the help of motion and physical activity, you can also affect other functions. The quality of sleep is one of the more obvious areas. And although there are no studies as to the relationship between sleep and physical activity in the autism spectrum, there is plenty of evidence generally about exercise and good sleep being closely linked. For those with sleep disorders and motor difficulties, unfortunately, there may be very few physical activities (or these may be on the wrong level both energy- and skill-wise). Last, we all know that physical activity is good for general health.

With physical motion you can also affect the sense of presence and energy. In a user staff co-operative daily service I supervise, staff have introduced 'smart movements' as an activity of 30 minutes each day. The type of movements they do are described in several books, and are often referred to as 'brain gyms', 'smart moves' and similar. The experiences are consistently positive. The participants, who are all adults with autism spectrum disorders, describe how they feel generally better and happier after a half-hour workout with the movements. They now also use the movements in joint meetings, and see a big difference in their presence and energy to attend the meeting. Previously long meetings were a worry, since users had a hard time coping with them, but now users do not only find the energy to cope, but also say that meetings are fun.

Last but not least, for those who, due to their difficulties with motor skills and perception, have not been able to develop a well-adjusted body perception, it is often difficult to understand sex education in school (if you do not perceive or understand your basic body functions, it is hard to assimilate the content of sex education). It is therefore important that the motor-perceptual training comes early, so that one can also understand the bodily functions and later make sense of how they are coherent.

Actually there is no reason at all not to work with motor skills, perception and body awareness for children, adolescents and adults with autism spectrum disorders.

8

One Person May Be of Many Ages

A Chapter on the Development Perspective

Being able to see the development perspective is crucial if you work with people with disabilities on the autism spectrum. In addition to the 'triad of impairments'[1] you could say that what characterizes the autism spectrum is a significant unevenness in development. This means that in practice *a person can be of many ages*. The individual can in one area be far ahead of their peers, in another just like their peers and in a third area far behind their peers. This places great demands on the environment to adjust levels of requirements and expectations for this particular individual's version of development.

Why is this so important, one wonders? Well, to allow pupils and users to develop a sense of self-esteem and a confidence in their own capacity they need to have an appropriate balance in demands, so that the expectations are neither too high nor too low. What we, as professionals, can always do when we encounter a behaviour we do not understand, is to ask ourselves:

Does this behaviour occur in normal development?

If the answer to that question is yes (and it often is), then the following question will be:

How can we understand and approach this behaviour if we see it from a development perspective?

EXAMPLE

My then three-year-old son (who does not have a disability within the autism spectrum) and I were out in the garden. Suddenly I notice that he has gone inside the house, and I go in to see what he is doing. When I enter there is a speaking silence (all parents know what this means; something is afoot). I call his name but get no answer.

---

1   Don't know what the triad of impairments means? Well, this can happen if you are a rookie. Want to know? You can read more in 'The Short and Boring Chapter', p.186.

I detect a trail of white crumbs that lead from the kitchen to the living room, and to the back of the couch. Behind the couch is my son. He is chewing, with his mouth full, and around his mouth and on his cheeks are white crumbs. I know (and so does he, apparently!) that there is popcorn in our pantry, and I ask him 'Have you taken popcorn from the pantry?' 'No,' replies my son with emphasis, and shakes his head.

What's he doing here? He flatly denies taking the popcorn. Only a year later, at the age of four, he would never flatly deny something that was so obvious in such a situation. That said, I can't say I have a fantastically well-behaved child, and that he would never take popcorn (or something else from the pantry) without asking permission at age four, or five or six…but what he would do when he got caught would be to justify his actions in any way that he thought I would 'buy'. He would perhaps try something like 'But Mum, it's Saturday, and we eat cookies on Saturdays, right?' or maybe 'I was *really* hungry and I found nothing else' or 'You promised me popcorn last weekend, and I didn't get any then'. But he would no longer flatly deny that he had taken something without permission.[2] What is it that has happened between three and four years of age in a child's development?

It is about something called 'theory of mind'[3] or 'mentalization'. I meet many people (teachers, care staff, social workers, etc.) who work in the autism field and have learned the *theoretical* meaning of mentalization (and you may wake them up in the middle of the night and they can describe the Sally and Anne test[4]). But they have absolutely no idea what this means – what the *consequences are* – to

---

2   Well, it might actually happen if he, or another child who had reached this stage of mentalization, was under extreme pressure. Children who have acquired age-appropriate and more mature strategies may lose them when there is a situation of high stress, maybe combined with tiredness and hunger and being very emotional. In fact, even adults lose their maturity occasionally under such circumstances. This is known as regression, and may happen to anyone from time to time.

3   The theory of mind groundbreaking research was conducted by Uta Frith (Baron-Cohen, Leslie and Frith 1985) more than 20 years ago. Uta Frith is Deputy Director of UCL's Institute of Cognitive Neuroscience, and has continued researching the area.

4   This is a test with two dolls, 'Sally' and 'Anne'. Sally has a basket and Anne has a box. Sally puts a marble in her basket and then leaves the room. While Sally is away Anne takes the marble out of Sally's basket and puts it into her box. Sally then returns and the children are asked where they think she will look for her marble. In a study where this test was used, it was shown that children with autism couldn't take another person's perspective (80% answered that Sally would look for her marble in the box, where they themselves now knew the marble was), while most children without autism (both normally developed children and children with Down's syndrome) answered that Sally would look in the basket (where she had put it before she left and therefore coming back would still believe it was there). (See Baron-Cohen, Leslie and Frith 1985.)

their pupils, users and clients. And furthermore, they are clueless as to how, or even why, they should adjust their interaction and approach when a client has a delay in the development of mentalization.

I will try to link theory to a practical understanding now. But since you, the reader of this book, may be new to the autism field you might never have come across the concept of mentalization before, I'll first describe it.

Theory of mind or mentalization is described as the ability to understand that other people have other feelings and thoughts than your own. Sometimes degrees, steps (or 'schemes') are mentioned when speaking of developing mentalization. The understanding of others feeling or thinking something other than I myself feel or think would then be the first step. The next step in the mentalization development is to understand that others can think and feel something about other people (and thus about you). In this step, you will also begin to develop what you might call the ability to perceive oneself from the outside, to see yourself in others' eyes. I'll come back to this shortly.

If we take a look at the typical development of a child, the ability to mentalize in the first step should be present at the age of four (but is often established earlier). When the child understands that others think and feel something other than what they themselves think and feel, they can begin to show consideration. The very young child who as yet has no mentalization cannot, in terms of adjusting their behaviour for example, take into account whether someone is sick or tired. An angry toddler, under the age of two, will act out his anger even if his dad says he is ill, or his mother says she has a headache. A two-year-old often understands the meaning of 'being ill'. He may show sympathy when you tell him you are ill; he might caress you, come running with a patch or his doctor's kit. But once a two-year-old is angry, he still cannot modify his behaviour because he knows that Mum is ill.

A three-year-old, however, who has begun to develop mentalization can often do this. A three-year-old can start to whine, and when Dad says 'Do you remember that I am ill today?' the child can often stop and show consideration.

Just to be very clear: a three-year-old is still not very well equipped in the area of controlling impulses, so even when the first step of mentalization is present they may not be able to control their behaviour for very long. Also, since the mentalization here is a newly developed skill it will be quite often lost in regression when the child is overly tired or under some other type of pressure. And speaking of regression, when regressing we often lose the most recently acquired skill.

EXAMPLE

Yosef is a depressed 17-year-old with autism. He was severely bullied in his previous school, not only because of his disability but also for being an immigrant and not mastering the language. In addition he has had a poor social situation; among other things his mother has schizophrenia. Yosef is now in a special education class where all the students have autism spectrum disorders. He is still depressed but doing a lot better. Here he has begun to mature, and he has achieved the first step of mentalization, but not the second.

One day, Marva, an adult with Asperger syndrome, visits the class. She speaks about growing up with Asperger syndrome and being bullied, and how she is now doing well. Yosef relates to this, and is thrilled. He gets to speak with Marva alone at break time. Marva gives him hope, and for the first time he thinks there might be a future for him too. When Marva has left, Yosef meets his teacher and says smiling, 'I spoke to Marva, I am all tingly inside! You must be all tingly inside too!'

So when becoming this excited, Yosef loses his mentalization skill, and expects other people to feel the same way he does.

8.1 Mentalization in practice

Consideration and mentalization can often be expressed in different ways between children than between adults.

EXAMPLE

Two five-year olds, Chloe and Jack, are playing in a small room.

Jack *(with raised voice)*: Bleah! It smells like fart in here!

Chloe *(embarrassed)*: Um... It may be that... um, maybe it was me who happened to fart... sort of... without noticing...

Jack: You know, maybe we *both* farted without noticing!

Here Jack gives an example of a well-developed mentalization where he understands the embarrassing situation, and wants to help his friend to feel less ashamed (in fact adults are rarely generous enough to claim someone else's fart). A typical consequence of mentalization skills is that we human beings can perceive when something is socially embarrassing for someone else, and then we try to make it easier for them, by glossing over, making a joke, smiling or changing the subject.

In children we can also see the development of mentalization in how they view gifts. Very small children who are going to a birthday party will often want to give away something they no longer want themselves (some of their own used toys). And when their parents (of course) prevent them from doing this, and later take their child to a toy store to buy a gift, the child will choose something she herself likes. Here the child completely sees it from her own perspective; the consideration is there (wanting to give a gift to the friend), but the ability to see the gift from the recipient's perspective, is not yet developed.

When the child is a bit older, she understands that when buying a gift for her grandmother, it should be something that her grandmother may like, maybe a soap or a candle. But because the child herself loves purple, she buys purple soap and a purple light – they are the best! An even older child, say a nine- or ten-year-old, however, would begin to ask themselves 'What does Grandma like?' and wants to buy a present that suits Granny.

All age suggestions here are approximate, of course. Even in 'standard development' there is a large range, completely in line with other areas of development such as when children learn to walk, stop using nappies, etc.

What I want to show with these examples is that an older person with an autism spectrum disorder may not be at all 'inconsiderate', although it may look as if she is. Let us look at Hannah, who is 15 years old. Hannah's older sister Emma is sad because her boyfriend broke up with her, and Hannah wants to comfort her. Hannah starts 'rambling' to her sister about caterpillars (which happens to be her special interest). Emma feels that Hannah is totally insensitive.

But Hannah simply thinks in a logical way, from the point of view of her mentalization level, that her big sister will become happy through what makes Hannah herself happy, which is to talk about caterpillars. There's a great deal of consideration and care in this! It is just like the small child who wants to kiss Daddy's feet when he hurt his toe to make it better; we don't call this child egocentric or inconsiderate.[5]

---

5   Let us not get the concepts of 'theory of mind' and 'empathy' mixed up; a person with
     delayed development of theory of mind does not necessarily lack empathy. Just like the two-
     year-old who comes with a plaster when you say you are ill, an older person with autism and
     delayed development of mentalization may want to be helpful or 'do good' in a situation.
     It' s just that the lagging development in the mentalization area is an obstacle to figuring
     out how you would show this in a way that suits the other person. In fact most people with
     autism I have met have been empathetic to a high degree, they just have an unusual way of
     showing it, which may result in others not understanding or seeing the empathy.

There are numerous other ways that children can express their ability to mentalize, for example by controlling their temper and behaviour depending on who they are with, they might behave in a certain way with their grandparents, and behave differently in kindergarden, etc. A child with no mentalization skills (which, as you understood, all toddlers lack more or less) will not behave very differently depending on who they are with (other than maybe being shy around strangers).

Back to my son behind the sofa. He was at the time three years old and one could not expect him to have reached the second level of mentalizing yet, and therefore he could not see the situation from outside his own perspective and be able to guess what conclusions I would draw. He could not understand how I saw him and the situation, and he therefore flatly denied having taken popcorn. Because of his age this is nothing to be upset about; rather it is quite sweet, and I am not provoked by his behaviour. Imagine if we could also adjust our expectations to the levels of development the client or pupil with autism has achieved.

We know then that the development of mentalization is delayed in autism spectrum disorders, but how much delay there is will vary greatly between individuals. With autism-specific knowledge, we understand the consequences and the most logical response, when we meet a 15-, 25- or 47-year-old with autism who flatly denies something that we know that he or she has done, is to pause and realize that this person is still three years old in this particular area of development.

Figure 8.1: A person with autism may be of many ages

This has obviously nothing to do with other areas of development; the person may have a high IQ, and be very proficient in other areas. It rather means that we as staff can be more relaxed when we understand that there is no point in being provoked, bothered or annoyed by this kind of behaviour.

Personally, I think that if we can see where the person is at developmentally in a particular area, it will be easier to help him or her forward in his or her development. And therefore we need to always do an assessment, something you will read more about later on. By knowing if Sonya has reached the first degree of mentalization but not the second, we can show her not just a better understanding, but also work in such a way that she is supported to progress in this particular area.

To understand the development perspective is obviously about understanding not just mentalization, but also any developmental level that might be delayed: linguistic, conceptual, cognitive, emotional or physical for example. We can find the irregularities in several of these areas, and each individual has his unique mix of strengths and, well, if not weaknesses, then delays.

Using the development perspective, we can understand these people with autism:

- Samantha, who has a difficulty perceiving signals from inside her body (for example, small signals of hunger, satiation, need to go to the bathroom). Like a newborn baby, she has not yet developed a 'refining' in the system. Samantha eats sparingly, and does not seem to feel hunger.

- Jessica, who requires food to be ready immediately whenever she is hungry.

- Gemma who is 11 years old and has autism, and soils her pants instead of going to the toilet.[6]

- Andrew, who can't understand why the bus doesn't immediately appear when he arrives at the bus stop (and is really upset).

Anyone who has not developed what we might call 'refinement' in the nervous system might only realize the need to go to the toilet when it becomes very urgent, and therefore not always get there in time; or they may need food as soon as they start to get hungry. Anyone who

---

6   You can read more about Gemma and her problems on p.263.

doesn't have mentalization skills may not understand why the rest of the world isn't ready when they are.

This is sometimes classified as 'immediate need-satisfaction', but this expression has (as do many others, such as 'being controlling' or even a 'control freak', being 'manipulative' or 'attention-seeking', and having a 'fixation') a very negative ring to it. Think of it instead from a development perspective. Try this thought with any behaviour you encounter that seems problematic.

We can even learn to embrace the positive in some phases that we see in normal development, and let them show us that person is in the process of development. Take, for example, the demand for extreme justice which we typically see in children at the ages of five, six or seven. They can be quite obsessive about whether their brother will get just a drop more soda, or want to bring a ruler when splitting a chocolate bar. We understand that this is a phase, from which the child later can move on to a new understanding. If we now find this obsessiveness with justice in a 25-year-old with autism, we can simply realize that he is – in this area – on a six-year-old level. Perhaps he is soon ready for the next step in his understanding of justice and distribution? Perhaps precisely for this reason we should be presenting him with simple tasks in which he may practise and reflect on just that.

EXERCISE 8.1

Developmental phases

Try to think of more developmental phases children go through and at what age they normally occur. Do you see any of them in your clients with autism? (You can look in the key in the footnote after you do this practice.)[7]

Finally, we must never confuse the understanding of the development perspective with assumptions about a general level of development. The 25-year-old is still 25, and although we understand that he is seven in one particular area (and perhaps three in yet another), we can and should not respond to him as to a child in general. But you probably already figured that out.

---

7   Here are two suggestions: telling the same joke over and over (very common in five-year-olds who are discovering the world of jokes and humour); love of repetition (this phase is present more or less during all preschool ages).

9

Say What You Mean and Mean What You Say

A Chapter on Communication

Problems with communication are common in autism, even, or should I say especially, in the people we are talking about in this book: those who are considered high-functioning and have good verbal skills.

9.1 Language comprehension being poorer than verbal expression

In my experience the over-estimation of language comprehension in individuals with autism spectrum disorders is one of the most common mistakes made by staff.

EXAMPLE

I was hired to support staff around Stephanie, a young woman with autism. Stephanie was perceived as very 'acting-out' to staff at the care home where she was a patient. To me it was obvious that Stephanie was the one who had the greatest difficulties of the seven people who were placed there (all with autism spectrum disorders). But Stephanie had the least aids and support! What was the difference between her and the others? Well, she was the most verbal resident.

It often appears to be difficult for the environment to understand that someone who is very verbal can have poor language comprehension. That is, the person does not understand as well as he or she can speak (or, I should perhaps say, as it *seems* he or she can speak).

9.2 Echolalia

As you may know, echolalia[1] is quite a common symptom in individuals with autism and learning disabilities. I think that echolalia is also often present in higher-functioning individuals, but their better verbal ability, better social skills (relative to autism with learning disability) and higher IQ, help the echolalia to 'fit in' quite well in social circumstances. This may lead to family and staff not understanding that it is a case of echolalia.

What characterizes it as 'delayed echolalia', in my opinion, is that it is learned by heart and is often used as a social strategy. It can also, just like echolalia in severe autism, be a sign of stress.

EXAMPLE

Yasmine is a young woman with autism who is perceived by all as highly social (which she is, even if her social understanding is impaired). Yasmine has three phrases which she switches between: 'Wow!', 'Cool!' and 'So how was that on a scale of one to ten?'

Using these expressions is sufficient for her to be perceived as more socially skilled than she is, and thus it is a viable strategy. But because she only has three phrases to choose from, it happens sometimes that the result is not so successful. When a classmate told Yasmine that her (the friend's, that is) grandmother had died, Yasmine said 'Wow!' Having said that, Yasmine felt that it wasn't really the right thing to say, and tried 'So on a scale of one to ten, how was that?' And then fell silent when she saw her friend's bemused (and hurt) face.

Afterwards, at home, when Yasmine realized what she had said and how inappropriate it was in the context, she felt really bad and dwelled on what a social failure she was.[2]

---

1   Echolalia is when you repeat words or whole sentences, for example in response to a question. This is called 'direct echolalia'. 'Delayed echolalia' can be words, sounds or whole sentences, which are repeated out of context.

2   People often tell me that Asperger individuals tend to dwell on things, as if this was a symptom of the disorder. In my opinion all people tend to dwell on certain things. Have you yourself ever failed socially (if your answer is no, I don't believe you)? Think of this time when you failed socially. Does it still embarrass you? Thought so. Sometimes we will blush only by thinking of it, even if it happened years ago. And when this happened, did you dwell on it? Thought so. We human beings tend to dwell on social failures, and that is being human, not having autism. But in autism you will have plenty more social failures (which means more to dwell on). And when the second level of mentalization begins to develop, you will start to become painfully aware of them.

EXAMPLE

Thomas is a very neat and polite young man with autism. Thomas has learned what one might call 'politician's echolalia', that is, a variety of empty phrases that sound authoritative. He chimes in with comments like 'We will look into this' or 'It is extraordinarily important.'

When Thomas is under stress his echolalia increases, and what stresses Thomas the most is when he does not understand. The consequence is that the less Thomas understands, the more competent he sounds!

The fact that people are misled by his appearance (meaning both speech and appearance) has led to Thomas being elected to organization boards and getting jobs he did not have a chance of managing (with greatly increased stress as a result).

Thomas did not want to have those assignments, but his lack of social understanding and social ability mean he did not know how to pull out of them. Consequently, he continued to keep up appearances as well as he could, until everything suddenly broke down. Only then did people understand that Thomas is not all he seems to be. Unfortunately, they had very little understanding of Thomas' disability and instead blamed him for his shortcomings.

EXAMPLE

Susanna, who has high-functioning autism, has trained herself to use short small-talk words, signalling that she is following, when someone tells her something. Susanna chimes in with small words like 'Oh, well', 'Really?' etc. These words signal to the other person that Susanna is understanding what they are telling her. But unfortunately it is not certain that she understands a word.

The real paradox here is that the more the person learns to 'blend in', to 'behave' or 'seem' like others (something that the environment too often tends to strive for and encourage!), the smaller the chances are that he or she will be met with an understanding of their difficulties.

Most people seem to find it fairly easy to understand that someone can have poorer verbal skills than language comprehension. We have all gone through a phase of that, when we learned to speak for the first time as toddlers. (And perhaps again later, if we learned a foreign language.) We understand more than we can express. But in autism, as you now have understood, it can be the other way around – someone can have poorer language comprehension than verbal skills. This means that visual aids are required as a support; that is, we as professionals need to clarify important information visually. And even if the person does understand occasionally, he or she may not be able to understand in a stressful situation, which is why we need to use the visual aids preventively.[3]

Figure 9.1: In autism you can have poorer language comprehension than verbal skills

9.3 Truths, lies and subtext

Making 'socially inappropriate' comments is usually attributed to a lack of theory of mind, but it can probably just as often be about a kind of echolalia (phrases learned by heart). What we see is often not the impairment itself, but the strategy a person has found to compensate for their lack of language comprehension and social understanding.

It may look like this:

---

3   We all, more or less, lose our language comprehension under stress. That is why, as I wrote in Chapter 6 on sensory processing, escape routes and fire extinguishers are marked with pictures (visual aids). Haven't you yourself been in a situation where you were under a lot of pressure (think: you are being fired, your partner is breaking up with you, someone tells you a relative died, or a doctor tells you you have a serious condition) and suddenly you couldn't make sense of what they were saying? And in autism (a) the language comprehension is often reduced in the first place and (b) you are under a lot more stress in your everyday life because of your deficits. This means that we must use visual aids in everyday life, even for people who are verbal and have a normal, or even high, intelligence.

- *Disability:* Lack of social interaction skills.

- *Effect:* Feeling stupid in many situations (and not wanting to feel stupid).

- *Strategy:* Rejects everything and everyone to avoid feeling stupid.

- *Disability:* Lack of social interaction skills.

- *Effect:* Feeling confused in many situations (and not wanting to feel confused).

- *Strategy:* Says yes to, and accepts, everything because it's easiest that way.

- *Disability:* Lack of social interaction skills.

- *Effect:* Feeling insecure in many situations (and not wanting to feel insecure).

- *Strategy:* Tells everyone else what is right and wrong.

EXAMPLE

Camille, a girl with high-functioning autism, responds 'Nope' or 'Dunno' and seems to reject what others say in all situations. This works out as a protection for her in social situations, and as we understand this, it is our responsibility to provide her with new strategies (which may have more constructive results) to handle these situations.

Therefore, we will help her to develop both a social understanding of the concept of 'uncertainty' and to use other ways to express her uncertainty. It is not a goal in itself to get her to stop using this strategy.

Naturally, the lack of social interaction is associated with communication, and it is not always easy to distinguish what is what. People with autism spectrum disorders experience many social failures.

EXAMPLE

Ben, a man with autism, was at a funeral where everyone filed past the deceased's mother on the way out of church. When it was Ben's turn, he could not think of a phrase that fitted in this situation. First he said 'Nice to meet you', then he felt that this phrase was not the right one and therefore continued 'How are you?' When the mother of the deceased didn't answer, Ben said 'It was a nice party', and then left embarrassed.

As I mentioned, social failures are often painful.[4] Inventing strategies to avoid them is therefore no cause for surprise. A rejecting or even threatening behaviour, or lying or telling tales, may simply be ways to mask social and communication difficulties.

As you may recall, I mentioned flatly denying as an example in the previous chapter about the development perspective. The lies baffle many professionals, as they have often heard that people with autism 'cannot lie'. Well sure, people with autism can lie. But they do not lie as often, and not for the same reasons as other people. Neurotypicals (i.e. people without autism) lie (in the sense of 'not telling the truth') quite often. Here are some examples:

How are you?
Fine.
The truth: I have a headache and I am worried about my finances.

What a nice shirt you have, is it new?
Yes, and it was only 20 quid!
The truth: It was £29.

Do you need help with that?
No, I'm fine.
The truth: I am not fine at all but I don't want to be any trouble.

My aunt has been given a new job.
How interesting.
The truth: I am not at all interested in that.

There are also typical phrases which in a way can be lies, such as 'Can I help you?' which does not have to be an offer of help, but can mean a variety of things such as for example: 'What are you doing here?' Or 'excuse me', meaning 'Get out of my way.'

---

4   As described on p.153 most people experience social breakdowns from time to time. We can be thoughtless, unprepared, or even plain stupid sometimes. Here is an empathy exercise: Think of a really embarrassing moment in your life (again). An opportunity where you felt really embarrassed and stupid. Now think about that moment for a while. How did you feel at the time? How did you feel afterwards? How does it feel to think about it now? Now imagine that you have a disability that makes situations like that occur several times a week, maybe every day. Doing this exercise now and then can help you to see things from the perspective of the individuals you are supporting.

Figure 9.2: Most people lie more often than they think

In most cases, these types of lies have 'good' intentions, they are there to protect others' feelings, or to make others feel better, and particularly to facilitate social interaction. These types of lies are not as common in people with autism spectrum disorders, not because they do not wish others well, but simply because of difficulties with mentalization. If you cannot see things from others' perspective, it is difficult to lie to make them feel better or to make life easier. Thus, people within the autism spectrum often lie in a different way.

EXAMPLE

Cal was a man with autism who was in a supported employment project. This meant he was on a regular work placement and after an introductory period he had some support from a couple of job coaches. His coaches would visit Cal at his job for weekly follow-ups. When the coaches arrived, they always followed the same routine. Cal would make tea in the office lunch room, and the coaches, Rodriguez and Maria, would bring some rolls. They would sit down, choosing the same chairs every time, and pour some tea.[5]

Rodriguez would make a comment about the weather, Maria would clear her throat and pick up some papers from her backpack. The coaches 'held' the meeting and steered the conversation by the questions they asked. After about 20 minutes the routine part of the meeting would be over, and the rest of the content was uncertain. There would be a silence and then Cal would start: 'I'll tell you what happened...'

---

5   As you may know, neurotypical people are very prone to rituals: they usually say the same things when they greet people, they like to sit in the same seat as last time, they express the same opinions as usual, etc.

What followed next could be entirely fictional depictions of how the day before there had been a fire or a bomb threat in the office, or of how he had seen something remarkable happen (for example, a robbery or an accident).

Maria and Rodriguez wanted my counselling, and asked me whether in these situations they should 'agree' with Cal, or if they should tell him that what he said was not true (a typical example of extreme positions as described in Pitfall 4 on p.76). They had tried to do both, but he nevertheless continued with these 'lies' every time they met him.

The key here is *when* Cal starts to tell stories. The fact that he did it every time there was a silence, when he was unsure of what to talk about, and having the feeling that 'he was supposed to say something' made me guess that Cal really tried to solve a problem – his lack of social interaction skills – in the most constructive way he could. The option for him had otherwise been to sit quietly and feel stupid and rude, and that he did not want, of course.

With Cal (and with some others I worked with), a way forward was to help him to put into words what was happening. This must be done with great care and sensitivity. If you, as Cal, have had a strategy for about 30 years or so, the 'exposure' might be unpleasant or might even arouse anxiety.

Rodriguez and Maria were given the task, the next time they got into this situation, to say to Cal 'I wonder if you might be unsure of what to talk about right now. Would you like us to help you with topics for the next time we meet?' The first time Cal said nothing to this. The second time he said 'No thanks' and fell silent.[6]

The third time the coaches instead said 'Today we have brought a little box into which you could stick some ideas of topics for conversation. But if you don't want to, you don't have to.' This time, Cal said 'OK'. (He needed to see what it was before he was able to say yes – the difficulty of envisioning, you know.)[7]

As you probably noticed, I cannot write about or discuss the communication of people with autism spectrum disorders without also touching on the subject of your communication as a professional. To do what Rodriguez and Maria now did is a kind of meta-communication; they are communicating about the communication. It is quite a sophisticated form of communication, and the fact is that

---

6   The professional autism worker has obviously learned the art of not giving up!

7   If your conclusion from this is that lying in autism is always due to lack of social interaction skills, this means you have drawn the 'Go to Jail' card, and you might want to read this book again while you are there.

many, without any impairment in this area, have difficulty with doing this spontaneously.

To meta-communicate is a matter of training; everyone who practises can be better at it. (And in my opinion, the world would be a better place if people in general could meta-communicate.) But in particular, your pupils, clients or users, can benefit if you have this skill. If you put into words what is actually happening – what an actor would call subtext, the hidden meaning – you can help someone find new and better strategies. (Another example is Joshua who did not recognize his own feeling of tiredness; read more in Chapter 15, p.220.)

EXAMPLE

A subtext situation

Marjorie is a teacher in a small special education class of pupils with autism. Phil is 12 years old and today's lesson is about the United Nations and human rights. Phil, who is an animal lover (you might even call him an animal rights activist, but without the activist part), is very upset that animals do not have the same rights as people. Phil is getting worked up, and becoming increasingly agitated and loud.

Listen to this conversation:

Phil: Those who hurt animals should be killed!

Marjorie: Phil, can you calm down a bit?

Phil: They should be boiled alive, they should not hurt animals – they are terrible people!

Marjorie: Can we talk about something else now, Phil?

Phil: They make furs from animals, and they should die. All animals should have a good life. I will kill them.

Marjorie: Change the topic now, Phil!

Phil *(now starting to yell rather than speak)***:** I'm going to boil them in a large pot and...

Marjorie: Phil, now you have to cut it!

Another pupil is now 'getting started' (which Marjorie knew would happen) and agreeing with Phil, with the effect that both pupils are growing less and less contactable, and 'running high'. Marjorie feels that the situation is derailing and that she must take control. Thus Marjorie simply changes the topic of conversation (good move!).

Marjorie: Does anyone want to know what's for lunch today? Something, actually, that all of you like!

The conversation now moves on to hamburgers, and after a while Marjorie can go on with her lesson on human rights.

Now, first I will discuss subtexts with you a little bit, then I will come back to a discussion of whether changing the subject really was the best strategy Marjorie could have used. Let us listen to this conversation again, but this time with the subtext elucidated, that is, what is actually expressed in the conversation – *what the communication is about*. It would sound like this:

Phil: Those who hurt animals should be killed!

Marjorie: Phil, can you calm down a bit?

Phil: I can't calm down.

Marjorie: Change the subject.

Phil: I can't change the subject.

Marjorie: Yes, you can.

Phil: No, I can't.

Marjorie: Sure you can.

Marjorie: I can change the subject for you.

If we imagine that Phil was having a maths lesson and had great difficulty with a calculation, then it would be quite unthinkable that his teacher would communicate in this way. If the pupil says 'I can't do it', the teacher would not respond with 'Sure, you can' several times, right? Nor would the teacher end up doing the calculation for the pupil! (Where would the learning be in that?)

No, the teacher would give the pupil the prerequisites to be able to do it himself. The teacher would create circumstances under which learning could take place. This is all about perspectives on independence and learning. In the case of Phil's difficulties, there is no reason to have a different approach to learning and independence, than that which pervades the educational activities in schools. The crux of the matter is:

> Do we want Phil to be dependent on an adult who can read his subtext throughout his life, or do we want to give Phil tools and teach him new strategies in order for him to sort out situations like this himself in the future?

If we keep doing everything for Phil, if we read him, and only respond by adapting, he will certainly have some kind of support, but no support leading to increased independence.[8] In this example he is not receiving the best help, and why shouldn't he?

Let me make a parallel for you who are not working in the school area, and might think this reasoning doesn't apply to your field of work. This certainly does not only apply to working in schools.

EXAMPLE

Harold is working in a residential care home. Stella has autism and schizophrenia, and is a resident. When Stella becomes restless and starts talking in a certain way, Harold knows she will feel better if he takes her out for a walk, or takes her to the art room for painting. So Harold reads Stella and takes her for a walk or encourages her to start painting when needed.

But, I say to Harold, what happens when you are not there? What happens when Stella is hospitalized for a period (which happens from time to time), or if there are staff changes, or Stella moves out? Would it not be better for Stella, through aids, to become aware of when she needs an aid and use it independently?

There are many ways of doing this. We can use social stories.[9] We can also try to make Stella herself recognize that feeling, and point out to others when she is getting stressed out and needs a break. Or we can make pictures (visual aids) of the activities (walking and painting) and let Stella choose if she wants to paint or go for a walk in these situations.

But, you might say now, why is it better that Stella looks at a picture (a visual aid) before going for a walk, than that Harold takes her directly out for a walk (or painting)? The result is, after all, the same (Stella comes together). True, but when Stella has visual aids, there are the following advantages:

1. Stella becomes aware that she needs an aid in these situations.

2. She has the opportunity to influence what strategy to choose (she becomes *involved*).

3. In that the aid is in the physical world (rather than in Harold's mind), others can more easily offer the same support for Stella.

---

8   Please note: I am not saying that we should never use adaptation as a strategy, just that if there is another way to support Phil, a way which gives him more independence and promotes the learning of new skills, we should choose this way.

9   My experience is that social stories work well with people who have schizophrenia or other psychotic illnesses, together with autism spectrum disorders. Unfortunately, they rarely have access to this method because the staff I meet who work with adults are often unable to (or perhaps, unwilling to, or maybe don't understand why they should) use social stories. For more information about social stories, see p.300.

The visual aid will itself become a documentation, which in an obvious way will follow Stella, for example to the psychiatric ward where she is admitted at times.

Now back to Phil. What should Marjorie have done? Phil, too, needs an aid and therefore I suggest Marjorie produces a 'chat box', a small box with suggestions for topics of conversation. So, one day Marjorie sits down with Phil and makes notes with topics for the 'chat box' (Phil being involved). The next time Phil gets all worked up about animal rights (or something similar) she asks him to go and get the chat box and select a new topic (independence and awareness).

So, yes, it is great when professionals can read 'the subtexts' of their clients, but they must also, when possible, work with strategies that allow the pupil or client to have as much awareness, involvement and independence as possible.

While we're on the subject of subtexts and communication I'd like to highlight another issue, closely linked to this. If you lack a thorough knowledge of autism, you can sometimes read a subtext in completely the wrong way. I sometimes meet with groups of staff that I almost have to 'deprogramme' from erroneous interpretations. (They have sometimes been 'programmed' in the first place by a sympathetic but ignorant, that is, ignorant in the autism field, psychologist.)

EXAMPLE

We are in the staff room. I've been asked here to consult with staff because they have problems with a client. We're talking about Myrna, who has autism and can be very challenging and act out at times.

Eve: Well, Myrna always wants revenge when she gets angry. She wants to get back at you.

Joe: Yeah, sort of an eye for an eye *(laughs)*.

GG: If we see Myrna's behaviour in a developmental perspective, it is not strange. How does this show with small children in normal development?

Eve: Sure, they get back at you, too…

GG: Right, so it may be that Myrna in this area is not much older than two. Earlier we talked about how Myrna's mentalization development is delayed and impaired.

Eve: Yeah, that's right.

Joe: So she's like a small child.

Eve: Yes, she wants to punish us.

GG: Punish you? What makes you think that?

Eve: Well, she wants to punish us, because we have done something wrong. Like when I grabbed her.

GG: But to want to punish someone, you must of course have a pretty well-developed mentalization. You have to take another person's perspective and figure out how this person will experience something. Does Myrna have such a developed mentalization skill, do you think?

Eve: No, that's right. She hasn't... You've said that before.

And we met, on a monthly basis, for a year at least, before I managed to get Eve to *really* understand what a delayed mentalization development means.

9.4 Announcing your actions

Regarding communication, there are a couple of other things that may be observed in the communication of people with autism spectrum disorders, such as that they do not 'announce' their actions to the same extent as others.

Some of the communication between people is about them saying things like 'I'm going to the bathroom' or 'I'll get the paper' right before doing it. This is probably both about you using theory of mind skills to take other people's perspectives, and thinking that they may be wondering what you are doing when you suddenly leave the room, and about the fact that meaningless small talk is a way to consolidate relations. According to the professor of psychology Robin Dunbar, our social chit-chat has the same purpose as when chimpanzees groom each other' – it creates loyalties.[10]

At workplaces, and in other social settings, you can see this clearly. The traditional female way[11] of chatting socially is commenting on appearance. It may sound like this:

'Did you dye your hair?' or 'What a nice sweater' or 'You look good today.' You have to give the 'right' reply to this: 'You think so?' or 'Oh, but this is just an old sweater' or 'Thank you, though

---

10   You can read more about this in the book *Grooming, Gossip, and the Evolution of Language* (Dunbar 1998).

11   As much as I am a feminist, I wish it were possible not to generalize like this about male and female ways of communicating, but after checking the reality closely, I must say that very often it looks like this (women say something nice about the other woman, which she denies/questions/appreciates), and men say something nice about themselves (which the other man reinforces/wants to know more about). This is also why someone who is deviant (breaks the social norm) very often is freezed out. Unfortunately.

I feel really tired'. The traditional male way is to make a statement (preferably related to a performance): 'What a great game there was yesterday' or 'I ran six miles the other week' or 'I've been offered a new job'. Here too you have to give the 'right' reply: 'Yeah, it was damn good!' or 'Well done!' or 'How interesting'.

An individual with autism can be very social in the sense of wanting to participate in social life, and having a social interest. He or she can also be very verbal. But it is often difficult to understand or handle this mechanism of language. To the person with an autism spectrum disorder the language is often used more as a means to share information than to build loyalties. Those who do not participate in this kind of chit-chat can often unfortunately be perceived as a threat to the group (without the group at a conscious level having understood why, of course). Anyone who breaks the norm is at risk of not being allowed into the group, being neglected, bullied, and perhaps at worst, becoming a scapegoat if anything happens.[12]

9.5 Literal language comprehension

As you probably already know, a literal understanding of language is one of the characteristics of autism. If we see this from a developmental perspective, it's clear that all small children have a literal language comprehension.[13] In autism the problem is often that although the overall intelligence is normal or even high, you misunderstand certain expressions. And you will still have a literal understanding, long after your peers have grown out of that phase. There are plenty of examples of this in several other books, so you may have already read about how crazy or even hilarious it can be when people with autism make a literal interpretation of what is said.

---

12   Let's say there is a theft in the office, and no one knows who is to blame. Everybody feels uncomfortable having suspicions without knowing in which direction to look. If you could point someone out the whole group would be at ease. And it is very easy to start suspecting the one who doesn't fit in: 'Well, I have always thought she seemed a bit strange.'

13   Let me tell you a beautiful story of a five-year-old, Amber, a 'standard child' (i.e. no developmental disorders) and her literal understanding. The kindergarden teacher had told the children she had a baby in her stomach, and that she would soon be on maternity leave. The teacher later that day lifted up little Amber. Amber looked down the teacher's shirt, saw her cleavage and exclaimed 'Miss, I can see the baby's bottom!' This is the type of literal understanding that all children have, of language and of the world.

EXAMPLES

- The mother said 'Can you get the door, please?' to her son, and the son, who had autism, went for the toolbox.

- The young man with autism who thought that the 'road to recovery' was an address.

- The woman with autism who was at a seminar on effectiveness where the lecturer advised the auditorium to jump-start their day at work. Thereafter she started every day with jumping up and down a couple of times.

- Perhaps most amusing is the father who, after nagging his son with autism to tidy his room said 'I'm not telling you this again' after which his son cheerfully looked up and said 'That's great!'

- Another fun example is the family that bought a nice new kitchen table and they wanted to look after it. They explained carefully to their son, who had autism, that he was not allowed to play with his cars at the table anymore. 'But,' they added, 'you can still draw there.' The next morning the son had made a lot of neat drawings *on* the new kitchen table!

This means that you as a professional have to be aware of your communication and how it can be misunderstood.

A lot of people with autism also have difficulty understanding vague expressions and imprecise words. We have so many of these in our language: 'later', 'perhaps', 'then', 'in a moment', 'soon', 'let's see', and so on.

EXAMPLE

A mother told me that her daughters had tasks to perform in the family's stable after school. Abby, the daughter with autism, might come home from school and say, much like her older sister (who did not have autism) often did: 'Mum, I'll do the stables later.'

'OK' the mother usually replied, as she thought that both her daughters must take responsibility for doing their chores. But the mother became more and more annoyed when the whole evening passed and Abby did not go to the stables. When the mother finally talked to Abby about it, Abby said: 'But Mum, I've been waiting all afternoon, waiting for you to tell me that "now it is later". *I* don't know when *later* is.'

Abby could also clearly express another problem about communication: 'In school they want me to say when there is something I don't understand, but I do not understand that I do not understand – so how can I tell them?'

9.6 Lack of 'auto correction'

Sometimes idiosyncratic expressions are mentioned as one of the symptoms in autism spectrum disorders; that is to say that those on the spectrum have more made-up (and unusual) words than others. I am not sure this is the whole truth. Most children invent their own words (which we usually think is pretty cute). But pretty quickly children learn what the actual word is, whereas the child with autism may retain their own word over time.

What could the reason be? I do not know for sure, but the impression I have is that children with autism spectrum disorders lack the sort of 'auto correction' that other children have. This is how auto correction works in 'standard development':

Child: Then we goed to the kiosk…

Adult: So you went to the kiosk?

Child: Yeah, we went to the kiosk and there…

Children correct themselves automatically according to others, and we as adults don't have to tell them '"goed" is wrong, it should be "went"'. Indeed, most highfunctioning children with autism do learn language well, they don't still say 'goed' as adults. (Do they ever say 'goed', by the way? Perhaps they do not make these linguistic mistakes as often when little?) But despite the fact that they learn to speak well, it is rare for children with autism to correct themselves like this when you talk with them.

This auto correction in normal development seems to apply not only linguistically but in a way that affects the view of reality. In 'standard development', children believe a lot of things (and can be rather gullible) but when they find out how things are they rapidly change their perception of reality. They do this by asking questions and communicating how they think it is, and by having the ability to quickly change their perception. Children with autism often do not seem to have these abilities.

This means that we as professionals have an extensive and important task of creating aids for communication and supporting the development of skills in this area.

Some professionals have noticed that the communication works out better if they give 'orders' rather than using 'nice' standard phrases to their clients or pupils with autism. And sometimes they tell me they are puzzled as to why this works.

EXAMPLE

John has chores, and is about to empty the dishwasher.

Anne: John, would you be so kind as to put the glasses on that shelf, please.

John slams the dishwasher and leaves.

Or:

Anne points to the shelf.

Anne: John, put the glasses here.

John empties the dishwasher and puts the glasses where Anne told him to.

Why is this so? We have to look at the subtexts again:

Anne: John, would you be so kind as to put the glasses on that shelf, please.

John thinks: *What does she mean? Did I get it wrong before? What has 'kind' to do with this? And what with 'would', could I choose not to? Pshaw! I don't get it! I can't do this, I give up!*

John slams the dishwasher and leaves.

Or:

Anne points to the shelf.

Anne: John, put the glasses here.

John thinks: *Aha, the glasses go on that shelf.*

John empties the dishwasher and puts the glasses where Anne told him to.

9.7 'Attitude'

When I am consulting with services and schools, it is not unusual for professionals to tell me that one of their clients or pupils with autism has a problematic *attitude*. Often, this is about how this individual communicates, what expressions he or she uses.

EXAMPLE

Shannon was 17, and a student at secondary school with units for pupils with speech, language and communication needs. The school had a special boarding house for the students with autism spectrum disorders. When the boarding staff asked Shannon to do her chores, she practically always refused, and when asked why, she provocatively stated 'I'm just a lazy person'.

In school teachers tried hard to get Shannon to do her assignments and to improve her skills in areas where she was deficient. When they tried to motivate Shannon by telling her that she would need these skills (and her grades) in the future if she wanted a good job, she replied 'I don't want a job anyway, I want to get paid for doing nothing'.

Boarding staff, as well as teachers, found it difficult to reach her; it was like talking to a wall. They perceived her as completely unmotivated and her attitude as deliberately provocative.

I interviewed Shannon, Shannon's staff and her parents. It was revealed that Shannon had moved from school to school, that she had been trying different placements; and that she had failed everywhere.

Failure is not a particularly pleasant feeling for anyone, and when you cannot make sense of your failures, when you are unable to figure out how and why you fail (to prevent any recurrence), you have to find another approach. I mean really *have to*, because I think it is very difficult to exist without having a theory about yourself,[14] a theory that makes you, in your own view, understandable in some way.

One hypothesis in the work with Shannon was that this 'attitude' may be a strategy for her, which both serves to avoid being disappointed (if you don't expect anything/have no ambitions, you will not be disappointed) and also has a social function, that is to say that she has more of this attitude when she feels socially insecure. Based on this hypothesis, it became easier for the staff not to be provoked by Shannon's attitude and to see it as a door (which they needed to find the key to) rather than a wall.

When I talked more with Shannon I found that there was another key to her 'attitude'. Shannon was extremely talented and found it incredibly easy to learn. Her ability to memorize was amazing. This meant that she had always learned without effort. Shannon was completely unaccustomed to having to work or strive to learn. With an understanding of this, we were able to reason with her that wanting to 'be paid for doing nothing' is not an especially strange wish, but perhaps we could talk about what this 'nothing' could be. For instance, if you do something you enjoy and are interested in, and get paid for doing it – could this be equivalent to (or even better than) doing 'nothing'?

---

14   Aaron Antonovsky is the one who coined the concept of SOC (sense of coherence), which determines whether an individual can experience health. Antonovsky argued that we need to have the basic perception that what is happening inside and outside the individual is *comprehensible and manageable*, and that there is a meaningfulness about life. I argue that many of the people with autism spectrum disorders who are perceived as 'difficult' or 'challenging' lack the prerequisites for SOC, and that we as professionals must help create the circumstances for SOC.

In this way we could see Shannon's communication with new eyes, and use our understanding in how we communicated with her.[15]

9.8 Restorative communication

A lot of people with autism spectrum disorders also often find it difficult to *repair communication*. If they say something and the recipient does not understand, they cannot change their way of expressing, but rather just repeat the same phrase, sometimes in a louder voice. A person who has this difficulty perhaps cannot become very skilled, but they can almost always improve in this area. You can practise the skills many times. We can help by describing – and then practise in role play, for example – how a message can be reformulated in different ways.

If we are working with practising enhancement of communication, it is a good idea to add flexibility into the mixture from the start. I remember a man who had been taught that it is always good to clear up misunderstandings. Then, when after a meeting he learned he had misunderstood a question, he wanted to call all who had attended the meeting (20 people) to explain this to them. We then had to work on explaining to him that this rule rather applies to family and friends. A misunderstanding that would call for sorting it out with your co-workers would have to be a bigger issue. And when it comes to people who you may just see at a monthly society meeting (which was the case here) you usually do not contact them to clear things up (except for things that have crucial consequences).

All this is of course difficult to explain. When is a misunderstanding big enough? When are consequences crucial, and when are they not? The problem is that all this varies from situation to situation, and people who do not have autism spectrum disorders make these assessments based on intuition and experience.

9.9 Repetitive communication

There are staff who describe their clients or pupils as 'rambling', a word that should not be in the professional vocabulary. I have never met a person with autism who rambles. What I have met, on the other hand, is people with a repetitive communication. The reasons for someone asking the same question over and over again, or going on

---

15   You can read more about conversational techniques in Chapter 22.

talking without interruption, can be many. And if we want to help someone to make progress in this area, we must (as usual) find out the reason in this particular case.

EXAMPLE

Maureen, who has autism, repeatedly, every day, asked 'What is for lunch?' Staff told her what today's dish was, but she nevertheless continued to ask. To me, as an advisor, the question was whether it was OK to tell her 'Enough now with asking.'

The staff had tended to be slightly unsympathetic in their responses, when they were asked for perhaps the twenty-seventh time. They found themselves responding with phrases like 'Yeah, what is it for lunch?' 'You know what it is for lunch!' or 'I already told you.' To me they said that it did not matter how they responded, because she just kept asking anyway.

But one thing we can be certain of is that there is a *reason* for her questions; there is a purpose and if she continues to ask the same question, it is to achieve that purpose. We cannot just decide that the fact that we have responded 'cottage pie' means that her purpose is achieved. We must find out the purpose and help her to achieve it faster or differently.[16]

Some ideas of what Maureen's reasons could be are:

- *Difficulties with the ability to envision.* If we only respond 'cottage pie' it may be that Maureen cannot see an image of this in her mind. (Hint: in other situations related to things happening in the future Maureen asks repeated questions.)

- *Difficulties with social interaction.* Maureen is perhaps eager to interact socially, but her lack of social skills means this (asking what's for lunch) is her only means to interact. (Hint: Maureen has a social interest, but we've never seen that she can start a conversation in any other way.)

- *Under-stimulation.* Maureen may lack meaningful occupations or activities. (Hint: she never asks repeatedly when she is involved in something that is meaningful to her.)

---

16   And sometimes – though very rarely – if we fail to find the key, we will have to learn to live with a repetitive communication. Then we need strategies that help us keep up the professionalism and compassion when we feel depressed or overwhelmed. What could it be? Well, a simple thing like asking a colleague to take over in such a situation can be the solution.

- *Difficulty with shifting.* Maureen finds it difficult to 'switch tracks' and will easily get stuck on one thing. (Hint: we see it in other situations, too.)

- *Stress reaction.* Maureen is overloaded by demands and situations she does not understand. (Hint: we see more of the repetitive questions during stress and less of it when she is in balance.)

- *Difficulty in understanding the whole, the context.* By asking again and again Maureen may be checking if she will get the same answer. Who really knows what it will be for lunch (and how do they know this?). If Al replies 'Cottage pie, I think' and Millie says 'Some meat dish', is this the same thing? (Hint: Maureen is 'satisfied' if they all give the exact same response.)

- *Ritualistic behaviour.* The asking has become ritualized in a compulsive way. (Hint: it will always end at a certain point, where the ritual ends, so to speak, in a similar way every time.)

…and so on. I cannot give you an exhaustive list, there's simply no such thing. Of course, not all repetitive communication comes in the form of questions, but it is the most common form.

'But how can we help Maureen?' you might wonder now. A good exercise is to bring these issues to your reading of Part 4 of this book. There you will find a toolbox with practical ideas, and as you read the chapters in that section, write down different ideas on how you could help Maureen based on what the cause of her repetitive communication is.

Finally: to communicate your needs, to speak up and make yourself heard, is incredibly important for the well-being of the vast majority of people. Thus, if you cannot use language to communicate your needs or have your way, perhaps you have either to become dejected, passive and 'compliant', or perhaps use behaviour to influence your life. In the latter case, the means you use may be perceived as 'challenging behaviour' by professionals. It is therefore extremely important that we understand the difficulties that exist and build strategies which can compensate for them; and that we do not blame a person who, lacking other means, tries to influence or take control of his life in the only way he can.

10

Living Without a
Spare Petrol Can

A Chapter on Energy and Stress

Most people have a certain amount of energy, with many individual differences, of course. You probably know people who have more energy than you, and people who have less. We often try to arrange our lives to suit our own level of energy. We want to have an individually adjusted withdrawal on the energy account. For some people this means for example that they go to the gym every day, for others that they do it once a week or not at all. Our job will cost us a certain amount of our energy, but most of us do not want a job that consumes all of it; we want sufficient energy also for family and leisure activities.

If we have a life in which withdrawals equal our available supply of energy, we often feel balanced and well energy-wise. If something out of the ordinary happens, something which means we need extra energy (such as having to do overtime at work, a traffic jam when we are in a hurry, and sick children, accidents, etc.), we will use our 'spare can'. There we find the extra energy which allows us to cope with the over and above as well.

But what happens when the spare can runs empty too, after several days, or weeks, of an energy account overdraft? Right! For most people it affects not only general well-being, but also their mood. You are more likely to become sour, irritated or even have a meltdown.

10.1 The drop excavates the stone
(and the straw that broke the camel's back)

Living with autism often means a very high energy withdrawal for things that for others do not cost much energy at all.[1]

---

1   It may even be that what for many works as a re-energizer (e.g. spending time with friends and family) will drain the person with autism spectrum disorder of energy.

Some ideas of what these might be:

- Social interaction (which the individual with autism certainly may like and want a lot of, but is still expensive in terms of energy currency).

- Household chores (which not only consume physical energy in performance, but also often have a high cost in planning, and launching and therefore, if the individual has motor difficulties, the actual carrying out costs a vast amount of energy).

- Sensory processing problems (which will result in cost of energy for processing – i.e. organize and co-ordinate – sensory stimuli).

- Uneven development (wherein the energy cost lies in trying constantly to figure out why you cannot do certain things, and still trying hard to do them).

...and so on.

You could say that your entire 'spare can' will be spent on an everyday basis. This means that for some people if only one small thing out of the ordinary occurs, there's no energy left. Which, as we just reasoned, logically often leads to exhaustion, mood drops and 'explosions'.

Figure 10.1: We need to avoid overdraft in our energy account

EXAMPLE

Kieran is not an unusual boy with autism, yet he was perceived as very difficult. He could explode at 'nothing'. When we looked closely through an assessment at Kieran's life, we could see that the demands his staff put on him – for example, he would get up by himself (but staff would knock on his door to wake him), he would get dressed by himself, and then eat breakfast with other clients – not only consumed all of his everyday energy, but even his 'spare can' was already used up by around ten o'clock in the morning.

From Kieran's perspective, these 'easy' things are very difficult. Kieran has sleeping problems and is constantly tired. He has difficulty waking up, if he manages to fall asleep in the first place.

Technically he could dress himself, but his organizational skills were much reduced. This meant that he sometimes slipped on his jeans, to discover that his underwear remained on the floor. He pulled off his jeans (to put on his underwear) but lost focus, and now took the shirt and shoes. And then off with the shoes to put on his jeans, then the pants... and so on.

At last he was ready to go down one floor for breakfast at the care home where he was a resident. At breakfast Kieran had to face the fact that, since he was late to breakfast, they were out of ham, which was his favourite. Kieran has an auditory sensory problem, and since the other residents now were on their way out of the breakfast room, there was an extra high level of noise: the scraping of chairs and rattling of plates. Already Kieran's stress level was so high that the potential energy gained from a night's sleep was consumed.

And now it might happen that someone on the staff suddenly (and in a friendly way, in their opinion) would make a joke with Kieran about how he had put on his shirt inside-out, or point out to him that he was late.

Kaboom! The explosion was inevitable.

When the service were eventually able to see things from Kieran's perspective (theory of mind, you know, not always so easy for so-called neurotypicals either)[2], it was not so difficult to figure out how they could help him avoid such an extensive energy withdrawal that early in the day.

The adjustments they made in the expectations and demands on Kieran, and the simple aids he was given, made Kieran much less prone to sudden explosions and losing his temper.

---

2   I would say that a high (and rather unusual) level of professionalism is where staff can have second-degree theory of mind and see the service itself (not just individual situations) with the pupil's/patient's/client's eyes.

10.2 Stress and stress management

The American researcher, June Groden, who also runs the Groden Centre, has for years been engaged in stress and stress reduction for people with autism (see Groden *et al.* 1994). She has drawn attention to how it often becomes a negative spiral of stress if you do not receive help and support. People with good coping strategies, on the other hand, often get positive secondary effects from these strategies, in turn.

People without developmental disabilities, argues Groden, often have a buffer to cope with stress. They can use their social networks or internal control mechanisms to handle stress. This buffer helps to reduce stress, and also enables positive emotions, such as increased self-esteem or a feeling of closeness to others and being understood.

A person with a developmental disorder, such as autism or learning disabilities, may have more stress triggers in their daily lives – such as unexpected changes or instructions that they do not understand – and may also have an inability to use a buffer. That is, the person may not have good self-control, may lack the ability to communicate about what stresses him, or not have friends to share his worries with. Then the stress can instead take the form of a behaviour, which is ill-suited to function in our social interactions.

Keys to avoiding stress are:

- a balance between demands and capability

- a balance between activity and rest.

Keys to coping with stress when it does occur are:

- relaxation techniques

- awareness and being able to leave or say 'when'

- taking a break or rest (which may need to be made clear as to the location, timing and content).

The important thing to remember is once again that what works as rest or recovery for most people (such as leisure activities, break time and socializing) may be the most challenging for people with disabilities within the autism spectrum. Every individual is unique.

EXAMPLE

For Mohammad, who had autism, a glassed passage between the school building and lunch room was extremely stressful (phobias and fear of certain places are not unusual in autism spectrum disorders). The mere thought of perhaps having to pass through there for lunch drained him of energy every morning.

EXAMPLE

When Dara expects her teacher to say that she should be getting on with her schoolwork (which to Dara means that she is 'bad', and has 'done wrong') she feels a negative expectation. The stress is already a fact when Dara sees her teacher (who might not be thinking about saying anything about it at all).

Stress can occur as early as the anticipation stage. Therefore, we must work to be a step ahead. If we know what Dara might expect, we can prevent her stress. We can, furthermore, by giving Dara lots of positive feedback in all those situations where she is expecting something else, teach her new expectations (thus producing less stress).

Since each person is unique, you need to make an individual stress profile (which should be documented) for each pupil who has a stress problem.

10.3 Sleep

It is well known that sleep problems are common in autism spectrum disorders.[3] Though some in the group sleep well and experience no problems, many do have sleep disorders. My impression is that among those who do have problems with sleep, challenging behaviour is also more common. (This means of course that there can still be a lot of individuals with sleep problems, but without challenging behaviour.)

As to why sleep is affected in autism, there is no clear answer. It might be about sensory processing issues, hormonal problems (sleep is controlled by a hormone called melatonin), activity control problems, as well as a fear of falling asleep or going to bed, or something else.

---

3   There are several studies investigating sleep in autism spectrum disorders, mostly in children. One study, however, investigated sleep in individuals aged 15–25 years with autism spectrum disorders. The sleep questionnaires were completed by parents and caretakers and revealed only a moderate degree of sleep problems. But a much greater sleep disturbance was recorded when actigraphy (an actimetry sensor worn by the patient while sleeping) was used. The findings were low sleep efficiency and long sleep latency in 80 per cent of the individuals. The researchers conclude that this 'study suggests that even though subjective complaints of sleep disturbances are less common in adolescents and young adults with autism, this may be due to an adaptation process rather than an actual reduction in sleep disturbances' (Øyane and Bjorvatn 2005).

However, what we all know is that sleep affects our well-being and that our 'spare can' will quickly run out if we do not get enough good sleep.

Therefore, I would say that the individuals who have disturbed sleep need more of our understanding and empathy.

Finnish researchers who examined the sleep of children with autism spectrum disorders consider sleep disorders very common and suggest that sleep problems in children with autism spectrum disorders should be routinely investigated (Pavonen *et al.* 2008).

10.4 Time perception

Time perception does not necessarily have anything to do with energy, but time and stress are closely linked for most people. It is not uncommon for people with autism to have problems with time perception, often a difficulty with experiencing time. If you have a difficulty with experiencing time, you will automatically have problems assessing time. Every assessment you do – when do I have to leave to catch the bus? When to set the alarm clock? etc. – has, of course, to be based on a personal assessment: how much time do *I* need?

EXAMPLE

Krystyna has autism and significant difficulty with time perception. Krystyna meets with her case manager Michael once a month. As Michael perceives Krystyna has no problems being on time (and this is certainly not true for all his clients with neuropsychiatric disorders), he gives her the first appointment in the morning, nine o'clock. Krystyna is always on time.

What Michael does not know is that Krystyna gets up at half past three in the morning to feel sure that she will be at his office at nine o'clock. She is often already in place at half past seven, and waiting outside the building for an hour and a half. The energy withdrawal is huge since she gets so little sleep. But Krystyna is not a person who questions or objects to anything.

EXAMPLE

Carl is diagnosed with PDD-NOS and judging time is very difficult for him. Carl is also very slow in everything he does. He does not perceive time at all. Carl is always late for everything, and since he hates to be late (he knows people will scold him) he often chooses not to show up at all, when he realizes that he will be late.

When asked why he didn't show up, he often comes up with excuses such as there was a stop in the subway, there was an accident and similar. This has made other people even more critical, because they feel that Carl is also lying.

In fact, Carl does his utmost to get everywhere on time, and as he himself does not understand why he can't be on time, he tries to give explanations that he has heard others use when they were late. He cannot understand why his apologies are not accepted when others' are.[4]

---

4   Honestly, me neither. If we understand Carl's difficulties, there is no need for us to be irritated at his behaviour. We can also help him, by giving him a better self-understanding and more knowledge about his diagnosis, in order for him to make better, and truer, excuses.

11

I Don't Give a Damn About the Chores!

A Chapter on Cognition

Cognition is about the mental processes. Cognitive processes are relevant to how we gather and process information, and how we make it into knowledge. It is for instance about thinking, judiciousness, reflection, problem-solving and memory. It is often said that people with autism spectrum disorders think differently, but I am not sure it's all that true. Perhaps many have a more concrete and logical way of thinking than others, but many are also very good at thinking. If you have a disability within the autism spectrum you are obliged to think a lot in order to manage, and what you do very often you will become good at!

11.1 Executive functions

'Executive functions' is a term to describe a set of cognitive abilities which, among other things, is needed for a targeted behaviour. With the help of these functions one can also predict possible outcomes and adapt to change. One can briefly say that it is about being able to plan one's actions and to change strategy if the strategy one has in mind does not work. It requires, among other things, persistence, impulse control, imagination (mental imagery) and a flexibility in thinking for this to work. If you have done your homework in terms of the development perspective, you will of course realize that very small children do not have developed executive functions.

Imagine a small toddler with a walker toy, who suddenly hits a threshold in the doorway. The child runs against the threshold again and again, and cannot get the toy over it. We often see that the child becomes frustrated (and hear their sounds of frustration as well: 'uh-uh'). If the child does not get help, maybe he starts crying or becomes angry (throwing the toy) or simply gives up and walks away.[1] Older children begin to think 'How can I do that in a different way?' They can imagine that there are alternatives to the first strategy and examine them. They can also draw conclusions from their experiences and generalize them to new situations.

Many people with autism spectrum disorders have difficulties with their executive functions, which create problems in their practical everyday lives. Let me illustrate with an example.

EXAMPLE

George A is 22 years old and in a boarding school for troubled teens with autism. The programme includes training for independent living.

Today George A is sitting on his couch watching his favourite movie. George's staff understands that there is much he cannot do independently, and now they knock on his door and tells him: 'George, it is time to do the dishes.'

The first thing that must happen in George's head is that he must get an internal picture of the washing-up-dishes process (using mental imagery); this is closely related to memory (i.e. remembering what doing the dishes means; 'How did I go about it the last time?').

If George A has difficulty with mental imagery, making pictures in his mind,[2] but does not understand this himself, maybe he cannot complete the task. He cannot see it before his eyes. Or, if George also has traits of ADHD, he may have problems with working memory and quick access to memory.

George B is in the same situation, watching a movie when the staff knocks on the door and tells him that 'it's time to do the dishes'.

---

1 Don't we all recognize this? We're on the computer, and suddenly it freezes, and there we are hitting the same key over and over again, although nothing happens, and making sounds of frustration. And when we realize the document has gone (we didn't save it), we become sad, angry or listless. Well, remember the regression thing? Even if we have developed a mature level of executive functions we may lose them under stress.

2 Pictures in your mind, what does that mean? Think of what happens in your mind when you read a fictional story. You see pictures, right? A person with difficulties in imagining has problems creating these pictures. This may be one reason why many with autism spectrum disorders prefer non-fictional literature to fictional. You need these inner pictures when you are to perform a task – make a bed for example. You have to be able to see in your mind (even if you may not be consciously aware of this picture) the final result of the task (what does a made-up bed look like?) to be able to perform it. Now you may ask, how does this correspond to a famous book on autism titled *Thinking in Pictures* (Grandin 1995)? Well, first, many people with Asperger I meet do not think in pictures so it does not seem to be that common a feature in autism spectrum disorders, and second, Temple Grandin, the author of *Thinking in Pictures* clearly describes a difficulty with *general* pictures. And third – and most important – in autism nothing is 'always this' or 'always that'; the variations are great.

George B has no major problems with either memory or imagination. He turns off the film and gets up off the couch. He is about to go to the kitchen and do the dishes. But just when he gets up, he catches sight of his computer and remembers that he bought a new game yesterday. He turns on the computer and begins to play.

Ten minutes later the phone rings, and George gets up to answer. When he finishes the call he sees a form to be filled in on the desk, and gets started with it. George B acts on every impulse that arises, and will never get into the kitchen. He has problems with impulse control.

George C is again a 22-year-old in exactly the same situation. But George C has no problems with impulse control, nor with memory and imagination (picturing things in his mind). When the staff say it's time to go and wash up the dishes, George C goes straight to the kitchen, turns on the tap…and discovers that he can't find the detergent in its usual place!

George C has no idea what to do; no options spring to his mind. He cannot do what most people can in this situation: figure out a solution or an alternative strategy (such as check if someone put the detergent in a different place, ask someone for help, go out and buy new detergent or do the dishes with shampoo).[3]

George C has problems with flexibility in thinking.

Well, this was only an example to illustrate the problems with executive functions. In reality, I meet some people who have all the difficulties of George A, B and C at the same time. Most do not understand their own difficulties (and the people around them do not always understand them either, unfortunately). Therefore they have developed different strategies to deal with their difficulties.

It may sound like this:

- I don't give a damn about the chores!

- I am too tired!

- You can't decide what I should do!

- I can't do it!

Another strategy is to go back to 'square one' when you cannot do the task. In this case, George A would have sat down on the couch again, and turned his favourite film back on. (And maybe, if his staff had no autism specific knowledge they would have said that George is so unmotivated, and he wants us to do everything for him!) Another strategy, or rather a reaction, is the one I just mentioned: anger (and

---

3　This works just fine. I have tried it.

a meltdown). Reacting with anger when you cannot do a task, and you do not yourself understand *why* you cannot do it, is completely understandable, as I mentioned earlier.

We can recognize this difficulty in individuals who get stuck or bogged down all the time. If we are talking about pupils with autism spectrum disorders in schools, it could be when they draw a picture that they are not happy with, when they make a mistake in an exercise book, when the zipper jams, or something else. They cannot think of anything else to do, but again and again examine the strategy (which does not work), much like the toddler at the threshold, until their patience is exhausted (and the explosion is inevitable). What we need to remember is to have as much patience with the ten-year-old, 25-year-old or 42-year-old with autism as we do with the toddler, as they may not be older than one year in this particular area!

There are aids that can be used for compensation to some extent: for example, pictures may be used as an aid. A person who has no internal images may need external images, which can be photographs or illustrations of the task. If you have difficulty with impulse control, you may need something that helps you keep your focus; and if it is hard to come up with options, you may have to have those written down. You will find several examples of how to do this in practice in Part 4 of this book. But first and foremost in importance, and most basic, is your understanding.

11.2 Working memory

Problems with working memory are typical of ADHD problems, but because there are quite a few people who have both autism and ADHD, it seems appropriate to include something about working memory in this book. Working memory can be described as the ability to process information which is stored for a short time, in the mind, and use that information in a complex way. If you have problems in this area, it will be difficult to listen to instructions and immediately turn them into action. It will also be difficult to reflect.[4]

---

4   Try to remember how it is when you are under extreme pressure, or very stressed. You are trying to think about something, or plan something, but you lose the first part of the thought as soon as you reach the second. You can't keep a train of thought in your mind and elaborate on it. For people with disturbed working memory it is like this all the time!

EXAMPLE

Erich is 15 years old and has ADHD and autism. Erich cannot 'hold something in his mind'. Erich listens to the instructions for the science experiment, but then when he is about do the experiment five minutes later, he has no idea how to go about it.

Erich's father has tried to show him how the washing machine works, and Erich has stood by and watched, and heard the instructions many times. But when he gets down to the laundry room, he has no idea what to do.

Erich does not know himself that he has a real difficulty with this; he has nothing to compare with, and his parents have not been informed about the consequences of ADHD in practice. The wrong level of the demands and expectations his school and parents have had for a long time, has made Erich conclude that he is 'plain stupid' (alternatively everyone else is).

Erich has also always found it difficult to wait for his turn to say something; he knows (quite rightly) that he will lose his thought if he cannot express it immediately.

11.3 Categorization

That people with autism spectrum disorders often find it difficult to categorize in the way that others do, is well documented. Temple Grandin, who has autism, mentioned in the footnote on p.181, has described how she indeed has inner images, but each picture is specific. The word 'dog' is a special dog she has met, not dogs in general, so she can't picture 'dogs' in general, but only a specific dog she has met. Difficulties with categorization are linked to central coherence (a function of overall perception that helps 'see the big picture'). People with autism spectrum disorders often have an extremely good perception of details (at the expense of wholes). Some have called this over-selectivity.

In the book, *Mum, Is That a Human Being or an Animal?* Hilde De Clercq (2003) has many examples of how her son Thomas, who has autism, thinks. Among other things, she describes how different glasses have their own name (instead of being called 'glasses'). One particular glass is, for example, called 'the furthest' by Thomas, as the first time he asked for a glass and pointed to a shelf Hilde could barely reach, which made her comment 'Well, you want the furthest'. De Clercq (2003) writes:

> Thomas came to a seminar with me. I had to wear a badge. Thomas was seven then and asked me what was written on it.

'Hilde de Clercq,' I said.

Thomas asked, 'What does that mean?'

'It's my name, I am Hilde de Clercq.'

'So why do you say you are Mum?'

For those who perceive the details so strongly, our culture's categorization is not obvious. We say 'fruit' and refer to a variety of things; what do they really have in common? We say that the tricycle is a bike and then we point to a cycle with two wheels and say that it is also a bike, but they're not quite the same thing!

12

The Short and Boring Chapter

A Chapter on Definitions, Incidence and Other Things You May Want to Know, but Which Are of Little Help in Practice

This far into the book someone may be wondering 'What about the triad of impairments?' or 'Does the author not know that autism spectrum disorders are primarily about social deficits?' There are shelf after shelf of books that pile up facts about autism, but with hardly any degree of understanding that is useful in practice. And how many lectures and seminars have we attended, both you and I, where the lecturer says the same things we've heard lots of times before?

Nevertheless, I am a coward. I dare not write this book without a chapter that describes those (useless) facts. But what I did was to hide this chapter really far into the book. And I've been very explicit with the chapter title, so anyone who wants to can skip it. So here it is, the chapter I think you do not want to read.

12.1 Definition

Autistic disorder and Asperger syndrome and pervasive developmental disorder not otherwise specified (PDD-NOS) are diagnoses of what we call autism spectrum disorders. Autism spectrum can be viewed as a category characterized by having symptoms within three areas. These are: qualitative impairment in social interaction; qualitative impairments in communication and restricted, repetitive, and stereotyped patterns of behaviour, interests, and activities. This is what is called the triad of impairments. Now with the changes proposed for *DSM-5* there is a discussion that it is really about a dyad of symptoms, which refers to qualitative impairments in social communication as one category and restricted interest and behaviour as the other.[1]

---

1   The *DSM-5* criteria will be published in the spring of 2013.

Another category of developmental disorders is attention and concentration disorders (ADD and ADHD included). These categories can be said to overlap; it is quite common for individuals with diagnoses from one category also to have symptoms from the other. Furthermore other psychiatric diagnoses such as for example Tourette's syndrome and OCD often overlap these neurodevelopmental disorders. Traditionally high-functioning autism is often diagnosed by psychiatrists (or in some cases by neurologists).

A person with an autism spectrum disorder, may in addition to this have, for example, an affective disorder (perhaps generalized anxiety disorder, obsessive compulsive disorder or depression), and some, although it is not very common, suffer from psychotic disorders.

Some individuals seem to have a mix of symptoms with 'a little something from everything' and although symptoms are having a great impact on their everyday lives it can be difficult to diagnose. A fairly new and unknown diagnosis is PANDAS (Pediatric Autoimmune Nueropsychiatric Disorder Associated with Streptococcus infection)[2] which is characterized by a very sudden onset of symptoms, always including tics and/or OCD. Other PANDAS symptoms can mimic those of above mentioned diagnoses, and there is new interesting research which links autism to the immune system too.[3]

12.2 Incidence

How common are these disorders, and are they increasing? According to Eric Fombonne, a professor of psychiatry in Canada, the more recent figures show a constant prevalence[4] of 0.6–0.7 per cent by summing up all of the PDD diagnoses (Fombonne 2009). Several others, including Professor Christopher Gillberg (Kadesjö, Gillberg

---

2   Read more about PANDAS here http://intramural.nimh.nih.gov/pdn/web.htm.

3   Here is an article on autism and the immune system: http://www.nytimes. com/2012/08/26/opinion/sunday/immune-disorders-and-autism. html?pagewanted=all&_r=0.

4   *Prevalence* means the number of people who are believed to have the disorder. Prevalence research is often done by screening (examining) all of a certain age group in a specific area, for example all seven-year-olds in an area. This will show many who fulfil the criteria. From this it is possible to draw conclusions and estimate the number of people in the whole population who might fulfil the criteria. *Incidence* is another term that means how many people who actually do have a certain diagnosis in the population, which can be measured by, for example finding out how many patients are diagnosed at a particular clinic. Prevalence is normally higher than incidence, since not all who fulfil the criteria for various reasons will actually search for or receive a diagnosis.

and Hagberg 1999), believe it is closer to one per cent. Childhood disintegrative disorder is the least common diagnosis, while PDD-NOS is responsible for 0.3 per cent. A comparison looking back in time shows that the numbers have increased. Most researchers believe that this can be explained by the following developments:

- The diagnostic criteria has been broadened to include milder cases than before.

- Awareness of autism spectrum disorders has increased.

- These diagnoses are nowadays more frequently made together with other diagnoses in children with more than one disability.

It is not completely possible to exclude the possibility that some portion of the increase is due to other factors, but at present there are only speculations of what these factors might be.

12.3 Causes

Today it is clear that autism spectrum disorders have biological causes. We have had more than 60 years of speculations of possible (and impossible!) causes. The most popular idea was for a long time that the mother is the root of all evil. Mothers have not only been accused of being the cause of autism, but also of schizophrenia and a number of other diseases, as you probably know.[5]

There are several biological factors linked to the causes of autism spectrum disorders, but in each individual case you cannot always determine the cause. In my opinion, relatively speaking, the cause is quite uninteresting. People with autism exist, have always existed and will (I hope!) always exist. So to me it seems a lot more interesting to develop the understanding and approaches, and create good living conditions, than to know what caused it. But that's my opinion.

If you want to delve into the biology of autism, I suggest you read *The Biology of the Autistic Syndromes* (Gillberg and Coleman 2000), which at 340 pages gives a thorough overview of what is known about the biology behind the autism spectrum disorders.

---

5   Is it not tiresome with all these films (Hitchcock's *Psycho* was perhaps the first), where the brutal/bestial behaviour of a psychopath is explained by a disturbed relationship with his mother? For those who want to expand on their view of the influence parents have, I suggest the book *The Nurture Assumption: Why Children Turn Out the Way They Do* (Rich Harris 1999).

12.4 Criteria

The triad of impairments, which I mentioned previously, is actually also the largest part of the definition of autism spectrum disorders. The three areas of symptoms are reflected in what is called the diagnostic criteria, which is basically a list of symptoms, of which a certain number must be fulfilled before a diagnosis can be made.

The criteria that are most widely and commonly used, are presented in the *DSM* (*Diagnostic and Statistical Manual of Mental Disorders*) which was published by the American Psychiatric Association (2000). DSM is based on a US collaboration between researchers and experts in the respective areas. There is a corresponding European manual called *ICD-10* (World Health Organization 1993) with a similar division of autism spectrum disorders. In addition to the triad of impairments it is usually also said that a profile of uneven development, and delay of development of theory of mind should be included in the definition.[6]

12.5 Work-up

The actual work-up for diagnosis is often done by a specialist psychiatric team. In the work-up several different surveys and interviews are included, and it is by a thorough assessment (a combination of neuropsychological test results, history, assessment scale/screening questionnaires, etc.) that one can arrive at a diagnosis.

Do you now think that this chapter was the best in the entire book and regret that it was not longer? Then I have to refer you to other sources. At the end of this book, on p.374, you will find suggestions of websites, books and other resources.

---

6   In practice, in many countries a profile of uneven development and delay of development of theory of mind are often included in the definition since they are part of the test battery performed by neuropsychologists in the work-up for diagnosis (e.g. False Belief Task, and profile on WISC).

PART 3

The Change Process

...An Important
Element of the Craftsmanship

13

Can We Make a Deaf Person Hear Better by Setting Limits?

*A Chapter on Punishment of 'Violations',
and Consequences of Actions*

Some clients and pupils who have autism spectrum disorders also, unfortunately and for various reasons, have behaviours that are problematic to themselves and their surroundings. Terms such as 'behavioural problems' and 'challenging behaviour' are commonly used. 'Challenging behaviour' works in terms of pointing to the fact that behaviour can challenge staff's ability to understand and respond. A colleague of mine coined 'challenging situations' as an alternative. This is even better as it makes it clear that it is all about certain situations and environments which may set off a reaction.

13.1 Ch–ch–ch–ch–changes

For several years I have worked with people with autism spectrum disorders and particularly with challenging behaviour. This usually means that a person harms people or objects, but it can also mean that a person only acts out verbally.

When you have to deal with such behaviours, there will always be (a lot of) other things the individual will need help with, which means it is always a process of change. And since what has been done in the past, the old approach, obviously has not worked out according to plan (if it had, there would be no reason for consulting me) the new approaches will be an element of the change process. And since the staff (and perhaps the family too) around this individual must change their approach, it will be a process of change for them too.

Change is not always easy. But it is possible. The first step is to really understand that there is a need for change. This is not that simple, because we humans are creatures of habit, and we like to do as we have always done. What we must understand is that if what we have always done (that is until now) has not worked – if Cindy or Toby still have uncontrolled breakdowns, a threatening behaviour, or whatever it may be – well, then we need to do something different. It is a process of change.

This work needs to be done on several levels. It starts at the mental level of the professionals who are around the person with the challenging behaviour. So, this is first and foremost about how your ethos shapes your approach, and this you have probably already read about in Chapter 2 'The Framework and Ideologies'.

You may wish to read that chapter again now, before continuing here. (And if you jumped straight to this section of the book, because you have a relative or client who has challenging behaviours, I want to make clear that it is absolutely critical that you also read all of Part 2, 'Understanding the Impairments'.)

I have consulted many staff groups, in short-term care, residential care, psychiatric wards (including forensic psychiatry), schools and day care, where there have been individuals with autism spectrum disorders and challenging behaviours. All these children, adolescents and adults I talked to who have had such behaviours, have experienced a great deal of suffering and have been very unhappy about their own behaviours (and situations). Even – or perhaps especially – in cases where they had an attitude that suggested that they really do not care at all.[1]

These people need our help, but for them to be able to receive it, we must show ourselves to be (trust)worthy helpers, giving the right kind of help. When you succeed in doing that, you will discover that just as the wrong kind of help provided a number of negative 'side effects', the right kind of help produces more positive ones: the ripple effect.

You may remember that in Chapter 2 'The Framework and Ideologies' (see p.20) I wrote:

The *implication* of an action can be destructive (at worst, someone is injured) but the *intention* is not destructive and thus, as I see it, nor is

---

1   You may recall the discussion in Chapter 9 on communication about what might lie behind an attitude (p.168). Sometimes, the explanation can also be a lack of theory of mind, with the result that the individual doesn't really understand how others perceive what he does; this is very common when there is a threatening behaviour (you can read more about the theory of mind in Chapter 16). Sometimes it's more about creating an identity for yourself, 'as if I care', which is common in people with depression and low self-esteem.

the act in itself. This may seem like a construction of thought, since I deliberately choose to see it this way. It is, however, useful because it has a significant bearing on how I respond to people.

So when the staff team says – about a man who trashes the staff room – that 'he does it to punish us', I must say that *if* that actually is the case (and to know that, we must first have found out properly why), then it was the most constructive thing he could do in this situation. And if we do not think that this is a good way for him to express his feeling of revenge, we must give him the tools to be able to do otherwise. At the risk of being over-explicit, I would say that most people I've met with this kind of problem very rarely have the desire for revenge as the reason behind their actions.

Let us return to constructive actions having destructive consequences.

EXAMPLE

Daniel is 15 years old and has been diagnosed with autism. He is in tenth grade. His teachers have been informed of the disability and also that Daniel has specific difficulties with touch and sudden, unexpected events.

His teacher wants the pupils to listen to what he says (quite understandable). In addition, it is not permissible to listen to music in class time. The teacher says to Daniel, who is not 'obeying' (or not hearing?) to turn off his music and take off his headphones.

The teacher requests this of him a couple more times and then becomes so provoked by Daniel's seemingly indifferent attitude, that he steps forward and pulls the headphones off Daniel (equals sudden event and touch).

In almost one hundredth of a second, Daniel has risen, thrown the chair he was sitting on out the window (which was not open), overturned a bookcase and run out of the classroom.

Who is responsible for the broken window? I believe that the teacher is. From Daniel's point of view, it was a panic reaction. Sure, Daniel needs more constructive ways to deal with his frustration, but it is for us to teach them to him.

13.2 Truth and consequences

At this moment I want to pause and discuss attitudes a bit and how the way we see 'truth' may be relevant. If Leia is 'yelling and messing around' when she has a breakdown, is it a truer truth than her own (that everyone is mean to her)? Or is it a truer truth than mine (that Leia lacks well-adjusted strategies to cope with stress and frustration)? The question of truth in the objective sense is not really possible to answer because the truth always has a subjective element. And the interesting question is hardly 'Which truth is the truest?', but rather 'Which truth serves Leia's possibilities for progress in this case?'

Let me give an example. Last week I presented the approach which is laid out in Chapter 15 in this book to a group of professionals. I described, among other things, the assessment in the form of a survey, where we can learn more about how the person himself perceives his existence. It includes the questions 'What do you do if you: are scared/ become angry/are tired/feel sad? One woman argued then that this was not useful to her client with autism, since he believes that he himself does not ever do anything wrong. 'Our client will never be able to answer it,' she said.

My first reaction was that she in fact could not know that he cannot answer because she had never tried using a questionnaire, and that in my experience you often get new and more thorough answers when using a visually supported way of asking (which of course is the point).

It is of course possible that he actually cannot answer these questions even when asked in the survey form, but if this happens it is also informative, in my opinion. Then we learn something about how he functions: namely, that he may not know what he does when he becomes scared or angry, or even that he does not know what he feels (or that he does not understand the questions). All of this gives us a key to why this man has such a high degree of stress and is unable to control his behaviour.

'OK,' she said, 'but we already know that he is yelling and going berserk, but he does not see this himself.' I answered her that I really did not intend to make her look (or feel) stupid now, but that her description is actually *not* an objective truth, that what she said he does, is not at all more true than his idea of what he does. She looked so puzzled, that I clarified that I would never use phrases such as 'yelling and going berserk' when describing a behaviour of a person with an autism spectrum disorder; it would never be a true description to me, however true she thinks it is. I would, for example, rather say that the client 'has difficulties handling his frustration in an appropriate way'.

But wait a minute, my truth is of course not truer than anyone else's – *that* is certainly true! Therefore, we must now look at what conclusions the various truths lead to.

- *Issue:* user/pupil/client yells and goes berserk.

- *Conclusion:* we need to get X to stop screaming and trashing places.

Unfortunately this truth with its conclusion, does not get us one iota closer to the solution. Let's try this instead:

- *Issue:* user/pupil/client is handling his frustration in a socially inappropriate manner.

- *Conclusion:* we must teach X new ways of dealing with his/her frustration.

And see, doesn't this immediately begin to stimulate some ideas of what and how this could be done?[2]

Once we have established the first step, that is, the entire staff group theoretically understands what a constructive ethos in this process means, we can move on. Initially, the new approach will not be automatic for them, nor have they (still) seen the benefits – the success – from it. Therefore, it is so far only superficial knowledge. When they keep on working with this approach, and are successful in this work, it will increasingly be a habit to think from this perspective. My hope as a supervisor or consultant is that staff eventually will have this view as a knee-jerk reaction, rather than their previous view, where they often felt vulnerable and powerless, and 'exposed' to the different behaviours of their client/pupil/user.

The second step is to understand that we affect behaviour by understanding its causes. *Why* is the key to change. To adhere to the behavioural level is a typical pitfall for staff, which I shall return to shortly.

If we ask ourselves 'How do we get Charlie to stop fighting?' or 'How do we get Jennifer not to trash her room?' there are no answers. When the question is posed in this way, one can possibly look for answers in a book or take a course in which a 'technique' is presented. But this 'expert', the lecturer or writer, knows nothing about Jennifer or

---

2   Issue: there are many descriptions that can be 'true'. Conclusion 1: the individual's own truth always says a lot about how he/she perceives the situation. Conclusion 2: use the truth that serves the individual and that promotes solutions.

Charlie – they've never met them. And since every person with autism spectrum disorder is so unique (in their deficits, in their personality and in their life situation) it is very likely that such an approach fails. For each failed effort, we risk building a situation where Charlie or Jennifer feels less and less helped, and more and more offended, and eventually perhaps we have a 'war' where the client lies in a trench and the staff in another.

I am not the one who should be credited for this approach. Division TEACCH described this more than 15 years ago as the 'iceberg metaphor'.[3] Unfortunately, it has not had sufficient impact on practice yet. According to Division TEACCH the behaviour is the tip of the iceberg (what we see), while the causes, just like the bulk of an iceberg, is below the surface, and thus not visible. Nonetheless, it is by understanding the causes that we can affect behaviour.

However, one cannot assume that an interconnection between a behaviour and its causes is always the same. Michael not being able to keep himself clean and tidy may be due to his motor difficulties, while Omar may have hygiene problems because of his difficulty getting organized and getting started, and Dara might simply not understand how others perceive her lack of hygiene. Jorge, on the other hand, may have difficulties with all these things. So, the variation is large, and when we see a behaviour, we should not just *guess* what is causing it. Or rather, guessing is precisely what we must do, but let us make as qualified and well-educated a guess as possible, not just pick the first idea that comes along.

An interesting note is that when I come to staff groups, it is not unusual for some of them to have very definite opinions about what the problematic behaviour is due to, or associated with (or 'there is no pattern at all, it may occur at anytime'). Often we find that the causes are not what they first thought, or that there most certainly is a pattern that can be detected. That does not mean that it is not worth listening to staff's perception of the situation, but it means it's even more important that we do investigative work together. Thus, we have to get below the surface of the iceberg to be able to help. We will need 'diving skills' in this work, which I will talk about in the next chapter.

---

3   See the history of TEACCH in *The TEACCH Approach to Autism Spectrum Disorders (Issues in Clinical Child Psychology)* (Mesibov, Shea and Schopler 2005).

13.3 Making the professional 'environmentally friendly'

I would like to take the iceberg metaphor a step further, and talk about the environment surrounding the iceberg. This environment consists largely of you professionals and family, who are around the person. And the environment is crucial to what behaviour we see in a person with the disability. The good news is that it is easier to start by changing yourself and your interactions, than trying to start with changing the user or pupil.

Sometimes you meet staff groups who think it makes sense to work with 'setting limits'. They may even have heard this from various 'experts': that they should be 'firm' and 'set boundaries', and 'not give in'. Other times, this approach has emerged from a staff group who felt so powerless and provoked that this was the only approach they could come up with (and unfortunately, much too often there is a substantial portion of punishment in this approach).

This way of working – or waging war, maybe – feels completely foreign to me. If you were working supporting a deaf person, would it seem reasonable to use 'boundaries' as a way of making this person hear better? Or would it rather actually be abusive?

EXAMPLE

Laura, who has autism, grew up in the 1960s. She has an atypical form of Rett syndrome,[4] with only mild autism and as a child her motor function was only mildly affected. (In the 1960s neither high-functioning forms of autism nor Rett syndrome in milder forms were well known.) Laura is today in a wheelchair.

At the age of six, her legs did not obey her properly, and she had difficulty walking. Since there was no (according to experts) obvious reason that she could not walk, they concluded that she was just lazy and oppositional. Consequently, a psychologist stood across the room and said to Laura 'Come to me, you can walk if you only want to.'

Was this reasonable?

Now you might think that you would never do anything like this. Sure, this was more than 40 years ago, and we know better today.

---

4   Rett syndrome is an autism spectrum disorder that affects mainly girls. They develop normally until 12–18 months of age and then experience symptoms that affect motor skills and behaviour. In its typical form these girls will have severe learning disorder, be in a wheelchair and lose speech. Now it is known that atypical and milder forms occur. You can read more about Rett syndrome at www.rettuk.org.

But the question is: where do we have our blind spots now? What is it today that we do not know that we are doing, that might be harmful for people with disabilities? It could be things such as using the 'setting boundaries' approach, when we instead should meet them with understanding and give them new solutions to their problems.

EXAMPLE

There is a staff meeting with me as a counsellor. The residential support staff want to talk about Mike, who is perceived as very difficult.

'Mike always changes the appointments with us, or wants us to meet in another location,' says one of the staff. 'Yes, and he checks on everything we do, follows us around to see if we do things properly when we clean his apartment,' another adds. 'He is so controlling!' says a third. 'Yes, it's as if he wants to take over, bossing us around'.

The staff say that now they want to set more strict boundaries as to when and how he should be supported, to limit his control. 'Maybe we should draw up a contract with him,' suggests one of the staff.

'In my experience people who want to control and steer others, are people who feel powerless,' I say.

I do not think we can best help those who feel powerless by taking away their power. On the contrary! We should give him *more* influence over his support. Otherwise, we risk ending up in a tug of war for power, which is not a particularly creative position for providing support.

It is easy to end up in this setting-boundaries approach if you do not have autism-specific knowledge. You may encounter a pupil with autism where there is a problem around eating. She will eat one thing, but not the other, and it must be cooked in a certain way, and you try to satisfy her. But after a while you begin to feel that 'she is never content, whatever we do'. And so you may eventually feel that you should 'put your foot down' and that 'she actually cannot always get her way'.

You're talking this through with your colleagues and you agree that you have really tried, and that 'now she must actually choose between two dishes, and if it doesn't suit her, she must go without'. It easily happens. But is this approach qualified support or something else? Are you rather acting out of your own feelings of powerlessness, and wanting to take control?

Or let's say you are a residential supporter and you have a client who does not want to go to the bathroom, but instead uses the buckets placed around his apartment (which he doesn't empty so they smell). Then you might try to convince him to use the bathroom. You and your colleagues explain to him several times why he should use the toilet. He says he will, but continues to do as he always has. And finally you and your colleagues reason that, well, then we stop emptying the buckets for him, we'll just leave them there smelling ('he must learn the consequences of his behaviour').

Real help or an offence?

Or maybe it's a man with autism who is calling and threatening his social worker over the phone. And you as residential staff try to talk to him and make him understand that he must stop, but he continues to do so. And someone in the staff group might say 'Well, we will just take his phone away', and another fills in 'Yes, and let him prove that he is able to have the phone, to earn it back little by little', and you think this makes sense.

Real help or a violation of his rights?[5]

Now you might never do something like this (although I have seen all these examples and many similar ones too often in schools, in residential care and other services).

Recently, I went to a school where a pupil with autism, 11 years old and with challenging behaviours, did not eat *anything* during the entire school day. 'We have tried everything,' the teachers said. 'There's nothing else we can do. So he will just go without food.' They also told me they had consulted with a doctor who said that a child can manage through the school day without eating.

I ask some questions:

GG: Can it be about the type of food?

Teachers: No, he gets the dishes he wants.

GG: Can it be about the environment in the lunch room?

Teachers: No, he has eaten there occasionally. And when we offered a space in another room, it still didn't work.

GG: Can it be that he doesn't want to miss out on anything particular at lunch break?

---

5   You may argue that threatening someone is against the law. But you are not a law enforcer, nor a judge; it's not your decision to make. You cannot stop someone breaking a law by breaking one yourself. If the social worker wants to report this man to the police, it's her decision. But most social workers I've met don't report everything, unless they feel it's serious.

Teachers: Eh… well, perhaps. He likes the swings, and he wants to get out there before they're occupied by other pupils.

GG: Can it be that he doesn't know how to get his special dishes in the lunch room?

Teachers: No, because we have shown him how he needs to go to the kitchen and ask for his special dish. But despite that, he just goes to the kitchen and stands there.

GG: OK, in four questions we have found two possible factors, one being there's something he is afraid of missing during the lunch-break, and the other being that he does not know what he should do to get his food.

Teachers: No, no, we *have shown* him how to get his food. We have gone with him, and we have told him how to do it.

GG: But you say he just stands there, and if he does not seem to know how he has to ask for his own dishes, then you *have not* shown him. Not in a way that works.

What I mean by telling you this is not that I have the magic power to solve all problems in three minutes, but that it is sometimes very simple questions on my part, that allow us to find a way of working. If we know what the problem is, we can start to work out the solutions. When you 'get stuck' with a pupil, user or client, you must start asking questions, and when you run out of questions you look for new ones.

There is a saying that you have probably heard before, but which is worth thinking about now and then: 'If you're not part of the solution, you may be part of the problem'. Even if the teachers had consulted the doctor who said that that there was no health hazard in going without eating during school days, I think most people only need to look at themselves to see the connection between frustration tolerance, and hunger. If there is a pupil with great difficulty controlling his temper, the least we can do for him is to ensure that he is not hungry. It is difficult enough for the pupil and the professionals!

If being without food the entire school day makes him have five meltdowns instead of two, or if his meltdowns are ten-pointers, instead of only seven-pointers, surely we don't want him to go without food, if we can do something about it. We cannot think 'We can only stretch ourselves so much' (to arrange alternative dishes, and a private space for lunch). We need to think 'We have to stretch ourselves as far as is necessary.'

It is exciting that sometimes it is the actual stretch that does the trick; our own attitude seems to influence the person as much as what we actually do.

13.4 Avoiding a financial crisis on the trust account

Occasionally the person with the disability is blamed for his difficulties, which is even more problematic since staff sometimes (unintentionally, of course) trigger the behaviour. In Sweden municipalities have even decided to have 'a policy' to report to the police any 'violent incidents' in their care services. That is the ultimate 'consequence'. This is especially problematic since staff, as we will see later in this book, are often responsible (unknowingly and unwillingly of course) for triggering such incidents.

In the UK staff tend to seek psychiatric help for a client with a challenging behaviour, which of course may be a good thing, but ever so often only has the result that the client is heavily medicated. Medicine may be a wonderful help to some people, but I have met several who have been so heavily medicated that the side effects actually cause more severe problems than the individual had to begin with.

What you need to understand is the mechanisms behind the 'blaming the client' syndrome. As staff you are a professional, but you also interact on a personal level with the client. This is inevitable; as I discussed previously, you cannot withdraw your own person from the professional role (then you would become a machine), and not everything we do in terms of interchange can be conscious and premeditated – sometimes we make a breakthrough by chance, luck or by using our intuition. Thus, there will always be an irrational element to work involving teaching or supporting human beings.

However, this leaves room for less desirable processes, too, and here we need our awareness and maturity to avoid them. As staff you may have a tough client, and you try and try and do your best and the client is still acting out. Finally you may come to a point where you feel 'offended' by the client (believe me, I have heard staff use such words more than once). But the fact that staff feel 'offended' signals to me that they do not have sufficiently good Management. I cannot understand how someone can be 'offended' by their client's difficulties, if they work with people with these types of problems.

(It may be uncomfortable, or being hit may hurt, etc.... but surely you don't feel 'offended'?) 'Offended' is what you become when you think you have 'done everything' and 'been fair', but are 'getting nothing back' or 'just ingratitude in return'. But in my opinion this is not possible within the framework of being a professional. Have we ever 'done everything'? Can doing your job ever be characterized as 'being fair'? Can the fact that one's disability prevented one from learning to express frustration and stress adequately be described as a sign of ingratitude? No staff I meet use these exact words, of course – but they are embedded in the word 'offended', in my opinion.

I also suggest that this is a management issue, since if a staff group reverts to ending up on a personal level (rather than on the professional one) in their approaches, it is the Management that has to snatch them back on the right track again. Above all, it is the task of the Management to give staff hope and the prerequisites to do a good job. When this happens (staff blaming the client) it is often about a staff group who feels 'vulnerable' (is powerless), and a person with autism who is very vulnerable (and feels powerless).

What do I mean by the disability preventing the client from learning to express frustration and stress in a more adequate way? Well, in addition to all the factors that may cause the individual to feel (extreme) stress, he may also often have an immature way of dealing with anger and frustration (feelings that are natural consequences of extreme stress). It is not that the individual has developed a mature and adequate way of handling frustration, and then still chooses to throw chairs and push staff (though often enough staff I meet seem to think that this is a fact).

And with regards to medication, Juan Fuentes' ten principles of Pharmautism from 1998 are still valid (Autism-Europe 1998):

1. No, there is no drug to treat autism. Many drugs were tested, but none has solved the main problems related to what is called autism.

2. Yes, some drugs can efficiently treat psychiatric disorders or behavioural problems experienced by people with autism.

3. No, in the case of people with autism, drugs should not be used if we are unable to achieve, through other methods, the necessary progress. For the time being, there is no treatment for autism, and drugs are likely to complicate even more the situation.

4. Yes, drugs can supplement a multimodal treatment and make other interventions more efficient.

5. No, drugs cannot substitute for other social or educational treatments and cannot offset structural shortages, i.e. a lack of qualified staff.

6. Yes, one should bear in mind that drug prescription is an attempt without any certainty as to the result. In principle, a drug should not be given all life long.

7. No, psychotropic drugs should not be given without the certainty that behavioural problems are not of physical origin, more especially in the case of children or non-verbal people (restlessness can be due to a toothache, a headache or otitis, etc.).

8. Yes, the instructions given by the medical staff must be adhered to: the dosage should not be increased or reduced without permission; the treatments should not be shortened or prolonged without necessary control.

9. No, there are no psychotropic drugs without side effects. Nearly all drugs have either positive or negative effects. Generally speaking, one has to weigh the pros and cons.

10. Yes, people with autism, to the best of their abilities, the families and the professionals concerned must be involved, warned about the limits, the potential risks and the beneficial effects of drugs. People with autism and/or their legal guardians are entitled to give their informed consent and it is up to the prescriber to provide the necessary information so that a decision can be made with full knowledge of the facts.

13.5 The development of mature strategies – how does it come about?

When a small child has these emotions – anger and frustration (perhaps triggered by such things as hunger, fatigue, stress, disappointment) – he often acts on them physically. The child will throw a toy on the floor, scream, bite an adult, push another child. It is not a behaviour that we think is remarkable for a toddler. Since what I now call 'socially appropriate behaviour in anger'[6] is not innate, it has to be learned. But how does this learning occur in the common developmental process?

Many adults probably think that reprimands are vital, and children certainly receive many remarks about their behaviour. Personally, I do not think that telling a child ever so often that a behaviour is inappropriate really has such a great impact on their behaviour. Sure, they can be compliant or non-compliant[7] but what we are speaking of here is the child's inner motivation to behave or not behave in a certain way.

But let us still dwell on the reprimands for a while. Two factors are required to make this work, the first is actually having the ability to regulate the behaviour (so that the remark serves as a reminder when they forget) and the second is that the child is emotionally dependent on being liked by the person who gives the remark, which we can call social motivation. Both these factors can be out of play in autism spectrum disorders.[8]

We say that children do not do as we tell them, they do as we do. This means that if I as a parent always scream 'bitch' or 'shit' when I'm frustrated, but am telling my son that he should not use such language when he is angry, he will most probably use these words anyway, although my son has social motivation as well as the ability to control his behaviour. Why would he curse anyway? Well, because the

---

6   Please note that having a socially appropriate behaviour in anger must mean that one is able and allowed to express anger. On one occasion I found a social story written for a pupil with autism, in which the essence was 'When I become angry and upset, I shall sit at my desk and rest my head against my arm'. It is difficult to see how this can be a means to express anger.

7   Compliance is in my opinion best viewed as a personality trait, just as musicality or something else. We are born different on a scale of compliance to non-compliance (as well as on a scale of absolute pitch to unmusicality, or something else). Most of us are somewhere in the middle range (well, not me, I was born at the very non-compliant end, which has been somewhat troublesome but also an enormous strength). This means we can't rely on compliance from a client or pupil who happens to be born more at the non-compliant end. Furthermore, it means that we have to really embrace the fact that even though we do not speak of compliance that much, we as professionals, subconsciously often want compliance, and we praise it – though, I would say, being very compliant is more troublesome for an individual than being more non-compliant. (But it is the other way around for the surroundings, and I am not just speaking of people with autism spectrum disorders here, this goes for everyone.) This is a paradox and, with the assignment we have in caring settings to support the individual, we must be aware of this paradox and handle it.

8   This paragraph is indeed a parenthesis, because I still think that not even in the child with 'standard development' it is the verbal cues, the remarks and reprimands, which, so to speak, do the trick.

primary learning strategy in child development is *imitation*. Children do as we do. In autism spectrum disorders we know that imitation is not the primary learning strategy.[9]

An interesting side note is that in standard development in children there is a very strong desire to *be big* and become older. You know how important it is for children that they are four-and-*a-half* years old (not just four). And how often do we use children's desire to be big to motivate them ('A big girl like you should be able to put her clothes on herself'; 'Now that you will soon turn six, it's time for you to learn…' and so on). Many children with autism spectrum disorders that I meet do not have this drive (and therefore that kind of argument will not work as motivation).[10] What am I getting at, you may wonder. Well, I believe that if nature equipped children with imitation as the primary learning strategy, of course it is 'wise' to ensure that they will mimic *older* children and adults, not younger children. And anyone who does not have imitation as the primary learning strategy, will then perhaps not have the drive to be or seem bigger than they are.[11]

Another interesting, and perhaps more important, factor that helps children learn to express anger and frustration in a socially appropriate way is associated with the theory of mind development. I usually call this *social embarrassment*, (OK, you may argue that all embarrassment is social, but I am speaking of the part of embarrassment that is linked to the socialization and maturing process) which seems to me to evolve gradually after the second-order theory of mind is established.[12] It tends to peak somewhere between the ages of 11 and 14 when children tend to perceive almost everything as socially embarrassing (especially what their parents say and do).

I believe that social embarrassment is one of the strongest factors influencing children to regulate their behaviour in this context.

---

9   NB: this does not mean that a child with autism is never able to imitate anyone, it rather means literally what I wrote: that it is not the *primary* learning strategy.

10   And I have always thought there is something deeply sympathetic to this: the idea that you are who you are, and why would it be better to be five than to be four?

11   However, I do meet many people with autism who are offended by being perceived and above all, treated, as younger than they are, but it's a different thing than the urge to be bigger.

12   Second-order theory of mind means that you understand that other people can think and feel something *about other people*, and consequently they can think something about *you*. Thus, the ability to see yourself through the eyes of others, to understand how we are perceived from outside ourselves, relies on having reached the second degree of theory of mind.

EXAMPLE

Courtney is a normally developed eight-year-old, a 'standard child' as a colleague of mine would put it. Courtney is going shopping with her dad. In the supermarket she sees a candy bar, and tells her dad that she wants it. Dad replies: 'No, we are not buying candy today.'

I believe Courtney, however 'normal' she may be, can become angry in this situation. (And, just as for all of us, her general well-being at that moment will determine if she gets angry at all, and if so to what degree on that particular day. Of course, another day she might not be as angry, a day when she had slept well, eaten well, not been disappointed in her older brother a few hours earlier, and so on.)

But now we are trying to differentiate between the actual emotion, and the acting on it, so let's assume that Courtney does become angry with her dad for not getting the candy bar. When you're angry, you can be tempted to do a lot of things which are perceived as destructive or inappropriate (again, this goes for all of us, even adults, right?). Thus, Courtney could have the urge to kick something in the shop, to tear down all the candy bars from the shelf, hit her father, or throw herself on the floor and yell.

I argue that in this respect Courtney and an eight-year-old with an autism spectrum disorder, let's call her Paige, are alike: they can both become upset, and they may both be tempted to act inappropriately.

I would say that it is Courtney's ability to imitate behaviours as a learning process that would help her to know how she should behave, but above all it is the social embarrassment that prevents her from acting out what she may feel. In her mind Courtney views scenarios that will inhibit her: what if the man at the counter sees me lying on the floor screaming! Or even worse, what if one of my classmates is here! Courtney wants to avoid feeling awkward and embarrassed, and she has a well-developed theory of mind that helps her to understand how others would perceive her.

Paige, being the same age but having autism, however, might not have learned through imitation, or even have developed second-degree theory of mind. If Paige has great difficulty with behaviour, she might not even have developed the first degree. She has no more idea than a toddler of how she should behave and, not being aware of how other people perceive her, it doesn't really bother her.

Now you might object that there are a lot of children and adolescents (and adults) with autism spectrum disorders who actually are able to display their anger or frustration in a socially appropriate way. This is quite true. However, it takes longer to learn for most of them, compared with their peers. And although several of those who are more severely affected by autism *can* learn this, it often requires (because of the mechanisms I have described) someone to explicitly teach them.

Thus Paige can certainly learn a more socially appropriate approach to deal with her frustration – there is in fact nothing wrong with her general ability to learn. However, the mechanisms for what we may call 'auto-learning' are affected by her disability, and therefore she (as often happens) is only referred to reprimands and remarks as the 'method' for learning – which in practice means she does not stand a chance.[13]

How can we teach her? What should we teach her? When are we going to do it? There are many possible approaches. It's best if we work together with Paige to come up with one.

Figure 13.1: An example of an 'anger-paper'

EXAMPLE

Natnael, a third-grader with autism stressed out every time he made the slightest error, such as if he needed to erase something he had written. He would throw his papers and books from his desk, shouting and

---

13   Of course, there are several factors that affect the ability to show anger in a socially appropriate manner, such as lack of impulse control. But this you have probably already understood because this book is full of examples of such factors.

cursing. Besides all the obvious efforts to reduce his stress, we saw a need to teach Natnael new strategies to deal with frustration.

Since he often crumpled up his papers before throwing them around, we decided to build on this. Kim, his teacher, designed an 'anger-paper' (see Figure 13.1) together with Natnael on the computer, and printed copies. They talked about how he could use these papers the next time he got frustrated in the classroom.

Kim and her colleagues were then watchful for when Natnael showed signs of stress. When she saw early signs of stress, Kim pointed to the pile of paper that was on the shelf next to his desk (she pointed since she knew that Natnael cannot handle verbal information when he is about to collapse).

Natnael had to be reminded and supported in this new strategy for about three weeks, after which he would independently use his 'anger-papers'.

14

CRAP

A Chapter with Thoughts on the Use of Confirmations or Rewards, the Idea of Being Affirmative, and Why Punishments Do Not Work

Since the previous chapter addressed 'setting boundaries', it seems logical to follow up with addressing the reward systems that are commonly used for people with autism spectrum disorders. When I encounter them in services and schools I consult, sometimes they are formalized, as in using token economy, and sometimes just quite arbitrarily invented by staff. It may seem like a great idea to reinforce the positive, and I understand that the idea appeals to many people.

As you might have guessed I am not all in favour of a reward system. Theoretically, such as in the token economy system, the importance of taking into account what individuals actually are able to do, which skills are present, and the difficulties involved, is often emphasized. In practice, it is unfortunately only a few of those involved in implementing and maintaining reward systems that have such knowledge.[1]

Let's look at an email I received. A staff group in a day service wrote this to me:

---

1 Some months ago I was asked for my view on reward systems at a lecture. When I put forward my criticisms, a woman in the audience became very upset. She was a licensed psychologist specializing in behavioural therapy, and she stressed that reward systems function very well if implemented right. I asked her if her opinion was that it took someone with her training and education to do it right. She agreed with that. Well, you see, in all the hundreds of services and schools for people with autism spectrum disorders I have visited while consulting, hardly any do have access to such a person, let alone have one employed in the service. This means we see a lot of brutal variants on the theme of rewards, and therefore I would rather stick with my opinion: don't use them, because they can go wrong – and because if you really understand what the problem is, you don't even need them.

Here in our day service, we work for our user right now with a plus and minus system that has worked so-so but, in general terms, the user gets a plus when he goes into the loo to 'scream, moan and nag' as it is permissible to do that there in a scheduled time. He gets a minus when he does not stick to the rule and is loud in places other than in the loo. The pluses and the minuses are the basis for the reward, which currently is in the form of snacks and Coca Cola, which he likes very much.

Let us focus on the plus part first:[2] is not reinforcing behaviour with rewards a good idea? And don't we use rewards with children all the time? Is it not natural to reward desirable behaviour? Well, not really.

When we reward children, or indeed efforts at work (in the form of a pay increase or bonus), we do that only if the person *has the ability*. We would not try to get a two-year-old to make his own bed or vacuum the house, using rewards, or a five-year-old to do advanced mathematical calculations, by dangling a carrot (or rather, a candy bag) in front of him. We would find it equally unfair if the head of our workplace just gave bonuses to those who could run 100 metres in under 12 seconds. The key here is:

DO NOT DEMAND A SKILL IF YOU DO NOT KNOW THAT IT EXISTS.

But, now you might answer: 'If the person can do it with a reward the skill is there.' Or you may join in the chorus of: 'He could do it yesterday, therefore he must be able today too.' In this book you have actually already found many examples of factors that may cause an individual with autism to be able to do things at one point that he isn't able to perform at other times. Another thing worth mentioning here, is something that everyone can recognize in themselves: that sometimes if you really want something, you strain every nerve to get it. Have you never, for example, though you were sick or had migraines or whatever it may be, dragged yourself to something that you really wanted to do, or felt that you had to. Does that mean you could do it every time you are ill? Maybe we need another key as well:

DO NOT DEMAND (OR DO NOT REWARD) A SKILL IF YOU DON'T KNOW THE COST OF IT.

---

2   There is certainly also a minus point system here, but I'll discuss this later.

EXAMPLE

Kevin has autism. When he was nine years old, he ate with his hands and refused to use cutlery. Kevin's parents found it troublesome; they could not for example take him to a restaurant. He looked like a normal nine-year-old and people would stare and look disapproving when he ate with his hands. They decided to try positive reinforcement. Kevin would now get a point every time he used cutlery, and a candy as a reward after a certain number of points.

In tears and agony (he wanted the candy of course) Kevin used the cutlery, trying to eat with them. The whole family found it very distressing and therefore eventually gave up on this training. Even if they thought that it perhaps could actually succeed, the price was as they perceived it, too high.

Some months later, the parents discovered by chance that if he could eat with plastic cutlery, he had no problems using it. Something about the metal (maybe a sensory disorder in hearing and/or touch on Kevin's part?) made using ordinary cutlery painful for him. In this case, is it a real help teaching him to use cuttlery by using rewards?

And another example:

EXAMPLE

A mother told me how her daughter with PDD and language disorder would only wear dirty clothes. She refused to put on clean or new clothing. The mother was advised by experts to use rewards. The daughter would receive a chewing gum every time she took off her dirty clothes and put them in the laundry bin. That part worked well, except that her daughter outsmarted her and would sneak up early in the morning before anyone else was awake, fish out her dirty clothes from the bin and put them on.[3]

Well, the mother had heard me at a lecture speaking of a person with a literal understanding of dirt (see the example of Adnan, p.27), and tried out a social story to explain to her daughter why and when to put on clean clothes. She also realized her daughter had a sensory problem and overdosing the fabric softener also helped. And she used the aid clothes-by-temperature-thermometer you can read about later (p.316) in this book. All in all, the mother solved the problem by using three different approaches, each one addressing a part of the problem. Sure, more effort on her part, but in a way that gave the daughter both a far greater degree of autonomy and understanding.

An aid, an adjustment and an explanation will get you really far, and no rewards are needed!

---

3   Excuse me, but I just love when people with autism spectrum disorders outsmart their parents or staff like this!

A few years ago I saw something that helped me to understand what it is a reward system really does. I visited a group of teachers who asked me to come round to advise them regarding a middle school pupil who was perceived as 'totally unmotivated'. When I was finally able to come (this was a period when, for various reasons, I could not take on new assignments), they told me that they had been about to cancel my planned visit, because they had now found an approach that worked well. They had introduced a reward system.

But now that I was there, it would of course be interesting to see how they were working.

This pupil had not previously had any adjustments or aids, but now with the implementation of a reward system, some changes followed. He had received a whiteboard where he could see various curriculum subjects, and choose certain assignments from them. He could also see clearly how many points he would receive from completing a task. Furthermore, the board made clear with colour marks how many points he needed to attain a certain reward (the more points the more desirable the reward).

For him to have an overview of his point system they had turned his desk against the wall, where the whiteboard was (the other students sat in a circle in the classroom). And now, as I mentioned, he did schoolwork as never seen before.

Why do I still think that this was not great, then? Well, what I realized was the outcome for the pupil of the method:

- It contributed *clarity* (the student could see all the relevant information).

- The pupil could *affect/influence* (choosing between different tasks).

- The tasks had a *purpose* (the reward).

- In addition the pupil was by sheer chance shielded off, facing the wall, which also helped him focus.[4]

I believe that for motivation to occur, you need these ingredients:

---

4   Sure, as you probably know, to screen off input from your workplace, and to put up a clear overview or schedule in a visible place is a very common adaptation for pupils with autism spectrum disorders, entirely without having a reward system involved. But this child had not had these kinds of adjustments made for him before. And even if inclusion is a great thing, I see far less knowledge of how to adjust the environment to make them autism-friendly in the mainstream classroom, than in the special-ed classroom.

- clarity/transparency

- influence/a sense of being able to affect things

- purpose/meaning.

The snag here occurs at the end. If the purpose is merely to collect a reward, it can be difficult to phase out, and you will continue to need rewards for you to get the person to perform. The drawback of this is that the person is perhaps deprived of the opportunity to experience other purposes, as well as having built a system where we have to continue with rewards.

My opinion is that you most often can provide these things – transparency, influence and purpose – without using a reward system. The first two speak for themselves, I hope, even if the same principle applies here as before: how the lucidity and influence is created for George is not the same as how it is done for Ahmed or Janet. All are unique individuals and their aids and adjustments need to be created for *their* individual difficulties. By using what we have in our toolbox (see Part 4), we can create an explicit clarity and overview for the client or pupil. Then we also see to it that the client can be involved in choices and feel they can affect their lives, in a manner and at a level that fits this person and his or her level of disability.[5]

The third is perhaps a bit trickier: purpose. Why should we have to bother with that? Other children in the school learn anyway, without us explicitly explaining the purpose. Sure. But the 'standard-developed' children often have a great deal of social motivation (as for example reflected in doing something just because 'everyone else' does it, or doing something to 'be liked' by others). It is not uncommon for this motivation to be lacking in people with autism spectrum disorders. 'Standard developed' children also have an ability to read between the lines when necessary. Those who do not have autism often see purposes even if they are never pronounced (as in getting good grades, or that you may have use for certain knowledge in the future). This kind of purpose can be completely hidden from the person with autism. Therefore, we must show the purpose in a more specific and concrete way to those who need this.

There are also comprehensive general purposes, as in 'it is fun to learn'. A person who never experienced (in a conscious way) the joy of learning things may need help to explore this joy, both the feeling

---

5   Let us not forget that people have a *right* to influence their lives, and that it is our job to make that possible.

and the learning process. And again: we must create the conditions for this to happen.

Sometimes it is sufficient to understand the purpose of the task.

EXAMPLE

Sarah, a girl with autism, refused to do anything as stupid as to solve a crossword puzzle in class time. Crosswords are a pastime, it is well known to all! The thing was that in her exercise book there was a crossword puzzle on page 29, and her teacher said to complete pages 28–30 of the exercise book.

Her teacher tried to explain to her that all the exercises in the book were included in the task, and that it actually was a school assignment, even though it looked like a pastime. They argued.

Sarah did not cave in, and the teacher who felt a bit pressured at being opposed with arguments he could not really understand came up with maybe not the most clever counter-arguments, such as 'I am your teacher and I decide what to do in the classroom.'[6]

Finally, in desperation, the teacher showed Sarah *his* exercise book (the one with a teacher's guide) and there was the purpose of the crossword in black and white, clearly depicting what it was intended that pupils would learn in this exercise. And when Sarah read this, she said 'OK' and then completed the crossword without problems.

And another example:

EXAMPLE

Dylan is quite skilled at maths, but he never shows off his skills and is reluctant to do maths in school. The biggest problem is that when he has completed one new calculation, and succeeded with it, he refuses to do the following pages of similar calculations. He says 'I already know that' in a grumpy way. He wants to go on to the next level, and even proceed with the maths-book for the next grade, but his teacher is unwilling because she feels he will only learn superficially. After taking a course about autism his teacher realized she must explain to him the idea of repetition. She searched the internet and found this text by Michael Tipper:

Why repetition is important

When you create a memory, a pathway is created between your brain cells. It is like clearing a path through a dense forest. The first time that

---

6   By the way, don't we all take a superior stance when we get into an argument where we do not understand the other person's perspective or arguments, and he stubbornly insists? But that was not hard to understand, you may say, Sarah had told her teacher what the problem was. And the teacher had heard and understood. But he apparently did not understand why Sarah thinks that crossword puzzles could only be a leisure activity.

you do it, you have to fight your way through the undergrowth. If you don't travel that path again, very quickly it will become overgrown and you may not even realise that you have been down that path. If however, you travel along that path before it begins to grow over, you will find it easier than your first journey along that way.

Successive journeys down that path mean that eventually your track will turn into a footpath, which will turn into a lane, which will turn into a road, and into a motorway and so on. It is the same with your memory: the more times that you repeat patterns of thought, for example when learning new information, the more likely you will be able to recall that information. So repetition is a key part of learning.[7]

She read this text with Dylan, and printed it for him. They returned to it a couple of times. And after that he had no problem with doing repetition calculations. (Or to be honest, he is still grumpy, but that's just Dylan.)

14.1 Attribution

But now I might have drifted a bit from the subject; it was rewards we were talking about. I want to get into something called *attribution*. Attribution theory is concerned with how people interpret events and relate them to their thinking and behaviour. It's a cognitive perception which affects motivation. It is interesting to learn something about attribution theory in the field of care or teaching. It concerns how we look at the cause of the behaviour of others, as well as the cause of our own. You could say that how we explain our behaviour to ourselves affects the likelihood that we will behave the same way again.

Lepper, Greene and Nisbett (1973)[8] published a study in which they looked at the result of a rewards system. The subjects were all nursery school children who devoted much time to drawing. The researchers divided the children into three groups. The children were one by one invited into a room where there were paper and magic markers, of a finer quality than the children normally had access to.

The children in the first group, the expected reward group, were offered an award – a nice certificate with a red ribbon and place for their name – for making a drawing. The children in the second group, the unexpected reward group, would also receive a diploma for the

---

7   Michael Tipper's text (and a lot more) can be found at www.happychild.org.uk.
8   OK, OK, you might say, but why even bother to mention such an old study? Well, in 1999 Edward Deci and his colleagues performed a meta-analysis of 128 studies of the impact of extrinsic rewards on internal motivation, and found as they also expected, that extrinsic rewards were undermining intrinsic motivation (Deci *et al.* 1999).

drawings, but without being promised this in advance. The third group received no reward (but encouraging comments). Those who carried out the study were blind regarding which group the children belonged to.

When the drawing session was over, those who carried out the experiment looked in a manual to see if the child would receive a reward (the first and second groups), or if they belonged to the third group and would only be thanked with a phrase: 'Well, it looks like our time is up. Thank you very much for helping me out by drawing these pictures for me. You did a really good job.'

For two weeks after this the drawing materials were removed in the nursery school, and when they were made available for the children again, the researchers observed how much time they would choose to spend drawing. Those now observing were also blind regarding which group the children belonged to. The children included in the unexpected reward and no reward groups continued to devote much time to drawing (on average 16.7 and 18.1% of observation time). But the interest in drawing was lower in children who had entered the group of expected reward (who on average now devoted 8.6% of their time to drawing).

This is worth contemplating, don't you think?

14.2 Penalty marking is banned!

Before I close this chapter on reward systems, I would also like to say something about minus scoring systems, or withdrawal of benefits[9] (whether it be candy, weekly allowance, computer gaming, favourite TV programmes or anything else):

- It goes against everything we know about learning psychology (i.e. learning best occurs in a positive context).

- It goes against common sense (in my opinion).

To withdraw 'benefits' for an adult is as I see it a coercive measure. It may be interesting to know that in Norway there is legislation

---

9   I am now speaking of people with disabilities who have a developmental profile which is characterized by unevenness, and who therefore do not have the necessary prerequisites to understand consequences, generalize learned skills, and who have additional immature reactions to stress, and a lot more to be stressed about than do their non-disabled peers. If you as a parent withdraw ice-cream, or TV-watching for a 'standard child' who behaved badly that's a whole different story.

on disabilities, which provides that before a coercive measure is implemented, *all other voluntary means have been tested and excluded.* In Norway they have seen that the use of coercive methods in care has decreased after the legislation gained legal force. So I can safely say that punishment systems of this kind are not desirable nor needed.

But should you really never ever use a reward system, then? I would like to put it this way: I would not say that you absolutely never should use it, but not until you've tried everything else. In those cases where I have encountered reward systems, I have never seen that it was preceded by such an accurate assessment of the problem, the individual and the environment, as should always be done when there is a challenging behaviour (see the next chapter). Not having done that, you won't know the causes of the problem (you remember the iceberg, right?) and then it will be difficult to find solutions. Conversely, in the services I've worked with where they earnestly and carefully work to carry out assessments before deciding how to try to resolve the problem, no reward systems are needed.

Sometimes it seems that schools give way to using something that motivates the student as a reward.[10]

EXAMPLE

Maya has high-functioning autism. Maya loves Pokemon. Abigail, Maya's teacher, thinks that when Maya has completed a task she can have a moment with her Pokemon pictures as a reward. Maya is very sensitive to demands and protests loudly at every form of schoolwork. There is a lot of time spent on her protests and even if she then does some tasks to get access to Pokemon pictures afterwards, she grunts while doing them.

In addition to the time these protests take and the energy exerted by Abigail (and by Maya too, presumably), there seems to be no progress with this approach. Maya continues to do the minimum necessary, and under protest.

---

10   We have in recent years increasingly been influenced by the American way of looking at rewards, although we still (hopefully) have a long way to go before children who are performing well in school get free food at McDonald's as an award. The message has not least been drummed in by 'Dr Phil' and countless 'Nanny-shows' – that one should know the child's 'currency' (such as video games) and use it to get the child to do such things as household tasks. If you want to read a clear, entertaining and relevant criticism of a school (and society) that is based on rewards, I recommend Alfie Kohn's *Punished by Rewards* (1999). By the way, speaking of currency, Alfie Kohn aptly writes: '*Rewards* and *punishments* are *just two sides* of the *same coin* — and that coin doesn't buy very much.'

EXAMPLE

Lewis has high-functioning autism and loves Pokemon. Lewis is very sensitive to demands and protests loudly at every form of school work. Lewis' teacher Tariq has made photocopies of Lewis' favourite Pokemon figures, and sticks them on his working sheets and school books. Lewis thinks it's fun to see which figure will show up on his next assignment. He is still not thrilled by doing schoolwork, but there are far fewer conflicts and Tariq perceives that Lewis is actually moving forward, and that he now does more school tasks than before.

14.3 A/C – Affirm and Confirm

If one reflects on the study by Mark Lepper and his colleagues (1973), the idea that positive feedback has a good effect on motivation quickly comes to mind. This is fully in line with the solution-focused work that I mentioned earlier and which you can read more about later. Sometimes staff tell me that their clients or pupils react negatively to praise. If that is the case with the individual you are supporting, you can think of being affirmative and confirmative, rather than praising someone in the traditional sense. Examples of this are phrases such as 'I saw that you made your bed,' 'What a great idea to…' 'Thank you for…' and so on. You can read more about positive feedback in Chapter 23 on working with self-knowledge, self-esteem and confidence.

Perhaps I have scored an own goal in this chapter, by telling you what you should not do (instead of what to do). But do you remember the chocolate cake recipe? It can be quite right to tell people what they should not do, but only if you also give them the tools to do it right. That is my endeavour in the chapters that follow.

15

Diving Lessons in the Ocean

A Chapter on How to Make
Assessments and Analyses

Have you heard that people with autism need structure and routine? If so, you are not alone, but I often maliciously say that it is *staff* who need structure and routine. Helpers who lack structure in their work cannot give their users, clients or students truly professional support.

Structure in this case means a systematic approach. This helps us to increase professionalism, and decrease the number of errors we make (we will probably never succeed in completely ceasing to make mistakes). Structure is actually one of the tools that you as a craftsman in the autism field need in your toolbox (or is it rather the box that other tools are in?). It consists of a systematic way of working to achieve results in your work. The structure is no 'method', but rather a consequence of what I earlier called the framework or a way of thinking. It also involves translating your ethos into practice. The routine is the part which makes sure that the beautiful structure is not just something we say we do, but actually do.

There are probably other (and perhaps even better) ways of doing this, only I haven't come across them (yet). The important thing is not that you do this exactly in the way I describe it; what matters is that you do *something* to make sure that you as a professional actually know what you are doing.[1] This means knowing the answers to these questions:

- *Why* do I do this for this client? (This includes knowing which options for intervention, human interchange and adjustments and aids are available and why we choose to handle this person/situation in this particular way).

---

1 No offence, you may be an extremely skilled professional in the field of teaching, psychology or something else; I am only talking about your professionalism as an autism craftsman here, which is much needed in addition to your other professionalism.

- Does what we do actually mean solving the problem or making progress (or even both!)?

Without a framework that provides the answers to these questions we subject our clients to ourselves making guesses.

Perhaps you attend a lecture on autism, held by a knowledgeable person, and when there is an opportunity for questions you ask the lecturer 'What should we do about Maureen's violent behaviour?'[2] Or maybe you just listen to the lecturer, or read a book on autism, and think 'I will try that with Raveena'. But neither the lecturer, nor the author has ever met Maureen or Raveena. The good news is that you have!

We can also establish that if Maureen's and Raveena's difficulties lead to challenging behaviour, it is probably a fact that what you and your colleagues do and have done until now is not working. Thus, this is the first practical step of what I in Chapter 13 called *a process of change*. The first mental step was, as you may recall, the insight that something needs to change and understanding of the iceberg principle.

The first concrete phase in the change process thus involves a dive below the surface. What do the parts of the iceberg that we cannot immediately see consist of? Since Maureen and Raveena are individuals, we cannot dive in a general glacial sea, but have to look closely at Maureen and Raveena, respectively. As you will, I hope, recall, we can sometimes see the same or similar behaviour in some individuals, but the causes of them can be quite different.

I am obviously jumping between metaphors and talking about diving here, but I will try to connect my metaphorical landscape. A professional diver must be a skilled craftsman in his area, too. So let me return to the craftsmanship a moment. What makes DIY different from the work of a craftsman? Well, the professionalism of course. And if you are a trained nurse, psychiatrist, social worker, psychologist, pedagogue, or have any other of all the professions that are relevant here, I do not think that you believe an electrician or painter could do your job just as well.

---

2   Believe me, as a lecturer I get a lot of those questions, and all I can say is: 'I have never met your pupil or client. I can only speak in general terms. If I come to your service and we together make a thorough assessment, *then* we can begin to find some answers to your question.'

Being a professional in autism is a separate profession, I would say – autism worker, if you like. This is (unfortunately) not a profession with a name, and as you know, you, in your education as a teacher or nurse, received little (if any) knowledge of craftsmanship in the autism profession.

Every profession has its craftsmanship and it is often the part of the profession that you do not see (and may also sometimes be perceived as the 'boring' part).

Have you for example ever got the urge to paint the walls in your house, or to sew something? I have. And my experience is that it is the *preparatory work* that is the real job. To stroke paint on a wall or a piece of furniture, to sew a seam on a sewing machine – it's the last little step, which often is both fun and relatively simple. Before doing that, it is necessary to grind, apply putty, clean, tape around the edges and protect flooring, or measure, cut, tack, try, and change tack again. Only then you can paint or sew!

An often hard-earned experience is that if you skip or forget to do preparatory work, the result is not nearly as good. I would say that the knowledge of, the ability to add weight to, and to skilfully perform great preparatory work is a huge part of professionalism. This applies whether you are a musician, painter, tailor, or 'autism worker'.

So we must do the thorough preparatory work before we put an approach or intervention into 'action', before we try a tool or use a 'method' or an aid, and the importance of doing this increases the more serious the problem is. Unfortunately, it often goes the opposite way in services for people with autism spectrum disorders, namely that the more serious the problem is, the more desperate and ill-considered actions we take.

If we work with Charlotte, who has autism and is intimidating and disruptive, or Rhys with high-functioning autism who is self-injurious, it is very likely that precisely because of the acute problems, you take a chance on the various approaches and interventions. Charlotte and Rhys are perhaps also moved around between services and care wards, because they are perceived to be 'too difficult'. This does, unfortunately, mean a significant risk of Charlotte and Rhys deteriorating, for several reasons.

The first reason is that, for every intervention that does not succeed, we are digging a deeper and deeper hole in the place where

Charlotte's and Rhys' trust in us would have presided. At the end of the day, they (rightly) have no trust left in us as professionals. Helping someone without having any of their confidence and trust is almost impossible.

The second reason is that for every intervention that does not succeed, Charlotte and Rhys risk concluding that nothing works, they are a hopeless case, and since nothing works it must be themselves who are the problem, rather than the help not being helpful enough (a conclusion which, unfortunately, sometimes their surroundings reinforce and contribute to). The consequence is often, therefore, loss of hope while their self-image is deteriorating.

So, professionals need a structure to work with assessments and analyses to have a better basis for deciding on action. Sure, there may still be guesses, but these can be educated guesses.

This structure is crucial for people with challenging behaviours, but it is fully applicable also for other iceberg peaks, that is, things we need to understand better. It can be anything.

In Chapter 3, 'Same, Same but Different', you for example read about a variety of causes of poor hygiene (pp.27–29). As you probably already realized when reading that, the intervention, adjustment or aid must be built on what is causing the issue. If Awela (see Chapter 6, p.109) cannot take a shower because she has a hypersensitive tactile perception, she will not be helped by 'a procedure' with step-by-step pictures on what to do in the shower. How then, can we know in advance what is the cause? Well, by thorough assessments.

15.1 Assessment

What we need to find out is what the factors are that affect the behaviour we see, and what the actual behaviour may be due to. To understand this we must first be aware that we have a lot of preconceived ideas. This is especially the case when a person with autism has a provocative, disruptive or threatening behaviour. Therefore, we must consciously put our preconceptions aside, and engage in an exploratory stage, being as unbiased as we can.

The structure is shown in Figure 15.1:

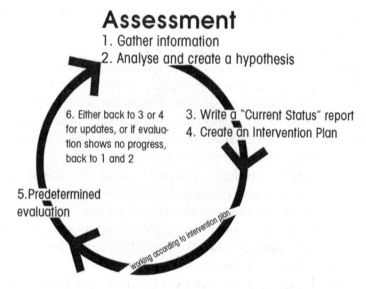

Figure 15.1: Assessment structure

I'll explain the whole illustration a bit further down. Let us start out by immersing ourselves in the beginning of the assessment. At this stage, we find out as much as possible. In this phase, we need to remember that we should still not draw any conclusions, just collect facts, and as objectively as possible record them. The information to collect includes: the history, the individual, what is actually happening in the problematic situation (if that is the issue), ourselves, and then the overall (life) situation.

We use the observations and we may also make a measurement. Subsequently, an analysis and hypothesis phase follows. All this I will now describe in more detail.

History

When did the behaviour occur for the first time? Has it always occurred? Has it ceased during some periods? Try to find out as much as possible about the background. It is important that you understand that you must have an open mind. There are no ready-made questions that I can give you – the variation between individuals and situations is too great and too diverse. I cannot make a template, but a sketch. You must have the curiosity to ask more questions.

With regard to history, you will need to talk to relatives and other services that the person may be attached to. If you work in a school you may want to talk to parents and staff from the pupil's short-term activities, the residential support may need to speak with day service, and so on. Everything that you learn can be a clue. If the day service says that they have never seen Aaron acting out the way he is doing in your service a couple times a week, this is of course valuable information.[3]

The individual

If Jeremy says 'I don't hit people at all', this is also important information for the pieces we are looking for in the puzzle (that we eventually will try to solve). Samantha, however, may say 'I hate everybody, that's why I beat you', but reveals herself much more when the subject of the upcoming Easter break comes up and she says 'It will be nice for you to get rid of me for a week'.

By also finding out how the individual looks at his or her situation, we get crucial information that will need to be addressed in the Intervention Plan. In fact, every difficulty we face in the individual – Charlotte's lack of self-esteem, Rhys' different perception of what is happening – will be addressed, with a proposed treatment, intervention, aid or adjustment of the environment for each part.

Now you might object that your client/pupil with autism will not answer such questions, and this is exactly why you should use a questionnaire.

What should this questionnaire look like? There is no right or wrong way, I've done them in different ways depending on the individual's age, level of functioning and what I know about the problem in advance. You can see some examples of questions in Appendix 1, but make your own. Why? Well, if for no other reason, if you have not written the questions yourself and your client does not understand what you mean (which happens a lot, trust me), perhaps you cannot explain them!

---

3   Such information immediately raises the idea of making a visit to the day service to see what there is to learn. But let us not jump the gun. Interventions will come later.

But 'Why not just ask?' you may wonder, especially if this particular client or pupil is very verbal. Many people with autism spectrum disorders, and those with challenging behaviours in particular, despite their verbal ability have significantly more difficulties understanding and responding to what has just been said. Using a survey has further advantages:

- When we use a questionnaire, we will sit next to the individual (rather than opposite them), and we will both focus on the paper. This means that the client does not have to try to interpret our facial expressions, consider how long they are going to look us in the eye, and so on. We thus relieve him or her of an obstacle.

- Written information is often clear (well, I must admit that I probably have messed up a number of times by writing the questions too vaguely or imprecisely, but through ignorance we make mistakes, and by mistakes we learn). As it is clearer than spoken information the client does not have to guess whether the question means something else because of our tone of voice or the way we look.

- The answers remain. If Aaron writes 'yes' when asked if he wants help with new strategies when he is upset, it makes it easier for us, when we later (maybe weeks later) launch the Intervention Plan, to pull out the questionnaire with his replies and say: 'Aaron, do you remember the paper where you marked 'yes' in wanting help with new strategies? I thought we would talk about this now.'

And then a few rules of thumb:

- We always include questions that clearly show that we actually care very much about how the individuals themselves understand and view their situation.

- We always include questions about how we can better help the individual.

- We never leave a questionnaire for the person to fill out on their own. We always do it together, both to help clear up ambiguities, but above all to be able to ask supplementary questions. Often, filling in a form is an excellent basis for a conversation – in my experience, this is frequently a conversation that would not have occurred unless we were sitting right next to each other with a piece of paper in front of us.

The questionnaire may therefore well be a basis for conversation. If the individual gives me additional information through follow-up questions I ask, I usually ask if I can take notes of them, so that we also have this information later in the assessment process.

What do we want to know about the individual? Important information is also that which may not always be obtained in the survey, but sometimes through observation or simply by our knowledge of the person. For example:

- How much does he/she know and understand about his/her own diagnosis?

- How is his/her self-esteem and self-confidence?

- What about frustration tolerance?

- How does he/she communicate?

- Is he/she able to ask for help and express his/her wishes and needs?

- Are there problems with fatigue and attention?

- Are there difficulties with motor skills and sensory integration?

- What are his/her strengths?

- Which are the stressors in his/her everyday life?

- What are the individual's early signs of stress, that is, what heralds a reaction to stress, such as acting out or being self-destructive? (It may be the tone of voice, facial expression, things he/she says, the way the person gesticulates, or something else.)

- Does he/she feel content and safe in our service/school?

- What does he/she like to do?

- When does it work well?

- Who has he/she most confidence in?

- From what does he/she regain energy? (It could be listening to music, playing a favourite computer game, engaging in a special interest, or something else – usually not by socialising though, even if they may enjoy it.)

- Can he/she handle choices?

- Can he/she recognize and put into words their feelings?

- How well/poorly does he/she understand shades and degrees (of emotions, as well as in general)?

- Is there – based on the individual perspective – a good balance between stimulating and developmental activities on the one hand, and opportunity to rest and relax, on the other?

- Does he/she feel they can influence their lives?[4]

- Is everyday life understandable and possible to survey?

Again, there are no exhaustive lists. I've probably forgotten something. The more you know, and learn, about people with these disabilities – the more curious you are – the more things you can add.

We must of course also consider whether there are medical problems and if so, ensure that the person will receive adequate treatment. A contributing factor in challenging behaviours may be side effects of medication, or lack of adequate medication – for example for conditions such as depression, compulsion, tics and anxiety. You may need to investigate and obtain medical or therapeutic help with the above, and also with sleeping problems, and any deficiency (which may have arisen because of a very unbalanced diet, or from being very sensitive to light and thus not producing enough Vitamin D). There may be common conditions such as migraines and PMS which are untreated and affect quality of life.

Measurement

If there is a challenging behaviour, the assessment will also include a measurement of how often the problem behaviour occurs. This is because we need to have a comparison later on, when we will evaluate

---

4   Please note that this is regardless of what *we* think he or she is able to influence; it's the individual's own perception here that counts.

our efforts. You will find an example of how a 'schedule' for such measurement can be designed in Appendix 2.

If this is an individual who has an acting-out behaviour several times a week, there is no need to measure for more than a week, because the measurement has one drawback, namely that we can focus too much on the actual incidents.

Observation

Through observation, you can get new information about the behaviour (and the person). When you observe, you have to leave your job mentally, that is, you cannot interact while you are observing. When you participate in social interaction, you lose your open mind, and a large part of your mental capacity is too busy with the interaction to take notice of new things.

'But how do we explain to our clients that one of us suddenly will be present and just watching. They will think it's really weird or be upset with being observed?' is an objection I get to hear every so often. Well, the best way is often to be honest.

Therefore you explain to your clients that you as a group are trying to learn to become better professionals, that you want to know how you can better help all who are in the service, and that means that one of you will only watch during the day. Most clients have no problem with this if you emphasize that it is about *you* (needing to do your job better), instead of putting forward the idea that you will be observing them (that their behaviour is problematic and needs to be changed).

And honestly, it really is about this – it is you who needs to become a better helper!

Another objection might be that it will not work in terms of schedule, that there is not a person to spare. So change the schedule! Talk to your boss and get the head to understand that in this change process you must occasionally have extra staff for observation.

In the case of older children, adolescents or adults it may be too difficult for them if you take notes during observation; they may wonder and want to read what you write. When I observe, I take as many notes in my mind as I can handle, then quickly escape to scribble down some words, and then come back and continue to observe.

When observing you should try to see everything; you may not always know at the time what is important or unimportant, especially if you are not used to working in this way. But you could say that you should be looking for what you do not already know.

When you have finished reading the next chapter, you will have some idea of what it could be you might encounter if it is a case of acting-out problems. But since every person and situation is unique, you may well come to learn something completely new from your client.

When speaking of assessment, the following issues are often considered important. I bear them in mind when observing, but as I mentioned earlier, it is important to be as unbiased as possible.

- What occurs right before the behaviour? (What does the person himself/herself do? What do others do or say? Are there signs that make it possible to predict a stress reaction?)

- What happens right after the behaviour?

- When does the behaviour occur? (A certain time of day? Is it linked with hunger or fatigue? Linked with failures? With too-low expectations – or too-high? When there is 'nothing to do'?)

- Who is present, who is not present? (Does it occur more often with a certain member of staff, or even never with some of the staff?)

The question of who is present is sometimes very interesting. It is not uncommon that with someone in the staff group the problematic behaviour occurs very rarely (or even never). If you ask the staff member what it is he or she is doing, they often do not know themselves. A couple of times we have had someone observing, or just being beside the person who has this 'magical' effect on a client.

What we have seen is that this particular member of staff is often very adept at picking up early signals of stress in the client. This natural talent distracts the client, or changes the situation, at an early stage, enough to prevent real frustration from occurring. The rest of us can often learn from him, while he also may be able to better look out for and articulate what he actually does.

Myself/us in the staff

I have already mentioned that during observation we will also look at ourselves, and I would like to put some extra focus on how we as helpers act and interact. It is not unusual that we are contributing to, or even triggering, a stress reaction, in our client or pupil. I'll try to list some aspects of our own behaviour that we may need to investigate.

Knee-jerk reactions

We have a variety of ways to respond and act; we do this or that automatically and we may find it difficult to reflect upon it, since we barely noticed what we did or said. All these behaviours can be pitfalls, and therefore we need to know that the mechanism exists.

EXAMPLE

Jacob is 11 years old and has autism. He often explodes, so the school called me for a consultation to help his teachers to understand and respond better to Jacob. We begin with an observation.

Jacob is in a special education class, and in the afternoon they have snacks once a month, as part of social training (and for training in practical cooking skills they prepare the snacks). In the morning the class made chocolate chip cookies, and now in the afternoon when I am there to observe it is time to savour them.

A moment of chaos occurs when the seven pupils are about to sit down, and glasses, juice and cookies are laid out. Jacob is already seated when his teacher, Ashley, puts a plate of cookies down on the table.

'How many can we have each?' Jacob cries out.

'We'll see,' says Ashley, who is a bit busy discussing with another child, wanting him to put away his markers, and simultaneously trying to set the table up.

Jacob, who seems to be a gifted and creative child – which, incidentally, many children with autism are – is perhaps thinking something like 'Well, I won't get any help from Ashley, so I'd better solve the problem on my own.' (The problem being knowing how many cookies he will be allowed to eat, and he really *needs* to know that, as uncertainty is difficult to handle for most people with autism).

Jacob is good at maths and starts counting the cookies and then dividing them by the number of people around the table. It is a bit tricky since the cookies on the plate are on top of each other, and he must really make an effort to get an idea of how many there are.

Ashley now notes that Jacob is stressed about not having received an answer to his question and, therefore, she says: 'We'll start with two each, and then we'll see.'

What happens now? Well, Jacob rapidly stuffs his two cookies into his mouth, and swallows them more or less without chewing: he needs his answer as soon as possible. Only to discover what you and I could have guessed, namely that *everyone* will have to have eaten their two cookies before Ashley will tell him how many more they can have.

Jacob, now on the very edge of despair, sits and taps his fingers and jumps in his chair.

He brilliantly makes an effort not to explode (something he rarely receives any appreciation for – who notices a meltdown that is held back?). He is now waiting for the last slow kid to eat his final crumbs of cookie. Then, eventually, when he thinks he will get his answer, Ashley says: 'We'll take one more each, and then save the rest'.

Jacob explodes.

What just happened? Well, actually Ashley drove Jacob into this meltdown, or to use another metaphor, she pushed him, step by step toward the abyss until he tipped over the edge and the fall was a fact. Why? Because she is a malicious person? Hardly. I would say that she did it because *this is the way we do it.*

It is not written in any books about raising children, but almost all of us adults do this with children – we stretch their frustration tolerance. We say 'Take one more bite' when they do not want to eat more, we say 'Sit a little while longer' when they want to leave the table – and it's not because we think that that particular bite contains important nutrition or that it is so important how long they sit at the table. We do it because we know that 'standard children' in this way are learning to wait, to endure or overcome their own frustration over something, to become more flexible. And because it works.

The snag is that when we are dealing with a person with an autism spectrum disorder, who also has difficulty with frustration tolerance, who does not have the prerequisite for that rubber-like flexibility we see develop in 'standard children', it will not work. In autism spectrum disorders there are several other difficulties that interfere with the mechanisms that make it work for 'standard children':

- low frustration threshold

- difficulties in understanding language and implicit messages

- lack of flexibility in thinking.

I think there are lots of knee-jerk reactions, things we just do, without reflecting, and that we need to look at them. We need to learn to question ourselves: why did I do this, what did it lead to? If we as colleagues also question one another, it's even better (do you remember the respectful questioning on p.52?).

Involuntary offender

In the book *Between Power and Help*[5] by Greta Marie Skau, she argues that the first step that should be taken to avoid violations of the helper–client relationship, is to recognize that we are all potential offenders:

> A phenomenon must be made visible in order to be able to do something about it. But it is not sufficient as a prerequisite. In order to work against offence and abuse, we must first learn to understand what they are about, and be prepared to shoulder the personal pressure that may result from fighting these phenomena in whatever social arena we find ourselves. (Skau 1998)

Anyone who *feels* offended *is* offended in Skau's opinion; it has nothing to do with the intention of the sender. The definition of an offence is at the recipient's end. However, people (e.g. children and people with disabilities) can actually be offended without being aware of it.

EXERCISE 15.1

Being offended

Think about how it feels to be offended. Sometimes you may not have been aware of the offence until afterwards. How did that make you feel? Have you ever watched someone be offended, without intervening? How did that make you feel? Did you intervene when someone was offended? How did that make you feel?

1. Is a perceived offence less offensive if you gloss over it and ignore it?

2. Is a perceived offence less offensive if the sender admits it and apologizes? Does it help if the sender (after having listened and apologized) explains themselves?

3. If anyone is offended by you, do you tend to be defensive immediately (as in 'it was not my intention to hurt you'), or first listen to the person in question?

4. Is it only people who can offend someone, or is it also possible to be offended by an institution or situation?

---

5   My translation of the Swedish title *Mellan makt och hjälp* (Skau 1998). The book is not published in English.

Skau again:

> While it can be experienced as painful, increased awareness of and sensitivity to the violation as a dimension of interpersonal relations is an important resource in efforts to halt the spread of an offensive culture.[6] (Skau 1998)

If we understand that this is so, our awareness can help us avoid the worst pitfalls. What is perceived as offensive to one individual need not be so for another. We cannot know in advance what is offensive to someone.

The awareness is rather that we understand that one does obviously not offend other people intentionally. (When someone offends another person intentionally, that is better characterized as wickedness than offence, and I have not seen it happen, although I know it does unfortunately occur in care settings, as we sometimes see when care scandals are revealed.) The awareness is also about us understanding that the fact that we had no intention to offend, does not make the other person's *experience* of being offended less painful or smaller. The result is that we can without hesitation apologize, and explain (i.e. *explain*, not justify or exculpate) our reasons for doing or saying what we did.

The issue here, since we are talking about assessment, is: are we doing something that may cause the client or pupil to feel offended? If so, what could it be?

There is of course no key you could look up to know what it could be, but one example worth mentioning is when we treat someone 'too childishly'.[7] We may be over-protective in a way that is perceived

---

6   My translation of the Swedish title *Mellan makt och hjälo* (Skau 1998).

7   Sadly enough, I have on several occasions consulted with staff who describe the client as 'extremely difficult' and who speak quite patronizingly of the individual in question; they see nothing of the strengths this person has. I have later met the client in other circumstances, and seen almost a completely different person. For example, a young man with Asperger's and ADHD, who was quite a requested DJ (and that job suited him perfectly as music was his special interest and the volume of the music made his social interaction problems invisible). To give another example, a man with Asperger's, seen by staff as a real nuisance since he, as they said 'denied his own disability' (and indeed, it was provoking that he rather would view staff as his 'servants', since he didn't like the idea of needing support). But this man is also one of the wittiest, wisest people I've ever met. He fights injustice and inequality wherever he sees it, and is a person of some status in the transgender area. But in both cases, staff chose to see nothing of this. To not see a person as a whole, complex, human being with both strengths and difficulties, is an offence in itself. I am not saying staff are 'bad people' for not doing this, rather that when we do see so much of a person's deficits in our role as helpers, we need to consciously make an effort to see the other sides of this person as well.

as condescending, or have too-low expectations. Or on the contrary, when we expect that a person can control something (their behaviour) that he or she actually cannot. Not to be taken seriously can also be offensive.

EXAMPLE

A team of staff in an autism-specific leisure service meet in the afternoon, before the people with autism arrive. They are having tea. Woe and horror: they are out of milk. Since they all agree on milk with the tea being necessary, one of them rushes to the supermarket. They are short of time, since in half an hour they are going to the nearby woods with a group of teenagers with high-functioning autism. But still, milk is so important to the staff, they make time for it. This despite the fact that the staff group do not have a disability that affects their flexibility, they have no real legitimate reason to be routine-bound, and to have difficulty with changes. They simply want milk in their tea (and all of us who like milk in our tea can sympathize with that).

But a couple of hours later, at the outing, when they make a small campfire to cook some hotdogs with the youngsters, it is discovered that they forgot to bring mustard. Now the staff's understanding of necessary paraphernalia is gone with the wind. So they – quite unsympathetically – tell the young people they must do without (this though they had cars nearby and it wouldn't have taken them longer to go and get the mustard than it took to buy the milk earlier that day). And amongst themselves they later air opinions such as 'They need to be challenged', and 'They are so bound to routines'. Actually, staff in this case even praise themselves on how they made a 'pedagogical opportunity to learn' out of this situation.

Someone may also be offended by something that for us as professionals is entirely 'innocent'.

EXAMPLE

Cody is a young man with autism and severe difficulties, and was severely bullied during his school career. Cody just recently moved into a supported living facility.

Cody knocked on the door to ask for something. At that moment we decided to take a break and Heather went to get the door and see what Cody needed.

While Cody stood in the doorway the rest of us got up from the table. Tiffany put her arm around the shoulders of her colleague, Wesesa. They turned their back to the door and Tiffany whispered something to Wesesa, and then they both burst out laughing. Cody's interpretation (a reasonable one considering his background), was that they were laughing at him.

Aren't we allowed to laugh, you might wonder? What I'm getting at is having an awareness of the risk that we will be offenders (which is not just there because we are human beings and therefore fallible, but in particular due to the balance of power in the relationship between professionals and users of a service) to make us prevent at least some of these situations.

Communication

It may also be a good idea to look at how we as professionals communicate, since many people with autism have difficulties here, including literal understanding of language and sometimes poor language comprehension in general. Below are some questions that I have used for reflections:

How do I communicate?
THE PRIVATE I

- I often communicate indirectly.
- I like joking when I talk about things.
- I am often direct and clear.
- Anything else?

IN MY PROFESSIONAL ROLE

- I often communicate indirectly.
- I like joking when I talk about things.
- I am often direct and clear.
- Anything else?

IS THIS YOU?

- I often communicate with questions, even when there's not really a choice.
- I may sound disputing, even when I do not mean to be.

ESTIMATE

- Are there some situations in my work where I become clearer or less clear in my communication?

- How understandable am I for my pupils/users/clients on a scale of 1–10? How can I make half a step improvement (say from 8 to 8.5)? When can I implement this change?

The whole

As part of an assessment we also always have to look up and survey the whole. The following questions need to be answered:

- Is there a life perspective around the client? (That is, do professionals look ahead, make plans for the future, and is the client involved in or aware of this?)

- Does the environment have adequate knowledge? (Are there other services, or relatives, who do not have sufficient knowledge of and understanding of the disability and its implications?)

- Does the person have access to the aids needed to function in everyday life? (In answering this question you must obviously have a solid understanding of the tools that are appropriate, and in particular what they are supposed to alleviate. You can find more about practical aids in Part 4 of this book.)

If any of these questions is answered with 'no', they will also be addressed in the Intervention Plan (see p.239).

To summarize

Once the data collection is finished, we have acquired as much information as we can:

- on the history

- on the individual

- about the problematic situation (if there is one)

- about ourselves

- on the entirety.

We have used observations, interviews with relatives and others, surveys, and perhaps we have also made a measurement (see Appendix 2). The analysis and hypothesis follow.

15.2 Analysis and hypothesis

Do you remember the picture of the structure (Figure 15.1)? We have done the first part of the assessment. We have gained as much information as we can about the individual and the situation as we can. Let's go through our material and make an analysis. When we meet at a staff meeting we start putting the pieces together. Based on the clues we have, we are trying to create some hypotheses (assumptions) about the reasons for the behaviours we see (the base of the iceberg). Someone at the meeting will take notes, and later put the notes together.[8]

We make a description of the current situation. It might look something like this:

Current situation: Ryan

- Ryan is a creative and talented boy with autism and an extensive unevenness in his developmental profile. In some areas, he is three and five years rather than his actual 14. The fact that Ryan is both a quick thinker and gifted can be somewhat of an obstacle; it may make us believe that he understands more than he really does.

- Ryan has very low self-esteem (which probably stems from his difficulty in identifying and describing feelings, which in turn is due to his disability).

- Ryan's breakdowns are usually seen in conjunction with him making a mistake and feeling like a failure. Ryan has no effective strategies to deal with failures, and we think he often feels stupid.

- The fact that Ryan is now bigger and stronger has made his breakdowns more problematic, as his stress and frustration reactions now have more serious consequences.

---

8   Why do I write such an obvious thing? Well, in my experience all good things do *not* come to he who waits, and in many services I have worked with there is lots of talking but less action. If we don't assign the task of taking notes to someone it may happen that we fall into the trap of not actually working as we say we are working (and that happens a lot). It's not for nothing that most cultures have sayings and proverbs like these: 'An idea not coupled with action will never get any bigger than the brain cell it occupied'; 'Talk doesn't cook rice'; 'It is not enough to stare up the steps – we must step up the stairs'; 'Between saying and doing, many a pair of shoes is worn out.'

- We also believe that Ryan's growing ability to see himself through somebody else's eyes (i.e. his development of theory of mind) now means that he suffers more from not understanding.

- Ryan has great difficulty coping with unforeseen events.

- Ryan likes metaphors, and has a good sense of humour, which can be used to teach him things.

- We believe that Ryan's environment needs more knowledge about his disability.

15.3 Intervention plan

Now it's time for the intervention plan. How can we best help Ryan with what we have discovered? This will always be about a combination of training of new skills, strategies for increasing well-being and reducing stress, new aids, and changes in our own way of interacting.

Now we need to get this down on paper. Any identified difficulty is now to get its own 'tag' with an intervention. If there are many things we need to do, some things will be on stand-by for a while (but still need to be written down). Other things will have to be built step by step; for example, we must always begin with the increasing of well-being and reducing of stress, before we try to teach a new individualized strategy to manage anger and frustration.

Let us return to the description of Ryan:

'Ryan is a creative and talented boy with autism and an extensive unevenness in his developmental profile. In some areas, he is three and five years rather than his actual 14. The fact that Ryan is both a quick thinker and gifted can be somewhat of an obstacle; it may make us believe that he understands more than he really does.'

Solution: We will give Ryan better aids, and adjust our expectations of him based on our understanding of his varying developmental levels.

Concrete support: A visual aid (Time Timer[9]); a coloured visual schedule to be more actively used than what he has today;[10] all choices must be made visually clear. Important information should always be written down.

Objective: For Ryan to have an overall situation which in terms of demands and expectations is well adjusted to his needs.

'Ryan has very low self-esteem (which probably stems from his difficulty in identifying and describing feelings, which in turn is due to his disability).'

Solution: We will work actively with much positive feedback about him as a person – both about how he is as a person and how he performs.

Concrete support: Ryan will be given working materials that will help him to recognize (and reflect on) feelings. We will help Ryan to a better means of describing himself as a person. We will make a list of all Ryan's positive qualities and miss no opportunity to mention them to him.

Objective: For Ryan to have a good self-knowledge and self-esteem, and to be able to describe himself, both in terms of personality and of his likes and dislikes.

'Ryan's breakdowns are usually seen in conjunction with him making a mistake and feeling like a failure. Ryan has no effective strategies to deal with failures, and we think he often feels stupid. The fact that Ryan is now bigger and stronger has made his breakdowns more problematic, as his stress and frustration reactions now have more serious consequences. We also believe that Ryan's growing ability to see

---

9   There are many visual aids for perception of time. Time timer is only one of them, but it works very well for many schoolchildren with time perception difficulties. Time timer is a visual timer. As time elapses, the signature red disk disappears, helping everyone to see how much time is left. It is also available as an app for smart phones.

10   Ryan is not unusual; he had a visual schedule, with different colours for activities and days of the week – all according to the general autism knowledge – but, just like many pupils I meet, he didn't use it much. An aid that is not used, that is just for show, seems quite pointless, right? Staff thought maybe he did not need it, or could not make use of it (since he didn't use it). But don't shoot the messenger; in order for an aid to be helpful we must *teach* the individual how to use it. This teaching means, for example, referring to the schedule when Ryan asks 'What's next?' or 'What class are we having tomorrow morning', rather than just replying to his question.

himself through somebody else's eyes (i.e. his development of theory of mind), now means that he suffers more from not understanding.'

Solution: We will prevent situations where Ryan could experience failures. We will help him with strategies for what he can do when the frustration becomes too great.

Concrete support: We will give Ryan clear and unambiguous instructions, and train ourselves to see how school assignments can be seen from his perspective. Exploratory tasks need to be prepared carefully, since he will be very stressed if he makes a 'wrong' guess. We will help Ryan to practise a new strategy (to 'growl' and stomp on the floor) when he becomes frustrated. Ryan must have two 'safe havens' that he can always go off to when he needs to get away.

Objective: For Ryan to feel safe and have a sense of well-being, and to be able to handle his frustration in a way that hurts no one.

'Ryan has great difficulty coping with unforeseen events.'

Solution: We will make an effort to always minimize the unexpected. (Ryan's lack of imagination, lack of ability to form mental images, means that he cannot predict or imagine things that he never experienced.)

Concrete support: We will create aids and strategies that compensate for the lack of imagination. We will use social stories as a way to prepare him. When Ryan has a reaction, we will use it as a reminder that we are not prepared enough and learn from it.

Objective: For Ryan to be able to survey his school day, and feel confident.

'Ryan likes metaphors, and has a good sense of humour, which can be used to teach him things.'

Solution: We use his strengths.

Concrete support: We will use his own train metaphor (when all is well the train chugs along) but try to develop it by talking about how there may be a switch further down the track – for example, when we finish one thing and start another. We will give positive feedback to Ryan for being so great at describing how things feel when all's well, and ask him to help us with more descriptions. As regards the feelings and nuances of emotion, we will try to use weather metaphors since Ryan is interested in weather phenomena. We will try to describe moods as sunny, cloudy, there may be a thunderstorm, etc., and see if this can be a tool for Ryan to better identify and express his feelings. We will use his sense of humour to create a sense of well-being around him.

New assessment: We will identify and document the type of humour that Ryan has. We already know that he enjoys wordplays and we will find new games he enjoys.

Objective: To create many situations where Ryan has fun and can have a laugh with others. To develop Ryan's sense of humour so he can be more involved in more social settings, and does not need to feel that he does not understand.

'We believe that Ryan's environment needs more knowledge about his disability.'

Solution: We will work actively to get Ryan's relatives involved.

Concrete support: We will invite them to future staff counselling meetings. When we notify them about our assessment and intervention plan we will ask them to offer their views. We will ask them how we can help or assist them, and how together we can raise awareness of autism in the network around Ryan (in his leisure activities, with the grandparents and so on). We will ask if they want help with reading recommendations, contact with the National Autism Society (NAS), etc.

Objective: To establish a good basic understanding of Ryan's difficulties in his network and good collaboration with his family.

Well, this was really just an example, and an Intervention Plan is often even more extensive and more concrete. At this meeting, when we write the Intervention Plan, perhaps the parents are already included – in my example, they were not there because my experience is that many staff groups (unfortunately) do not invite family to participate to the extent they could. When I tutor or counsel staff, I often propose that both parents and representatives of other services in the individual's life are invited to attend right from the start. It is cost-effective from a human as well as an economic angle.

When we write the Intervention Plan we also decide, and document, who does what and when to start. Sometimes the whole plan is launched on a certain date, and on other occasions, different parts at different times. One important thing is to decide who informs absent staff, and to have a target date for when this should be done. Only then can we launch the Intervention Plan, and that date is specified in the plan.

Sometimes there is a very concrete and precise way of responding written into the plan, and then of course all concerned must know of it. Sometimes it may be that *all* staff in an entire school must be informed (and this may take some time!).

EXAMPLE

Joshua was 13 years old and diagnosed with PDD. He had been in this school since fourth grade. He had, according to his teachers, a tough and threatening behaviour. In the corridor of Joshua's school, there were cabinets with school supplies, and these cabinets had glass doors. Joshua would, every so often, at break, walk up to any adult who happened to pass by and threaten to smash the cabinet glass.

The adults (teachers as well as school managers and caretakers were affected) were very upset because it felt like whatever they did or said, it did not help. They had tried to be calm, to rebuke, discipline and distract Joshua, but whatever they did Joshua would always be even more agitated.

During his time in this school, he had in fact shattered the glass twice, so it was always a possibility (albeit unlikely given that he threatened thousands of times, but had only done it twice) that he would actually do it.

An assessment yielded, among other things, that Joshua was a tired boy with attention problems. Joshua had what I call 'a nervous system with a screen saver'. When Joshua had no input from outside, when nothing happened, you could see how he would slowly sort of slip into his own mind. He would not fall asleep, but it was as if he pulled the plug, so to speak. We could also see that Joshua was trying to avoid this (it is probably quite uncomfortable to detach like this). Our hypothesis was that 'a little adrenaline makes you alert'.

A good threatening and angry conversation was pure self-medication for Joshua.

Once we understood this, we had to come up with options. The assessment had also revealed that Joshua had great difficulty identifying and putting words to feelings and emotions.

The new strategy was that all adults who were 'targeted' by Joshua's behaviour would meet him with a friendly 'Now I think you are tired and need to cheer up? Would you like to…?'

Here Joshua was given three options to choose from (and of course we knew from the assessment that Joshua had no difficulty with choices; if he had, we would never have entered a choice here).

The alternative Joshua by far the most frequently chose was the (for all) brand-new sport of 'throwing pots on the school steps'. This activity was invented because we needed an activity that could fulfil the same function (loud and noisy), which was fun and workable. A box of old used aluminium pots was bought cheaply at a flea market. And the sport was performed exactly as it was named – Joshua and an adult would together throw the pots at the stairs (outside). Wonderful bangs echoed across the schoolyard.

The challenge was to inform *all* those who worked in the school (a large school has many employees) about the new strategy. Everyone would know how to deal with Joshua, and what things he could choose from. If you yourself did not have time to practise throwing pots with Joshua, you had to find another adult who could do it. But there was no need to find a stand-in that often, because the truth was that many adults actually also enjoyed throwing pots.

We explained to Joshua's classmates that this was a new means for helping Joshua, and that they would get help and support where *they* needed it (as it otherwise would seem unfair to them that Joshua would get this fun new activity). Since all the school friends knew that Joshua needed special support in many situations, it was not very hard to get them to accept this.

From being a threatening and upsetting situation which all involved suffered from, it got to be a fun activity, which in addition taught Joshua to recognize and understand that he had a fatigue and alertness problem, and that he needed help with this. (There were also other things arranged around Joshua, such as he would receive a preventive rest during the school day, and exercises in recognizing other emotions).

Joshua did not have to use the pot throwing very often, and with time there was no need at all, as he would have other strategies for handling his attention problems.

But with our new approach Joshua would also get the message that we did not believe that he was 'mean', or that he himself should be able to control his behaviour – he understood that we realized he had a real problem that he needed help with, and the climate of our interaction changed to positive, from both sides.

Back to the Intervention Plan. We have written Ryan's Intervention Plan and we need to decide from when it takes effect. Let us say we decide that the plan must be launched next week. Before this week is over, all staff who are involved in the Intervention Plan have to sign it.[11]

---

11   Why? Well, because if someone then does not work according to the Intervention Plan, he should at least not be able to say that he did not know we now had these new approaches. Therefore, everybody signs that they have read and understood the plan. It works as an extra commitment to follow the plan, for those we might call 'I-do-as-I-always-have-done-rs'.

But before the plan is complete, we must also determine the date for evaluation.[12] When should we do the first evaluation? Maybe in two or four weeks? How long a time we need before we make the first evaluation depends on the situation as well as on the interventions. We need to give it enough time for us to expect to see some change.

When we decide a date, we also write it into the Intervention Plan and in the diary, and allocate time for such a meeting. If the evaluation is four weeks ahead, we might already after one week have a mini-meeting just to check how we are doing. Especially if it's a service that has regular staff meetings or collegial meetings once a week.

The obvious question, in such a first meeting within a week, is 'Have all followed the intervention plan?' If the answer to that question is no, usually it's because you do not think you have 'had time'. Thus, it is important that you understand from the outset, that working with this structure is most challenging and time-consuming in the beginning. It will take an effort on your part.

Why is it more demanding at first? It is because you have almost always been a step behind. You run around and sweep up the remnants of 'disasters' like breakdowns, conflicts, disputes, and so on. Now you are working to be one step ahead. But before you can reap the benefits of being one step ahead (and it may take a while), you will both have to do all the preliminary work, and continue to 'take care of the remains'. Count on it to take time.

Perhaps you can cut down on time spent in other areas in the service for a couple of weeks; maybe bring in some extra staff. But I can assure you that it's worth it in the long run. It pays (both financially and timewise) to be a good autism-craftsman with skills, who knows how to do their preliminary work properly. There is so much less taking care of your own mistakes afterwards!

If you do not have a quality craftsmanship, you might do as I did when I wanted to paint a stool in the kitchen (I am not a professional painter, obviously). I was thinking 'Well, I won't spill anything when painting this little stool' and I just put a newspaper underneath. And then I get down on my knees afterwards and try to remove paint stains from the floor. But your paint stains will be clients, pupils or clients exhibiting stress reactions because you and your colleagues have not yet caught up with making adaptations, creating aids and new strategies and supporting the individual to make progress.

---

12   We must always, always have a date for evaluation!

15.4 Evaluation

Now is the time to evaluate. Are we on track? Is Ryan making progress? If necessary we record whether his incidents of acting out and threatening have decreased in size and number. But often we do not need to measure; we see so clearly how well the client responds to the new approach and support.

In the evaluation we will review the various components and adjust the Intervention Plan. Perhaps we have come up with something new that we want to add. Maybe it was one of the strategies that did not work so well. Then we rewrite the action plan accordingly, and give it a new date for evaluation. In this way we always know where we are in the structure of the Intervention Plan. The Intervention Plan must be an active and live document. The more crossings-outs and coffee stains on it, the better!

15.5 Documentation

The Intervention Plans are of course also excellent documentation, and a good basis for writing what Hilde De Clercq once called the 'manual'. Hilde is the mother of a boy with autism (and the author of a couple of books on the subject (see De Clercq 2003, 2006). Hilde has described that when her son was to change schools, she brought a textbook about how he understands the world, and what type of approaches and practical aids he needed. The new teacher asked, 'Do you have a son with a manual?' Hilde thought for a moment and then replied 'Yes, I have a son with a manual.'

I do not think that we really can make extensive manuals that cover everything for our clients and pupils with autism spectrum disorders. However, we can become better at documentation. We may know in our service that Ramesh cannot take a shower in the mornings because he is too tired; that Jennifer cannot handle the word 'no' or that we speak in terms of 'right' and 'wrong'; that Omar is stressed by all situations involving choices; and that Sun can talk better about difficult things if we take her for a drive.[13] But that knowledge may stand or fall with the personnel group that Sun, Omar, Jennifer or Ramesh have today. What if they are replaced? What happens when the person moves or changes school? If the clients and pupils have documentation (a 'manual') of their special needs and the way to interact with them – which, if they are old enough, they have read and accepted, of course – it can be really helpful. Why should Jennifer or Ramesh be a 'guinea pig' for each new staff member to make their own mistakes?

15.6 Troubleshooting or 'HELP – it does not work!'

Finally, I would also like to say something about when it does not work. I've noticed that quite often in a staff counselling process (especially when we have a client with an acting-out problem) at first it moves forward as on rails. The staff are so happy to see the challenging behaviour being reduced and the well-being of their client or pupil improve. They are surprised that it was that 'easy' to change something they previously felt was so difficult. But then suddenly everything is hard again.

I will arrive at a counselling session and be met with sighs and resignation. My experience is that it can be about a few different things that I'll try to explain here.

Sloth

Man is by nature quite lazy, as I mentioned earlier. That goes for you, as well as for me (most certainly for me!). We want to do most things with minimal effort. Wisely so. But not always that effective. It could mean that when our pupils or clients have received new aids that work well, our relationship with them has improved and a calm presents itself, we imperceptibly begin to think those tools, those visual strategies, all the

---

13 Travelling by car may even be described as a tool to work with. Significantly many of the acting-out individuals with autism spectrum disorders I have worked with have a higher level of well-being when going by car, and can have better conversations in the car. I think that it can be because of the car's direct effect on the nervous system (vibrations and sound) – many parents of infants with colic have noticed travelling by car (or the sound of a dryer) has a soothing and calming effect on the baby. But for conversation, the car is also perfect as the one driving has to keep her eyes on the road. So you will sit next to each other and look straight ahead, making it easier for those who have difficulty (and find it challenging) to interpret facial expressions and eye contact.

positive feedback is probably not really necessary We lose momentum in the preparatory work, and begin to be half a step behind.

If this is the problem, then get back on track again! There is no escape from preliminary work. The painter cannot skip the grinding and plastering; the tailor has to tack; and you, as an autism craftsman, have to do your groundwork.

New problems

Sometimes we succeed so quickly and well in solving the acute stress around a person with challenging behaviours, that it liberates a substantial amount of time and energy in our service or classroom. Time to catch your breath and relax, one could wish. But it is not at all unusual that what then happens is that a new (or really an old) problem surfaces and becomes more visible.

Now that Joanne no longer trashes the place (or runs screaming out of the classroom), we may see Ben's difficulties more clearly. They become more visible because the staff no longer have to run around and sweep up the remains (literally or figuratively, or both) from Joanne's breakdowns. Or it could be that another problem that Joanne herself has surfaces when her overall stress level is reduced.

Maybe what happens is even that Joanne and Ben together now start with 'something new'. Joanne no longer has breakdowns, but she and Ben suddenly start teasing Emily (which leads to Emily's stress increasing and now Emily is acting out). This is not surprising; if there are unresolved difficulties[14], they'll get more space when we have solved the most acute problems. What to do? Well, just start with the assessment process again. The good news is that the second (and third and fourth and so on) time, it takes less time.

Another aspect here is that I sometimes come across groups of staff who have worked in a 'war zone' for so long that they have become accustomed to it. They seem to expect work to be like this. And that's

---

14   What could the difficulties be leading them to start teasing Emily? A general question to ask is often what function does it fulfil? Excitement? Well then, offer them other things that are exciting. To have a fellowship (us against her)? Well, then we will help with new forms of togetherness. Or perhaps it is something as 'simple' as the lack of ability to form mental images (affecting the possibilities of thinking of alternatives) making Joanne and Ben not be able to break this new 'habit'.

why they sometimes see serious problems where there actually are none.[15]

Groups of staff sometimes have developed a common identity in that they are to be pitied by colleagues and even their boss, because they are exposed and they struggle with very difficult clients or pupils. It may have given them a special 'status' at school, or in the service. If they no longer have such serious problems, they can have difficulty recognizing the new situation, and suddenly they come to counselling and with grave seriousness paint something pretty trivial as a giant problem.

Not the right strategy

Maybe the new approach and aids had a positive effect the first few weeks, but due to Jaydon's low self-esteem and sense of powerlessness, this was not enough. Maybe we made a miscalculation?

Perhaps we have, without being aware, sustained focus on the behaviour itself rather than the causes? We go back to the assessment process and look at our material. Have we missed something? Do we need more knowledge?

15.7 Finally, about assessments

This was an attempt to, as clearly and in as much detail as I was able to, describe to you the process that I believe is the foundation of quality craftsmanship in the autism field. It takes time to recognize this. Actually, we can't know it until we're there. When you have only a little knowledge about something, it is often difficult to see what you lack. It is easy to think that you know it 'all' if you have worked for a long time in the field.

EXAMPLE

When I began to study autism at university, it was a new field (not in practice, but in the academic sense). Many fought for the few places

---

15 Let me give you an example: a group of teachers in a special ed class did a fantastic job in supporting a pupil who had huge behaviour problems. Together we assessed and addressed the issues. Everything was fine! But at our next meeting, I see worry in their faces. And in dead-serious voices they tell me that Kaleigh now has... has... [shock horror] started a blog! (Well as it turns out, even if she had some minor problems with this blogging in terms of unwanted comments, it turned out to be a great way for her to express herself – and practise writing too.)

on this course, and the admission requirements were at least ten years' professional experience (or equivalent) of autism. We all at the beginning felt we were pretty good at this and knew what we were doing. We were the skilled few, with this long experience, who had managed to get in to this course.

But about halfway into this course we were all collectively struck by a realization that we in fact knew nothing at all. We suddenly saw the (frighteningly large) gaps we had in our knowledge, and how (awfully) unaware we had been of it.

A few months later that feeling of paralysis gradually was released, and when the course came to an end, I think many of us felt empowered in what knowledge and experience we had, and the new knowledge now added to this. But we also had brought away with us a remaining awareness that we will never be fully skilled. Simply, because there is no such thing.

A classic mistake when you start working with assessments is that you think you can skip them. Don't.

EXAMPLE

I supervised the staff of a daily service. Dwayne had challenging behaviours that affected the entire service. After about six months, Dwayne was fine, and there were no longer any major problems around him. I left my assignment, and wished the service good luck.

Six months later the staff contacted me and told me that now they had a new user, a woman, who also had challenging behaviours.' We've tried all your strategies, but they do not work.'

Of course they do not work! The strategies we had used were based on an assessment of Dwayne and his difficulties. If you are near-sighted and visit the optician, you do not think she should give you the same glasses as she gave the last customer, just because both of you 'have a vision problem', do you?

You cannot skip the assessment process. You cannot skip the assessment process. You cannot skip the assessment process, and so on…

We know accurately only when we know little; with knowledge doubt increases. (Johann Wolfgang von Goethe)

16

An Underwater Guide

A Chapter on Common Contributing
Factors in Challenging Behaviours

Remember the iceberg metaphor (p.197)? I hope so! In the previous chapter I spoke of the structure you as a professional need in order to know what you're doing and that your interventions are working. Now I want to highlight some factors beneath the surface of the iceberg. That is, difficulties and skills, which can be present or absent in the individual with the disability, that affect the behaviour we see.

Each 'iceberg' is of course completely individual. Although it is, in general terms, possible to say that challenging behaviours are often triggered by stress, the stressors are different for each person. There are several common stressors that I have already written about, including sensory processing problems as an important one.

In this chapter I will attempt to describe some areas which quite often show up when I dive into the glacial sea (or however I should put it to make it fit my metaphorical landscape). I gave you the diving lessons in the previous chapter (and you understood that the diving equipment can be a bit heavy before you get used to it), so you now know how to dive (make an assessment). Now I want to give you some idea of what I think you might run into down there.

This chapter is very strongly linked to the whole of Part 2, 'Understanding the Impairments'. That is to say, all the symptoms and difficulties mentioned there belong to the things you might find under the surface, and I will not mention them again here. The examples I take here are those things people often miss, or do not really understand when it comes to challenging behaviours, and therefore they get to have a chapter of their own.

But let me start by saying that people with autism spectrum disorders in many ways are just like everybody else. I let some participants in a course (all were staff of various kinds) list what could affect their mood.[1] Here is the list:

- lack of energy and lack of sleep

- the weather (too hot, too dark, etc.)

- hunger

- stress/time pressure

- addiction (not having an addiction satisfied, such as coffee, nicotine, Coca Cola)

- feeling crowded

- being scared and worried

- physical pain (including such things as headaches, sickness, PMS)

- the mood and attitude of others

- grief/depression/dysphoria

- concerns over finances, relationships and other life circumstances.

Of course it is often the same things that affect the mood of your pupils, clients or users; the difference is mainly that they, because of their disability, are stressed, scared and worried about more things than other people. In addition, energy shortages are often larger since many of the difficulties in autism often drain the individual of energy.

As you saw, the participants at my course pointed to the fact that fears and worries affect your mood, and I would argue that fear and anger are two emotions which for most people are closely linked to each other. It is very common to react with anger when you get scared. But often, a person who has a disability within the autism spectrum can also become afraid of things that other people are not afraid of, and perhaps even more frequently. A person may be scared due to motor difficulties (if you have poor co-ordination or balance, many places can be frightening), sensory issues (you may be very startled by a sudden noise or touch), or difficulty with mental imagery (when you

---

1   Take a moment to think about what affects your mood. Things that may cause you to be upset over something that deep down you know you would not be all that upset over at another occasion?

cannot foresee the outcome of a situation, it may be really scary), and then reacts with anger.[2] In people with acting-out problems, there are things we may need to have a special radar for. Our radar needs to have a sensitivity to discovering problems with self-esteem, imagination, communication and to the development perspective (again!).

16.1 Self-esteem

Most people with challenging behaviours that I meet have very low self-esteem. They believe they are stupid, not good enough for anything. They furthermore feel they know nothing, have no skill, nothing to contribute and that they are not needed.[3] They lack the feeling of competence, the 'I am able' feeling.

Sometimes it has gone so far that the client is in a state of chronic powerlessness. If staff in turn also feel powerless, this can create a scenario with 'a war' between two trenches: a dejected, powerless and frustrated client in the one trench, and a dejected, powerless and frustrated group of staff in the other. In your trench, you are by definition better off – you are in company; you have chosen to be there (well, not in the trench, but on the job) and you are paid for being there. The client is completely alone in his trench!

The sense of powerlessness should always be broken; thus we must create better conditions for self-esteem, while also building self-confidence. This applies to both the staff group and to the people with disabilities.

How? You will read more about this in Chapter 23, 'Can You Be Yourself When You Do Not Know Who You Are?' Here, I just want to alert you to the fact that low self-esteem is common, and that we can rarely reverse a situation in which a behaviour has destructive

---

2   Believe me: it will not be better if the professionals, in turn, are afraid of the client's reaction and react with anger to it.

3   Being needed, in a broad sense, seems to be extremely important for the general well-being of all human beings. Many people without autism spectrum disorders accomplish that by having a job and/or a family where they are needed. We need to think really hard about how we can help our clients to find an area where they feel needed. It can be letting them use their skills to help us or other clients with something; getting a pet; doing some volunteer work; or something else. Because, if for nothing else, increased well-being reduces challenging behaviour. Here's what Herbert Lovett says: 'Being needed is a genuinely important status. When we are needed, we belong and we have a reason to speak up; and when people are needed, that is when we most often find the ways to listen to them' (Lovett 1996).

consequences, unless we also help the individual to improve his or her self-esteem.

Low self-esteem can take a variety of expressions.

EXAMPLES

- The teacher Annie says to Liu, her pupil with autism: 'Now, it will be nice to have Christmas holidays, right?' and Liu replies: 'Yes, it will be good for you to get rid of me.'

- Amir, residential support employee, tells the user Oscar that next time, he will help him to sort the laundry so that the white laundry is not discoloured. Oscar replies: 'Right, I am really stupid!'

- Marcela, staff in a short-term service, takes some children with autism to McDonald's. Marc refuses to eat his hamburger (though everyone knows he loves it). He says 'I'm not worthy of a burger, because I am a freak.'

But also in the following cases, there may be low self-esteem:

EXAMPLES

- The maths teacher, Gemma, points out that it would be good if Charles could try to write more than one calculation per paper next time. Charles replies that he can damn well do what he wants and he at least is smarter than everyone, even smarter than the dumb teachers who do not know anything.

- Danielle who is 19 years old and has just received her diagnosis screams 'I don't have any fucking autism, you bloody idiots!'

- The teacher Milijan tells the student Adam (who loves to bake) that if he does not come in on time from the break next time for domestic science class, he cannot bake in domestic science. Adam throws a fit and crushes a plate against the wall.[4]

---

4   How is this related to low self-esteem, you may wonder? Well, Adam, who has autism, and huge difficulties with picturing things (envisioning consequences) was late in from the break (that's why Milijan told him off). His low self-esteem in combination with his symptoms makes him feel stupid, and the teacher's comment is a confirmation of this. But can you as a teacher not say things like this? No, if you want to inform about a consequence (however reasonable it is), you do it in *advance*, and in a visually clear way (for example, before the next domestic science lesson, using written or drawn information).

16.2 Ability to form mental images

The lack of ability to form mental images that is common in autism spectrum disorders often creates problems. It is particularly important to understand this when we work with people with challenging behaviours. Sometimes I hear people say that people with autism have a need for control, which is basically something they have in common with the vast majority of people on earth.

We all want a picture of what we have ahead of us, what we can expect of a situation. The difference is that anyone who has a good ability to create pictures in their mind, can use their experience of similar situations to build a notion of a situation they have not yet been through.

Let us say you are going to the movies in a new city. You know nothing about what this cinema looks like, nor have you seen this particular movie before. Yet you *expect* certain things. You've been to the movies before. So you take it for granted that there will be toilets (there have been at all cinemas you have been to before), you assume that there is popcorn (but perhaps you think that you cannot be completely sure) and so on, and you do this (whether you are aware of it or not, by using pictures in your mind).[5] Then when you arrive at this new cinema you are able to adjust your view of how your evening will be in accordance with what you see: 'Aha, there is a cafe'. You constantly build a picture of the future, based on both previous experience and new impressions.

Those who have difficulty with imagination[6] cannot do this, at least not as quickly and as smoothly as you can. It can often lead to a feeling of uneasiness and anxiousness (which you would also feel if you could not envision what your day would look like), and can mean that you are scared, angry or upset when things do not turn out as you expected.[7] In terms of behaviour we may see a client who always

---

5   Most people are not aware of how they use pictures, their ability to form mental images, but most do. A common example is that if you speak with someone over the phone (or hear them on the radio) you form a picture of the person. Then you may be surprised when you meet the person in real life, that he or she does not look anything like you pictured. As I said, we do this all the time, but we are also great at quickly adjusting the image according to the new reality.

6   Now, I don't speak of imagination in the sense of 'thinking new thoughts'; many with Asperger's can do that. I am speaking of the 'image' part of the imagination.

7   Wait a minute, how could someone expect something if they lack the ability to foresee? Well, many with difficulties in this area use their experience in an inflexible way; either they believe things will happen *exactly* as they did last time, or they have no clue at all.

refuses to participate in certain things, or acts out when confronted with things he or she cannot picture.

We may see a pupil screaming and kicking at things, because the trip to the museum was not what he (literally) had in mind.

EXAMPLE

Jonathan could use only one previous experience with a museum (the Science Museum he had been to last year) to anticipate this excursion to a completely different museum (which he had never been to).

He expected the museum to be equal to his exact memory of the Science Museum. To him 'a museum' was 'the Science Museum'. Now when the class arrives at the British Museum he is both disappointed (he had been looking forward to what he expected), and confused. (How does it all come together? What is a museum?)

He also feels stupid (why is it that I do not grasp something that seems to be obvious to everyone else?), and a bit scared (how will this day turn out?) What lies in front of him is becoming a 'black hole', since he cannot use any prior experience to know what to expect.

Question: If within a second (when the bus stops and the teacher says 'Here is the museum') you are hit by something that makes you disappointed, confused, feeling stupid and scared – is it then surprising if you lose control over your behaviour?

Answer: No, it's not strange at all (you would too, if it happened to you).

Many of the tools we can work with compensate for the lack of imagination. You can read more about the tools in Part 4 of this book.

There is an extremely important point in understanding the lack of ability to form mental images. It is the reason why many people with autism spectrum disorders cannot learn from consequences, as do others (especially children). In parenting and education we often use consequences as a management tool. When we tell a child that they have to eat some of the first course to get dessert, we expect them to learn and be able to apply this rule to future eating situations. But for those who cannot use imagination in a flexible way to generalize the rule, the rule may apply only if it is fish and chips; only if Dad has a blue t-shirt on; or only if it's lunch. If the conditions are different (there is sausages, Dad has a green shirt, or it is not lunch but dinner), you cannot understand that the rule applies.

This also applies when the rule takes the form of punishment, as in: 'She must learn the consequences of screaming and having a meltdown in the computer room; now she will not be allowed into the computer room for a week, then maybe she will learn!' Or 'We cannot let him get away with everything, right? We have to put our foot down and teach him that his behaviour has consequences! We should take away his video games until he shows he can behave.' Or 'If she continues to run away without telling us where she goes, we'll make it clear that it is not OK, and we will simply not let her into the joint activities when she gets back. She must learn that she can't just disappear and appear as she wishes.'

Besides concern that none of these 'strategies' will help the pupil or client with what is the real problem (the iceberg under the surface), it is furthermore a serious problem that the client probably lacks the ability to learn through consequences. And when the ability is missing, well then, this type of treatment risks becoming abusive.[8] And with abuse we risk making the problem worse. Aggrieved people may, for example – quite understandably – become vengeful and want to 'get even', and suddenly we have created a war we did not want.

EXAMPLE

A few years ago when I gave a lecture on working with challenging behaviours, a woman came up to me in the first intermission. We can call her Clare.

Clare told me that she was a teacher and that she had a pupil, 13 years old with autism. She knew the pupil well, she said, and had known her from previous grades. Now the semester had just started and today was the first time Clare was absent on a school day.

The substitute teacher at school called Clare. The pupil had locked herself in a room at school, where there was a CD-player. She had put on music at high volume, and refused to come out. 'What should I advise the substitute teacher?' Clare asked me.

'What does the substitute teacher want to do?' I asked. 'The substitute teacher thinks it is important to "set a limit" and to "make clear" to the pupil that this behaviour is not OK,' said Clare.

I was glad I was asked and could advise them to do otherwise.

I sometimes think of this situation, and reflect on the fact that something as trivial as this kind of situation could be the beginning

---

8   Why is it abusive to make a 'benefit' conditional on an achievement that the individual does not have the prerequisites to perform? Well, it goes without saying, I hope. If you still need examples of this, see the reasoning on p.211.

of an approach that leads to a negative spiral. Sometimes I have used this example in lectures and asked the participants at the beginning of the lecture what they would have advised the substitute teacher, and then at the end of the day asked them if they now think differently. In the morning, it is not uncommon for participants to reply that the substitute teacher should 'call the janitor with the master key, and open the door', and similar.

I think the most obvious interpretation of this situation is that the pupil was not sufficiently prepared for Clare's absence. ('But we *have* prepared her,' Clare objected. 'Well, you have most certainly done something to prepare her, but what we see in terms of her behaviour, I think is an obvious proof that you have not prepared *her well enough or in a way that works for her,*' I replied.)

So what is the gist of this? Well, that we should put the responsibility where it belongs. Consequently, I proposed that the substitute teacher should insert a note under the door that read something like:

> I understand that you have to be inside. We apologize that we did not prepare you enough for having a substitute teacher today. You may stay in there as long as you need, and you are welcome to come out to us when you feel ready.

The lack of imagination can have further consequences. I have seen that many with autism spectrum disorders create their own theories about things. A person who does not really have the ability to get a picture in his mind of what might happen (if he has not experienced the exact same event before) will perhaps try to – in a rather 'mechanical' and fixed way – premeditate a chain of events (if I do this, then that will happen, then if I say A, she will answer B, and so on). Then this becomes a rigid conception of what will occur: a conception which does not include all the variables that others would add.

As the individual himself may not know or understand that his ability to form mental images is reduced (it is very difficult to understand what you do not understand – try it for yourself!), it may be that he firmly believes that certain things *will* happen on the basis of what he himself says or does. If the reality then does not play according to the 'script' he had figured, he can be shocked, as well as confused, disappointed, angry and sad. And all these emotions can in some individuals manifest themselves as challenging behaviours.

The remedy for this is obviously *not* to 'tell the person that reality does not work this way,' but rather to create aids, adjustments and approaches (such as 'Informed choices' – see p.294); in short, things that give the person a better opportunity to review various outcomes of a given action. Preferably you do this using visual aids, that is, text and images.

16.3 Developmental perspective and theory of mind (mentalization)

Yes, that's right, you've read about this earlier. But here I want to highlight some particular perspectives on this, and link this to challenging behaviours.

Sometimes I meet people with diagnoses within the autism spectrum who have a special interest in making others angry, annoyed or upset. As you probably know, people with autism are often proficient in their special interest, and this behaviour may seem very provocative to those around the person because they feel that it really is deliberate and directed against them.

EXAMPLE

Milo has a special interest in making people annoyed. There are some people in his life (his uncle, the landlord, a neighbour) that he knows exactly how he will 'get started'. Milo thinks that people look very funny when they become irritated.

It is important that people around Milo understand that wanting to make people annoyed is not the same as wanting them to 'feel bad', a conclusion that is otherwise easy to draw. His lack of theory of mind (mentalization) means that he does not understand how they perceive the situation from their perspective. He has no idea that what he thinks 'looks fun' really is painful for other people.

For the same reasons, some individuals with autism spectrum disorders use bad language or sexual words, etc. – simply because they get such exciting reactions!

And before you get the wrong idea: I do not think it's a good idea to try to 'extinguish' the behaviour by simply not giving the expected response. If we do that, we have forgotten our diving lessons – we have to get below the surface, where we might find not only problems with the theory of mind (which we may address with social stories), but also a need for excitement.

A need for excitement, for something to happen, can both signal an attention problem, that is, an attempt to 'stay awake' by making things happen, and a need for excitement in everyday life.[9]

Whatever it is we find below the surface, it must be addressed. If we are looking at this and working to find an approach, well then, it is of course easier for us to keep calm when Milo is trying to irritate us. Not primarily to make him stop doing that and for us to feel better, but rather because when we understand *why* Milo is doing it, we can help him with new strategies.

Another perspective on development is to look at the ability to regulate one's mood and behaviour; we do not expect a very small child to be able to do this. And with the uneven development characteristic in autism spectrum disorders, we cannot expect everyone with these conditions to be 'there' yet. But, before one can affect one's surroundings with language (by arguing, for example), how does one affect the environment, then? With behaviour.

Do you remember the example of my three-year-old who flatly denied taking popcorn (see p.144)? When he got older, he would start arguing with me instead, but this occurred only after development of theory of mind reached the level where he could form an idea of what I was thinking (and what arguments I might buy).

When we can manipulate people, in the positive sense of the word,[10] we are not at the mercy of only being able to act or react with our behaviour. Some people with autism spectrum disorders (not all!) are lagging behind in the development of mentalization and have no other ways of affecting their lives than with their behaviour. When we understand this, we also understand that we need not be more upset

---

9   Meaningful activities often prevent challenging behaviours. The other day I gave a lecture to staff from residential support. I said: 'I have not been to your specific services and have not met your clients, but unfortunately the fact is that many of the clients I meet, have quite an empty existence, and in the same individuals we often find challenging behaviours.' Many of the participants recognized this from their own services. Many of us, and probably you too, find the strength to get through difficulties by having things that we look forward to. Maybe we book a trip for the holidays, and during the months until we're actually taking off, the dream, and expectation of that holiday is something that gives us strength and energy. Unfortunately, I meet a lot of adults with autism who have nothing exciting to look forward to, ever – nothing to anticipate. No wonder then if they try to create the excitement they can!

10   Manipulation has such a negative ring to it. But don't we all manipulate people all the time? We want to affect people around us. If you want to go to the movies with a friend, and are discussing what film to see, you might try to affect (manipulate!) your friend to want to see the film you had in mind (e.g. by telling her something good you read about this particular film).

about the inappropriate behaviour, than we would be about a two-year-old's way of acting or reacting for the purpose of getting their way, or in different emotional states.

EXAMPLE

I was asked to consult with staff on a forensic psychiatric ward. There was this young woman they could not make any sense of. She was convicted because she had tried to strangle her little sister, only because the sister had Tourette's syndrome and made noises. She had been evaluated but not diagnosed with anything other than mental retardation, a diagnosis which the nurses (rightfully) questioned. But the doctors at this forensic psychiatric hospital did not, as the nurses put it, 'believe in autism'. I was not called there to make a diagnosis (and I do not do that as a line of work), but to give my opinion and help out with practical interventions. From spending two hours with Emma, she struck me as a typical person with high-functioning autism. Not just her extreme sensitivity to sound, but also her uneven development in several areas. She was perfectly able to read quite a complicated text out loud for me, and tell me what it was about (so much for the mental retardation). But she was clueless about everything involving seeing things from another perspective than her own.

Anyway, when it came to behaviour, the nurses told me, she had the oddest behaviour they had ever seen (and nurses in psychiatric wards have seen a lot!). If she couldn't get her way when she wanted something, she would just lie down on the floor and refuse to move or get up. They had tried to punish her for that (there's a lot of punishment going on in forensic psychiatric care, even if it goes by names such as 'detention' and 'withdrawal of benefits'), but it didn't work. 'Well,' I said, 'the first rule is if something doesn't work, then stop doing it and try something else.' But before trying something else we preferably need to understand something about the behaviour.

I asked the nurses if this behaviour (refusing to move/get up) ever occurs in normal development. They looked at me as if they didn't understand what I was talking about, so I asked if they had children – or ever had met small children – and if they'd ever seen a small child throw themselves on the floor and refuse to move. Well, practically all of them had this experience as parents: lifting a screaming two-year-old who refused to put on clothes or go home from nursery school. 'I believe it's the same thing with Emma,' I explained, 'but the thing is that it is way more difficult to just carry a 22-year-old.'[11]

When we speak of the 'terrible twos', we speak of a child who has matured enough as an individual to have the will to affect the environment, but who yet lacks the language and the mentalization skills to do it by other means than behaviour. In high-functioning autism the language may be age appropriate (although the understanding of language can be reduced, generally or in certain situations), but above all, the mentalization development is delayed. Thus, we may (as here) see the 'terrible twenty-twos'. And the person is as little to be blamed for this as is the toddler.

If you read Part 2, 'Understanding the Impairments' you understand that it is not only about cognitive processes and social maturity, but also in concrete terms about how the nervous system develops.

EXAMPLE

Matthew, 19 years, was in a care facility for young adults with autism. Matthew had the 'peculiarities' to pass his stools here and there, in a closet or in his bed, for example. Often, he covered it passably with something that was at hand, and then would not admit to having done it.

The staff had consulted a doctor, who investigated if there was something physically wrong with Matthew's bowel function, but this was not the case. In addition, Matthew used the toilet *sometimes*, which led staff to believe that he always could, 'if only he wanted to' – a relatively common but erroneous conclusion.

A year earlier they had had a psychologist (without autism-specific knowledge) as supervisor, who thought that Matthew's behaviour here could be interpreted on a symbolic level. 'It's a protest,' the psychologist said. Matthew was communicating, according to the psychologist, with

---

11   This was to exemplify the development perspective, but of course you may be curious as to how we solved the situation. As always, it was a combination of several strategies. Emma would get a schedule with activities for all the time she was awake (with rest as an activity too), in order to reduce the 'black holes' where she had no idea what to do. She would get less punishment (as the nurses understood we cannot punish someone for not having developed certain skills, and that having meaningful activities – which were the ones they would withdraw by punishment – often work as a prevention of challenging behaviour). And the nurses started to use social stories, both as a means to explain others' perspectives and to get her development in that area started.

his faeces that he 'doesn't give a shit about you'.[12] Since staff could not see any other explanation, and trusted the psychologist as an expert, this led to the approach that Matthew himself had to take the 'consequences', which could mean that if Matthew had faeces in his bed and had not voluntarily changed the sheets, he had to sleep in it.

EXAMPLE

Gemma, who was 11 years old and went to school, in a normal class, passed her stool in her pants every so often. 'And she doesn't even seem to mind!' exclaimed the astonished teachers. 'We ask her if she does not think it's messy, or that it smells, but she says she does not notice it.'

This may not come as so big a surprise, if we put this into a development perspective. What do we know about the ability to control bowel and bladder? Well, it's a developmental skill, in which individual variability is high even in the 'standard development'.

We know that in the development of children bladder control can happen very early – with or without training – even before the age of a year, or as late as three or four years. We also know that the ability to control the bowel will come later (*after* having learned to control the bladder). For some children, it's only a matter of weeks, while there are other children who use the toilet for emptying the bladder, without having 'accidents' at three, but still use a nappy for their stool at the age of four and even five, in late cases.

Really small children often do not feel, and do not suffer discomfort or distress from, the stools in their nappies, while slightly older children definitely do if they have their stool in their pants. It is of course a matter of the development of the nervous system, sensory systems and body perception. As you perhaps recall, there are often many ages within a single person in autism spectrum disorders.

So after an assessment we made an informed guess that both Matthew and Gemma in terms of ability to control their bowel movement were typical two- to three-year-olds (although they in many other areas were as skilled and well-developed as their peers).

---

12 Excuse me, but that's as stupid as the psychoanalyst who at a lecture talked about the psychoanalytic treatment of a child with autism. And when the child pulled and twitched the doors to a cabinet that was locked (which the child knew held paper and crayons) the analyst told us in the audience that it was his way of saying that he was 'locked in the relationship with his mother'. Or the psychologist who told me that a boy with autism obsessed with 'the delusion' that the sun is going to burn out (which by the way happens to be true, even if it won't happen in our lifetime) was speaking about his father, as the 'sun represents the father, and the moon the mother'. I'm not sure whether to laugh or cry.

In the case of Matthew, he had developed a bit further, since he actually could use the toilet *sometimes*. The thing was that he perceived the signal only when the need was acute, 'I need a toilet *now*' (while Gemma did not even feel that). If Matthew at that moment happened to be next to a toilet, he could certainly go in there. But if there was no toilet within easy steps, then it had to be the closet or anywhere else.

The solution for both Matthew and Gemma, was to schedule the bathroom visits. We decided on a time that could be the same every day. It therefore needed to be a time that worked for all the activities that the person attended, even at home.

For Gemma, for example, it was at ten o'clock in the morning, based on what her family said would work for them, since they usually did not go off somewhere at the weekends before 11 o'clock, and Gemma had never had her stool in her pants before ten o'clock in the morning. Subsequently, both the parents and the school told Gemma that starting tomorrow, she would have a specific time to go to the bathroom. The first day they told Gemma, to 'go to the bathroom to do a poo' at ten o'clock. She also learned that she could sit in peace as long as she needed (and was provided with some comic books while sitting there).

It was thus made clear to Gemma (and to Matthew) that the purpose of the toilet visit was to pass their stool, although it obviously was not presented as some sort of coercion. No one knows if Gemma and Matthew really pass their stool every day when they go to the toilet 'on schedule', but the fact is that neither of them have passed their stool somewhere else after this routine was implemented.[13] Bowel function is actually quite easy to 'time control' – the bowels seem to like a routine.

16.4 Communication

I have already touched on several aspects of communication in this book, but here I want to highlight a few that can be found 'below the surface' when it comes to challenging behaviours.

I have occasionally met adolescents or young adults with autism spectrum disorders who have a very intimidating, unpleasant and aggressive in its content 'verbiage'. My experience is that this often

---

13   Actually, come to think of it, Matthew has had some accidents when he has been out of town and his toilet routines have been disrupted, but in everyday life it works fine.

'masks' another problem (such as social difficulties and lack of communication skills).

I have also met some people who have something I call 'a noise channel'. It is difficult to describe this in words unless you have experienced it, but I'll try.

EXAMPLE

Jake, who was 16 years old and had autism, could blurt out long, bloody and menacing harangues against adults.

I cannot really even try to write what he said but it could be something like 'I'll cut your throat, you bastard, and then I'll hang you upside down and pull out your guts', and so on. You can think of the worst splatter movie you have seen (or heard of) and raise it to the tenth power; then you have Jake's 'noise'. Moreover, his harangues were very long.

Adults around Jake reacted differently to this but most were fairly provoked (even if they acted out different amounts of their feeling). Some felt the need to 'put a foot down and show him that it is not OK'; others refused to talk to him unless he stopped; some still felt that we should kindly ask him to stop; some were calling for a psychologist; some were afraid; some thought he should not remain in school.

I had already, before I met Jake, encountered a similar 'noise channel' of another guy, Ali (although Ali's noise had a completely different content). Ali's noise channel could sound something like, 'I'm so fucking stupid, I'm an ass, I'm a sicko, so fucking dumb, a daft', but much longer. Why I call this 'the noise channel' has nothing to do with the content of what is said, but with a quality that is almost impossible to describe. I perceive the quality of the speech in these cases as forced and obsessive-compulsive or 'Tourette-like' – it sort of flows, or rather wells, out of the individual, but in a rather monotonous and (especially with regard to its content) atonal and unemotional manner. It is as if the person himself is not really present in what is said.

The reason I call this 'the noise channel' is that when working with Ali, I discovered that this verbiage was occurring on one frequency (imagine a radio). Talking to him actually worked well if you 'called him on a different frequency', while the noise was going on in the background. I will not deny that it was demanding to have a conversation this way, but *it was possible*. There was communication.

I decided to try the same approach with Jake.[14] I knew that Jake was interested in cars and therefore I (who know nothing about cars)

---

14 But have I not just taught that you have to make an assessment before choosing an approach? That you cannot just take an approach that worked with one person, and believe that it should work with another. Completely true! But now I stood there with Jake at our first meeting and I had no time to make an assessment first. I used my intuition – you can allow yourself a little 'artistic freedom' when you have reached the higher levels of craftsmanship in the autism field.

had prepared some questions about his interest. I noticed that just like with Ali it worked just fine if I ignored the verbiage and just talked to him on a 'different frequency'. I asked a question and he replied clearly with a normal tone of voice in the midst of his verbiage. The voice he replied with was different from the one he used for his 'noise', which reinforced my belief that these tirades were a kind of vocal tic rather than aggression.

Now we just had to get all the adults in the school to embrace the new strategy: ignore the noise completely and talk to Jake about other things. It was not easy to reach everybody with the message at such a large workplace, but eventually we did. Did Jake cease with these tirades? No, neither he nor Ali did, but they became less frequent as they became more involved in conversations and socializing (none of them could have the 'noise channel' running while talking themselves, and the more they talked, the less noise).

But for Jake the threatening aggressive noise also had offered an identity, because many were afraid of him. And in earlier grades he had been bullied and scared. Therefore, the content of the 'noise channel' had a function (to get respect), and we also had to work with that. For Ali, part the content of the noise was so incredibly destructive of his self-esteem, that we worked very hard to raise his self-esteem.

Figure 16.1: A verbiage perceived as a wall may actually be a door

16.5 There and then, here and now: when someone fights or injures himself

But what can you actually *do*, when someone has a challenging (often acting-out) behaviour? I refer you to Part 4 'Practical Intervention'. That is where we find the tools we need. Actually, we have no special tool just for acting-out behaviour, because the problem cannot be seen as separate from the disability. If there is something specific to challenging behaviour, it is perhaps that the individual may need to learn new skills to deal with frustration and anger.

In the actual situation, when someone has an actual explosion, there is not very much we can do. We back off, lower our voices, refrain from escalating the situation. If we are provoked, we abstain from acting on that feeling.

If a person is verbally provocative, one can say something neutral like: 'Well then, I know what you think.' Or 'OK, I hear what you say (but I like you anyway).' And perhaps, 'I hear that you probably need to be left alone for a while, I will go now but I will be back shortly.' Of course, if our evaluation (assessment) has shown that the stress will increase as a result of spoken language we do not talk at all.

But you might object, 'What if we have a client or pupil who actually harm others?' Yes, that could be the case. I have met clients who have become accustomed to being wrestled down or put in a belt, as I mentioned earlier.[15] Then of course we must try to gradually get them to be accustomed to another way.

For those accustomed to be held down (and where you cannot just stop holding them down because, if you don't, they will hurt someone) we start by putting something in between us and the client; we can, for example, use a chain, a weighted blanket and ball covers.[16]

If we know that the client scratches or grabs us with his hands very hard, we can prepare something to put in the hands of the person (I have cut pieces of pool noodles, a foam swimming toy, but you can probably take anything that is just the right size and provides a good grip). And then we try to back away from the holding by gradually (several times) getting further and further away from the person and leaving him or her with just the blanket.

I am not really comfortable writing about this because I am afraid that someone might perceive it as a 'method' or 'an approach'. It is not. This is an absolute emergency solution to a crisis and can never ever replace the long-term efforts aimed at preventing situations that create stress by using preliminary work, to help the person to develop skills and strategies to handle frustration without acting out. This can be achieved with the help of thorough knowledge of autism and of the individual.

---

15   See Pitfall 3, 'That's the way he wants it!' on p.75.

16   Chain-weighted blankets and ball covers are heavy blankets that apply deep pressure to the body, for some users creating a feeling of safety and 'boundaries' giving a calming effect. See www.weight2goblankets.co.uk and www.sensorydirect.com for more information on this.

17

The Danger of Focusing
on the Behaviour Itself

A Chapter About What Could Happen
If You Do Not Learn to Dive

When I see services where there are individuals with very serious challenging behaviours, I can see that there are some things that these cases have in common. Often, over time, the individual living space has shrunk (both literally and figuratively) and the number and quality of activities have been reduced, instead of, as they should have, been increased and broadened. The staff has simply focused excessively on the behaviour itself and not looked at the big picture. Remember the iceberg metaphor? You could say that they have just stayed on top of the iceberg and not bothered with what is below the surface. There are great risks with this, I'll give you a few examples shortly.

First, let me just show you a picture of what I mean:

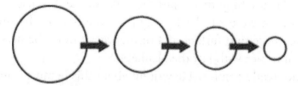

Figure 17.1: Activities and living space may shrink

Because of the problematic behaviour, activities are restricted as well as the living space, which leads to less and less content and space in the individual's life. The reduced space can go from many square feet to zero, from living in their own apartment (perhaps 500 square feet) to being belted in a psychiatric ward (here we're talking about inches of living space!). The content of life, both in terms of intellectual and physical stimulation, becomes less in quality as well as quantity, the more restrained a facility is.

The lack (or non-existence) of meaningful activities in the daily lives of the patients I have met in forensic psychiatry amazed me at first, together with the seemingly complete ignorance of the fact that being engaged in something meaningful is extremely preventive of challenging behaviours.

EXAMPLE

A young woman with autism, OCD and severe self-injurious behaviours was placed in psychiatry under coercion and moved around between different locked psychiatric wards. Her condition would just get worse, and she was considered extremely difficult, hence the moving her from place to place, hoping the next one would succeed better than the previous. Finally, she made a turnaround and was slowly making progress. (And now she lives in her own apartment with only out-patient treatment). When the last facility was asked what they had done differently than the institutions where she had spent the previous ten years, the chief psychiatrist replied: 'I'm not really sure, but here we focus on our patients being occupied with meaningful activities throughout the day.'[1]

Well, let us now get back to an example of how reducing activities and space leads to increased behaviour problems.

EXAMPLE

Richard, who has autism, was 14 years old when he started to get difficult on the school bus. Richard's behaviour worsened – he could, among other things, beat and kick other children. After several warnings, it was decided that it was 'untenable' to allow him to be on the bus, and that he would now have a disability taxi card and take a cab to school.

As you can see, here the focus is on the behaviour without looking at the big picture.

---

1   If you have never been in a locked psychiatric ward you may be surprised how much of the time is unstructured, and just passed hanging around waiting for the next meal, or for your therapy (which may sometimes at the best be 2 × 45 minutes out of the week's 10,080 minutes). And since very little is happening, there's very little to talk about, which means people with poor social skills may even deteriorate in that area. My estimation is that substantially more than 50 per cent of the conversation going on between patients and caretakers is about sleep, since obviously many of the patients have trouble with sleeping. But is that meaningful conversation? Sure, they do good work too, and the therapy and medication can be very helpful – but they certainly could do better. Of course it is a matter of finances, number of staff, etc. But it is also, to a high degree, a matter of culture; it has 'always been like this' (i.e. mostly 'storage', combined with medical treatment and seeing a therapist twice a week) and therefore it is not questioned. And sure, at an acute stage of psychiatric illness you may need a lot of rest, but when spending years and years in coercive care you need meaningfulness and activity.

Questions like these were never asked and answers found: 'Is Richard depressed?',[2] 'Is Richard bullied?' (i.e. is there a reason why Richard hits those other children?); 'What does Richard's everyday life look like, and is there something happening right before or during the bus trip that triggers his behaviour?'; 'Does the trip work out better with some drivers than with others, and if so, why?'; 'Does Richard have strategies for dealing with anger and frustration?'; and so on.

Since Richard has autism and 'fights', it is taken for granted that the problem lies with him and the focus is on 'eliminating the behaviour'. This is typically done with reprimands, complaints and nagging, resulting in a lot of negative feedback to Richard ('You cannot…'; 'You must learn to…'; You must understand that you are not allowed to…) Also, typically, focusing on what he should *not do*, as opposed to what he *could do instead*.

Negative feedback often breeds negative emotions, which in turn reduces the person's self-confidence and sense of competence.

As the activities and living space (and yes, a taxi is smaller than a bus) is reduced, Richard may feel an increased frustration. In the absence of adequate strategies to express and deal with his frustration Richard will now have *even more* of the behaviour that was originally identified as the problem. And this can, paradoxically, lead to Richard's life shrinking further.

Now Richard starts to exhibit a behaviour (now interpreted as 'aggressive' and 'violent') also in the cab. Cab drivers say they cannot drive safely with a child going berserk in the car. Therefore, this solution too becomes 'untenable' and adults are perplexed – how will Richard now get to school?

They see no other way than that Richard should be home-schooled, but with support from social services and the school. A teacher and a social worker will visit him now and then, and he will be in email touch with other teachers. Now Richard's world is very small; he rarely leaves home at all. That Richard is a person with a great desire for social interaction (even if his disability means that this is difficult for him, he likes being around people) was never considered.

Now Richard is under-stimulated and bored. He perhaps also feels 'punished' – it is a fact that because of his disability, he is no longer allowed to attend school (of course, his surroundings would not put it this way, since they see the behaviour as distinct from the disability rather than as a consequence of it).

Richard now (still) handles his frustration in the only way he can, by beating and screaming. This affects the teacher who provides home-schooling, and the social worker, and they are both ultimately so afraid of Richard that it is considered a work hazard, and they stop coming. Now Richard has no schooling at all, and will almost never get outside the house. It becomes more and more unlikely that Richard ever will improve.

---

2   Increased irritability is a common symptom of depression in teenagers.

Now Richard is 16 years old, his self-image is that he is violent and unsuccessful, and the likelihood that Richard will ever be functioning in the community seems very small.

EXAMPLE

Laila had mild mental retardation and autism, and was living in an apartment with a group of personal assistants who would help her around the clock. Laila had earlier lived in a group home for people with learning disabilities, but was considered 'too difficult'.

Laila would, when she was stressed or upset, destroy things. She could trash furniture to smithereens, and shred clothing and other textiles beyond recognition. If you could call it a skill, she was extremely skilled in trashing and shredding. But her staff group had no autism craft skills, so they never asked the relevant questions, but focused only on her behaviour (the peak of the iceberg). Subsequently they stored away and locked up all the stuff that could be broken. In the room where Laila now lived there was nothing – *absolutely nothing* – other than a couch fastened to the floor.

But what do you think happened when Laila no longer was able to smash things, and the cause was not yet addressed?

You guessed right! Laila started smashing *people* instead. This resulted in bruises and injuries among staff. Laila was extremely strong and soon became equally adept at breaking people as she had ever been at breaking things (practice makes perfect, unfortunately). Long-term sick leave, health and safety problems and redundancies were part of the result.

When I arrived at Laila's place there were 13 people employed on a schedule that meant that you were never fewer than three simultaneously, in order for staff to be able to overpower her, and if necessary, take her to a psychiatric ward where she would be restrained with a belt. Many of the previous staff had left, and most employees were now men who had courage and physical strength, rather than knowledge of care on their CVs (and they certainly had no autism-specific knowledge).

The approach continued on the beaten track. If Laila injured personnel, they never asked themselves why or what triggered it. Instead they would overpower her, as before, and additionally they had a grille door installed to divide the apartment into two parts, with staff on one side and Laila on the other. But what do you think happened when Laila was no longer able to hurt people, and the cause was not yet addressed?

You guessed right again! Laila began hurting *herself* instead. Now she did not have many tools at her disposal of course. (On her side of the grille gate there was only the one bed that was bolted to the floor, with no sheets, cover or anything. Nothing more. Really, nothing.)

But Laila was inventive and would pull a plug from the wall and put her fingers in the socket and scream that she did not want to live.

And even after this had been going on for a while until the plugs were covered too, it had not led to an inquiry into possible depression! Well, having no other means, she pulled out her own fingernails and, even worse, she put her fingers behind her eye ball and was trying to rip out her own eyes. The very sad thing in this story is perhaps that staff in their ignorance actually prompted a serious self-injurious behaviour which had not been present at the beginning.

How did we help Laila? Well, this is also a sad part. Laila is unfortunately one of those that I could not help. The people in charge thought that the educational effort that I felt necessary was 'too expensive', and therefore my contribution amounted to next to nothing. But I have heard that after things had gone badly for Laila for a long time, she had an entire new staff group, with a better understanding of autism, and things have now begun to take a turn for the better.

Figure 17.2: Can the individual be expected to fit the service?

How to help and support is described in many other places in this book, and the meaning of this chapter is really to try to make clear the risks of focusing on the behaviour, and specifically warn you about becoming part of the problem instead of being part of the solution. Perhaps you will not meet as 'difficult' cases as Laila in your line of work, but I would guess that working in the autism field means you will occasionally encounter a 'Richard'. And if you contribute to the excessive focus on the behaviour itself (and seek the solution only in trying the easiest way 'to remove the behaviour'), you can also contribute to a worsening situation.

Well, unfortunately, the list of cautionary tales could be long, but I guess I have made my point, so let's not dwell too long in despair.[3] Just one more thing.

There is another thing that these people have in common, those whom I call 'the most difficult' – namely that they have had to move many, many times. 'Richard/Laila does not fit our services' is a common phrase. And then they do not fit the next service, nor the group home after that. Can you imagine? 'It will be better for Richard/Laila at another service' is now the phrase of the day. 'And now we found this care home, they will surely know how to help.' Then after six months, this new care home says 'Richard/Laila does not fit our services.' But, let me ask you this: if this is a service specializing in autism and Richard or Laila has such a diagnosis, where would they be better off? And perhaps the most pressing issue (excuse me for shouting):

IS IT LAILA AND RICHARD WHO SHOULD CHANGE TO FIT THE SERVICE OR SHOULD THE SERVICE CHANGE TO FIT THEM?

Thus, do we not need to make some changes in the way we work, here and now, if we are not successful in supporting Laila or Richard? Especially if we know that many moves increase the risk of very serious behaviour problems. Naturally, there you should never generalize; there are times when a move can be for the better. But most often it is not. Often it is better to use counselling and education to radically alter the approaches and the social interchange to better suit the client.

Here I finally just want to say that if your current approach – the type of support and the tools you currently use – does not work, well then, doing more of the same thing will not work either. You must do things differently. There are several ideas in this book on how you can work (for practical ideas see Part 4), but above all you need to reverse the movement. Richard's and Laila's lives must be *extended*, the meaningful content of everyday life and activities must become *more*, not less, the frequency of *positive feedback must increase* – in

---

3   Do you know what makes me really sad when it comes to people who are acting out or have other challenging behaviours? That it is so easy to help many of them, but they do not receive the support, aids and adjustments they need, but must live with a significantly lower quality of life than they could have. But do you know what makes me very happy when it comes to people who are acting out or have other challenging behaviours? That it is so easy to help many of them, and that *you* can be one of them contributing to getting adequate help!

that self-esteem and sense of competence increases. The circles must become wider. The movement must be reversed:

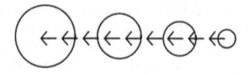

Figure 17.3: Shrinkage in activities and living space must be reversed, and the user's life expanded

PART 4

Practical Intervention

*The Things You May Need
in Your Toolbox*

18

The Toolbox

An Introduction to the Tools

In line with my metaphor of craftsmanship, I believe you also need to have a well-stocked toolbox. But if you skipped the previous chapters, I would urge you to read Chapter 15 about the assessment before you read this chapter. There is a purpose in having this chapter at the end of the book – in my experience many helpers actually have lots of the tools but lack craftsmanship. There is an idiom that says 'Bad workmen always blame their tools', and it may be true here too. If one lacks a quality craftsmanship, perhaps one does not understand how to use the tools, or why a particular tool is appropriate for a particular purpose.

What should we have in our toolbox as 'autism workers'? Well, perhaps first I should clarify that this toolkit is dynamic, and as far from static as you can imagine. It must be developed constantly, and each tool necessarily tailored to the individual. As for the tools: it's about such things as practical aids; developing skills for the future; adjustments of the environment (including people in the environment); information; professional development; specific approaches and methodologies (such as social stories, and CAT-kit), conversations and communication. The tricky thing is that what one moment is a tool, is found in the next moment to be a way to practise skills. These areas all blend into one another and are thus not easy to categorize.

But let me first draw some basic guidelines. Our tools must, to the largest extent possible, compensate for the difficulties the individual has, increase autonomy and create a life that is meaningful, understandable and lucid. This is why, when we are using a tool, we should also know what it is compensating for, and deliberately have chosen the tool that provides most autonomy. In my experience this is often not the case. If staff have a toolkit where a few tools rattle at the bottom of the case, but they lack quality craftsmanship, they can come to use their tools in a relatively inflexible way, and without really knowing why.

The more I work with tools and compensatory strategies, the more uncertain I become of what it is about a particular aid that *really* makes it helpful.

In my experience, an aid, strategy or adjustment certainly offers something that compensates for a difficulty, but the fact that we offer a tool is also a major part of the help, because our offer conveys a message: 'I understand that you have a difficulty, I see that you need support.' And for people who are often blamed for their difficulties, who often get the message (even if not in so many words): 'You can do better if you just want to', I believe the mere offer of support is a substantial part of the help.

It is also a fact that we cannot always know exactly what an aid compensates for. Sometimes, when I believe that an aid will compensate for lack of imagination, it may in fact be that it offers a moment of shift of focus, and that is what helps. A tool can also be an approach, and a person who over a period of time needs many adjustments of the environment, may eventually need more training and development of skills. Thus, tools can change.

What I am trying to say is that we cannot always, in every moment, know exactly why we do what we do. But in my opinion it still must be a goal to get as close to always knowing as we can.

The point to make about the examples I give here is that they are *examples*. Once you understand the clients or pupils with autism spectrum disorders in your service or school, you can use the principles of compensation and autonomy to invent your own specific tools and strategies. And then they will be suited to your clients. Therefore, the chapters in this section are to be seen more as pointers for the various tool categories, rather than an exhaustive description of every possible tool that could be used.

In the case of using adjustments as a tool, I meet some staff who are afraid of making too many adjustments.

EXAMPLE

Kevin, seven years old, who had autism, had a behaviour in school that staff called 'acting police'. He would tell all the other children what they could and could not do, what was allowed and what wasn't. This was a problem since it made him unpopular with his peers.

When we had done an assessment, we saw that his behaviour was the result of stress, and that environments that made great demands on his sensory system were one of the things that stressed him most. The time and place where he would exhibit this behaviour most often was in the queue for the school canteen (a time of day when he also, of course, was hungry, which we all know can affect our behaviour). A canteen queue is noisy and there are lots of unpredictable movements, and Kevin was sensitive to both sound and touch.

'Let us begin by reducing stress for Kevin,' I suggested, 'Let him go before the others in the queue.'

'But what will happen if we do that? How will life turn out for him if we just make exceptions and he never learns to stand in line and wait?' the teachers exclaimed.

The first question that arises is whether he can really learn to stand in line by simply standing in line? Has not experience already shown that this is not so? The second question we must ask is whether 'to stand in line' is an important skill? The answer to this may be both yes and no, or maybe later, but not right now. It depends on Kevin, his difficulties, the environment, what his family thinks, and so on.

But even if we conclude that it is an important skill for Kevin, we cannot train this skill in a situation where hunger and sensory stress are at their peak. If we are to teach a new skill, we find – as every teacher knows, but sometimes forgets when it comes to learning outside the curriculum – a positive learning opportunity. If we want to teach Kevin to stand in line, we let him jump the queue at lunchtime, but find other opportunities to practise the skill itself, in a positive context, and beginning on a small scale.

I could take many similar examples from real life but will limit myself to one more.

EXAMPLE

Julie, who had high-functioning autism, was 15 years old. Julie's teachers felt that Julie must do a group project to get her grades. The special education teacher agreed, saying 'You can't go through life without working in a team anyway'.

Again we must ask ourselves whether to work in groups is an important skill, and here the answer was yes; even Julie herself thought so. But is it reasonable that she should practise on something that her disability makes very difficult for her, while she has to perform intellectually at the same time?

Is it reasonable to work on a difficulty, to train a skill, while doing a project that will be graded?[1] Or should we create positive learning opportunities where the pupil can practise just being in a group and then eventually, when the skill is learned, work in a group?

Another experience I have of using aids and adaptations is that sometimes the staff do not see the need for an aid, and instead make the individual more dependent on their environment. There are already several examples of this in this book, as in the example of Harold and Stella on p.162.

If we are able to create a tool, an aid, that provides more autonomy, we should. But there is a time for everything.

Kevin, for example, was too stressed out to start using a tool in the queue situation, which is why we used an adaptation instead (letting him jump the queue). It is not uncommon, especially if we are to start working with someone who has not had that much autism-specific support before, that we start with adjustments and then, when stress is reduced, get on to the practice of new skills and the use of aids.

In the next chapters, each group of tools will have a specific chapter, but they are not ranked in any kind of 'most important to least important' way. All are important, and what will be useful for an individual varies a lot. And, as I already mentioned, even if it looks as though the tools are quite distinct, they blend.

---

1 Do you think it would be fair if I demanded of you to ride an exercise bike *while* reading this book, just because it is important that you exercise?

19

Not Having to Learn to Be the Same as 'Others'

A Chapter on Adjustments

Being willing to make adjustments is of course essential. I am thinking of a teacher I once had a discussion with. One of his pupils, Daniel, would explode every time he received a vague answer to a question. Daniel, who had autism, could not handle the vague expressions that are quite common in spoken conversation. If Daniel asked his teacher something and the teacher replied 'We'll talk about that later' or 'We'll see about that', Daniel would become very upset. It was not unusual that he threw the book on the floor and shouted and cursed. The teacher saw this as a behaviour problem, while I perceived it as a language comprehension problem.

We discussed for a while, and eventually, the teacher understood what I meant and could see the situation from another perspective. I breathed a quiet sigh of relief. But I should not have counted my chickens until they had hatched, since the teacher – after having thought about this for a while – stated: 'OK but it is really hard for me to think about how I talk! And besides, people talk like this, and kids with autism will just have to learn to be like others!'

I am completely convinced that it would be entirely alien to this teacher to reason like this if he had a physically disabled student who used a wheelchair. He would hardly say: 'OK, the classroom is located on the third floor but it is really hard for us to rebuild or to change classrooms. Besides we all use the stairs, and kids with no legs will just have to learn to be like others!'

Resistance to adjustments is often based on lack of understanding of the difficulties, paired with a fear that people will become 'lazy', or even 'spoilt', if you make many adjustments. What could an adjustment involve for Daniel? An adaptation of the teacher's communication is what first comes to mind. Many people with autism spectrum disorders need to be with people who adapt their style and their social communication to make it understandable for the individual. (Of course, one could – outside of the classroom situation – also support Daniel in learning language comprehension skills).

Adjustments can furthermore be about making changes in the environment (for example, for those who have sensory problems),[1] or in what activities one participates, as well as how and when to participate.

As I said earlier, if you can create a tool that will make the client able to participate on a nearly equal footing with others, it is obviously preferable compared to making an adaptation (which may mean that the person is not participating in the activity at all).

EXAMPLE

A nursery school was about to get a teacher's assistant for Hedda, a five-year-old girl with autism, who also had great difficulties with motor automatization. Hedda often did not, due to her difficulties, have the energy to make the walk to the nearby park. The staff were now going to make an adjustment, and planned that when the resource teacher had arrived, she could stay indoors with Hedda while staff took the other children to the park. It is not uncommon to reason like this. But here we have to ponder: what is the *purpose* of going to the park? Is it *walking* to the park or *being in* the park? And if the purpose is to *be* in the park (which the pedagogues usually say when asked) then surely it is better to use the resource teacher to take Hedda there in a buggy?

The main thing to understand about adjustments is that they are never general to the impairment, but are based on an assessment of the individual. It means that we can never say that it 'should' be this or that, because of a certain diagnosis. Adjustments are very much about finding a good balance between demands and capacity.

Adjustments should be based on individual needs, not the needs of the service. By this I mean that sometimes I have seen examples of how the reference to adapted curriculum has excluded pupils with autism from, for example, parts of physical education, when the actual reason is that the school found it 'too difficult' or lacked resources to include them.[2]

---

1   Please, do not forget that *you* are part of the environment, and therefore an adjustment can be a matter of doing or saying (or not doing or saying) things in a certain way.

2   By all means, I am not saying that an *adapted curriculum cannot be useful, I am saying that it is the pupil's needs that should rule the intervention, not the school's.*

At times an individual can need more and extensive adjustments, as when the level of stress is high. But be sure to really take stock of which situations are stressful, so you do not make the wrong kind of adjustments.

Finally, adjustments can also of course be what are known as home adaptations. For this you typically need a visit from an occupational therapist, and the social security department of your local council can make an assessment of the home. Examples of housing adaptations for people with autism are a bath (instead of a shower) in the case of tactile over-sensitivity, sound insulation of the apartment for auditory over-sensitivity, and blackout curtains to help with light sensitivity.

20

Inform More – and Well!

A Chapter on How We Can Work with Information as a Tool

I believe that information is a tool that you should have in your toolbox, and also a well-thought-out strategy for how to provide information when needed. It may be informing family and relatives as well as informing our client.

Mainly I am thinking of information about autism spectrum disorders, the diagnosis and its consequences. Of course, it is related to how we will provide information about other things, and about having a joint plan in our service for how we communicate with families.

20.1 Surroundings

If we have a thought-out approach to information, it can mean that we will arrange information evenings for families, or that we (together with the client/pupil) put together a dossier on what support we perceive that she needs and why. This becomes a documentation which we can easily communicate to parents (or other services our client uses). It can of course also be that we invite the parents and other relatives to network, since we know that many may have a need to share their experiences. We can invite siblings to meet, and why not arrange a meeting for the grandparents, if we work with children?

What I mean by using information as a tool, is that we have a strategy for it, a plan for how and when we use it. This includes, of course, that we have developed an 'information package' for these occasions. If you find it difficult to lecture or lead a discussion about the disability, you can use materials from, for example, the National Autistic Society (www.autism.org.uk). We may also have put together some text about our service, how we work and the ethos of our approach, which, together with tips on literature and support groups can be put into the hands of the relatives.

It can also be a good idea to contact the local branch of the autism society. Perhaps someone from the branch could come and speak at a meeting? If we know what local support there is, it is easier for us to refer families to them. When informing younger peers you can use films such as 'Asperger's syndrome explained for children', an episode of the children's show *Arthur* available on YouTube.[1]

20.2 The individual

Regarding information for the child, pupil, user or client, this is something I am often asked about. Perhaps the most common question concerns the idea of how to help the client with something that staff and family call 'disability awareness'. One of the problems associated with this inquiry is the notion that you could actually provide anyone with an awareness, since this is not possible. Awareness is closely linked to insights, and an insight can be obtained, but not given. Awareness is raised within a person; it is not an 'implant' that can be put there by someone else.

Furthermore, how Ivan views the fact that he has autism and what this means to him in his life can differ completely from how Ann and Peter view the same fact. It is not even the case that one kind of 'disability awareness' is predominant. This is true for all disabilities – for example, not that everyone with hearing loss has the same opinion of what it means for them to have no hearing, or a hearing that differs from others. How one understands and relates to one's diagnosis is as unique as the individual you are. What the people closest to you can do is not put an implant of a complete (their own) belief into the mind of the person with the diagnosis, but create conditions for the person to (in their own way) understand and reflect on what the diagnosis means to him.

In my experience absolutely the best way to do this is to go into an exploration together. I am surprised sometimes when I hear staff take on the 'expert role', and tell Ivan or Ann what the diagnosis means. It can sometimes be staff who do not have much knowledge at all, while we can assume that Ann and Ivan actually have the best opportunities of having knowledge about themselves.

---

1   Go to www.youtube.com and type 'Asperger's syndrome explained for children' in the search field. You can find more useful material on YouTube (but you may have to search a bit since there is a lot of nonsense on YouTube too).

Going into a joint exploration can be reading texts together. You can start with texts that are autobiographical, or similar. You can prepare, look for articles or sections of books that you think the person is reasonably able to recognize something in. It is good if you've looked at the texts in advance so you can be prepared for questions that may arise. It is about you being a conversation partner with whom the individual explores his or her strengths, personality traits and difficulties, and reflects on how and where these have to do with the diagnosis. It can be laid out in the form of a 'course' or a programme, where you do this one hour per week.

In some services it fits in well to do this in groups, and participation is of course always voluntary. In my experience even those who are a bit reluctant to participate, and who never say anything, at these occasions can hear and take in a lot.

In Chapter 3, I talked about reaching a conclusion about which side of 'normal' you are, and I used the runway as an analogy for coming down on one side or another. I actually think 'landing the diagnosis', is a better term than, for example, 'disability awareness'. Of course there is no 'right' or 'wrong' side of the normality 'border'– there isn't even such a border. But in most people's (especially young people's) minds, there is. And receiving a psychiatric diagnosis means you need to handle this, 'to land the diagnosis'. And as I wrote in Chapter 3, since the runway looks different for each individual, the 'approach' will too. The person with the disability is the pilot, and your role is rather to be air traffic controllers, cabin crew and marshall,[2] namely to serve the pilot to make the landing safe.

It does not require that you have all the theoretical knowledge (this you can, as I mentioned, search together), but is more about your interest in, attention to, respect for and support of the process.

I want to emphasize again that as staff it is not your job to say what is right or wrong, as in these examples.

---

2   Aircraft marshalling is the visual aid the pilot receives from the ground crew, known as marshalls, leading the plane right when it is about to park.

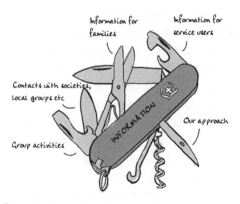

Figure 20.1: Information is a multi-tool

EXAMPLE

Ivan: I think it's quite hard to know what to say when I come into a library.

Staff: Well Ivan, that happens to all of us. I also think it's very difficult to know what to say sometimes.

If Ivan just now was beginning to explore what the diagnosis means for him, how it affects him, the staff's comment in this example can effectively put a lid on the continued exploration. The staff communicates that they know better than Ivan, that what Ivan is experiencing has nothing to do with his diagnosis, and is not to be taken seriously.

EXAMPLE

Ann: I do not have autism. Those who have autism are totally unsocial, and I am not!

Staff: But Ann, you *do* have autism, you know that. And we can see that you have difficulty with social interaction as well.

Here staff are steamrolling Ann, and telling her that they are in possession of the answer to who she is.

EXAMPLE

Peter: If I have trouble sleeping, is this to do with autism?

Staff: No, having trouble sleeping has nothing to do with the diagnosis.

Here staff give a dead sure answer to something they actually do not have enough knowledge about.

But what to do and what to say? There is no template, but if you try using a more open, conversational style, the answers can then be something like:

- Well, I also wonder how it all comes together. Let's look on the internet, and see if there are others with autism who have similar experiences.

- How does it feel when it is difficult to know what to say?

- Let's see if we can find out more about how people with autism are, if they really are as unsocial as you say. I do not know for sure, but I do not think it has to be so.

- I would like to learn more about how you think, can you tell me?

A good idea is to read texts written by, or about, people with autism spectrum disorders together with the client, and encourage the client to reflect on such things as similarities and differences. To not recognize some things is just as good (and just as important) as to recognize. What we want to do is start the reflective process.

If you read interviews in magazines, take the opportunity to also critically discuss journalists' knowledge of autism – not everything is correct. Journalists often have no detailed knowledge of the subjects they write about.

Figure 20.2: 'Everything begins with building a trusting relationship'

'I do not have any bloody autism!'

Some do not accept their diagnosis. This is particularly common among adolescents who received their diagnosis in their teens. There may be many factors that contribute to this. It is a balancing act to meet those who are unwilling to accept their diagnosis (and who often do not want to receive the help they need). It requires sensitivity, and everything begins with building a trusting relationship. Before you and your client have a relationship, before he or she has confidence in you, there's no use trying to make the individual 'accept his diagnosis'.

Amongst those who are negatively disposed to the diagnosis, it can work out better if we start by discussing the legal rights that come with the diagnosis, that is, to make the entrance to the subject more about actually having certain rights (and strengths), rather than having particular difficulties. The strengths are of course always important, but some already know what they're good at and are not particularly susceptible to 'flattery', and then speaking of legal rights can be a way forward.

Sometimes I have stressed that with knowledge about autism, you also have the opportunity to make more reasonable demands on those around you; you can get them to listen to you and your needs if you understand them better yourself.

Here are some ideas of what questions you can start with (various issues fit differently, of course, depending on whether you are talking to children, adolescents or adults):

- Why do you have specific rights when you have a diagnosis?

- What is the Equality Act?

- What kind of support is possible:
  - when moving out?
  - with leisure?
  - with employment?

- What kind of support is common for adults with autism in their daily lives?

- What is an occupational therapist, and what can they do for you?

- Is it hard to get the support you are entitled to, and how do you go about getting the support?

- Which support or adjustments are you entitled to if you have trouble doing certain kinds of assignments in schools, such as team work or oral presentations?

Occasionally I meet a person with autism in a service who believes that he or she does not have any disability at all, but in fact is more of a member of staff. It is common for staff groups to feel frustrated and find it difficult to know how to interact with this person. Some of the staff advocate frankness (sometimes to the point of bluntness) and want to tell the client that he is certainly not working there. Others want to be 'softer'.

As usual, I think we need a common approach and that it should be a long-term one. To just hammer a message of what *you* perceive as 'reality' into someone who is not ready for it (and does not share the same perception of reality) has rarely, if ever, worked. We must build a strong long-term relationship where we provide the client with increased self-esteem and a sense of competence. And this is how easy and wonderful it is: when you get your everyday life to function well, when you feel at least somewhat good about yourself, then you become more ready to see and understand your difficulties.

Sharing experiences with others

Information in a group of children, adolescents and adults can sometimes be more open in its nature, with discussions of different themes that you might first read something short about and then allow participants to exchange experiences.

Some years ago I, together with two psychologists (Siw Hogberg and Pamela Wilkner) had a project where we informed children of the diagnosis. It was quite a few years ago, but much of what we did then is still valid. We had two groups, one with teenagers 13–16 years old, and one with children 9–12 years old. Many, both parents and families, raised concerns about informing children as young as the youngest group, but in fact we found that group was the easiest to handle. At nine you are old enough to understand many things, but do not yet have as many prejudices or ideas of how things 'should be' as a teenager. The participants in the younger group also spontaneously shared many experiences, while the older group were more hesitant. We had plans for the content of each session, but we also had to be flexible, as for example bullying was a theme brought up by the participants, which they (unfortunately) had many experiences of and needed to discuss. We found (in both groups) that the children were strengthened (and this was confirmed by parents) by getting adequate information about their disorder, and by meeting others who shared similar experiences.

The structure for the group was 12–15 participants and two group leaders. Everybody received an 'out' card and were instructed they just had to hold up their card if they for any reason wanted to leave the room. We had a postbox for questions in case participants wanted to be anonymous or found it difficult to ask their questions out loud in the group. The group met five times in total, for one hour and 30 minutes each meeting. Topics were, among other things 'Why is it called Asperger syndrome?'; 'What does it mean (with some basic information about the brain and how you can know that you have it)?'; 'Difficulties and strengths'; and 'How can you explain it to others?' Our goal was that each one should have a written-down explanation of autism, that made sense to themselves, that they could use to explain to others. All in all, the experiences of the project were extremely positive and resulted in it becoming a model for the work of the habilitation centre in Stockholm.

In this project we had no adult groups, but later, in other services I worked with we did have such groups for adults. Here are some examples of themes to discuss with adolescents and adults:

- *Getting up/getting going/getting out.* Problems with your 'start engine'? Difficulty finishing things? Difficulty choosing and prioritizing? Exchange of experiences and tips.

- *Night and day, sleep and wakefulness.* Advantages and disadvantages of being up all night and sleeping in the daytime. Fatigue although you slept? Difficulty falling asleep, waking up many times during the night? Exchange of experiences and tips.

- *Attention and concentration.* When is it easy or hard to focus? Exchange of experiences and tips.

- *Public transport – problems and solutions?* Experiences and tips.

- *Time.* Are you fast/slow? Is it hard to make changes in plans, for example cancel scheduled events, or spontaneously do something not planned?

...and so on. I am sure you can come up with other interesting and useful topics.

Speaking about the actual disability to those whom it concerns is a balancing act. Sometimes I meet with groups of staff who tiptoe around it, and hardly dare mention the 'A' word. Occasionally I meet staff groups who use the diagnosis in almost every circumstance. Neither of these extremes are especially successful. With a well-thought-out plan for how to provide information it is easier. There are of course a lot of staff who can converse about the diagnosis in a balanced and respectful way, but in my experience many of them feel insecure.

Finally, some general advice about when you should inform the individual about the diagnosis:

- View yourself as the one who plants the seed for the ability to reason about and respond to their diagnosis, but try to avoid having too much of an opinion on what it is that is growing. You sow and water the plant but let the plant take its own form. You are not the chief horticulturist, but rather provide plant support.

- Avoid putting on the expert's hat. You are not the one with all the answers; instead volunteer to be a sounding board and to make a joint exploration.

- Be curious. If you're curious, about people in general and the individual in particular, it can be contagious, and the client can become curious too, about himself and others.

- Avoid negatively charged words such as 'illness', 'disability' and 'problems' and instead use more neutral words such as 'autism' or 'diagnosis'.

21

Written, Drawn and Other Visual Aids

An Important Chapter on Aid
That Too Many Get Too Little Of!

A tool can be so many different things, look so different, and in the services I am working with new ones are constantly invented. That is why I cannot give any definitive list, but have tried to include examples that can inspire you and give you new ideas.

There are many traditional aids that may be considered, such as the time aids (there are several), hand-held computers, schedules (such as whiteboards and other day or week planners), and the ball covers I mentioned in Chapter 16. You will read more about traditional aids in the last chapter of this book. Even though I call them 'traditional', a Swedish survey (Stälhardske and Hägg) shows that as few as ten per cent of people with psychiatric disorders receive aids in Sweden (this figure includes all psychiatric disorders). I doubt the situation is much better in any European country.

In this chapter I am thinking more of the aids we may invent or create ourselves – ways to compensate for deficits and increase autonomy and independence. Many of the tools work to make things clear and lucid, and they often compensate for the lack of imagination. I'll try to give you ideas and inspiration through my examples, but this is no recipe to cook an aid soup. You must yourselves – based on the knowledge you have (knowledge of disability and knowledge of individuals, obtained through assessments and other means) – develop the aids that best suit your client or pupil.

21.1 Choices and ability to form mental images

It is not uncommon in autism spectrum disorders to have problems with choices; some individuals become very stressed by situations that require a choice. When there is a choice you need your imagination to see the options in front of you (if they are not visually made clear for you) and you also need to be able to predict the consequences of the choices made. It is no wonder that one can be stressed out by this if the ability to elaborate alternatives in your mind is reduced. As I've mentioned, many people with autism spectrum disorders have difficulties creating the kind of pictures that, for example, you may see inside your head when you read a novel. This not only makes novels uninteresting for these people (and non-fiction books more interesting), but can also affect the ability to see the result of a task while performing it, and can make choices very difficult.

EXAMPLE

Nicole, who had autism, had great difficulties with choices. She would get stressed, and sometimes threw herself screaming on the floor.

Nicole was in a service where supper was served as a buffet. The management felt it was nice that there was plenty to choose from, and that the young people themselves could pick just exactly what they wanted. A lovely idea, although not for Nicole. The staff discussed whether they would, for Nicole's sake, let go of the buffet idea. Perhaps they should just serve one course? Or should Nicole have a single dish served before the other residents ate?

I suggested that we should choose a solution that gave Nicole the highest degree of independence possible, and that also meant that we did not prevent the other residents (who had no problems with choices) from choosing from a buffet. This meant creating an aid for Nicole, rather than making adjustments in the environment.

Since Nicole liked maps, we made her a 'buffet map' (had Nicole had another special interest, we might have used this if possible). The map of the dining hall had a path drawn from the entrance door to the big table with the buffet, and then to her seat. On the picture of the buffet table we put velcro. Then we made pictures of every meal, cut out and laminated and with velcro on the back. The next day, Nicole was told, before entering the dining hall, that she had her own map, where her choice of dish and drink was already made. It went splendidly. Nicole looked at her map, and followed the visual instructions, and no screaming (read, no stress) occurred.

Now, since this went so well, we could not resist trying to increase her independence further. So a few weeks later, one of the staff said 'Psst, Nicole, come into the kitchen!' before the meal.

When Nicole came into the kitchen the staff member showed her pictures of two different meals served that day and said: 'Which one will we put on your map today, Nicole?'

Nicole made a choice without difficulty, both because she could see the choices visually, and certainly also because she could make the choice in an environment that was not nearly as difficult for her sensory system as when in a dining hall with ten other teenagers.

Today Nicole, before meals, independently goes into the kitchen and chooses from pictures of today's meals and drinks, puts the ones she wants on the map and brings it to the dining hall. This is a typical example of how something that starts as an aid, also can contribute to the development of skills!

To be clear, let me point out the benefits of this strategy (an aid): Nicole feels no stress; others do not have to adjust according to Nicole's needs; Nicole can develop new choice-making skills; Nicole is participating in the meal situation independently; and last but not least, Nicole has an aid that can be used in other settings. If we are going with Nicole to a restaurant we can obviously not call and ask them to only have one meal on the menu, but with her map she can cope with such an environment; that is, we call the restaurant and ask for the menu and put a choice on Nicole's map beforehand.

If we in the assessment find that an individual has difficulties with making choices, we always try (as with Nicole) to show choices visually. Thus we never just ask 'Do you want pizza or hamburgers?' without showing our suggestions (or pictures of them).

21.2 Informed choices

Another aspect of choices is what I would call informed choices. By that I mean that rather than telling a person what is 'best' or imperceptibly choosing for him or her, we try to clarify (in pictures and text if necessary) the consequences of different choices.

So when Joan, who is 22 years old and has autism, wanted to put out a nude picture of herself on her blog on the net, we did not tell her that this is inappropriate. Instead, we helped Joan to understand the possible consequences of her choices, in order for her to have more information to inform her choice. The choice, however, is hers to make.

Her disability makes her unable to imagine different possible outcomes of her actions. We sat down, together with Joan, and drew on a paper (to compensate for her lack of internal images). We made a simple sketch of her computer with the nude picture of her, and then of other people's computers, where they might see her picture. We then drew some scenarios. We said that this is John, at his computer, he might think you are good-looking and write a post on your blog about it. We discussed with Joan what this would feel like.[1]

And then we said that at a different computer is Charlie, and he may think that if you show yourself off like this on the internet, this must mean that you want to have sex with anyone, and perhaps he will post suggestions about sex (and how would you feel about this?). And here is Lisa at a different computer and she might be provoked by your picture, and she might write some nasty posts on the blog about you (and how would this make you feel?).

After we had in this manner visually made clear some of the possible consequences, Nicole was better equipped to make her own choice. Perhaps she would still want to post the picture – she might feel OK with the risks – or she might decide not to. The choice was hers. We helped her to understand.

21.3 Stress, overview and time

Another example of visual clarification is a very simple device, an almanac or a calendar. This can obviously compensate for difficulties with memory and time perception.[2] There are plenty of aids for memory problems (for more suggestions see Chapter 25). A schedule like that devised by TEACCH (see p.299), with velcro and pictures, may be helpful for some. But many with high-functioning autism want something more discreet as they grow older. Unfortunately the calendar on a cell phone is not that useful for many, as it is still quite difficult to get an overview of activities there.

But a calendar may also have other functions.

EXAMPLE

Lotta, a woman I know, has both ADHD and Asperger syndrome. She uses her calendar to have an overview of stress. She is easily stressed

---

1   Now you may be surprised, since you may be one of the staff who hear warning bells in all situations where a client may be about to make a mistake. Well, firstly, I don't know about you, but I myself would certainly not be who I am, or have reached the level of maturity that I have, had I never made any mistakes. We need to make mistakes, and learn from them, to evolve. Just protecting people would be doing them a disservice. Secondly, if we do not include the possible positive outcomes of a choice like this, we will not be credible, and if we're not credible Joan will probably not listen to us. We always need to think of the balance on the trust account!

2   Remember that an aid always compensates for something! And you should know at least what it is supposed to compensate for when you suggest or produce it.

out, and knows she needs a balance. She colour codes activities in her calendar with a highlighter pen in order to quickly see that she's not planning too many stressful activities in a week. She uses orange for things that consume energy and green for things that produce energy. Her calendar can look like the one below for a regular week.

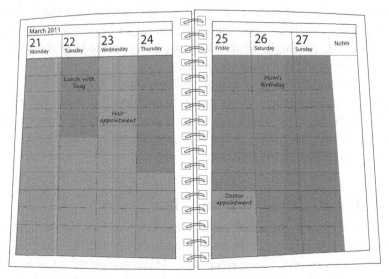

Figure 21.1: Calendar for reducing weekly stress

As she pointed out to me, one event could also easily change from energy-producing to energy-consuming. A couple of months ago her sister invited her over for her birthday. Well, to Lotta, this was a green event. Cake and family! But just before the party her sister called again to let her know that she had also invited some other friends that Lotta didn't know. Unknown people at a social gathering means it turned orange. To Lotta one activity can also be 50/50; for example, if the activity is energy-producing, but she has to go there by public transport, which is energy-consuming.

Speaking of stress and energy, it is also useful for many of the clients I meet to get a clearer idea of how much energy different activities cost them. We sometimes do stress inventories with clients. This may make it clear both to us and the client why it doesn't work with some activities on certain days.

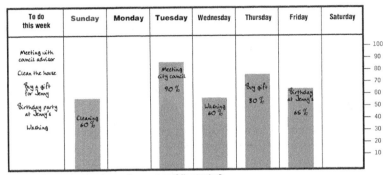

Figure 21.2: Measuring how much energy different activities cost. We do it visually of course!

Back to the calendar now. As I mentioned before we cannot always know what an aid is compensating for.

EXAMPLE

Bridget and Steve have a son, Anthony, with autism. Anthony is 42 years old and lives in his own apartment. He can do without residential support but is very dependent on his family for social contact. The highlight of his life is when every other weekend they go to the family cottage together. But recently Steve, who is over 80, has not always been able to manage to drive to the cottage. And Bridget does not drive (nor Anthony). Therefore, they sometimes have to cancel the trip.

When Bridget has to call Anthony to cancel, he just goes ballistic, she says. He screams and swears. Bridget feels very uncomfortable, because hearing all this verbal scolding is unpleasant, and she also feels sad that Anthony is this upset and disappointed because of the trip being cancelled. What to do?

Bridget is advised, together with Anthony, to buy an ordinary calendar. Anthony has never had one, because his life is so structured and compartmentalized that he does not need to have anything written down. Now Bridget instructs Anthony to write 'cottage-weekend' in the calendar. (Note that this is not a memory aid, since Anthony knows exactly when to go to the cottage without having to write it down). Bridget and Steve also instruct Anthony to use this aid for other situations. When Anthony, for example, has an appointment at the dentist, Bridget will tell him to note it in his calendar. This, again, is *not* for him to remember to go to the dentist (he has a remarkable memory); it is to help him handle changes.

When the time comes for Bridget to call Anthony to cancel the trip to the cottage, the conversation can sound like this:

Bridget: Hi Anthony, it's Mum. How are you today?

Anthony: I'm OK.

Bridget: Anthony, can you go and get your calendar and a pen?

Anthony: Wait a second.

Anthony: I'm back.

Bridget: Do you have a pen and the calendar now?

Anthony: Yes.

Bridget: Can you browse through the calendar to the day after tomorrow, Saturday, May 8… Have you found it?

Anthony: Yes.

Bridget: Do you see that it says cottage-weekend there? Can you take the pen and cross it out, and browse to next week and enter the cottage on May 15 instead?

Anthony: Okay.

Voila! No going berserk.

Now what does this compensate for? Well, for lack of imagination. The calendar (an aid) can thus help Anthony to handle change by making it visually clear. It may also be that other factors that contribute, such as:

- Anthony is 'busy' while he gets the information and this may distract him from his usual response (a verbal outburst).

- Bridget becomes more distinct, clearer and more straightforward in her message. (She might previously have tried to wrap it up somehow because she did not want to upset Anthony, but this may have had precisely the opposite effect since Anthony has difficulty interpreting implicit messages.)

- The aid can make it clear to both Anthony and Bridget that Anthony needs help, and being aware of a need for compensatory aids, often prevents feelings of guilt.

So, even if you know what the purpose of an aid is, this does not exclude the aid from having more than one string to its bow. Let us take another example of an aid.

EXAMPLE

Bethany had extreme difficulty with thresholds in life. All transitions were problematic (from home to school, from school to leisure, and so on). Bethany had a visual schedule but it was not enough for these situations.

We made Bethany tickets; a ticket to go home, for example. Bethany was then given the ticket at school and left for home. The tickets were decorated with pictures of various music groups Bethany liked.[3] At some places, as in the hallway at home and her classroom at school, she had a clearly marked spot where she put her ticket when arriving, but the tickets could also be received by a person.

What helped Bethany was probably that she got something to focus on when getting from one point to another. Here, we therefore believe that the aid works as a compensation for the difficulty of switching; it shifts her mindset from one thing to another.

21.4 TEACCH

The TEACCH programme was founded by Eric Shopler in the 1960s as part of the Department of Psychiatry of the School of Medicine at the University of North Carolina in the US. In the 1990s trainers from TEACCH often travelled to Europe and taught us a lot about adjusting services for people with autism spectrum disorders. Many schools have incorporated elements of TEACCH into their curricula, as have group homes and day services in their practices.

In TEACCH, assessments as well as individualization are important, which means that the approaches described in this book lean heavily on the TEACCH programme. Many of the strategies brought to Europe by TEACCH are very useful, but unfortunately I see in many services that the strategies have been watered down to using 'schedules', 'work systems' and 'task boxes', and sometimes TEACCH is used as an 'alibi'.[4]

The use of visual schedules has had a major impact. Sometimes they are well-made and personalized, but sometimes they are just one template which the person does not use independently. In these cases staff have totally forgotten (or did not ever know) that the most basic

---

3   If you know your TEACCH you may be wondering why we did not have a traditional schedule where you check in an activity by bringing a picture to the activity. The tickets can obviously be seen as a variant of such a schedule, but this was much more flexible as staff, parents and others could issue a ticket completely spontaneously.

4   By alibi, I mean: 'We have schedules, thus we are professional.' But using a hammer does not make me a carpenter.

feature about TEACCH is the use of assessments to individualize all strategies. Every so often I meet staff who announce their service as 'having TEACCH', but who are lacking the very basic knowledge of autism and have no clue as to *why* they are using task boxes and schedules (i.e. what the strategy is supposed to be compensating for) and no idea of how to adapt the strategies to a particular person.

A schedule is supposed to create an overview of what is happening during the course of the day. It is supposed to give the individual more control, better skills to handle changes, and answer the questions that others read between the lines, such as: What should I do? With whom? When? For how long? What happens next? But if the schedule does not work for Adan, we must ask ourselves: how can we create transparency and an overview for Adan? How can we compensate for the particular difficulties Adan has? How can we answer his questions? There we will find the answer. Not in just the notion of a schedule.

21.5 Social stories™ and comic strip conversations

Among visual aids, we also find social stories and comic strip conversations.[5] When lecturing, I often ask participants if they know about social stories (i.e. have heard of, read books about, or perhaps even taken a course in the approach). Wherever I go I get similar results. Out of 200 participants, perhaps 190 raise their hands (the ten who don't are usually new to the field).

When I then ask if they are actively working with this approach, using it in everyday life with their clients or pupils, there tend to be between five and ten of the 190 who raise their hands. And then, when I ask these five to ten professionals if they find the approach useful, they tend to reply with words such as 'very useful' and even 'invaluable', and 'I do not know how we would manage without it', and so on. It is funny (or rather sad) that so many know of it but so few use it.

My experience is that social stories and comic strip conversations are tools that you actually *have to* have in your toolbox. They do not fit every client, and are no panacea for every difficulty, but occasionally

---

5   As many of you probably know, this approach was developed by the American teacher Carol Gray (www.thegraycenter.org). She has written several books on the subject, for example Gray 1994, 2005, 2010 (see the References section).

(quite often), they are indeed invaluable. One might ask why there are so few using these approaches if they are that good? My experience is that many people feel insecure and uncomfortable with the approach. Now I am talking about the professionals.

The only way to overcome this, is to start using the approach, as practice makes perfect (or at least good). As with everything else, you'll be more secure and skilled, the more experience you have. I believe that you should not withhold from the individual the opportunity to understand and learn through social stories and comic strip conversations.

When having worked for a long time with social stories and comic strip conversations, as I have, you end up in what I call 'beyond social stories'. This means I no longer think in terms of 'strips' or a certain kind of sentence in a social story, and I will not always make them according to the rules. I rather work with visually demonstrating and concrete contexts, contexts that would not otherwise be obvious to the person with the disability. Nowadays I do it just like I talk, that is, without thinking out in advance how to do it.

EXAMPLE

Crystal, who has autism, is a trained architect but has never been able to work in her line of occupation. Now she is in a day service with an art programme which she likes and thrives in. Crystal's parents, however, are of the opinion that it is appalling that Crystal, with a higher education and university degree, has to be in a day service for people with disabilities.

Crystal herself does not feel this way. She says that out in the open job market, (if she even managed to get in there) she would succumb to the pressure and stress she would experience. To Crystal all social relations cost her a lot of energy, and there is an understanding of this in the day service.

To Crystal, the day service is meaningful, and she is content. The snag is that Crystal does not have that many other social contacts besides her parents, with whom she spends her weekends. However, Crystal cannot really distinguish between her parents' views and her own opinion. (This can of course be understood from a developmental perspective, as younger children also tend to not always be able to separate their parents' opinions from their own.)

Every Monday when Crystal arrives at day service, she expresses the view that 'it is crap that you should be in a day service when you are a trained architect'. The staff have tried to point out to Crystal that this is her parents' opinion, but it has not helped.

When I meet Crystal the matter comes up, and since I always have pen and paper to hand, I draw while we're talking. First I draw three stick figures on paper. I write Crystal's name on one and the parents' names on the other two. Then I ask Crystal what her parents think about her being in a day service. She says 'You ought not to be in a day service if you have a university degree'. I draw thought bubbles from the parents and write 'You ought not to be in a day service if you have a university degree.'

It is exciting to see how Crystal, who otherwise just says 'Yes, yes' when you try to talk to her about this, now begins to respond and reason in a more reflective way. Crystal now says her parents are sort of 'old-fashioned' and that they probably do not understand that she is content with her life as it is now.

I think the image I made compensates for Crystal's lack of imagination (inner pictures) and her difficulties with theory of mind. When I draw the perspectives (her own in relation to her parents'), they become more obvious and *that's when she can start thinking about it.*

I then ask Crystal what she thinks of being in the day service, to which she replies 'I like it here'. I go on asking what in particular it is that makes her like being at the day service[6] and Crystal says such things as:

'It is peaceful and quiet here.'

'You get to work at your own pace.'

'Everyone is nice.'

I write down what she says on the same piece of paper.

Figure 21.3: Stick figures used for talking to Crystal about her parents

---

6   As you can see, I throw in some of the solution-focused techniques here. We are looking for what is functioning, what is good – the 'success-factors'. (It is possible that too many cooks spoil the broth, but mixing ingredients is often a good idea!)

Then I ask Crystal if it might be a good idea if someone from her staff goes through the list with her when she arrives on Monday morning, to remind her why she likes being here. She thinks it's a good idea. After three Mondays of using the approach Crystal no longer expresses her parents' view, and the problem is solved.

Or to be honest, Crystal can now distinguish between her own perception and opinion, and those of her parents. But she is a bit sad that her parents think that what she is doing (and wants to do) is that bad. That leads us to keep on working, to help Crystal with strategies of how she can, if she wishes, answer her parents, tell them she does not want to talk about her job, or explain to them how she views it.

Obviously we will also talk to Crystal (using visual communication again, of course) about how it is not that unusual that parents have different views than their children about life choices. We will explain that it's actually quite common, and that there are many people who must find a way to handle their parents' disapproval of their choices.

By the way, Crystal also has her communications saved in a binder so we can easily refer to them if we need to.

EXAMPLE

Stanley had only one goal in life: to get a girlfriend. 'You should have a girl,' Stanley said. Over and over again. He did not talk about much else and the staff asked me (as usual) if they should agree with him, or be brutal (being brutal meant that some of the staff thought it might be best to tell him that he would not get a girlfriend... now how could they be so sure about that?).

I felt that neither approach would benefit him very much and suggested we should do an assessment. As you recall, all interventions should be based on an assessment.[7]

Well, to cut a long story short, we noticed that Stanley really could not see the causal chains (imagination again!). To him, things just seemed to happen (or not happen), but how or why they happened was a mystery. Stanley also had great difficulties reflecting upon thoughts, and distinguishing between thoughts, feelings and actions.

I told Stanley that having a girlfriend was his *dream*, and that I know several people with dreams. 'I have a friend who dreams of sailing across the Atlantic,' I told him, 'and having a girlfriend is your dream, Stanley.' The thing about dreams, is that we don't know if they will come true. But it often feels good to us to work on making our dreams possible. I also told Stanley that my sailor friend is working on getting closer to her dream coming true – she takes classes in navigation, she saves for a boat

---

7   Of course, even though we use assessments on a regular and structured basis, it happens quite often that we make quick decisions on an approach without launching all the major assessment work.

big enough for sailing the Atlantic, and so on. But still she does not know if she will achieve her goal.[8] While talking to Stanley I drew a staircase:

Figure 21.4: Drawing of staircase used for talking to Stanley about achieving his dreams

And then I told him that there could be steps to take to get closer to his dream. I asked if he knew any such step. He did not (and I was not surprised).[9] I told him that an important step was this:

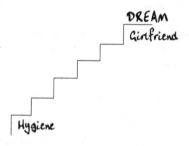

Figure 21.5: Drawing of step to illustrate what Stanley could do to make achieving his dreams possible

---

8   We are talking about meaningfulness here. Knowing that you are actively working on your dream creates a sense of purpose in life. My sailor friend will be happy about everything she did and learned, even if it turns out that she never actually crosses the Atlantic. The skills will be useful to her when sailing smaller waters, and – most important – she has taken her dream seriously, she believed in herself and started to work on making her dream come true.

9   Often, I notice clients at first are reluctant to answer. Previously I thought it was because of the difficulties that come with the disability, but lately I have come to think it is mostly due to a mechanism present in most of us: they think there might be a 'right answer', and since they don't want to give the wrong answer they would rather say nothing. I think this since I see that after a while many clients have quite a few (and good) suggestions about important steps towards a goal. But they will tell me only when they understand that all answers can be right.

Now it is important that you understand that I never would have mentioned this solely for 'educational purposes'; nor if I had not known Stanley as well I did – well enough that I felt pretty confident that he would not lash out because I brought this subject up. I told Stanley that I've met some men and women with the same diagnosis that he has, who also had difficulties taking care of their hygiene. I told him that I had sometimes seen that this could be the biggest obstacle to having a partner as there are actually very few people who want to be with someone who is dirty and smells bad, and that this reduces the likelihood of meeting someone. I made sure that Stanley understood that if he could get around his difficulties and start taking care of his hygiene, this was no guarantee that he would achieve his dream; rather it was a step that made the dream more possible.

Now of course this conversation was not a magic wand that made Stanley shower every day. He still needed support with personal hygiene matters, a support which we had to develop for him. But Stanley had not wanted to have assistance with this earlier. Now he suddenly saw that hygiene was part of a context that was important, and meaningful to him. There was a link between hygiene and his dream of a girlfriend that he had not previously understood.

Then we pursued this road in the conversation, and placed a few other things on the steps. For instance, we talked about how even if you do not know what a girlfriend that you have not yet met would be interested in doing, there are some things that many couples like to do together, such as going to the cinema, going out for a burger, and so on. Stanley had difficulties with these things too, and we made a plan to support him in practising these things.

The staircase became a tool that we have often come back to (a tool which compensated for Stanley's lack of understanding of context and lack of imagination, and that helped him to communicate about these things.)[10]

Using the same kind of strategy (taking small, visually clear steps) I know several clients who are close to fulfilling their dreams (and some who have); not just dreams about meeting a partner, but getting a job, an education, taking a trip, and other things.

Some clients I meet also have difficulties with prioritizing. Anna, a colleague of mine came up with the simple strategy of using parentheses. It started out when she was job-coaching Farrah, a client with autism. The boss had made Farrah an extensive 'to do' list, to

---

10   And no, no, no: it is not enough to just *say* to Stanley that he must address his hygiene to increase his possibilities of meeting a girl. I tell you this because I meet so many professionals who say 'We have already told him so'. But did you *show* him? We *must* use tools to compensate for the difficulties with organizing thoughts, categorizing and the lack of inner pictures (imagination).

keep her busy. All the things on the list were things that Farrah could do independently. What happened was that when co-workers arrived the next day, Farrah was still at the office. She never went home the night before – she hadn't finished what was on her list! So Anna started to put things on the list in parenthesis for Farrah, saying that these were things that could wait. Now this has become a strategy we use with several clients, and we see that they start speaking of things as 'parentheses', saying things like: 'This is a parenthesis, right?' This helps them prioritize not just things at work, but also household chores, social contacts, etc.

There are other ways of making prioritizing visible.

EXAMPLE

Sharon personified the word 'perfectionist'. Sharon has autism, and put so much emphasis on every detail of everything she did, that every task took her an infinity. It was OK for her staff, who were supporting and accepting, both at home and in day service. But for Sharon it wasn't. Everything that had to be done was an ocean of demands, and the pressure that she felt was overwhelming. Yet she wanted to do a lot of things, and she wanted to do them thoroughly.

Sharon is, for example, a wonderfully caring and generous person, and she kept track of everybody's birthdays (even staff's children's birthdays), and people would often receive a small but carefully chosen gift, and beautiful greeting cards made by Sharon. (If Sharon was only writing a shopping list, or a message that someone had called, it was always laid out with perfect calligraphy). As for many with autism spectrum disorders, there were of course a number of professionals around her. Thus this meant gifts and cards for one council advisor, one psychiatrist, six staff in day service, seven colleagues, four staff in residential support, as well as her family (parents, siblings and cousins).

When Sharon did something, whatever it was, it was always important – to her nothing could be more or less important – but everything was equally (very!) important to do, and to do perfectly. Sharon enjoyed carrying out everything as thoroughly as she did, but at the same time felt under pressure by the number of 'have-to's'.

We invented a priority board for Sharon. The board had three columns with the headings: *Important – needs to be done; Important – but no hurry; Not important – if there is time*. Additionally, there was a column called *No thanks!*

Figre 21.6: Sharon's priority board

On sticky notes, there were various things that Sharon wanted (or had) to do and then they could be moved about on the board, depending on their priority. Having the space with 'No thanks' was a way to show Sharon that it was possible to choose not to do some things, and that it was OK to say 'No thank you' (to Sharon it was extremely important to be polite and not to hurt someone).

This did not solve all Sharon's problems in one fell swoop, but it made it easier for her and we began a process of how to prioritize.

All of these examples are about visual aids that in a concrete way show what is otherwise hidden, and which compensate for the difficulties that individuals have. As you can see, these aids are also often tools for developing and practising new skills.

Visual aids can also compensate for communication difficulties (for example, the chat box, p.161). A simple (yet difficult[11]) and important visual aid for many is that you write down important information.

EXAMPLE

Salina had landed a placement in a day service which was very popular and had many requests for places (people with disabilities were actually queuing to be accepted by this particular service). Salina had a difficulty with leaving home, and therefore did not attend very often. Authorities

---

11 Difficult because people are so accustomed to information transmitted verbally, and because many with autism themselves are so verbal, that many professionals over-estimate their ability to understand, or forget that they can 'lose' information if only received verbally. And, not least, in 'care culture' many staff seem to feel that it is too 'technical' and 'cold' to write instead of talking. But if you give information more concretely and visually, this does not mean you are not a warm and supporting professional!

told Salina that unless she did attended more often, she would lose her placement in the service.

One semester went by, and each month Salina filled out a form showing her attendance, which she signed and submitted to the head of the service. At the next meeting with the department of social services Salina learned that she had lost her placement. She was very disappointed. In particular, she was disappointed that she had not received any information about this.

It seemed, however, that the head of the day service and the social services department's officer both felt Salina *had* received information, as they had warned her about this several months ago. I would like to say that Salina is right, though – she had not received information, because it had not been made clear to her. In fact, the visual clarity of the actual attendance report lulled Salina into a sense of 'doing the right thing'. She had happily filled out the form each month and felt that she had 'done her job'.

Salina would have needed written information on the decision that if she did not have a certain percentage of attendance over time she would lose her place. (The officer at social services should have provided her with this.) Then constant demonstrations in her everyday life Salina would also have needed by both the staff in her housing and in day services, of how much presence she needed to achieve 'quota'.

They could, for example, have added colour and shown clearly in a week how many days she had to attend day service. (And of course, they should also have made a comprehensive assessment to find out what prevented Salina from showing up at the day service.)

None of these examples show a social story by the book, and since I've written about how important it is to have social stories in your toolbox I will of course give an example of such, before we leave the topic. Carol Gray (2005), who has developed this tool, has divided the story into four types of sentences:[12]

- *Descriptive sentences* about what is happening, who is present and what they do. Carol Gray points out that one should avoid using 'always', 'never' and similar words.

- *Perspective sentences* provide different people's perspectives on the situation and explain what they feel or think. The person's own perspective is given in the first person.

- *Directive sentences* are the sentences that provide options. It is important that they are positive and not written as 'orders'.

12 Actually there are seven types of sentences that can be used according to 'the book'. But let's go with the basic here.

There should not be too many directive sentences in a social story.

- *Control sentences* are usually sentences that complete the story. They identify personal strategies the individual will use to recall and apply information. The sentence should help the person to remember the story or to deal with the situation.

Often you write a social story together with the person, and it's not just children who are helped by this strategy, but also many adults with autism. I will give you two examples of social stories below. The first is for a child and the second is for an adult. But please remember that social stories are always written personally for the individual; you cannot take a social story from another person and just recycle it.

Social story 1: 'Locking people out'

- Among the funniest things I know is to lock the door when someone has gone out and I know that the person must go in again.

- The person who is standing outside does not think it's funny.

- Nor do I think it's funny to be locked out. When it happens I become angry.

- I will try to leave the door unlocked.

- If I leave the door unlocked, others will be happy with me.

Social story 2: 'Letting people in'

- I do not usually open the door when the doorbell rings. *(Describes the situation.)*

- I'm not sure who it is and I am ashamed of the mess in my apartment. *(The person's own perspective.)*

- When the residential support is coming, they want to help me to clean up the mess. *(Other people's perspective.)*

- I feel better when my apartment is tidy and I can find things when everything is in order. *(Person's own perspective.)*

- Residential support always texts me half an hour before they arrive. *(Describes the situation.)*

- If the doorbell rings, I can check my phone and see if there's a text from the supporters; then I will know if it's them. *(The directive, describing a strategy.)*

- I will try to open when I know it's residential support calling at the door; then they can help me, and I can have order at home. Then I feel better. *(Positive conclusion.)*

A useful resource when working with comic strip conversations and social stories is the software Triple Stories, developed by Kenth Hedevag, a pedagogue whom I have worked with and known for several years.[13]

21.6 Nag-free information

As a professional it is easy to get caught up in reminding your clients or students about things so often that it becomes tedious, to the point of nagging. People rarely react particularly well to nagging. One way to get around this is to make information visual, as this makes it more free from nagging. Well, you may object to that, and say that having reminding notes and pictures can be perceived as nagging too. Sure. But at least with visual reminders there is no irritation in the tone of your voice, or expression of 'haven't I already told you this a hundred times' in your face. Furthermore information that is made visual does not immediately disappear (as do spoken words).

EXAMPLE

A teacher, Susanna, has a pupil with autism, Cathy, who reacts with stress to nagging, especially when it comes to schoolwork. Cathy screams and curses when Susanna reminds her of homework. (For Susanna it was initially not that obvious that this was about stress; she rather viewed Cathy as 'sensitive to demands'. Well, when in chronic stress we all become sensitive to demands).

In counselling with Susanna and her colleagues I had for a length of time nagged them (well, I too can probably become a little tedious as a counsellor) about the importance of writing down information. At one counselling session Susanne told me: 'Last week I thought I would try that written information you always talk about. So instead of reminding

---

13   Read more at www.triplestories.com.

Cathy to take home Wednesday's homework, I just put a note on her desk that said "Remember the Wednesday homework". When Cathy came in from break, I watched her go to the desk and then I heard how she read the note to herself: "Remember the Wednesday homework" and then she said to herself "Will do", and put the homework in her school bag. It was actually quite amazing – Cathy usually always shouts and swears when you remind her of homework!'

Yes, this is as simple (and as difficult) as it is! I say 'difficult' because people are so used to communicating with spoken words, that it often feels a bit awkward (or even 'callous') to communicate with text.

Of course neither relationship nor conversations are unimportant, but to many the actual information may need to be communicated in writing, or made visual. It is when we see that the spoken word is stressful, or that the person does not really understand or take in what we say, and when there is important information, that we replace it with visual communication. Otherwise there is no need.

On the whole, Post-it notes have been a useful communication aid for many people I work with. They are easy to have at hand, they are highly visible and can be stuck to most surfaces. (A teacher I know sticks them at times directly to the arm or hand of her pupil. Of course this is done with humour and compassion in the context of a good trustful relationship where she knows it is not perceived as offensive!)

Sometimes we need to cancel or stop a person who has a repetitive or compulsive behaviour, or is talking about the same thing at endless length. One problem is that the professional often lets the behaviour cross the (professional's own, that is) line, before trying to put an end to it. At that point it will be difficult for the professional to stop the person without letting her own emotions show.

21.7 The time model

Now, the time model... what was that about? Well, we invented this visual model for a client who was frustrated by out-patient housing staff not being able to do everything he felt needed to be done. John had been allocated two hours of residential support per week, but he had great difficulties understanding time. Staff always left his apartment feeling bad because John was being so disappointed by them. With this model, we could show John what was possible to do in an hour, and he could make an active choice, using velcro to stick to the circle the things he felt were most important today. Here's what the model looks like:

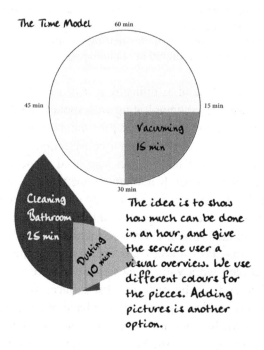

Figure 21.6: Example of a time model

21.8 Five-point scale

There is another visual tool called 'The incredible five-point scale'. The American teacher Kari Dunn Buron developed this tool. It is a scale from five to one, with a specific colour for each number. The book is titled *The Incredible 5-point Scale: Assisting Children with ASDs in Understanding Social Interactions and Controlling Their Emotional Responses* (Dunn Buron and Curtis 2003). I have found this tool very useful with children with autism. The book includes examples of how to use it to find the right tone of voice and regulate behaviour. I have used the scale for various issues, both as suggested by Dunn Buron, and in other situations, as with Patrick who had not really got the grasp of the difference between being in public and being in private (and what behaviour goes with what environment). We made a scale of being in public, to have a visual aid for our discussions. We filled in the text together with Pat as we discussed the different environments.

Here's our example.[14]

In public		I will think of
5	On town, e.g. in the mall	When people are together in public you need to behave differently than in private
4	At the movies	To be quiet during the film, other people are disturbed if I talk loud or make noises
3	At school	I know many people in school but it is still being in public. It is not okay to show my bottoms at school.
2	On the bus, on my way to and from school	If I curse and speak loudly to myself people may be disturbed and wonder if I am ill
1	At friends'	Being at friends' is a little private and a little public. I have to think more about how I act than I do at home.

Use colours for point 5–1. According to Buron the colours are: 5- red; 4 orange; 2 - yellow; 2 - blue; and 1 - green.

Figure 21.7: Scale for public and private behaviour

21.9 Escape routes

Unfortunately, I sometimes see that it is considered a problematic behaviour when a pupil runs off from the classroom, or hides, while in reality this is often the most basic and obvious strategy for all of us – if a situation is overwhelming get yourself out of it. With regards to flee or fight, we would rather see that our clients flee, right?

For some pupils with autism, especially those with acting-out behaviour, it has been very helpful to have their escape routes both approved and visually clarified. Of course this could be done by the use of a social story that says that it is OK to pull away, and where to go when you feel overwhelmed. It may also be done as in this example.

EXAMPLE

Evelyne is ten years old and has high-functioning autism. At school she runs away and disappears when she gets angry, her teachers say. (When she is stressed out and overloaded, I say – anger is often a reaction to something that happened.) 'One problem is that we do not know where she is,' the teacher adds, 'and another that she does not want to get

---

14   You can find other examples of how to use the scale in the book (Dunn Buron and Curtis 2003), as well as on the website: www.5pointscale.com.

back into the classroom again. ('Not want' or 'cannot', I wonder as a counsellor.)

Long term, we obviously will work to reduce stress for Evelyne, but what should we do here and now? Firstly, it is reasonable that we tell her it's OK to go off, especially since the option might be to stay and break things in the classroom, which has happened (and isn't it actually just brilliant that she has found that she can just run out of the room instead!?). And then we tell her where she can go (for us to have some control, and to know where she is).

As Evelyne does not have difficulty making choices, we give her two choices – you can run off to the cloakroom (where you like to be) or into the disabled toilet on the first floor (if you really need to be completely alone). We put a picture beside the classroom door (on the inside) of the two sites and a coloured pin she can use as a marker. We ask Evelyne to use the pin to mark which site she chooses before running off.

There is a point in doing this: namely that we want to make Evelyne aware that she is using an aid (and later on what it compensates for), and we want to make her participate. While we say it is OK to go away when she needs to, we also give her a part of the responsibility – to let us know where she is.

At the risk of being too obvious, I would say that this definitely would not have worked if we had only said all this to Evelyne. First, because of her lack of language comprehension, and second, she is so used to hearing complaints and reprimands that she often (quite reasonably) closes her ears to what adults say.

Then there was getting Evelyne to come back into the classroom again, when she had pulled herself together. Her teacher could not understand why she did not come back in, as they often could see her peering through the glass pane to the classroom. If the teacher opened the door and asked her to come in, she ran off again, which eventually could lead to a kind of frustrated 'hide-and-seek-game'.

Here we had help from the assessment we made. It was clear that if there is anything Evelyne cannot stand, or cope with, it is to feel foolish or insecure. She needs to save her face in every situation.

Although Evelyne herself is an emotional girl, she actually loves *neutrality* from others in these situations. Why is that? Well, because she finds it so difficult to interpret other people's tone of voice, gestures and facial expressions. She is unsure whether they might be ironic, or really mean what they say, if she is made fun of, and so on. If there is a microscopic risk that she might feel embarrassed, she would rather be safe than sorry, and runs off again.

So we created a tool capable of both showing concretely what we mean, which is neutral and clear, and which compensates for her primary difficulty with interpreting and understanding, and her secondary fear of humiliation. A note on the glass window was the solution: 'Evelyne: you are welcome into the classroom when you feel ready.'

Just as in the example of Joshua and the pot throwing on p.243, Evelyne too needed less and less of her escape strategy as school staff eventually had more knowledge, became more skilled in the autism craftsmanship, and thus were more able to respond to her, which in turn led to fewer situations that were overwhelming for her. Nevertheless, I think it is important that she may retain the right to use her approved escape routes in the future. Pulling back an aid and saying 'now, you don't need this anymore', can be very counterproductive.

21.10 The clothes-by-temperature-thermometer

In Chapter 14 I mentioned the clothes-by-temperature-thermometer, which is a simple but genius invention by a supported living service for young adults with autism. As they noticed many of their residents had a hard time knowing how to dress and when to change to warmer and cooler clothing, they just simply painted a thermometer in colours, laminated the instruction and put one of these in each apartment. Very helpful!

Figure 21.8 can be used as a guide for creating a 'clothes-by-temperature thermometer'. Place an outdoor thermometer where it can easily be seen when the person is indoors (e.g. on an external wall next to a window). You can adapt the illustration so that it resembles the real-life thermometer and also tailor the list of clothes for a male or female service user for the individual's personal clothing preferences.

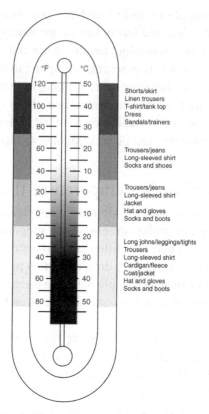

Figure 21.8: Example of a clothes-by-temperature thermometer

Finally it is always important when using or inventing aids that we do not become too authoritarian, 'over-educational' or 'dictatorial'. We easily end up trying to control our client's behaviours when we think that the behaviour is 'inappropriate'. It is, as I mentioned earlier, our task to provide them with the information (which they themselves cannot otherwise deduce or understand) that allows them to *choose* if they want to 'follow the rules' or not. And, of course, to provide them with the means or the support they may need to follow rules or conventions when they want to.[15]

Aids can look very different, and trying to enumerate all possible means of this kind would be impossible; and many tools we use are invented in direct response to someone's specific needs.

---

15   In my experience most people want to follow the 'rules' when they understand them and are supported to do so. But again, it's their free choice.

Sure, we could say that there are some general problems common to many with disabilities in the autism spectrum, but often it is not the general tools that 'do the trick' when it comes to actually giving someone a better quality of life and increased independence. This is partly because each person has his individual 'twist' on their impairment, and partly because we are working as much with the individual's difficulties as with his or her own strategies (sometimes not so good) to conceal or handle these difficulties. And let's not forget their individual strengths!

You could say that the disability, which appears in different variations, is also filtered through the personality. Therefore, different people need different types of aids and strategies. I am well aware of having mentioned this earlier in this book. But what is important here is that you understand the principles:

- Identify strengths and difficulties and then create an aid or strategy which may be based on the strengths, but which above all compensates for the difficulties.

- An aid is never static. It must change and evolve with the individual. Many people grow out of their aids after a while, or if they keep them, the aids might change shape.

And an individual should receive them according to need (and what the need is we know after making an assessment), not because a person with autism 'should have' this or that.

22

Talk and Babble, and a
Little About How to Play

A Chapter on How to Use Conversation as a Tool

Conversation is a part of life for those who communicate verbally, but can also be a needed intervention. Obviously, there are the professional conversations, such as those we have with a psychologist or therapist. Some clients need such interventions, but if you are not a psychologist, you will not be the one to provide it.

In my opinion we all – educators, residential supporters, nurses, etc. – can (and should) use conversations as a tool, and find ways for talks to help the client to progress. Some types of conversations are the ones that you have when you are working with social stories and comic strip conversations (these have already been mentioned. Here, I want to mention a few other aspects of, and types, of communications.

22.1 Conversations for 'landing'

Some clients may have difficulty with thresholds, that is, with the transition from home to school, from home to day service, and vice versa.

EXAMPLE

Amber is in a special education class for pupils with autism. When she arrives at school in the morning she can't really settle down. She moves around in the classroom; one minute she is being silly, and the next she is cursing school. When her teachers introduced a new routine, namely that the school day begins every morning with some 'computer talk'[1] they noticed she calmed down. While Amber still curses a lot during computer talk, it is as if she can get something out of her system, and the transition to school works better.

---

1   Computer talk is a conversation where you are both sitting in front of a computer and write to each other, by using the keyboard in turns. It makes the turn-taking simple and clear, and the client does not have to interpret facial expressions, tone of voice, and so on.

Sometimes a few minutes of computer talk is an opportunity to talk about something important, sometimes just a way to 'land'. For Amber, it is perhaps not the content that is important, but a great opportunity to 'land', to get over the threshold. Here's how a shortened version of a computer talk with Amber could look:

Teacher: Good morning, Amber! :-)

Amber: No.

Teacher: No? What do you mean, no?

Amber: Grrrrr.

Teacher: Are you angry today?

Amber: I hate polluters. :-(

Teacher: Sure, so do I. But you like the weather today, right?

Amber: Those who are polluting the environment are just fucking idiots who are sick in the head!

Teacher: OK, I can see that you are upset about their behaviour.

Amber: THEY ARE BLOODY IDIOTS!!!!!!!!!!!!!!!!

Teacher: OK, now we'll stop for today. Thank you for the talk, Amber. Now we have English as first class.[2]

A computer talk that is about more essential things and gives the client or pupil an opportunity to express something important she would not have been able to express in an ordinary conversation could look like this:

Teacher: Riona, we need to talk about this morning.

Riona: What?

---

2   Actually the teacher was reluctant to embark on this strategy. She said she did not have time to sit down with Amber in the morning, as she had to start teaching the whole class. But as it turned out, she could not start the class anyway, since Amber would wander around the classroom, and the computer talk in the morning took less time from teaching than before. Another concern was whether it really could be productive to have these types of conversations, since the content was so negative. But first, this is how Amber communicates (verbally too, but of course the cursing stands out as more obvious when you see it in writing); and second, this strategy worked – after five minutes of computer talk Amber was ready to start to concentrate and listen.

Teacher: I understand that it was not your intention to hurt Keira, but I wonder what happened?

Riona: I hate Keira.

Teacher: I see that you say you hate Keira, but what was it that made you throw a book at her?

Riona: Keira is always yelling.

Teacher: Aha, was it that Keira yelled that made you throw books at her?

Riona: Yes.

Teacher: Well, Keira really has a shrill voice.

Riona: ??

Teacher: Do you know what 'shrill' means?

Riona: Nah.

Teacher: Shrill means high-pitched, loud.

Riona: OK.

Teacher: How do you feel when you hear that kind of sound?

Riona: PAIN! I can't stand it. :-(:-(

Teacher: OK, now I understand what happened. Thank you for telling me.

Riona: OK.

Teacher: I think we should figure out together what to do in the future, if Keira or someone else is yelling.

Riona: ??

Teacher: Something that will help you but does not harm Keira. Is it ok if we talk about this tomorrow?

Riona: OK.

Teacher: Thanks for the conversation, Riona!

22.2 Solution-focused conversations

Another form of individual interview is the solution-focused conversation. Actually, I would recommend you to take a course since this type of conversation needs practice. But I will still try to describe what a solution-oriented talk can be about and what techniques are used. One way to do this is to use 'scaling'.

The question should be about something you want to change, and it can be either a specific change or a general change. You can open a 'scale conversation' with a question such as 'Is there anything you want to change?' and then proceed with what the pupil or client responds. But as some people with autism spectrum disorders can find such open questions difficult, you can either choose something that the person himself often complains about, or be more general.

Then the conversation can for example be opened with 'You often say that your parents nag you. I wonder if you would like to see if we can find a way to solve it?'[3], or the broader 'I wonder if we can talk about how you like it here at day service?', or '...how satisfied are you with your schoolwork?' Actually, whenever someone expresses dissatisfaction with something (and you have time for a conversation), there is an opportunity to initiate a conversation using scaling.

Now, what does scaling mean? Well, the question goes: 'On a scale from zero to ten, where zero represents the worst it has ever been, and ten the best you can imagine, where are you today?' Because of the difficulties with inner pictures you will often need to draw the scale on a piece of paper.

Figure 22.1: Example of a scaling picture

---

3   A desire to change someone else's behaviour – for example, to get someone to stop nagging – is as common in people with autism spectrum disorders as in people without, but in the solution-focused conversation it often becomes very clear that the only one you can change is yourself.

The phrasing options are many:

- 'On a scale from zero to ten, where zero represents when you were least satisfied, and ten represents how you wish it was, where are you today?'

- 'On a scale from zero to ten, where zero stands for how you measure when it was at its worst, and ten the best you can imagine, where are you now?'

When the client gives a number, you will only be working with what is between zero and that number. The question you now ask is 'What is it that makes it a three?' (or whatever figure the client gave). Then you ask the question (which is also possible to formulate in a number of ways) 'What else?', and go on asking questions until you have exhausted the subject.

It may sound like this:

Carol: Eric, you say you do not like school. I wonder if you want to look at this scale? Zero represents the worst it has ever been, and ten the best you can imagine, where are you now?

Eric: Two.

Carol: OK, so it is a two! What is it that makes it a two and not a zero or a one?

Eric: Playing with David.

Carol: So to play with David makes school more fun! What else makes it a two?

Eric: I'm good at maths.

Carol: Yes, you are, and you really like maths. What else?

Eric: …

Do not be afraid of silence. We give the person time to think, and we do not stop asking until we get a response like 'I can't think of anything else'. Also, sometimes the responses do not seem very relevant to the issue, but do not be afraid of that either or try to steer too much. If you keep going you will get to the point sooner or later. And here Eric's points are the important ones, not yours.

Eric: Pancakes.

Carol: OK, pancakes. What else?

Eric: …Well, uh… you and Joan. You really listen to us.

Carol: So you like that we listen to you pupils. Is there anything else that makes it a two?

Eric: …the boat…

Carol: Oh, you mean the boat that you made at crafts last week. It was really good! The boat then, and perhaps crafts class in general, is that right?

Eric: Crafts is fun!

Carol: What else?

Eric: Now I don't know anything else.

The conversation does not end here but I want to pause and reflect on what is happening. My experience is that both the professional and the client are smiling more and more the longer the conversation progresses. It's fun to talk about what you are good at and what you like! When we're talking about positive things, we feel good and when we feel good, we become more susceptible to change.

Here, for instance, it was not until towards the end that we learned that Eric was pleased with the response from the teachers, and that he likes crafts. This is why it is important that we continue to ask 'what else?' until there is a stop.

Carol: OK, Eric. Thanks for all the good answers. My question now is this. If you were to feel *half a step* better about school – that is, to get up to two and a half – what would have happened?

Eric: What?

Carol: I mean, what could it be that would make you say two and a half. What could make you feel a little better about school?

Eric: That I was better in English. And that there was more stuff to play with in the school playground.

Carol: OK, what could you do to get better in English?

Eric: I dunno.

Carol: Let's see, who could help you become better in English?

Eric: Ms Johnson, perhaps?

Carol: Yes, I think she could. We can talk to Ms Johnson about how we can plan this. Is there anything that *you* could do?

Eric: Read some more?

Carol: What good ideas you have! When would you be able to do some more reading, do you think?

Eric: Um... today, after school...

Carol: So you're taking the first steps to getting better at English today! And what about the school playground? I know we do not have a lot of stuff there, but I wonder what you could do to make it more fun to play in the school playground?

Eric: Me? It's boring in the school playground. There's nothing to play with!

Carol: Well, that is true. Perhaps the school board can do something about this in the future. But right now, I wonder if there is anything you can do, perhaps together with others, to make it more fun?

Eric: We could build a hut.

Carol: What a great idea. Who do you want build a hut with?

Eric: Samantha and David... and Leonardo!

Carol: What do you need to build a hut? Where can you get the materials?

Eric: We can get long sticks in the woods behind the school playground! Can we? And we could take leaves and make a floor, sort of.

Carol: When can you start building the hut?

Eric: Tomorrow at lunch break. If we can go and get the sticks?

Carol: I'll go with you to the woods to fetch sticks in the lunch break. You really have a lot of good ideas, Eric. Now I just wonder, when you're there at two and a half, how will you feel? How do you know that you have achieved that half step, I mean?

Eric: I'll know because it will be more fun to go to school.

Carol: Well then, you know how it will feel at two and a half. But of course I would have to know when you are at two and a half so we can celebrate it properly. How can I know when you have made that half-step?

Eric: I can tell you.

Carol: That's a good idea, but I wonder if I also could see it in some way?

Eric: That I look more cheerful?

Carol: Yes, it can be one way of knowing. But could we also say that when you have passed the exercise book in English, and when the hut is built, you're at two and a half?

Eric: OK.

Carol: Great! Thanks for letting me talk to you about this. It's always fun to talk to you, Eric!

As you understand from the first part of the conversation, we are only interested in what is between zero and two, and we try to find all the factors that contribute to the situation being as good as it is. In the second part of the conversation, we introduce the idea of making it half a step better (and what could contribute to that).

It is important to move forward *one small step* at a time, otherwise it will often be perceived as overwhelming. In the traditional solution-oriented conversation you also try to put lucid goals further into the future, and also you use something called 'the miracle question'.[4] My experience is that these strategies do not work so well with those who have difficulty with imagination, it is better to stick close to the present moment in a very concrete way.

It is important to understand that even if it is only myself I can change, this does not mean *without support*. That is why it is important to use creative questions such as 'Who can help you to...?' And 'What would you need to...?'

Other examples of creative questions are:

- When has it been a bit better?

- How did you make it succeed at that time?

- Which of your strengths did you make most use of then?

- How can I help?

- At which times is this not a problem?

It can happen that the client answers 'I don't know'. A creative way to reply to this might be 'I don't know either. How could we find out?'

As you may have noticed in the conversation between Eric and Carol, Eric is not really accustomed to think and respond in this way.

---

4   The miracle question that is often used in solution-focused work is: 'Suppose a miracle occurred during the night, and when you woke up in the morning, your problem was solved. What is the first thing you would notice?' But as I mentioned, for those who have great difficulty with imagination this does not work that well.

He still hangs in there as best he can. Sometimes it happens that the client continues to focus on problems. Eric says, for example, 'It's boring in the school playground. There's nothing to play with!' Carol reassures him that she hears what he says, but pilots him further in the conversation. This calls for (as always in working with people) a certain sensitivity.

John Sharry, solution-focused social worker and psychotherapist, and his colleagues say that we may have to work hard to inspire our clients to become co-detectives in solution-focused work, and to be aware of the fact that they at the beginning can be more like problem-detectives, than solution-detectives. They conclude that our intention is ultimately to be solution focused, not solution forced (Sharry, Madden and Darmody 2003).

Why should we have this kind of conversation? Well, because people are more susceptible to change when they themselves are active and formulate their goals, and when the conversation takes a positive form.

> People are usually more convinced by reasons they discovered themselves than by those found by others. (Blaise Pascal, mathematician, physicist and philosopher)

Carol persisted, as you probably noticed, in asking Eric how he would feel after the change had occurred. We might also ask 'How will you notice that...?' or 'How will others see that...?'

There are reasons for these questions. The first is an idea of the power of thought – just as athletes use goal images to envisage that the achievement has already been reached, to make it (at least a little) easier to achieve. Of course, with a client who has difficulty forming mental images this may not work as well, but on the one hand, there's no harm in trying (and not everybody with autism has this difficulty), and on the other hand, for those who do, we can try to use visual (drawing) communication to compensate for that.

The second reason – Carol also asks how *she* can know – is about the goal needing to be measurable. An important principle in solution-oriented work is to celebrate your achievements, so we need to know for sure when that half-step is taken. This is absolutely not the same as using rewards in a traditional reward system. This is about something we should all get better at; enjoying our progress!

The solution-oriented conversation may seem easy, and there is certainly a lightness in this way of working. But in fact it is also, as I noticed when I started working with this kind of conversation, oddly difficult not to give advice. I often think I have such good ideas, such good suggestions for solutions, and to hold them back can be really difficult. It's a matter of practice, and gradually you get better at it.

Many who work with solution-focused approaches tend to point out that humour is important. I agree with this. So far I have never met a person with autism without a sense of humour, but sometimes it has taken time to discover. This applies especially to the clients who have developed a great fear of failure, and who have low self-esteem. Some people with autism spectrum disorders also have developed a 'negativism' as a way of life (usually for the reasons mentioned above – namely low self-esteem and fear of failure). It is a challenge to meet them. They can turn everything you say into something negative, and 'pull down' the conversation all the time. Sometimes they say things like 'I want to be on welfare' or 'Everything is just shit anyway' or 'There's no point'. As a professional, it is not unusual to leave this conversation with feelings of failure, heaviness and hopelessness.

If you want to try to turn the conversation in a more positive direction, I have noticed that some tricks are helpful. One trick is to give positive feedback on those very small (sometimes microscopic) positive moments that occur. It may be comments such as:

- I saw a glimmer in your eyes when we talked about dogs. You like dogs, I take it?

- I saw you smiled for a moment when your sister came and visited.

- You leaned forward a bit when I took out this book. I wonder if that means you were curious about it?

But be careful not to be too cheerful (people who suffer from negativism are often, understandably, not keen on 'happy-clappiness'). With these individuals, turn down the volume of your voice, do not talk with too many exclamation marks in intonation, and give feedback in a way which does not make the client feel compelled to respond. Just make it a quick, positive feedback comment.

Another approach is to use contrary questions, for example:

- If I was to really make an effort to get you to do *nothing* at school, what would I have to do?

- If you really wanted to come to day service, and I said that you couldn't, what would you say to convince me?

- If you got to decide what rules existed here, and everyone had to follow them, what would you decide?

- If I wanted to stop you doing your homework, how would I do it?

- If we were to try to stop you ever going out, how could you convince us that it was important to you?

- If things were the exact opposite of what you want, what would it be like?

- If my goal was that you would be on welfare for the rest of your life, how could you work against me?

This type of question can often break the pattern of a conversation where the client has the same (negative) standard reply to all questions. In addition, they open it up for humour. I have in several conversations where I used this approach ended up laughing together with the client.

As I have mentioned before, motivation is often an issue in services, I have countless times heard clients described by staff as 'unmotivated'. Sharry and his colleagues (2003) write that if clients successfully do resolve their problems, or deal with them, it is because of their strengths and resources, not because of their weaknesses and shortcomings. In the solution-focused approach, motivation is not regarded as something just for the client, but rather as a joint effort of the therapist and client.

22.3 Furnishings

I have visited many consulting rooms and offices where individual meetings and conversations with clients take place. Although the kinds of services I visit are very different (psychiatric wards, care homes, group homes, school counsellor's office, etc.), these rooms are confusingly similar, and the furniture is always organized in the same manner. It is understood that you should sit opposite each other (often the chairs are just somewhat angled so that you don't sit completely face-to-face), and there is often a small, low table which is not particularly useful for anything.

Since I know it is difficult for many with autism spectrum disorders to read body language and handle eye contact, I usually, if possible, rearrange the furniture so we can sit next to each other. Then we can both look at the paper I always bring (for reasons you have by now understood, right?).

Since it is a norm to sit opposite each other, which most people with autism spectrum disorders are aware of, I usually say something like 'Is it OK that I am sitting here next to you, so that we can both look at the papers?' It is fine with most of them. And in my experience many of the conversations I have when not facing each other work out much better than otherwise.

22.4 Conversations in groups

Many services have different kinds of group activities. They may serve the purpose of practising social skills, sharing experiences or just socializing. It can also be user councils or class councils, or morning meetings/circle time. Since taking turns is difficult for many with autism spectrum disorders, we can use aids in these settings. A simple way of making turn-taking visible and concrete is to have two items – a pillow, a stick or whatever – one green and one yellow. The person whose turn it is to speak holds the green item, and the one waiting for his or her turn has the yellow one.

In the case of morning meetings or circle time with children, it is interesting that adults often think that many children find it difficult to sit properly and to focus on the meeting. When I've given lectures for preschool teachers I have asked the audience what they prefer: to hold the meeting, or to just sit in on one (not being the person holding it). All of them prefer to hold the meeting. Why is that? Mainly because it allows them to be active. The truth is, most of us get 'ants in our pants' when we have to sit and be passive for a long while. Adults can regulate this with the help of small movements that are not very noticeable, while children do it with bigger (more noticeable) movements.

Trying to get a sensory stimulus when you have sat still for a long time is perfectly natural, and therefore, some children (with or without autism spectrum disorders) need something to fiddle with during circle time. Some children have what I call 'a nervous system with a screen saver'. By this I mean that they may have difficulty holding a steady alertness (see the example of Joshua on p.243). If nothing happens to stimulate them directly (for example, in a circle time when another child tells at length what she did during the weekend) the 'screen saver' turns on; you can see the child is slipping away mentally. Sometimes also physically – the child may slide, lean or lie down. Some children seem to experience this condition as uncomfortable. Then they try to find different ways to stay alert. It can show up in a range of behaviours, from having to pick something up, spin, nudge your buddy next to you, or something similar. If we do not think that the child's strategy is 'appropriate' we must help them to find a better one. The issue is that we understand that the behaviour fills a function for the child and that we cannot simply tell the child to stop (or to 'sit properly').

EXAMPLE

Alfie, who was four years old and diagnosed with autism, would always play in a room with a toy castle and knights in the mornings. When it was time for the morning meeting he always brought one of the toy knights. And each morning he was told to put it away (you cannot have toys at circle time). Every meeting he was alert during the first three or four minutes and then he slowly began to 'drift off' and slipped into a semi-recumbent position. Every meeting he was – again and again – told to sit properly.

In these situations when Alfie lost his ability to keep his body upright, he started making noises which were perceived as disruptive. Every morning meeting, he was – again and again – told to be quiet. (Five days a week, approximately eight times each meeting, this makes a lot of remarks in a year…)

When we decided to try a new strategy and let him keep the toy knight at circle time, we saw what he did when he was about to lose alertness. He pressed the knight's hard edges into his palm, and thus he could stay alert. Now he could sit upright and made no disturbing noises. The knight was his own clever solution to a problem!

For conversations in groups with adolescents and adults, we have sometimes used conversation cards.[5] The cards have questions that can stimulate conversations and reflections about your characteristics and desires. There may be questions such as 'What does a perfect day look like to you?' and 'If you had a shop what would you sell?' Other cards can have unfinished sentences such as 'One thing that bothers me is… because…' and 'A nice compliment to give to someone is…because…'

---

5   These are typically made as conversation starters and sold by companies such as Table Topics (www.tabletopics.com).

Of course, you can make your own cards for this purpose. The cards provide a visual aid and turn-taking is made clear. Moreover, they have led to topics of conversation that never would have come up in the group otherwise. Since the ready-made cards are not all suited for individuals with autism spectrum disorders, I always browse the cards in advance and put aside the ones that I think may be too difficult for the group (for example because of age, experience or degree of disability).

Another tool that can be used in group conversations is to use the Socratic conversation model. The Socratic method requires a conversation leader. It uses open questions, which are sometimes difficult for people with autism spectrum disorders, but I have also seen several people who had difficulties at the start 'grow into it'. The Socratic model is fully in line with the solution-focused conversations; this is also about investigating and finding out more about a topic, rather than giving advice.

Wisdom begins in wonder. (Socrates)

The leader starts the conversation with the suggestion of a subject and gives some background on this subject. You can also start with a picture, and pass pictures around for everybody, in turn, to describe what they see. Or you can discuss a film. There are many possibilities! In the conversation you use open-ended questions such as:

- What do you mean by...?
- Can you rephrase that, please?
- Can you give me an example?
- When you say...do you mean that...?
- Do you agree or disagree with...?
- How do you know this?
- What evidence is there to support what you are saying?
- Please explain why/how...?
- What would happen if...?
- How do you know that it is so?
- Is there another perspective to this?

It is often a good idea to open the discussion with a question to answer in turn. This should be a question which has no 'right answer'. It might be 'What do you think that this picture represents?' and then 'Why?', or more philosophical questions like 'What does the word kindness mean to you?' and then 'Why?' If you have seen a film, or read a text together, questions like 'Would you like to have been in the main character's place?' and 'What would you have done if it was your sister who...?' may be useful.

As a leader (or rather the moderator) of the conversation, it is your role to see to it that everybody participates, by using phrases such as 'Hannah, what do you think about what John just said?' You can look for particularly interesting or confusing statements, and invite participants to elaborate or clarify. At the end you summarize what was discussed and what points were made.

In a Socratic conversation you practise your ability to converse. And even if people with autism spectrum disorders may have difficulties with open questions, I have many experiences of the opposite. In fact, questions that are not open often tend to 'close' the conversation with people who are not so adept at social interaction.

Sometimes a conversation with a person with autism becomes almost sort of staccato:

Professional: How are you?

Client: Fine.

Professional: Well, what have you done today then?

Client: Cleaned up.

Professional: What nice weather it is today!

Client: Yes.

The professional must take responsibility for this entire conversation since the client cannot 'invent' the answers, or ask questions back, which normally makes the conversation flow. In a group where several individuals give only short and monosyllabic answers to a question, you can feel unsure as a professional. Here, the Socratic questions can be useful. The aim is a dialogue containing everyone's feedback and where everyone's opinion is respected and listened to. You practise listening and arguing, reflection and critical thinking, and these conversations are often deep and interesting.

22.5 Younger children: play skills

With younger children we can help them to participate in conversations in groups by using simple 'conversation games'. We can start a round of questions with 'My favourite food is... What is your favourite food?' where the child has to reply and then pass on the question to the child next to her. This 'game' can be varied *ad infinitum* (favourite movie, favourite toy, something I think is boring, and so on). These conversations have the advantage of a very clear turn-taking, and the child with difficulties will get the opportunity both to practise 'conversational skills' and to reflect (to think of what they like and dislike).

But if we are working with younger children we may not work as much with conversations as a tool, but rather with play. Developing play skills should be an important aim when working with younger children with autism spectrum disorders.

In the preschool and younger school age we in the Western world often emphasize free play as important for children. Although we believe this to be so important, it is quite striking that preschool teachers have more tools at hand for how to teach a child to dress himself, to hold a pen, to cut with scissors, than to teach a child how to play. When I visit services for younger children who are included with peers without disabilities, I see that the children who have difficulties playing are often left without any support. I think you can agree with me if I say that the ability to play grows through play experiences. The children we view as being competent playmates have a lot of practice in playing. The child who has difficulty playing is too often left without the necessary experience of play.

What can we do? Well, the teacher can, for example, enter a role play with the child and stay for the entire playtime, so that the child with the difficulty gets an experience of participating in a role play from beginning to end (and the other children get an experience of this child being a playmate). In this situation we choose an easy role. If the play is about family, the teacher may choose the role of being a pet together with the child. Some of the children with these difficulties we are talking about find it difficult even taking a role at all; they are who they are, and to imagine being a 'daddy' or a 'dog' may exceed their imagination. The child might say 'I'm Jessie, I'm not a dog'. Then you can still assign yourselves (teacher and child together) the role of being Jessie in the play. Just the fact that the teacher is 'Jessie' along with Jessie is a first step in the imaginary world.

Some children have a hard time entering a play situation. These children can be taught (preferably also using social stories) how to do it (just as we teach children a lot of other things). Experience shows that children who have no difficulties joining a group of children playing do first look at the play for a while. If they don't understand what the game is about, they ask 'What are you playing?', and then they ask if they can join in, or they come up with a proposal of their own that fits the game. Here, you as a professional can do this together with the child, showing the steps of entering a play situation, and letting them practise the process.

EXAMPLE

Cameron: Harrison and Max won't let me play with them!

Teacher: Come on Cameron, let's go and look at what they're playing. *(Goes over to the children playing).*

Cameron: I want to play too!

Teacher: Wait a minute Cameron, let's check out what the game is all about. What are they doing? Watch closely.

Cameron watches.

Cameron: They're building!

Teacher: Well, what are they building?

Cameron: A castle.

Teacher: Mmm, I don't think they're building a castle, though. How could you find out what they are building?

Cameron: I don't know.

Teacher: We can listen to what they're talking about. Let's see if we can guess after we've listened?

Cameron: OK.

Pedagogue and Cameron listen for a while.

Teacher: Do you have any suggestions?

Cameron: Nah.

Teacher: Did you hear that they said there would be an engine over there?

Cameron: Um.

Teacher: So it's something with an engine, but how do we find out what?

Cameron: I don't know.

Teacher: Let's ask. Do you want to ask 'What are you building?'

Cameron: What are you building?

Harrison: We're building a rocket.

Cameron: Can I join in?

Teacher: Wait a minute Cameron, let's propose something for the rocket. Do you have any idea? Look at the boxes over there, can you come up with something that would fit into a rocket?

Cameron (having trouble with imagination, and still stuck at his first idea)**:** You can build a castle with them.

Teacher: A castle may not be so common on a rocket, but what do you think about calling it a 'space fortress'? Could you propose to Harrison and Max that you can build a space fortress over there?

Cameron: Can we make a space fortress over there?

Max: OK.

22.6 Rule play

Some children have such great difficulties with pretend play, that trying to involve them in make-believe play is out of the question. It is important that we can make these children feel involved and competent in playing too, and then usually rule games are a good alternative.

Sometimes you see adults who hold the child with autism spectrum disorder by the hand through games such as 'Grandmother's footsteps', 'What is the time, Mr Wolf?' and 'Simon says'. The child often does not have a clue what this is all about, but is rather being led along by an adult's hand. Of course, this can give a sense of inclusion, but what about the feeling of competence, the 'I can do it!'?

Instead, we can try to teach the child, in concrete terms and step by step, how the game goes and what it is about, with the goal of the child being able to participate independently. We start by doing it one-on-one, and then we can invite a few other (socially competent) children to participate, and increase the group gradually, until the child understands and masters the game.

In summary, what we as professionals need is to have tools in our toolbox, to facilitate the social interaction and build experiences of being competent and included. This goes for work with people with autism spectrum disorders of all ages, and in all kinds of settings.

23

Can You Be Yourself When You Do Not Know Who You Are?

A Chapter on Working with Self-knowledge and Self-esteem

Self-esteem is the sense of competence and worthiness, the belief that you are 'good enough' and that you are capable of dealing with things. I think that to develop good self-esteem, you need a fundamental self-knowledge. By this I do not necessarily mean having reached an emotional maturity (although this obviously can be good for your self-esteem, too), but a basic sense of, and knowledge about, who you are and what you are feeling.

I meet quite a lot of children, adolescents and adults with autism who have difficulties in this area, and as I mentioned earlier, low (or no) self-esteem is most significantly common in those with challenging behaviours. I believe that if you grow up with a disability within the autism spectrum, it may be particularly difficult to develop this fundamental self-awareness. For example, if you grow up with autism your perception of reality is typically not confirmed by others. When a child with sensory integration problems, or an extreme detail perception, is talking about how she experiences something, those around her (most especially if the child has not received a diagnosis) will often send the message 'this cannot be'. As a child you have no other option than either to accept that your reality is non-existing, or to have a double agenda where you know your reality exists, but that it is not accepted by others.

Another side of this is that in childhood, children cannot express their feelings and experiences in words. The learning in recognizing them happens when adults name them for you. This goes for both bodily sensations, and emotions. We say to the child: 'Do you need to pee?'; 'Now you're over-tired!'; and 'Oh, were you disappointed?' Over time the child learns to recognize and eventually to name emotions.

But the child with autism may not be as easy to read, and perhaps the environment will put the 'wrong' name on their feelings in different situations. For many children with autism spectrum disorders, there also appears to be a difficulty with the shades of emotions, and they may just perceive and thus understand the very strong emotions.

EXAMPLE

I used a survey in the assessment of Nick, who was 18 years old. The survey included questions such as: 'What do you do if you become sad/ scared/tired/angry/insecure? Nick replied 'Get angry' to all questions. His staff felt this was correct (Nick was a guy who broke things frequently). But as it turned out Nick did not recognize any other emotions but anger.

If you feel things you do not understand, it is perhaps not surprising that you become angry. With Nick, we began long-term work with emotions, first with the 'big' feelings, then with the nuances of them. Eventually Nick learned to recognize and label emotions as 'disappointment' and 'uncertainty'.[1] And the fact is that as Nick accquired this new vocabulary he became less angry in these situations. Just as with small children with 'standard development', feelings were not expressed in a (disruptive) behaviour when he had the language for them.

23.1 Thought–feeling–action

Perhaps you could say that with self-awareness comes the language and with the language comes communication, and when communication is improved, almost always we see an improvement with regards to behaviour. (Of course there are also clients who have the same difficulties, but who are not acting out, who instead become passive, timid, or shielded.)

Owning the language of emotions (together with being able to recognize them) is not just about being able to communicate them to others, but also about being able to reflect upon them, and to reason with yourself about your feelings. If a client cannot do this, to expect

---

1   Is uncertainty really an emotion, you might ask. I say, yes, and an important one to recognize and know the name of. In texts on affect theory, usually only fear is mentioned. But fear is a bigger emotion, which we (I hope) do not experience that often. Uncertainty, however, we experience, and need a strategy to deal with, quite often.

him to be able to regulate his behaviour is in my opinion too much to ask for.

When I have worked with 'emotional literacy' for individuals with disabilities on the autism spectrum, I have had some help from the book *Teaching Children With Autism to Mind-Read* (Howlin, Baron-Cohen and Hadwin 1998) and perhaps particularly from many of the ideas contained in Paul Stallard's books (Stallard 2002, 2005). The tools of the CAT-kit[2] have also been useful, as well as the pictures and photos in the software Triple Stories (see p.310).

But often we have not been able to follow a 'method', since the need for individualization is so strong. We have picked a bit here and there, and also used photos from magazines and pictures from comic books. With help from Stallard's books I discovered the importance of helping people with autism to distinguish between thought, feeling and action. Some thoughts automatically lead to a feeling which has an action as the result. (Or, sometimes, an emotion leads to a thought, which results in an action).

EXAMPLE

Madison's teacher says that Madison needs to practise some more on maths. Madison thinks 'I'm completely useless'. This thought instantly creates feelings of frustration and despair, and the action that follows is that Madison throws down her maths book and shouts 'I don't give a crap about maths!'

Madison got to work on identifying her feelings, thoughts and actions with inspiration from the worksheets in the book *Think Good – Feel Good* (Stallard 2002). Madison got to practise seeing whether something was a thought, a feeling or an action. We made a small 'curriculum' for Madison during one term. She would have one lesson a week which was about self-knowledge, and was to start with learning the difference between thoughts, feelings and actions. (Later, it could be about filling out a sheet of thoughts that make me feel good, a writing assignment about actions that make me happy, and so on.)

Madison's teacher would also use herself as an example in the classroom. She could come in one morning and open class by saying: 'Today on my way here, I saw that there was a traffic jam, and then I *thought* "Oh no, now I will be late". It made me *feel* stress and frustration. At the same time my son called me on my mobile to ask me something, and I was irritated and snapped at him. First I had a thought which led to a feeling, and from that came an action, which was not so good.'

---

2   See www.cat-kit.com.

The next step was that the teacher made Madison (and the rest of the class, who did not have autism, but probably gained from this too) aware that if you change your *thought*, then you can also automatically change your feeling and your reaction. It took time, but after one term Madison was significantly more aware of how what she thought could lead to certain feelings and certain actions.

In particular, it was noticeable that we affected her tendency to perceive any form of requests as criticism, which had previously automatically led to her thinking that she was hopeless. Madison was not as sensitive to requirements, and there were fewer books thrown around in the classroom.

What I am saying is that many people with high-functioning autism I have met, have a difficulty understanding the difference between feeling, thought and action, and there may be a point in teaching this. (And quite a few I have met without autism – even if they do understand this in theory – have difficulty separating them in practice, in an ongoing situation.) Now perhaps you are not a teacher, but with the pedagogical approach we all need to have when working in the autism field, you may need to do this kind of 'teaching' even if you happen to be a residential supporter, a psychiatric nurse, a social worker, or something else.

The thoughts are our means to steer our behaviour, and therefore we would like to help the person to become more aware of how a thought can lead to a certain reaction. By changing the thought, we can change both how we feel and how we act.

EXAMPLE

Scott had a meltdown as soon as something went wrong, or if someone tried to show him how to do something. He had terrrible difficulty learning how to start and use the washing machine, and when his supporters tried to show him he would scream and curse when he still couldn't do it. Scott had a regular meeting with his contact staff once a week, and staff now decided to devote half an hour of the meeting to reasoning and writing about feelings and thoughts. After a couple of months of consistent work, Scott himself could say 'When something goes wrong, I think that I am an idiot and then I get angry.'

Aha! It's not things going wrong that makes him angry, but rather it's the thought 'I'm an idiot' that creates the feeling.

Then a project to help Scott to form a new thought began: 'When something goes wrong, I think I need help', and staff strengthened the new strategy using social stories. It also became clear that Scott did not know how to ask for help; he had no 'template' for this. Thus, staff also had to work with teaching him this.

This meant that he had concretely and practically learned how to say 'Can you help me?' in these situations. The staff had to remind him by whispering the phrase to him in the beginning, but after a month with reminders and support Scott could independently ask for help.[3]

23.2 Getting your reality confirmed

A first and rather simple step we can make to help the individual on the road towards good self-esteem is about confirming and validating[4] her perception of reality. Here is an example to illustrate this. This is about children, but the example is transferable to all ages. This is what it often sounds like:

Anthony: She hit me!

Samira: I did not!

Teacher: What just happened?

Samira: I just touched him.

Teacher: Anthony, I think she just brushed against you.

Anthony: She hit me, it hurt!

Teacher: But Samira says she did not hit you, Anthony.

It could sound like this instead:

Anthony: She hit me!

Samira: I did not!

Teacher: What just happened?

Samira: I just touched him.

Teacher: Anthony, did it hurt?

Anthony: Yes!

Teacher: And you, Samira, felt that you just touched him?

---

3   This is about understanding the idea of working long term. Too often we just offer support when a client needs it, without teaching the person how to ask for support. If we want to help the person build new skills for the future, and if we really have increased autonomy as a goal, then we need an awareness of the importance of teaching the person to use an aid (also when staff are the actual aid).

4   Yes, there are two parts in this. Confirming, which means 'Yes, it is possible to feel/ experience something like this', and validating, which means approving of the feeling 'It is okay to feel like this'.

Samira: Yes!

Teacher: Sometimes there are two sides to a thing. You can both be right. To Anthony it hurt and it felt as if you gave him a punch. To Samira, it felt as she just stretched out her arm and brushed against you. Your truths are equally true.

Anthony: But she did hit me! For sure.

Samira: Did not!

Teacher: I can hear it hurt you, Anthony, and I can hear that Samira did not know it could hurt when you just touch someone. Can we stop there? It doesn't still hurt, does it, Anthony?

Anthony: Nah.

Here you see both children have their reality confirmed. In addition to the need for us as helpers to confirm what the person is experiencing, we often also need to teach the individual to put words to their emotions.

When we put someone else's feelings into words, we must be aware that we are *guessing*. We can never know what someone else is feeling. Therefore we must be both sensitive and humble. We can say – after having made an assessment and formulated a hypothesis, of course! – things like: 'Now I think you are tired', 'It looks as if you were disappointed' and 'How happy you seem today!' There are many ways to vary the wording, and there are many occasions in everyday life where you in this quite simple way can support your client in the development of self-knowledge.

23.3 Positive feedback

Another part of this work is to give the client a lot of positive feedback. This requires practice and a conscious effort. We may think we are positive in our approach but the fact is that people often say more negative things than positive. We are all generally pretty bad at giving positive feedback in our everyday lives. (For example, ask yourself, how often do you tell your friends how much they mean to you?)

I would like to distinguish between positive feedback and praise, even if the praise is not too bad either. But praise is narrower, and typically given on performance, as in 'Well done!' There are some people with autism (and, certainly, some without as well) who find it difficult to accept praise.[5] It is easy to think that you will not be able to give positive feedback in these cases. You can! There are plenty of ways.

Examples of positive feedback that is not about performance:

- It was clever of you to...

- I see that you care a lot about...

- You really are a person with a sense of humour!

- How thoughtful of you to...

- What patience you have when you...

A standard description of yourself must be included in basic self-knowledge, in my opinion. Most 'standard' adolescents and adults (and even children) are able to provide a short and positive description of themselves in answer to the question 'Who are you?' They can tell you something about their personal qualities as well as what they like and dislike. I meet a lot of people, of all ages, with autism who cannot. Sometimes they have no description at all of themselves, and in other cases they only have a negative description such as 'I am a person who fights' or 'I am a bloody sick-head'. This is why it is important that we give positive feedback on personal characteristics. We need to help the person to reach a positive standard description of themselves, such as 'I'm curious, I have a sense of humour, I am a person who cares about nature, I am considerate'.

If you have trouble seeing your client's positive qualities (which is often the case when it is a client with challenging behaviours), you will have to make an effort. You must become a detective in finding

---

5   This could be the aversion to 'happy-clappiness' mentioned earlier (see p.327), and these individuals may perceive praise as manipulative or false. Sometimes it is about the praise received being 'too childish' (I have seen people praise adults with disabilities with a tone of voice they would use with a three-year-old). In some cases it is simply about not knowing what you are expected to reply to praise, and if that is the problem we have worked with teaching the person some standard phrases such as 'thank you', or 'I'm glad you think so'. You might think that the person would know this already, as verbal as he might be. But actually the communication and social interaction around praising is quite complicated. The response is often a question such as 'really?' or 'you think so?' But these are not really questions. It is the same way with the British idea of politeness, which often goes something like this: 'Please, have another cookie!'; 'No, thank you, I'm fine'; 'Are you *sure* you don't want another cookie?'; 'Yes, they were lovely, but I'm full.'; 'But there's plenty left! Are you really sure?' and so on. It is not easy – if you have a difficulty with social interaction (or if you're from another culture!) – to know when to stop, and how to follow this and say no without being rude.

clues to your client's good traits, and actively look for opportunities to provide feedback on them.

This positive feedback also has the effect that it builds a good relationship. It is critical that we work actively to build a good and trustful relationship with our pupils or clients. If we make an overdraft on the trust account it can be very difficult to get new loans. However, if we have built a good and trusting relationship in a conscious way, it will be possible to make small withdrawals from time to time when we happen to mess things up (and if we apologize we can often restore the balance).

'But shouldn't positive feedback come from the heart?' a residential supporter asked me when we talked about one of her clients, who was perceived as violent, intimidating and extremely 'difficult'. Of course, it should be honest. In the case of clients who in the current situation are surrounded by staff's feelings of disgust, fear, apathy or powerlessness, it can be challenging to see positive things about this person. The staff can be so blinded by their resignation that they cannot see the client's strengths and competences. In these cases we can benefit from the solution-focused counselling, described in the example of Beth on p.59.

23.4 Balance of power

Powerlessness is mentioned earlier in this book, and this is another part of working with building a client's self-esteem: to break the sense of powerlessness. We do this best by finding more opportunities where the client can be included in decisions, and make him truly involved in decisions. It may feel awkward and challenging to work like this, especially when it is a client who is perceived by staff to have (too) much of the power (e.g. a threatening or violent behaviour).

It is fundamental that you understand that the staff always have more power than the individual with the disability. The balance of power is always biased toward the staff's benefit – it is in the nature of the relationship. The staff are paid, they can go home, they can quit their job and so on.

If you have a disability it may sometimes mean a sense of powerlessness (or at least that the power balance is skewed). You are more dependent on others – family, staff and authorities – to make decisions on where you will live, how much support you will get, etc. Furthermore, as is the case for many, you are financially more powerless than others – you can't just go out and get a job like everybody else, and even if you have an education, you may not get the job you are trained for, or if you do, you do not have the same ability to advance or get a raise as others do.[6]

If a person has autism, he might not have been able to break free from his parents in the natural sense that they no longer have the power to affect him. Now it may sound as if I am opposed to parents; I am certainly not! What I mean is that in the relationship between a child and a parent a change needs to and should occur when the child reaches adulthood, in order to, emotionally and practically, stand on his own feet.

I sometimes ask staff if they have ever made life choices that their parents have disapproved of. Many have. But when you grow up and perhaps also have formed a family of your own, you can say to yourself: 'Well, Mum thinks I should not do this, but I choose to do it anyway.'

Some young people with autism free themselves in a natural way from their parents, but others have difficulties with it. I think in part it is the disability that makes them more dependent on their parents since the parents may be their whole social network. But also the process may not have started by itself in adolescence, as it does for 'standard' teens.[7]

EXAMPLE

I was at a meeting aimed at teens with autism. The participants were 16–18 years old. Several of the parents had accompanied their children there. Before we went into the auditorium Tom's mother took out a comb from her pocket and combed Tom's hair (to make him look good at the meeting).

---

6   The Office for Disability Issues states that although 'the employment-rate gap between disabled and non-disabled people has decreased from around 36.2 per cent in 2002 to around 28.7 per cent in 2011 [...] disabled people remain far less likely to be in employment. In 2011, the employment rate of disabled people was 48.8 per cent, compared with 77.5 per cent of non-disabled people. [...] Disabled people are around twice as likely not to hold any qualifications compared to non-disabled people, and around half as likely to hold a degree-level qualification', and 'over a quarter of disabled people say that they do not frequently have choice and control over their daily lives' (Office for Disability Issues 2012).

7   If we look at 'standard' development (I'm sure you remember the development perspective?) we can see that the liberation process is gradual and ongoing over a period of years. It is closely linked to the development of abilities, being able to predict what can happen and plan ways of dealing with it. Thus, it involves both imagination and executive functions.

I cannot imagine a 'standard' 17-year-old who would have allowed his mother to comb his hair publicly (or ever). I am not saying that it was wrong of Tom's mum (well, maybe a bit wrong), and I can certainly sympathize with her. It is only natural to want to make your child look good, and it is the child who tends to prevent us from doing this when they reach a certain age! It is the *child* who starts the process of pushing parents away, and the parents just have to learn to deal with it.

But what if the child does not do this? Well, it takes a lot of awareness and maturity in order to, as a parent, launch this process. It will feel somewhat 'against nature' to do this.

But is it necessarily a bad thing not to have freed yourself from your parents? No, it might not have to be. But for the sake of the feeling of personal freedom and the opportunity to achieve what you want, it may be helpful. As professionals, we cannot directly do anything about this, but indirectly we can create the *conditions* – by using tools which compensate for difficulties, by contributing to increased self-knowledge and self-esteem.[8]

A client who suffers from a feeling of 'chronic powerlessness' often indeed has very little real power. And sometimes, a (not very fruitful) power struggle will occur.

EXAMPLE

Helen is enrolled at a care centre for 'difficult' adolescents with autism. Helen will sometimes show 'inappropriate behaviour'. When Helen throws a chair across the floor in frustration and anger, she learns that her allowance will be withheld this week. But last week when she turned over a table no one withheld her pocket money.

How can Helen understand this? Is it that chairs are worth more than tables? Is it the sum of a table last week, plus a chair this week that makes 'the crime so serious'? Or is it about which staff are present when this

---

8   As a parenthesis, I will just mention that many parents have told me they were greatly helped by professionals who indicated that they needed to be aware that their children actually now were teens or adults. It is terribly easy to be blind as a parent, and in some way one's children always are *children*, however old they are. But how to point this out to the families, is very much about how good and strong a relationship we have with them, and it is therefore difficult to generalize about.

happens? (Yes! And this is also where power becomes arbitrary,[9] which by the way is a shortcut to placing someone in chronic powerlessness.)

Even if Helen had had a well-functioning ability to form mental images and a good social understanding (she did not have either) it would have been difficult for her to understand and predict when and why spending money withdrawn sometimes was. And if she does not understand this, how can withdrawal of allowance help her to regulate her behaviour? How can the message be something other than 'We have the power', and how can Helen be expected to respond in any other way than, through her behaviour, trying to regain some power?

So when Helen yells 'You are fucking sick, you bloody freaks!' and throws the coffee maker on the floor, it is not only an understandable, but a healthy reaction, in my opinion.[10]

How do we break a power struggle? Well, since it is the staff who are professional, it must be them who relinquish some of their power.

Paradoxically, staff often feel powerless and that these clients have a lot of power. They might say 'Bob controls the entire service' or 'Joanna play us off against each other'. A meeting between a powerless individual and a powerless group of employees is seldom fruitful. But the staff (who do not have a disability that affects social understanding and imagination) are much more likely to be able to start changing their behaviour than the individual with the disability is.

But how do you relinquish power in practice? It's more of an attitude, than about actions, and therefore it is difficult to describe. But I want to be specific so I'll try to give an example, or rather two.

EXAMPLE

James has autism and a difficulty with regulating his behaviour. He also lacks constructive strategies for coping with stress. What is stressful to James is, among other things, when he does not understand; when things do not turn out as he thought they would; when staff give different

---

9 Individual staff do not make 'withdrawal of benefits' decisions at this care unit. But all staff know (although they never speak about this) that Mary reacts more strongly to 'furniture throwing' than does Tony; and that's why, when Mary at the staff meeting presented the proposal to withdraw Helen's spending money emphatically, the others agreed and the decision was made. Tony, who was present when the table was turned over last week never thought of raising this as a reason for suspension of allowance. (Tony is a quiet guy and does not protest against Mary's proposal either.) So, as you see, it will be quite arbitrary, and up to individual staff.

10 If you feel somewhat provoked by my opinion, and cannot understand how a destructive behaviour can be constructive, you will have to go back to Chapter 2 and read it again. Or, of course, you might just disagree with me. Well, that's OK.

answers to the same question; when he fails with something; when he feels stupid.

The staff examine, together with James, what stresses him. They document this, and then ask James to read and review the documentation and make changes if there's anything they have got wrong.

Then they set up an Intervention Plan together with James, which describes how the staff will support him in different situations and suggests strategies that they want to help James to use.

I hope you see the difference.

Another way to break powerlessness is to change the means of communication from helpers to clients. One way is to communicate on intent, rather than on guilt, when something 'inappropriate' has occurred. And to carry your own responsibilities in a clear way. Here's what the communication too often sounds like:

Helper: Nadia, I want to speak with you. You know you are not allowed into the medicine cabinet! Why did you go into the office at all. Clients are not allowed to be in the office!

Nadia: But the door was open…

Helper: Only staff are allowed in the office, you know that!

Nadia: I don't give a damn!

Let's look more closely at this communication:

Helper: Nadia, I want to speak with you.

This is not true in this case, the helper does not really want, or does not have the ability, to speak with Nadia. She wants to talk *to* Nadia. She wants to tell her what's right and what's wrong, and to make Nadia stop doing 'wrong'.

Helper: You know you are not allowed into the medicine cabinet!

This is a phrase designed to make Nadia feel bad, to be ashamed. To start by blaming someone is rarely a good entry point for bringing about a true communication.

Helper: Why did you go into the office at all, clients are not allowed to be in the office!

The helper is not particularly interested in 'why'; the question is mostly rhetorical. The word 'why' can also be extremely accusatory if used with a particular intonation.

Nadia: But the door was open…

Here Nadia actually gives a good and reasonable explanation. Nadia's difficulties include problems with impulse control, and at this moment in fact both the office and the medicine cabinet were suddenly unlocked.

Helper: Only staff are allowed in the office, you know that!

The helper is not listening to Nadia's explanation; instead she blames Nadia once again.

Nadia: I don't give a damn!

Nadia's response is quite adequate as the helper (a) is not listening and (b) on two occasions blamed her. If you do as the helper did, this is the response you usually get.

Here's how it could have sounded, had the helper had better communication skills:

Helper: Nadia, I heard you went into the office yesterday. It was really careless of us to leave the door open!

Nadia: Mmm.

Helper: I can understand that you were curious about what was in there. I wonder what it was you were looking for in the medicine cabinet?

Nadia: To see what was in there…

Helper: Were you just curious to see what was in there?

Nadia: Yeah, I am wondering why I don't get medicines, since Mark does.

Helper: OK, I understand. You have no medicines, since you don't need any. And it's a good thing that you don't need medicine. Many medicines have side effects. Do you know what that means?

Nadia: Yes.

Helper: I want to tell you about how it is supposed to work here. What I am saying is that both the office and the medicine cabinet are supposed to be locked, and the reason for that is for your protection. We must ensure that none of the clients gets the wrong, or too much medicine. And then we have to protect your papers in the office. The information about you, and the other clients, is confidential. This means that if you want, you are entitled to look at your records, but not the others', and they can't look at yours. Can you understand me?

Nadia: Yeah… Can I look at my records?

Helper: Sure, we can arrange a time for it. You know, in some ways it was good that this happened, because now we must learn not to be careless about locking the doors – that is our responsibility! Thanks for letting me talk to you about this.

Nadia: OK. When can I look at my records?

Figure 23.1: Keys to communication on intent

Some keys in this communication are taking responsibility for your own part in what happened (there is usually a large part), and the phrases that communicate intentions and normalize the event, for example:

- I can understand that…
- It is quite understandable that…
- It is common to…
- I should have…

Now perhaps you are thinking that if a client is acting out, and might have hit or kicked someone, it will be difficult to communicate positively about it. No, it need not be.

EXAMPLE

Helper: Michael, I certainly understand that it was not your intention that Cathy would be hurt. I wonder how we could prevent this from happening again?

Michael: I dunno.

Helper: You know, Michael, I certainly understand that you don't have the answer to that. How about we try to go through together what happened.

Michael: OK.

Helper: I've been thinking about one thing that I did just before you had that meltdown. I said that you should take another plate. I think you understood it to be me saying you had done something wrong.

Michael: Hmm.

Helper: I should have known better; I shouldn't have expressed myself as I did, because I know how stressed out you are when you get the feeling that you've done something wrong. You did nothing wrong. It was I who was so rigid in my thinking, that I thought you must take one of the plates on the table.

Michael: Mmm. You did wrong.

Helper: Yes, indeed I did. But I would like for us together to find a way for you to tell me when I make mistakes, so that no one is injured again. Can we try doing that?

Michael: OK.

This type of conversation is often done with the aid of other tools that I have already mentioned. It may be a 'comic strip conversation', where you illustrate with stick figures what happened and what people felt or thought. Or you can have them in the form of a 'computer talk', where you sit and 'talk' (i.e. type) in front of a computer keyboard. You also need to remember how you sit (and that sitting opposite each other may not be the best option). If you want to become skilled in communicating positively about difficult things, you have to practise.

Breaking powerlessness is also about creating a meaningful content in life, and making sure that the individual has influence and can really affect his life. Aren't many of the good things in life about looking forward to things, as well as enjoying the here and now? When I meet clients I am sad to say many of them have very little fun in the here and now, and not much to look forward to. Of course this varies with the type of services, being worst in forensic psychiatry. (I never really got that, by the way. So they are sentenced to being locked up and treated because they committed a crime. I get that part. But do they really have to be sentenced to be in an ugly environment with boredom as the main companion?) Amanda is a 20-year-old woman who was sentenced to forensic psychiatric care for trying to strangle a learning disabled co-resident at her group home. (The person survived, and the reason Amanda, who is terribly sound sensitive, presented was that the person made such awful noises all the time.) When Amanda in her second year of serving a forensic psychiatric sentence goes berserk over the broken promise of having ice-cream on New Year's Eve (because the kitchen had a problem), you may consider whether the decision to put her in detention for this really is reasonable. I mean, she's been looking forward to that ice-cream for months. Getting ice-cream four to five times a year is about as fun it gets for her.[11]

23.5 Better communication skills break powerlessness

Discussion groups with the aim of practising having your say, being assertive, and arguing for your opinion are a good idea. If your mentalization skills are delayed, it may be difficult to understand what information others need in order to comprehend what you are saying. We can help the person with this, both by understanding the deficiency, and through the use of tools (such as social stories) to clarify what is not 'visible'.

EXAMPLE

Chelsea is 12 years old and has autism. The class is going to the swimming pool. There's construction work going on along the route they usually take, a shortcut, and therefore they turn left at a point when they normally don't. Chelsea screams, throws herself on the ground and refuses to get up. 'That way,' she yells, pointing in the direction they normally take.

Eventually they manage to get her to get up and arrive at the swimming pool. But Chelsea is so tired after her meltdown that she

---

11   Sometimes I am appalled by how little some staff use their mentalization skills, although they have them all right!

cannot manage to shower and put on her bathing suit (even though she loves to swim).

When they arrive back at school, her teacher sits with her for a while and makes a conversation with pictures:

Teacher: Chelsea, this is when we were going to the swimming pool.

The teacher draws stick figures and write names on them.

Teacher: You wanted to go the usual route, but it was closed for construction work. I was thinking like this: 'It's best to take the big road, where we can walk straight ahead. It will be faster.'

The teacher draws a thought bubble and writes what she was thinking.

Teacher: What were you thinking, Chelsea?

Chelsea: I wanted to go the usual route.

Teacher: Yes, I understand that you wanted that. I wonder what you were thinking.

Chelsea: I don't know... I wanted to go to the usual pool.

Teacher: Aha, you thought you did not know where we were going?

Chelsea: I wanted to go to the usual pool.

Teacher: I see. You probably thought that if we took a different route we would go to another pool, is that true?

Chelsea: Yes.

The teacher writes Chelsea's thoughts in her thought bubble.

Teacher: That's great, now I understand what you thought. If you remember, it's a great help for me if you tell me what you think when this stuff happens.

Helping people with autism spectrum disorders to improve their communication skills is always a part of our work. This may be (and is often) written in the Intervention Plan, but on an everyday basis, you can have as a pervasive purpose: 'How can I help the client to improve his communication in this situation?' I try to keep this in mind in all situations (that said, I do not always succeed).

The fact that we as helpers always want to do just that – help – can sometimes be a disservice. For the person to be able to communicate better, he or she also needs to have a greater self-knowledge. So when Linda calls home to her parents and threatens to kill herself, or when Chris throws frying pans, what should we do? Well, you've probably already understood that we do not lock up the pans or the phone.

And you already know that we make an assessment to get below the surface of the iceberg, and from this create an Intervention Plan.

But one additional step is to help Linda and Chris to understand what we understand. It could be that the telephone calls have an anxiety-reducing effect for Linda (where we of course can offer other methods), and/or that her anxiety is triggered by a certain type of stress, perhaps combined with hunger or, alternatively, that it becomes a way of filling time when Linda is bored. It could be that Chris throws frying pans when he is stressed out, and someone speaks to him; or that the pans go on the floor when he feels he has failed; or when he has a feeling (for example, disappointment) which he cannot name and recognize; or something else.

Our goal is not only to make the threats cease and the pans stay where they should be, but also to enable Linda to say things like 'Now I feel like that again, maybe I need to eat something', and for Chris to be able to say 'Do not talk to me!' when he stands there with frying pans in his hands.

Much of the approach outlined in this book works by increasing communication and breaking powerlessness. If this is a timely subject for you in your service right now, I would particularly refer you back to Chapter 4 'Just Doing Your Job or Being a True Professional?' I would also suggest you be sure to read the quote by Herbert Lovett at the end of this book.

Finally, I'd like to recommend Michelle Garcia Winner's work on 'social thinking' (Garcia Winner 2008). She has written several books on the subject, and I have found her approach very useful in teaching social interaction skills, and discussing with people of all ages with autism.

24

Methods and Approaches

A Short Chapter About Some
Specific Techniques That May Be Useful

Elsewhere in this book I have spoken of the importance of making the purpose of a task clear. As you might recall, I did not think highly of the so-often-used reward systems, as they make the reward equal to the purpose, and I think this is not what we need to teach people. Making the purpose clear can be difficult as we as human beings do many things without knowing the purpose, or just for a social purpose (the feeling of togetherness, of not standing out in a crowd) and this may not be a valid purpose for an individual with autism. Sometimes we need to find the purpose of certain behaviour, in order to serve that purpose in a more appropriate or well-functioning way. Here collaborative problem solving (CPS), as described by Ross W. Greene (2001, 2006, 2008) can be very helpful. This is an approach where both parties put their concerns on the table and then look for a solution that can satisfy both. You can read more about this in the excellent books by Ross W. Greene; just let me give you two examples from real life here.

EXAMPLE

One mother with a teenage daughter with autism was concerned that her daughter didn't care much about hygiene. The mother said 'If you don't take a shower you will smell bad, and then your friends at school will not want to sit next to you.' Well, being the evidence-seeking scientist, her daughter took no showers and found that her classmates did not seem to care; they sat next to her anyway. 'So Mum, you see, I don't have to shower,' she said. After finding out about CPS, her mother tried this method, and asked her daughter what her concern about showering was. It turned out her daughter was concerned with her hair-dye being washed out every time she showered, and since she had to use her allowance to buy it she did not want to shower. By collaborative problem solving they together decided that the mum would buy all the hair-dye she wanted as long as she took a shower every other day. Problem solved!

The thing is, as long as we do not know how the problem looks from another person's perspective, it will be difficult to solve it. Here is another example, this time of 'accidental collaborative problem solving'.

EXAMPLE

Doris, the mother of Joshua, who had autism, had such trouble buying shoes for him. He just hated new shoes, and even more so shopping for new shoes. And every time it was time to go shopping for shoes she tried her best, and it ended in tears and yelling (on both parts). The thing was, Joshua always wanted them to buy shoes that were three or four times too big.

Doris tried everything she could. She looked for wide shoes, and shoes in soft materials, thinking this was about a tactile sensory problem. But no, Joshua always wanted these enormous shoes which made him look like a clown.

Finally one day, in the shoe shop, Doris fell apart, crying out 'WHY DO YOU WANT SUCH BIG SHOES?!' Whereupon Joshua looked at her and replied calmly 'Well, I thought if we buy them really big I won't have to buy new shoes for a couple of years.' This made perfect sense of course, from his point of view. Now, the solution to this was that they go out and buy shoes in several sizes for the years ahead.

Some could argue that CPS, like several other approaches are just 'common sense'. True, they have much common sense to them. But the bad news is that there is so much 'uncommon sense' out there that we often need these approaches.

24.1 Social stories and drawn conversations

I have already explained this method in a previous chapter. Here I just want to mention the usefulness again, and illustrate that this is not only an approach to be used with children. Camilla works in a day service for people with autism spectrum disorders and ADHD. She tells me she makes great use of 'draw-talk' with the users, especially since conflicts arises from time to time. In the service they find it most useful to draw on a big whiteboard. Camilla writes:

'Sarah, 24, who has ADHD, comes to me one day and wants to talk about something. She brings Frederick, 27, who has ADHD and Asperger syndrome. We sit in a room where we have access to a whiteboard. Sarah and Frederick tell me that Thomas, 25, who has ADD and Asperger syndrome has told both Frederick and another person in the service that Sarah is in love with him. Sarah is very worried by this.

Since I need to get the same picture that Sarah and Frederick have of what has happened, and also since Sarah and Frederick need to become clear about the different perspectives, I begin to draw on the whiteboard. I draw a stick figure who is supposed to be Sarah (she laughs and says this skinny type looks nothing like her). I explain to Sarah that most important is the "thought bubble" above the figure. Now I ask Sarah: "What are you thinking right now?" She replies: "I'm angry."

Then I draw stick figures representing Thomas and Frederick. Sarah now informs me that I should draw Frederick in the middle rather than at the side since "he's like in between what has happened" (this is interesting information, which I will use when we later come to Frederick's "in-between role"). Now both Sarah and Frederick are satisfied with the picture.

I then ask: "What did Thomas say?" Frederick replies: "He said 'Sarah is in love with me'." I ask: "What did you say?" Frederick replies: "Did she really say that?" We keep on like this until both are satisfied. It is important to include thoughts, questions and reflections such as: "Could it be that Thomas, who has trouble expressing himself at times, may have meant 'I think that Sarah is in love with me?'" If so, this makes things somewhat different.

It is also important to address Frederick's "in-between role", and to show that when he made the decision to tell (blab to) Sarah what Thomas had said, he created this situation. This is not about blaming someone, but rather making visible how "my own actions" affect the situation.

After this meeting we came up with three important things:

- To think about what signals you send out to others.

- To think about when you have an 'in-between role'.

- Sometimes when people say things and have difficulty expressing themselves they might mean something else.

There was another turn in this conflict before it could be closed. At this point we had a meeting between Sarah and Thomas, and a support person (but without Frederick). As it ended up they resumed the friendship they had before this happened, and nobody needed to come to the service and feel bad.'

Furthermore Camilla tells me that if they as staff do not help to resolve conflicts, it will very easily end up in clients wanting someone to say they are 'sorry', but it's not that simple. Camilla says that it always tends to be the same person who should be apologizing, but that this person must be allowed to give his version of the situation. The goal is of course that the person himself will understand what happened, and why, in order to avoid the same things happening over and over again.

To me this shows how important drawing conversations is as a tool, and how sad it is if not all professionals have this tool at hand for people who cannot resolve conflicts on their own.

24.2 Solution-focused methods

This approach has been described on p.63 and p.320. For me it is perhaps the most useful additional approach I have learned. Having a solution-focused perspective helps create a positive working climate, both with clients and among ourselves as colleagues. It completes the 'problem-focused' approach we have when we dive to see what's under the surface. There's to my knowledge only one book about solution-focused therapy and Asperger syndrome specifically: *A Self-determined Future with Asperger Syndrome: Solution Focused Approaches* by E. Veronica Bliss and Genevieve Edmonds (2007).[1]

24.3 CAT-kit

The CAT-kit (Cognitive Affective Training-kit)[2] is developed for people with autism spectrum disorders and thus has the advantage of not needing to be adjusted other than for the individual (with approaches developed for other target groups we always need to adjust them to make them autism-friendly too).

24.4 Cognitive behaviour therapy

Cognitive behavioural therapy (CBT) has many useful components, but exists in a variety of approaches. It is well documented as a successful treatment for depression and phobias, for example. But I also see a lot of reward systems which are 'laundered' by the name

---

1   You can also find useful tips at www.chanceuk.com.

2   See www.cat-kit.com.

CBT. To me CBT is basically about how we feel (emotion), how we think (cognition), and how we act (behaviour), and the notion that these concepts interact. When we understand this better, are made aware of this, it will be easier for us to affect our thoughts, feelings and behaviours. To have basic knowledge of CBT is useful when working in the autism field.

24.5 Motivational interviewing

I am not myself trained in motivational interviewing (MI)[3], but I work together with people who are, and I understand this to be a useful tool too. The method has a lot in common with solution-focused practice, but with both CBT techniques and solution-focused conversation, a starting point is the client's wish for change. If that wish isn't (yet) there, MI might be a useful approach. Also, MI is not developed for autism spectrum disorders, and tools may need to be altered or adjusted to fit this group. For instance, colleagues tell me that the expressing empathy part (using the client's wording to summarize and reflect back to them what they have said) is not particularly useful, as many people with autism will not see the point and simply ask 'Why are you saying what I just said?'; but on the other hand, I'm told that other parts of the technique, called 'Roll with resistance' are very useful (such as avoiding argumentation and encouraging the client to come up with alternatives).

To summarize: there are several approaches and tools we can borrow from other areas, as long as we understand and are skilled enough in our area to adapt them to our clients. I am sure there are more than those described in this book, I am always in the process of learning and curious to find out what could be around the next corner. It's a good thing the toolbox is infinitely expandable!

---

3   You can read more about motivational interviewing at www.facilitatingchange.org.uk.

25

Tips, Tricks and Gadgets

A Chapter on How Some Problems Have Been Solved

I cannot leave the visual aids just yet. As many of the clients I meet have additional difficulties and disorders, for example ADHD, there are also often problems with attention and memory. And many young adults I meet really desire an independent life, therefore we need to find out what aids can help them to achieve that.

Among the visual aids there are many relatively simple things such as:

- Tagging places in the home for mobile phone, keys and other such things since it's important to know where they are. *Compensates for lack of attention, difficulty with memory and overview.*

- Writing down instructions and checklists for those who find it difficult to know in which order you should wash the dishes, shower, or how to get things done. *Compensates, for example, for difficulties with executive functions and working memory.*

- Making clear schedules of the contents of days or weeks. *Compensates, among other things, for difficulties with imagination.*

It is not possible to make an exhaustive list. The possibilities of creating aids are many. In this chapter I just want to give you some ideas of how some people have solved their problems, taken from interviews I have held with them about their aids and support.

25.1 Learning to shop

It is not uncommon to need support to shop for groceries, but sometimes we are so focused on support that we forget to help people to do things independently. Neppe, a woman with ADHD, tells me how her residential supporters taught her this. She's very particular in describing that she's not all about 'deficits and difficulties'.

'It's not that I couldn't drive myself, or go to the shops. I am 43 years old, and I have three children. I am skilled in many ways. But the shopping was really chaotic. I would run down to the supermarket several times a day, and yet I often didn't have what I needed at home. And with three quite small children, it was jumbled,' she says.

She tells me that what was helpful was that the residential supporters added a long-term plan and that this could take time. They began by setting a time and date for shopping. The first five weeks, they came home to her house, and they accompanied her throughout the shopping, and then followed her back. In the next step, she started to do the grocery list by herself and the supporters met her at the supermarket, they shopped together, and they said goodbye at the supermarket. 'What I needed to understand was that the shopping takes time, and see it as something that must be planned. Shopping is a big task and I cannot schedule something else that day. Now I have a particular day a week for shopping.'

The supporters also taught her to self-scan at the supermarket. 'Self-scanning is great, I had not wanted to learn it before – it just stressed me, I felt "Oh no, not more technology."'

The supporters scanned together with Neppe for five or six weeks before she did it on her own. She says that it is great, because now she doesn't have the stress of getting the goods on the conveyor belt and then packing them again. She can also calculate how many bags she will need and that she can carry them.

Neppe says that it actually was not very difficult either to learn to shop effectively or to self-scan in the supermarket. But it was important to have a clear routine at the supermarket, always shop at the same supermarket and to take the same route round the shop.

The attitude of the supporters is important. 'An aid should be a joint project,' Neppe says, and continues 'I think it is unusual to get help to become independent in an activity, and for it to be able to take such a long time. I think that many people who have residential support may get too much help; you might go shopping with them every time, even though they could learn to do it themselves. It's just that this help, learning how to manage things on your own, takes time.'

25.2 Structure in the fridge

Eve is the mother of two adult sons, both diagnosed with autism, and one of them also with bipolar disorder and ADHD. Both sons have a great wish to live independently, and to make that possible they have built a structure for shopping and cooking. Basically they meet once a week to make a weekly menu and from that a grocery list, and then they go shopping. When they come home from the shop they have seven plastic boxes in the fridge, marked 'Sunday', 'Monday', etc. The groceries go, together with the recipe in the corresponding plastic box. In this way the sons know what to cook and eat, and have what they need at home.

25.3 Belt bag

One woman who always lost her phone and keys (and sometimes her wallet too) found the belt bag to be 'revolutionary'. She realized she often lost things when she put them down because she needed to hold or pick something up (for example while unlocking the car, she might put her wallet on the car roof, and then get into the car and drive away). 'Now I am truly hands-free,' she says. 'I always know where I have my things. Whether I'm indoors or out, I always wear my belt bag.'

25.4 Smart phones and apps

Smart phones have many useful functions for people who need support. Jenny, for example, would put a load of laundry into the machine but having great difficulties with memory and impulse control, as well as time perception, she would forget all about it. Now she uses the timer function on her mobile phone to remember. It is easier for her to set the time with a timer, than to calculate the time by looking at a watch. Some people I have talked to, who have specific troubles with time perception, often use music on an iPod or smart phone as time measurement. They know that this will take 'three tunes', or decide that 'I will be on the computer until this playlist is done', and then turn off and go to bed.

Making voice notes has been useful for many reasons, but I just want to mention a man I interviewed here. He had Asperger's as well as OCD and he would go back to his flat several times to check if he had locked the door and turned off the stove. He started making voice notes on his phone, beginning with the date and time and then saying, 'Now I am turning off the stove', 'Now I am locking the door', etc. And while at work he just needed to listen to his message to feel reassured he had done this. A global positioning system (GPS) is very useful for some people with Asperger's I know, who have trouble with their sense of direction and are always afraid of getting lost.

Apps are still very much about games and entertainment, but these can also be helpful. I have talked to several people who have had trouble with public transport, both in terms of waiting for the bus, and of crowds and sitting next to people they do not know. For some of them, the possibility of shielding themselves by playing games on their phone, or listening to music has been an important aid. Then there are several apps that are helpful in a more practical way. For example there are apps for finances and several calendar apps (which provide a better overview than the built-in ones). There are apps for locating your phone by texting it, and by GPS if you lose it, which will work even if it is put on silent mode. But listing apps here would not be meaningful since the market changes so rapidly. Probably we will see more apps in the future that specifically target the difficulties that people with autism and ADHD have.

25.5 Brushing teeth and hygiene

Due to motor difficulties some people with autism and ADHD do not brush their teeth as thoroughly as they should. Special toothbrushes (such as Collis Curve and Dr Barman's) can be very useful. Some clients have a difficulty with knowing how much soap or shampoo to use in the shower and have found it helpful to buy a set of travelling packs, and use refills, to always have the right 'portion' available.

25.6 Other stuff

Key finders such as 'Find One Find All' will also help you to find your wallet, your glasses and mobile phone (if you just find one of them you can 'beep' to find the rest), and have been useful for some people. As many clients have difficulties getting up in the morning, some of the more demanding alarm clocks may be useful. There are some that you have to chase around the bedroom in order to shut them off, some of them have a propeller that takes off so you have to find them in order to shut the alarm off, etc. These are not laid out as aids, but can be used as such. On the same theme there are today a lot of smart organizing and home decoration things that can be used as aids, for example there are self-adhesive images that can tell you what is inside the kitchen cabinets, which make it easier to keep things in order (and find things). (One man with high-functioning autism used to buy new pots all the time because he couldn't find the ones he had. With the help of an occupational therapist he got a basic working structure in the kitchen, with every cabinet and drawer tagged with a picture of its contents.)

26

Finally

The Last Chapter

This is the last chapter of this book. It is not even a chapter. Just a little something to finish this up. If you have read the book from the beginning till the end, I have hopefully brought you along with me on a kind of journey: I picked you up at the station where you were when you started reading, and here I am letting you off.

Now is the time to take your luggage with all the tools you have gathered, and start a new journey. If you want to share with me what has been useful, or have any suggestions or opinions about this book, please feel free to email me. I cannot promise that I will reply (I *want* to reply, but whether I am able to depends on how many people are emailing me, and what my daily life looks like at the moment). My address is gunilla@pavus.se.

I have worked on this book for years, thus it is with some sadness I wave you off here on the platform. Perhaps our paths will cross again, who knows?

27

But Wait a Minute?

Wasn't the Previous Chapter the Last Chapter?

Sure, it was. Almost. But as we are living in a modern world, we need some bonus material. Thus, I serve you this message from Herbert Lovett, as a dessert – enjoy!

Herbert Lovett, a brilliant psychologist and advocate for people with disabilities and their families who tragically died in a car accident in 1998 wrote a beautiful paragraph in his truly great book (1996), in which he compares the process of liberation of women, African-American and gay people to those with disabilities.

Lovett says there are two steps an oppressed minority need to go through to become liberated. In this first step, according to Lovett, people have found the pride of being a women, an African- American or a homosexual. The next necessary step is that the people around this minority have to acknowledge that labels have nothing to do with rights and dignity.

As the liberation of people with disabilities begins, we can no longer talk about the 'tragedy' of having a physical or mental disability any more than we can speak of the 'tragedy' of having been born female, Lovett says. And this means, that we can't speak of sufferers in respect to disabilities. One doesn't suffer from having Down's syndrome or autism any more than one suffers from being born a woman or a homosexual. There can be suffering but this is rather due to prejudices against these groups.

In the future Lovett predicts that we cannot continue to presume that a certain group of people inevitably should live lives that others have chosen for them, and that our professional roles will be restored to their original premise of helping people to be what they want to be rather than assessing who we think they are and getting them to accept our assessment as their reality (Lovett 1996).

Appendix 1

As mentioned in the book, a questionnaire, or rather a structured interview, can be a good way of getting more information about how a service user or pupil perceives the environment and himself. Even if the person finds it difficult to answer the questions, this is too valuable in helping us to understand what is problematic in his everyday life.

In my experience, I obtain much more information this way than by just talking to the person. What is helpful is that the individual does not have to process and interpret a lot of my body language and facial expressions; if eye contact is difficult for him, this approach automatically avoids it, as we are both looking at the paper. It can also help the person to focus, to stay on track and see that this conversation has a structure. The Q&A style seems to work well with many clients as it is clear and 'matter of fact'.

Absolutely the main thing to understand is that although this may look like a survey, it isn't really one (i.e. it is, in my opinion, pointless to give this paper to a person just to fill out as a form – rather, this is a visual and structured basis for a conversation).

What questions should you ask? That depends on what you want to know, of course. You also have a choice in how to ask them. Questions with statements, where you can circle the ones that fit, work best for some individuals. Such a question can look like the one below (and here, of course, we use our autism-specific knowledge when we come up with the statements):

If you sometimes find it difficult to get going, which factors affect you? Circle the statements that fit:

- getting out of bed in the morning

- getting dressed

- the transport

- remembering to bring or finding the things I need (keys, wallet, phone, etc.)

- handling possible changes that might occur during the day

- finishing what I am doing

- keeping track of time.

- Other: ....

Of course, if the person circles one or more of these statements, we should ask questions about this, such as 'Why is the transport difficult?'; and if the person cannot answer such an open question, again we may provide alternatives, such as 'Is it because it can be crowded?' or 'Is it because it is hard to be on time for the train?', etc.

If possible, it is a good idea to have the person write these things down too (although I offer to write for those who have difficulties writing or who just don't want to). I also ask if we can keep the paper, in order to refer back to it and see how we can help the person with whatever is a problem.

We may also want to ask the person about general things he or she might have difficulties with, such as sensory problems, other symptoms or energy levels. The questionnaire may look like this:

Questions about sensory processing

Are you sensitive to any of the following?

Light:	Yes	No	I don't know
Sound:	Yes	No	I don't know
Smell:	Yes	No	I don't know
Touch:	Yes	No	I don't know
Taste:	Yes	No	I don't know

Other: ....

Again, if the person circles 'Yes', you should follow up with further questions, such as 'In what situations?'; 'Do you have any strategies which are helpful for this?', etc.

You may also want to ask about how the client perceives the staff in general, as in:

Do you feel you receive the right level of support?	Yes	No	I don't know
If no:			
Do you have an idea what additional support might look like?	Yes	No	I don't know
Do you know in which situations you need more support?	Yes	No	I don't know
Do you feel the staff listens to you, and that you can make your opinion heard?	Yes	No	I don't know

These are just examples. You have to use your knowledge of autism and of the person to create the questions for your client. What questions, how many questions, open questions or questions with choices, or a mix of both types – it all depends on the client's difficulties, his age and the situation. Sure, you will make some mistakes (e.g. a question might not be clear enough, or perhaps you don't get the information you wanted), but that is how you will learn to do it better next time!

Measuring Challenging Behaviour 1

Note that we would only measure the frequency of such behaviours in order to be able to evaluate our efforts to enhance the individual's skills, reduce stress, etc. Here is an empty form, and the next page is an example of a form with notes.

	Monday	Tuesday	Wednesday	Thursday	Friday
8–12 A.M.					
12–5 P.M.					
5–8 P.M.					
	Comment	Comment	Comment	Comment	Comment
	Informant:	Informant:	Informant:	Informant:	Informant:

Measuring Challenging Behaviour 2

V=Verbal, P=Physical, P+=Physical where someone was hurt

The idea is to do this over a short period of time, in order to see if we, after implementing new methods, approaches and aids, can see a decrease. Otherwise, we refrain from focusing too much on the actual behaviours.

	Monday	Tuesday	Wednesday	Thursday	Friday
8–12 A.M.	V P+				
12–5 P.M.			V P		
5–8 P.M.	V V	V	P+ P P		P+
	Comment	Comment	Comment	Comment	Comment
	Tired! Tough weekend according to mum		No lunch, many disappointments		
	Informant: GG	Informant: SW	Informant: GG	Informant: SW	Informant: SW

References

American Psychiatric Association (2000) *Diagnostic and Statistical Manual of Mental Disorders Fourth Edition Text Revision DSM-IV-TR.* Arlington, VA: American Psychiatric Association.

Anderberg, M. (2002) 'Omsorgstagares inflytande över vardag och framtid: en kvalitetsundersökning i två gruppbostäder för utvecklingsstörda.' Master's degree thesis, School of Social Work, Lund University. Available at www.uppsatser.se/uppsats/f63935bbb4/. Accessed 19 October 2012.

Autism-Europe (1998) *Code of Good Practice on Prevention of Violence Against Persons with Autism.* Brussels: Autism Europe.

Attwood, T. (2006) *The Complete Guide to Asperger's Syndrome.* London: Jessica Kingsley Publishers.

Ayanian, J.Z. (1999) 'Quality of Care by Race and Gender for Congestive Heart Failure and Pneumonia'. *Medical Care 37*, 12.

Ayres, A.J. (2005) *Sensory Integration and the Child: 25th Anniversary Edition.* Los Angeles: Western Psychological Services.

Baron-Cohen, S., Leslie, A.M. and Frith, U. (1985) 'Does the autistic child have a "theory of mind"?' *Cognition 21*, 1, 37–46.

Barton, J.J. *et al.* (2004) 'Are patients with social developmental disorders prosopagnosic? Perceptual heterogeneity in the Asperger's and socio-emotional processing disorders.' *Brain*, August, 127.

Bliss, E.V. and Edmonds, G. (2007) *A Self-determined Future with Asperger Syndrome: Solution Focused Approaches.* London: Jessica Kingsley Publishers.

Bogdashina, O. (2003) *Sensory Perceptual Issues in Autism and Asperger's Syndrome.* London: Jessica Kingsley Publishers.

Children's Hemiplegia and Stroke Association (CHASA). Information on sensory processing problems in those with hemiplegia available at www.chasa.org. Accessed 22 October 2012.

Cytowic, R.E. (2003) *The Man Who Tasted Shapes.* Cambridge, MA and London: MIT Press.

Cytowic, R.E. (2009) *Wednesday Is Indigo Blue: Discovering the Brain of Synaesthesia.* Cambridge, MA and London: The MIT Press.

De Clercq, H. (2003) *Mum, Is That a Human Being or an Animal?* Bristol, UK: Lucky Duck Publishing.

De Clercq, H. (2006) *Autism From Within: A Unique Handbook.* Kungsängen, Sweden: Intermedia Books.

Deci, E *et al.* (1999) 'A meta-analytic review of experiments examining the effects of extrinsic rewards on intrinsic motivation.' *Psychological Bulletin 125*, 6.

Department for Education (2011) *National Strategies.* Available at www.education.gov.uk/schools/toolsandinitiatives/nationalstrategies, accessed on 25 July 2012. (The National Strategies website is now closed, but this page gives links to find the relevant materials.)

Dunbar, R. (1998) *Grooming, Gossip, and the Evolution of Language.* Dunbar, Cambridge, MA: Harvard University Press.

Dunn Buron, K. and Curtis, M. (2003) *The Incredible 5-point Scale: Assisting Children with ASDs in Understanding Social Interactions and Controlling Their Emotional Responses.* Kansas: Autism Asperger Publishing Co.

Ekstam, K. (2003) *Vardagens etik.* Lund: Studentlitteratur.

Fombonne, E. (2009) 'Epidemiology of pervasive developmental disorders.' *Pediatric Research*, February, 11.

Garcia Winner, M. (2008) Information and book titles available at www.socialthinking.com. Think Social Publishing. Accessed 10 August 2012.

Gillberg, C. and Coleman, M. (2000) *The Biology of the Autistic Syndromes*. Cambridge: Cambridge University Press.

Grandin, T. (1995) *Thinking in Pictures*. New York: Vintage Books.

Gray, C. (1994) *Comic Strip Conversations: Illustrated Interactions That Teach Conversation Skills to Students with Autism and Related Disorders*. Arlington, TX: Future Horizons Incorporated.

Gray, C. (2010) *The New Social Story Book*. Arlington, TX: Future Horizons Incorporated.

Gray, C., Howley, M. and Arnold, E. (2005) *Revealing the Hidden Social Code: Social Stories for People with Autistic Spectrum Disorders*. London: Jessica Kingsley Publishers.

Greene, R.W. (2001) *The Explosive Child: A New Approach for Understanding and Parenting Easily Frustrated, Chronically Inflexible Children*. New York: Quill.

Greene, R.W. (2008) *Lost at School: Why Our Kids with Behavioral Challenges Are Falling Through the Cracks and How We Can Help Them*. New York: Scribner.

Greene, R.W. and Ablon, J.S. (2006) *Treating Explosive Kids: The Collaborative Problem-Solving Approach*. New York: The Guilford Press.

Groden, J. *et al.* (1994) 'The impact of stress and anxiety on individuals with autism and other developmental disabilities.' In G. Schopler and G.B. Mesibov (eds) *Behavioural Issues in Autism*. New York: Plenum Press.

Howlin, P., Baron-Cohen, S. and Hadwin, J. (1998) *Teaching Children With Autism to Mind-Read: A Practical Guide for Teachers and Parents*. Chichester: John Wiley & Sons.

Hilliard, L.J. and Liben, L.S (2010) 'Differing Levels of Gender Salience in Preschool Classrooms: Effects on Children's Gender Attitudes and Intergroup Bias'. *Child Development 81*, 6, 1787.

Holm, U. (2001) *Empati: att förstå andra människors känslor*. Stockholm: Natur och Kultur.

ILSMH (International League of Societies for Persons with Mental Handicap) (now Inclusion International) (1994) *The Belief, Values, and Principles of Self-Advocacy*. Cambridge, MA: Brookline Books.

Jørgensen, M. and Schreiner, P. (1985) *Fighter-relationen: barns kamp med vuxna*. Copenhagen: Hans Reitzels.

Kadesjö, B., Gillberg, C. and Hagberg, B. (1999) 'Brief report: autism and Asperger syndrome in seven-year-old children: a total population study'. *Journal of Autism and Developmental Disorders 29*, 4, 327–331.

Kinge, E. (1999) *Empati hos vuxna som möter barn med särskilda behov*. Lund: Studentlitteratur AB.

Kohn, A. (1999) *Punished by Rewards*. Boston: Houghton Mifflin.

Lawson, W. (2001) *Understanding and Working with the Spectrum of Autism: An Insider's View*. London: Jessica Kingsley Publishers.

Lenke, B. and Wennberg, I. (1999) *Instinktsfällan: om människoskap, ledarskap, gruppens dynamik*. Sweden: Svenska Civilekonomföreningen.

Lepper, M., Greene, D., Nisbett, R. (1973) 'Undermining children's intrinsic interest with extrinsic reward: a test of the "over-justification" hypothesis.' *Journal of Personality and Social Psychology 13*, 28, 129–137.

Løgstrup, K.E. (1994) (originally published in Danish in 1956) *Det etiska kravet*. Göteberg: Daidalos.

Løgstrup, K.E., (2007) *Beyond the Ethical Demand*. Notre Dame IN: University of Notre Dame Press.

Lovett, H. (1996) *Learning to Listen: Positive Approaches and People with Difficult Behaviour*. London: Jessica Kingsley Publishers.

Mesibov, G.B., Shea, V. and Schopler, E. (2005) *The TEACCH Approach to Autism Spectrum Disorders (Issues in Clinical Child Psychology)*. New York: Springer.

National Autistic Society (NAS) (2012). Information about PDA is available at www.autism.org. uk/about-autism/related-conditions/pda-pathological-demand-avoidance-syndrome. aspx. Accessed 22 October 2012.

Normell, M. (2007) *Pedagogens inre rum   om betydelsen av känslomässig mognad*. Lund: Studentlitteratur AB.

Office for Disability Issues (2012). See http://odi.dwp.gov.uk/disability-statistics-and-research/disability-facts-and-figures.php#imp per 2012.08.28. (The statistics are reviewed and updated throughout the year as new data is published.) Accessed 22 October 2012.

Øyane, N. and Bjorvatn, B. (2005) 'Sleep disturbances in adolescents and young adults with autism and Asperger's syndrome.' *Autism 9*, 1, 83–94.

Paterson, B., Bradley, P., Stark, C., Saddler, D., Leadbetter, D. and Allen, D. (2003) 'Deaths associated with restraint use in health and social care in the UK: the results of a preliminary survey.' *Journal of Psychiatric and Mental Health Nursing 10*, 3–15.

Pavonen, E.J *et al.* (2008) 'Sleep in children with Asperger's syndrome.' *Journal of Autism and Developmental Disorders 38*, 1.

Powell, S. and Jordan, R. (1997) *Autism and Learning: A Guide to Good Practice.* London: David Fulton Publishers.

Rich Harris, J. (1999) *The Nurture Assumption: Why Children Turn Out the Way They Do.* New York: Free Press.

Rogers S.J. and Ozonoff, S. (2005) Annotation: What do we know about sensory dysfunction in autism? A critical review of the empirical evidence. *J Child Psychol Psychiatry, 46*, 12, 1255-68.

Rubio, R. (2009) *Basic Pathfinder Mind/Body Techniques for Asperger's Syndrome.* (DVD). London: Jessica Kingsley Publishers.

Rutherford, M.D. *et al.* (2007) 'Differences in discrimination of eye and mouth displacement in autism spectrum disorders.' *Vision Research 47*, 15.

Sayer, S. (2010) 'Politicians must recognise that people with learning disabilities have a right to vote too.' *The Guardian,* 20 January.

Sharry, J., Madden, B. and Darmody, M. (2003) *Becoming a Solution Detective: A Strengths-Based Guide to Brief Therapy.* London: Routledge.

Skau, G.M. (2005) *Gode fagfolk vokser: personlig kompetanse i arbeid med mennesker.* (*Good Professionals are Growing: Personal Expertise in Working with People.*) Oslo: Cappelen akademisk.

Skau, G.M. (1998) *Mellan makt och hjälp: om det flertydiga förhållandet mellan klient och hjälpare.* Stockholm: Liber.

Skau, G.M. (1998) *Mellan makt och hjälp.* Skau, G.M. (1998) Mellan makt och hjälp: om det flertydiga förhållandet mellan klient och hjälpare. Stockholm: Liber, (*Between Power and Help.*) Stockholm: Liber Utbildning.

Söderlund, G., Sikström, S. and Smart, A. (2007) 'Listen to the noise: noise is beneficial for cognitive performance in ADHD.' *Journal of Child Psychology and Psychiatry 48*, 8, 840–847.

Stålhandske, M. and Hägg, B. (2011) *HIP Hjälpmedel Inom Psykiatri.* Hjälpmedelsinstitutet.

Stallard, P. (2002) *Think Good – Feel Good: A Cognitive Behaviour Therapy Workbook for Children.* Chichester: John Wiley & Sons.

Stallard, P. (2005) *A Clinician's Guide to Think Good – Feel Good: Using CBT with Children and Young People.* Chichester: John Wiley & Sons.

Sterling, M., Jull G., Vicenzino, B. and Kenardy, J. (2003) 'Sensory hypersensitivity occurs soon after whiplash injury and is associated with poor recovery'. *Pain 10*, 509–517.

van Manen, M. (1991) 'Can Teaching Be Taught? or Are Real Teachers Found or Made?' *Phenomenology and Pedagogy 9*

Waltz, M. (2010) 'Great expectations: The Autism Act meets hope, misconceptions and realities'. Available at www.publicservice.co.uk/feature_story.asp?id=13684. Accessed on 22 October, 2012.

Waters, G. and Watling, R. (2000) 'Interventions to facilitate auditory, visual, and motor integration in autism: a review of the evidence.' *Journal of Autism and Developmental Disorders 30*, 5, October.

World Health Organization (1993) *The ICD-10 Classification of Mental and Behavioural Disorders: Diagnostic Criteria for Research.* Geneva: World Health Organization.

Resources

On the web (free stuff)

As you are no doubt aware, the internet is constantly changing, but I have tried to gather tips and information that are likely to be out there for some time. I have also tried to choose 'broader' kinds of information – things that will be of general interest to all UK professionals. The following is just a selection, and you can find many more national as well as local resources on the web.

Autism-specific information

The National Autistic Society (NAS)
www.autism.org.uk
On this website you can find lots of interesting articles about autism, information about upcoming conferences and much more. NAS also has a group on Facebook: www.facebook.com/NationalAutisticSociety.

Nursing Standard
http://mentalhealthpractice.rcnpublishing.co.uk/supplements/booklets-and-guides/autism/
At this address you can download the guide 'The Autism Act 2009: developing specialist skills in autism practice' and also a great poster with information you will constantly need to be reminded of – print it and pin it up in your staff room!

The Autism Education Trust
www.autismeducationtrust.org.uk
On this website you can download the report 'What is Good Practice in Autism Education?'; the section called 'Case studies' provides you with inspiring examples of enhancing education for pupils with autism.

Social Care Institute for Excellence
www.scie.org.uk
On this website you can find two videos on autism and the guide 'Improving Access to Social Care for Adults with Autism' (type in 'autism' in the search field to find them).

Education Scotland
www.educationscotland.gov.uk/resources/r/genericresource_tcm4587661.asp
Here you can find the extensive pdf 'Relationships, Sexual Health and Parenthood Resource for Young People with Autism Spectrum Disorder'.

Independent Parental Special Education Advice (IPSEA)
www.ipsea.org.uk
IPSEA provides free, legally based advice to families who have children with special educational needs.

Ambitious About Autism
www.ambitiousaboutautism.org.uk
Here you will find, among other things, information for parents about special education. The section 'Real Life Stories' is great reading. It is very parent orientated, but is useful since as a professional you will need to know what is out there for parents in order to point them in the right direction (information as a tool, remember?).

Talk About Autism
www.talkaboutautism.org.uk
An online discussion forum for parents, carers, family members, people on the spectrum and professionals. This is run by Ambitious About Autism (see above).

The Scottish Government (Riaghaltas na h-Alba)
www.scotland.gov.uk/Publications/2009/07/06111319/129
At this address you can download 'The Autism Toolbox: An Autism Resource for Scottish Schools', which is designed to support Education authorities, schools and pre-schools in the delivery of service and planning for children and young people with Autism Spectrum Disorders (ASD).

Healthtalkonline
www.healthtalkonline.org/Autism
Healthtalkonline lets you share in other people's experiences of health and illness. It has four sections: one for people who themselves are on the spectrum, one for parents, one for grandparents and the last one for siblings. It also contains articles, videos and forums.

Not about autism, but useful and interesting

Nidotherapy
www.nidotherapy.com
Nidotherapy is about changing the environment in all its forms so that a better fit is established between a person and every aspect of their surroundings. It was developed by Professor Peter Tyrer, who explains: 'It is essentially a

complicated matching process whereby people's deep desires, vague wishes, fundamental opinions and lifestyle are understood sufficiently to ensure that environmental factors in all their forms are adjusted sensibly and specifically to make the best fit for the patient'. Workshops in nidotherapy are held for professionals in psychiatry and social services.

The art of constructive conversation in schools: Interview with Kerstin Måhlberg and Maud Sjöblom

http://interviewscoertvisser.blogspot.se/2007/11/interview-with-kerstin-mhlberg-and-maud.html

At the interviewer Coert Visser's blog you can find many more articles on solution-focused work: www.articlescoertvisser.blogspot.se.

There are even more texts at

www.solutionfocusedchange.blogspot.se

OCD-UK

www.ocduk.org/

A national charity, working with and for children and adults whose lives are affected by Obsessive-Compulsive Disorder.

Tourettes Action

www.tourettes-action.org.uk

A national charity working to make life better for people with Tourette Syndrome.

ADDISS (The National Attention Deficit Disorder Information and Support Service)

www.addiss.co.uk

A charity that provides information, training and support for parents, sufferers and professionals in the fields of ADHD.

British Institute of Learning Disabilities

www.bild.org.uk

A website offering fact sheets, conferences, training, links and more.

And some (not altogether free) other stuff

As you have probably already guessed, I wouldn't recommend that you read every book in the Reference section of this book. That would be tiresome, and, to be honest, not every book I have referred to is that interesting. Sometimes you just find one golden nugget in a book or article of many pages. But the material I list below are things I think are really worth your while investing in – in terms of time as well as money.

'Triple Stories'

www.triplestories.com

'Triple Stories' is a great piece of software for PCs which helps improve communication, social skills, language and imagination for children with autism or special needs. In the 'studio' of the programme you can create your own personalized visual supports. I have found this very useful!

The Incredible 5-Point Scale

www.5pointscale.com

Ideas and tips on how to use the 5-point scale. Here you can download Kari Dunn Buron's 'Structured Student Interview', 'Social Cognition Paper' and more. In the section 'Smart Ideas' you will find the very useful 'Anxiety Curve'.

Social thinking

www.socialthinking.com

This is Michelle Garcia Winner's website, where you can buy her great books. There is also Michelle's blog and many articles explaining the concept of social thinking. I believe Michelle Garcia Winner is a pioneer in her work, explaining and teaching social skills to children, adolescents and adults with autism, or otherwise socially challenged individuals. Michelle mainly lectures in the USA (where she lives), but if you ever get a chance to listen to her talks, take it!

Studio III™

www.studio3.org

Studio III™ offers training in non-aversive behaviour management. Their Low Arousal Philosophy goes hand in hand with the way I work.

The CAT-kit

www.cat-kit.com

The Cat-kit is a very useful practical tool for enhancing self-insight, assertiveness, behavioural strategies and social interplay.

Finally, in short

Paul Stallard's books Think Good – Feel Good (John Wiley & Sons Ltd, 2001, 2005) are very useful in a practical way.

Tony Attwood's books are useful for theoretical understanding.

All Rita Jordan's books on autism and education are great and well worth reading.

And, of course, since I am still on the road of learning, there are probably many great books on the subject that I haven't read (yet!).

Index

acting out 59, 93, 192, 229,
254, 266–7, 273
adaptation 161, 162, 279, 281
ADDISS (The National
Attention Deficit Disorder
Information and Support
Service) 376
ADHD *see* attention deficit
hyperactivity disorder
adjustments
accepting the diagnosis 289
assessments and analyses 223
reward systems 212, 214
sensory processing issues 127
toolbox 276, 277, 279,
280–2
adventure trails 139
affirmation 219
aids
assessment 162–3, 223, 237
communication 154–5
executive functions 183
good aids that no one uses
93–4
motor skills 133, 135
reward systems 212, 214
sensory processing issues 103,
126, 127
toolbox 276, 277, 279
visual aids 292–317
Aikido 138
alarm clocks 362–3
alarm system 122–3
alcohol 117
alertness 329, 330
almanacs 295
Ambitious About Autism 375
American Psychiatric Association
189
analysis 238–9
Anderberg, M. 73
anger
challenging behaviour 203–5,
207–9, 252, 267
executive functions 183
self-knowledge and self-
esteem 337, 339
'anger-papers' 208, 209
announcing your actions 164–5
Antonovsky, Aaron 169
apps 361–2
Asperger, Hans 129
Asperger syndrome
assessment 234
definition 186
echolalia 153

motor skills 129
smart phones and apps 361,
362
solution-focused techniques
357
surroundings 284
theory of mind 146
assertiveness training 91
assessment 220–50
analysis and hypothesis
238–9
assessment structure 224
communication 236–7
documentation 246–7
evaluation 246
history 224–5
the individual 225–8
Intervention Plan 239–45
involuntary offenders 233–6
measurement 228–9
observation 229–30
overview 220–3, 223–37,
249–50
of staff 230–1
troubleshooting 247–9
visual aids 299, 300, 304
the whole 237
work-up for diagnosis 189
attention 136, 290, 359
attention deficit hyperactivity
disorder (ADHD)
cognition 181, 183, 184
definitions 187
gender trap 92
motor skills 139
sensory processing issues
113, 123
tips, tricks and gadgets 359,
359, 361, 362
attitudes 168–70, 194
attribution 216–17
Attwood, Tony 133, 377
audio-posture synaesthesia 121
auditory perception 111–15,
123, 128, 282
Autism Act 14
Autism Education Trust 374
Autism-Europe 203
autism societies 283–4
autism-specific knowledge 15,
16, 17, 57, 87, 88
autism spectrum disorders
causes 188
common pitfalls for staff 77,
87–8, 90, 92, 96–8
definitions 186, 187

development perspective
144–51
diagnostic criteria 189
incidence 187–8
liberation of people with
disabilities 365
motor skills 129, 131, 136
problematic behaviours 24,
26–30
professionalism 14–15,
49, 50
sensory processing issues 100,
101, 102, 108, 117
work-up for diagnosis 189
'auto correction' 167–8
automatization 130–6
autonomy 30, 71, 277, 279,
292
awareness
common pitfalls for staff 69,
85, 88, 93
the individual 284
professionalism 37–44, 58
Ayanian, J.Z. 92
Ayres, Jean 124

balance 116–17, 139, 141
balance of power 343–51
ball covers 267
bans 76–8
Baron-Cohen, S. 145
Barton, J.J. 108
belt bag 361
biological causes 188
bipolar disorder 361
Bjorvatn, B. 177
blackout curtains 282
bladder control 119, 263
blame 20, 83, 165, 202–3, 347,
348
blankets 267
Bliss, E.V. 357
blogging 249, 294–5
body language 26, 329
body perception 117–18, 137,
139, 140, 142–3, 263,
336
Bogdashina, Olga 107, 122
boundary setting 49, 198, 199
bowel control 119, 262–3, 264
brain function 100–2, 110, 112,
113, 118
brain gyms 142
break times 94, 96, 126
British Institute of Learning
Disabilities 376

brushing teeth 79, 131, 362
'buddy' role 73–5
bullying 26, 146, 165, 270, 289

calendars 295, 296, 297, 298, 362
careers 301–3
car travel 247
categorization 184–5
CAT-kit (Cognitive Affective Training-kit) 338, 357, 377
CBT *see* cognitive behavioural therapy
cell phones 296, 359, 361–2
central coherence 184
cerebral palsy 82, 100
chain-weighted blankets 267
chairs 133
challenging behaviour
assessment 221, 223, 228–9
avoiding blaming the client 202–4
change process 192–4
common contributing factors 251–67
ability to form mental images 255–9
communication 264–6
fighting and self-injuring 266–7
overview 251–3
self-esteem 253–4
theory of mind 259–64
danger of focusing on the behaviour itself 268–74
development of mature strategies 204–9
factors affecting mood 252
making the professional 'environmentally friendly' 198–202
measurement 369–70
punishment and consequences 192–209
truth and consequences 194–7
change process 191–274
assessments and analyses 220–50
challenging behaviours 251–67
common pitfalls for staff 87–8
danger of focusing on the behaviour itself 268–74
professionalism 39–42, 65
punishment and consequences 192–209
reward systems 210–19
chat boxes 163, 308
checklists 38–9, 359

childhood disintegrative disorder 187–8
Children's Hemiplegia and Stroke Association 100
choices 73, 292–4, 294–5
chores 92, 131, 134, 135, 174
circadian rhythm 29
circle time 329, 330
cleaning 29, 30, 92, 131, 135
client/helper relationship model 85–6
climbing 138
clothes 89–90, 91, 109, 111, 141, 175
clothes-by-temperature-thermometer 212, 315–17
clumsiness 122, 129, 130, 141
coercive care 218, 269
cognition 180–9
categorization 184–5
executive functions 180–3
working memory 183–4
cognitive behavioural therapy (CBT) 357–8
Coleman, M. 188
collaborative problem solving (CPS) 354, 355
Collis Curve toothbrushes 362
colours 119, 120
comic strip conversations 300–10, 350
common pitfalls for staff 67–98
excessive empathy 80–2
falling into the buddy role 73–5
falling into the parental role 69–73
gender trap 91–3
good aids that no one uses 93–4
lack of empathy 82–6
'more normal than normal' 89–91
normality produces quality of life 96–8
other children will never accept... 95–6
overview 67–8
prohibiting or allowing 76–8
restraints 75–6
steering the will of others 79–80
universal truths 86–7
'we know this' 87–8
'what if everybody?' 94–5
communication 152–72
announcing your actions 164–5
assessment 236–7
'attitude' 168–70
challenging behaviour 264–6
echolalia 153–5
falling into the buddy role 74

lack of 'auto correction' 167–8
language comprehension and verbal expression 152
literal language comprehension 165–6
professionalism 45, 48
repetitive communication 170–2
restorative communication 170
self-knowledge and self-esteem 337, 347–50, 351–3
truths, lies and subtext 155–64
compliance 91, 205
computer talk 318–19, 350
concentration 112, 290
Confucius 15
consent 204
consequences 194–7, 256, 257
constructive actions 21, 193–4, 346
constructive criticism 53–5
controlling the person 69
conversational skills 73–5, 159, 163
conversation as a tool 318–35
conversations for 'landing' 318–20
conversations in groups 329–32
furnishings 328–9
rule play 335
solution-focused conversations 320–8
younger children and play skills 333–5
cooking 86–7, 135, 361
co-ordination 117, 139, 141
copying movements 136, 137
CPS *see* collaborative problem solving
craftsmanship
assessment 221, 222, 245, 249
professionalism 12–16, 18, 38, 47
toolbox 276
CRAP (Confirmations, Rewards, Affirmative, Punishments) 210–19
affirm and confirm (A/C) 219
attribution 216–17
overview 210–16
criticism 43–4, 45, 53–5
Curtis, M. 313
Cytowic, Richard E. 119, 120

DCD *see* developmental co-ordination disorder
deaths 75

Deci, Edward 216
De Clerq, Hilde 184–5, 246
delayed echolalia 153
delayed perception 122
demand avoidance 92
denying 157
Department for Education –
    National Strategies website
    63
depression 187, 193, 228, 270,
    357
depth perception 103
desensitization 122–4, 128
detail orientation 107
developmental co-ordination
    disorder (DCD) 129
developmental disorders 21, 84,
    102, 119, 176, 189
development perspective 28,
    129, 144–51, 259
diagnosis 82–3, 88, 187–9, 286,
    288, 289, 291
Diagnostic and Statistical Manual of
    Mental Disorders (DSM) 189
dialogues with parents checklist
    39
diet *see* food
direct echolalia 153
direction 104, 362
disabilities 77, 79, 81, 82–3, 91,
    95, 97, 365
disability awareness 284, 285
discussion groups 351
distance assessment 103
distorted perception 122
documentation 38, 55–7, 58,
    66, 246–7
Down's syndrome 84, 89, 145,
    365
drawn conversations 355–7
Dr Barman's toothbrushes 362
driving 130, 131, 134
drugs 203–4
DSM (Diagnostic and Statistical
    Manual of Mental Disorders)
    186, 189
Dunbar, Robin 164
Dunn Buron, Kari 313, 377
dysgraphia 105

earplugs 126
eating 199, 200, 201
echolalia 153–5, 155
education 344
Edmonds, G. 357
Education Scotland 375
Ekstam, Kjell 46
embarrassment 147, 206
emotional maturity 41–2, 44,
    50, 54, 203, 336–8
empathy 45–51, 64–5, 80–2,
    82–6, 148, 157

energy
    motor skills 131, 132, 142
    sensory processing issues 101
    sleep 177–8
    stress management 173–9
    stress, overview and time
       296–7
    teenage behaviour 29
    time perception 178–9
environment 127, 198, 237, 281
envisioning 159, 171, 254, 255
equality 85, 91, 96
Equality Act 288
escape routes 61, 314–15
ethics 45–51
evaluation 245, 246
excessive empathy 80–2
executive functions 180–3, 359
exercise 138, 140, 142
expert role 284, 291
eye contact 97–8, 108, 226,
    247, 329

face recognition 107–8
False Belief Task 189
families 38, 242, 283
fear 176, 252, 337
feedback 53, 62, 270, 341–3
feelings 42, 338, 339
fighter relationships 49
fighting 266–7
finances 362
'Find One Find All' key finder
    362
fine motor skills 129
five-point scale 313
'fixations' 124, 125, 151
flexibility in thinking 182, 232
Fombonne, Eric 187
food
    challenging behaviour 199,
       200, 201
    mental imagery 293–4
    mentalization 150
    sensory processing issues 115,
       115–16, 119
'foreground–background
    perception' 110, 116
fragmented perception 122
frameworks 20–3
free play 333
fridges 361
friendships 73–5
Frith, Uta 145
frustration 183, 194–6, 201,
    203–7, 209, 232, 267,
    270
Fuentes, Juan 203
furnishings 328–9

Garcia Winner, Michelle 353,
    377
gender 91–3, 164–5

generalized anxiety disorder 187
gestalt perception 107
Gillberg, Christopher 114, 187,
    188
global positioning system (GPS)
    362
goals 55, 56, 326
Goethe, Johann Wolfgang von
    250
Golding, Margaret M. 90, 91
GPS *see* global positioning
    system
Grandin, Temple 181, 184
Gray, Carol 300, 309
Greene, D. 216, 219
Greene, Ross W. 48–9, 96, 354
grocery shopping 359–60, 361
Groden, June 176
gross motor skills 129
group homes 13, 73
group work 278, 329–32
guilt 16, 45, 347

habituation 122–4
Hagberg, B. 187–8
Hägg, B. 292
headaches 104, 112
headphones 127
Healthtalkonline 375
hearing 111–15
hearing voices 114–15, 121
Hedevag, Kenth 310
hidden meanings 160, 161
high-functioning autism 25, 63,
    92, 167, 187, 339
Hilliard, L.J. 92
history taking 224–5
Hogberg, Siw 289
holding 75, 76, 267
home adaptations 282
home schooling 270
homework 107, 311
homosexuality 44
hormones 177
household chores 92, 131, 134,
    135, 174
Howlin, P. 338
humour 151, 241, 242, 327,
    328
hunger 118, 119, 150, 201,
    204, 278
hygiene
    assessment 223
    challenging behaviour 197
    collaborative problem solving
       354
    motor skills 140, 141
    professional role 27–8, 29
    social stories 305, 306
    solution-focused questions 63
    tactile perception 109
    tips, tricks and gadgets 362
hypotheses 238–9

ICD-10 189
iceberg metaphor 197, 198,
    218, 221, 251, 268
ideologies 20–3, 38, 83
ILSMH (International League of
    Societies for Persons with
    Mental Handicap) 73
imagination 125, 255, 256, 258,
    293, 298, 359
imitation 26, 206, 207
immune system 187
impulse control 145, 180, 182,
    208, 348
The Incredible 5-Point Scale
    313, 377
independence 73, 161, 162,
    163, 292, 293
Independent Parental Special
    Education Advice (IPSEA)
    375
influencing others 79–80
information as a tool 283–91
    accepting the diagnosis
        288–9
    the individual 284–7
    sharing experiences with
        others 289–91
    surroundings 283–4
informed choices 72, 78, 294–5
informed consent 204
Inge, W. R. 95
injuries 266–7, 271
instinct traps 42
interoceptive senses 118–19
Intervention Plans 225, 226,
    237, 239–46, 352, 353
involuntary offenders 233–6

joint sense 117–18
Jordan, Rita 90, 91, 377
Jørgensen, Margot 49, 50
journalism 287
justice 134, 151

Kadesjö, B. 187–8
key finders 362
Kinge, Emilie 31, 48
Kirkegaard, Søren 13
kitchen 363
knee-jerk reactions 42, 231–2
knowledge 35, 88, 250, 287
Kohn, Alfie 218
Kopp, Svenny 92

language comprehension
    adjustments 280–1
    assessment 232
    communication 154, 155,
        165–6
    sensory processing issues 102,
        103, 126–7
    thought–feeling–action 337
    verbal expression 152

laundry 27–8, 89–90, 89–90,
    92, 135
Lawson, Wendy 122
learning
    challenging behaviour 205–8,
        256, 257
    communication 161, 162
    learning opportunities 278,
        279
    reward systems 214–17
learning disabilities 18, 59, 73,
    75, 77, 79
learning to shop 359–60
legal rights 77, 288
leisure map 93, 94
Lenke, Björn 42
Lepper, M. 216, 219
Leslie, A.M. 145
Liben, L.S. 92
light sensitivity 97–8, 105–7,
    128, 228, 282
limit setting 75, 83, 93, 198,
    199, 257
literal language comprehension
    165–6
living space 268, 269, 270, 274
locks 78, 89, 349
Løgstrup, Knud Ejler 45, 66
Lovett, Herbert 21, 22–3, 84–5,
    253, 353, 365
lying 157, 158, 159

Måhlberg, Kerstin 39, 376
manipulation 260
martial arts 138–9
maturity 41, 44, 51, 73
meals 119, 293–4
meaningful activities 260, 269,
    273, 304, 350–1
measurement 228–9
mechanical restraint 75
medication 202, 203–4, 228
meetings 142, 329
melatonin 177
meltdowns
    common pitfalls for staff
        76, 90
    executive functions 183
    knee-jerk reactions 232
    motor skills 136
    professionalism 45
    self-knowledge and self-
        esteem 339, 350
    sensory processing issues 126
    setting limits 201
memory 181, 183–4, 215–16,
    295, 297, 359
mental imagery
    challenging behaviour 253,
        255–9
    choices and ability to form
        mental images 292–4
    cognition 180, 181, 184

good aids that no one uses 93
professional role 26, 28
solution-focused conversations
    326
visual perception 102
mentalization 145–6, 147–51,
    158, 163–4, 259–64
Mesibov, G.B. 197
meta-communication 159–60
methods and approaches 354–8
    CAT-kit 357
    cognitive behavioural therapy
        357–8
    motivational interviewing 358
    social stories and drawn
        conversations 355–7
    solution-focused methods 357
migraine 104, 228
minus scoring systems 217–19
mirror neurons 136
mistakes 45, 69, 73, 208–9, 295
mobile phones 361–2
mobile phones 296, 359, 361–2
moods 90, 252, 260
moral competence 45–51, 46
motivation
    affirming and confirming 219
    challenging behaviour 205,
        206
    communication 169, 328
    executive functions 182
    motor skills 131, 132, 133,
        134
    reward systems 213, 214,
        216, 218
motivational interviewing (MI)
    358
motor automatization 130–6, 141
motor skills 129–43
    balance 116
    challenging behaviour 197,
        253
    hygiene 28
    motor automatization 130–6
    other motor difficulties 136–7
    overview 129–30
    practical implications 137–43
muscle sense 117–18
music 113, 127, 362

nagging 69, 270, 310–12, 321
'Nanny-shows' 218
National Autistic Society (NAS)
    92, 242, 283, 374
negative feedback 270
negativism 327
nidotherapy 375–6
Nisbett, R. 216, 219
noise 111–15, 126
noise channel 265, 266
non-verbal communication 137
Normell, Margareta 41–2
Nursing Standard 374

objectives 55, 56–7
observation 229–30
'obsessions' 124, 125
obsessive compulsive disorder
    (OCD) 78, 187, 361
occupational therapists 32, 282,
    288, 363
OCD see obsessive compulsive
    disorder
OCD-UK 376
offence 202–3, 233–6
Office for Disability Issues 344
olfactory sense 115
open questions 331–2
overviews 223–4, 295–9, 300
overwhelming situations 75
Øyane, N. 177
Ozonoff, S. 122

pain perception 110, 123
PANDAS (Pediatric Autoimmune
    Neuropsychiatric
    Disorder Associated with
    Streptococcus infection)
    187
parental role 69–73
parents
    balance of power 344, 345
    information as a tool 283
    professionalism 38, 39
    professional role 22, 30
Pascal, Blaise 326
pathological demand avoidance
    (PDA) 92
Pavonen, E.J. 178
PDA see pathological demand
    avoidance
penalty marking 217–19
'perception of rear' 118
perfectionism 306
perseverance 27
personal instinct traps 42
personal values 44
perspective taking 47, 48, 57,
    58, 140
pervasive developmental disorder
    (PDD) 126, 187–8
pervasive developmental disorder
    not otherwise specified
    (PDD-NOS) 123, 178,
    186, 188
Pharmautism 203
phobias 123, 176, 357
physical education (PE) 103,
    118, 126, 137–41, 281
physical restraint 75
pitfalls for staff see common
    pitfalls for staff
play 128, 139, 333–5
positive feedback
    affirming and confirming 219
    challenging behaviour 273
    Intervention Plans 240, 241

professionalism 53, 62
    self-knowledge and self-
        esteem 341–3
    solution-focused conversations
        327
    stress management 177
Post-it notes 311
posture 121
Powell, S. 90
powerlessness 83–4, 199, 253,
    343, 345–7, 350, 351–3
power relations 68, 73, 83,
    85–6, 199, 343–51
praise 53, 219, 341, 342
prioritizing 306, 307
problem-focused work 64
process of change see change
    process
professionalism 19–98
    assessments and analyses 220,
        221
    common pitfalls for staff 67,
        68, 70, 76, 84, 88
    definitions 31–6
    framework and ideologies
        20–3
    overview 13, 15–17
    stairs of professionalism 36
    what professionalism could
        mean 31–66
        ambition levels 36–7
        awareness, development
            and change 37–44
        constructive criticism 53–5
        documentation of
            approaches and tools
            55–7
        empathy, ethics and moral
            competence 45–51
        making it right when
            doing wrong 44–5
        overview 65–6
        practice reflection 52
        prerequisites for
            professionalism 35
        professionalism in
            exchanges with
            clients 57–65
        questioning respectfully
            52–3
        some ideas 52–7
    prohibitions 76–8
    proprioception (muscle and joint
        sense) 117–18
    prosopagnosia 107–8
    psychiatric care 202, 269, 271,
        351
    psychoanalysis 263
    psychodynamically orientated
        services 24
    psychologists 32, 34, 67, 68,
        263
    psychosocial services 24–30

psychotic disorders 162, 187
psychotropic drugs 204
puberty 29
public behaviour 313
public transport 290, 362
punishments 76, 194, 198,
    217–19, 257, 261, 262
purpose 214, 215, 304, 354

quality of life 96–8, 273
questioning respectfully 52–3
questionnaires 37, 195, 225–7,
    366–8

'rear' perception 118
reason 46
reducing activities and space
    268, 269, 270
reflection 41, 52, 65
regression 145, 181
relationships 70–2, 303–6
relaxation 125, 176
repetition 215–16
repetitive behaviour 124, 125,
    151, 311
repetitive communication 170–2
responsibility 41, 45, 46, 88
restorative communication 170
restraint 75–6, 271
Rett syndrome 198
reward systems 76, 210–19,
    326, 354, 357
Rich Harris, J. 188
rights 73, 77, 288
rituals 158, 172
Rogers, S.J. 122
role play 38, 58, 333
roles 69–73
routines 42, 43, 220, 264
Rubio, Ron 138, 139
rule play 335
rules 76, 139, 316
Rutherford, M.D. 108

Sally and Anne test 145
Sayer, S. 77
scaling 321–5
scapegoating 165
schedules 93–4, 93–4, 213,
    264, 299, 300, 359
schizophrenia 63, 162, 188
schools
    challenging behaviour 270
    common pitfalls for staff 75,
        94, 96
    escape routes 314, 315
    Intervention Plans 243–4
    motor skills 133, 143
    professionalism 63
Schopler, E. 197
Schreiner, Peter 49, 50
scoring systems 217–19
The Scottish Government 375

second-order theory of mind
206, 207
self-confidence 97, 118, 253
self-esteem 336–53
balance of power 343–51
challenging behaviour 193,
253–4, 274
common pitfalls for staff
72, 97
communication skills and
powerlessness 351–3
definition 336
getting your reality confirmed
340–1
motor skills 142
overview 336–7
positive feedback 341–3
thought–feeling–action
337–40
self-injurious behaviour 266–7,
271–2
self-knowledge 336–53
balance of power 343–51
communication skills and
powerlessness 351–3
definition 336
getting your reality confirmed
340–1
overview 336–7
positive feedback 341–3
thought–feeling–action
337–40
sense of coherence (SOC) 169
sense of direction 104, 362
sensory integration problems
122, 123–4
sensory processing issues
100–28
adjustments 282
balance 116–17
different is not always a
problem 124–5
energy and stress 174
habituation 122–4
how do we know, what do we
do? 126–8
interoceptive senses 118–19
introduction to the tools
277–8
olfactory sense 115
overview 100–2
proprioception 117–18
questionnaires 367–8
sensory integration problems
122
synaesthesia 119–21
tactile perception 109–11
taste 115–16
visual perception 102–8
sensory training 128
sex 26, 44, 71, 72, 91, 142–3,
259, 295

SFBT see Solution-Focused Brief
Therapy
shape-auditory synaesthesia 120
Sharry, John 63, 326, 328
Shea, V. 197
Shopler, Eric 299
shopping 359–60, 361
showering 27, 28, 109, 141,
223, 282, 362
sitting 130, 131, 132, 133, 134
Sjöblom, Maud 39, 376
Skau, Greta Marie 17, 39, 40,
57–8, 68, 85, 87–8,
233–4
sleep
assessment 228
energy and stress 175, 177–8
legal rights 77–8
motor skills 142
sensory processing issues 105,
106, 112
sharing experiences with
others 290
'sliders' 132, 133, 330
sloth 247–8
smart phones 361–2
Social Care Institute for
Excellence 374
social embarrassment 206, 207
social failures 156, 157
social interaction 137, 139, 156,
158, 159, 171, 174, 353
socially appropriate behaviour in
anger 205, 207, 208
social motivation 205, 214
social services 58, 91
social skills 153, 154
social stories
challenging behaviour 205,
259
play skills 334
self-knowledge and self-
esteem 339, 351, 352
truths, lies and subtext 162
visual aids 300–10, 355–7
social support 34, 67
Social Thinking 353, 377
Socratic conversation model
331–2
SOC (sense of coherence) 169
Söderlund, Göran 113
'soft' values 72, 73
Solution-Focused Brief Therapy
(SFBT) 63
solution-focused conversations
59–62, 320–8
solution-focused techniques 37,
53, 59–65, 219, 302
soundproofing 128, 282
sound sensitivity 100, 111–15,
120, 123, 128
spatial relationships 103, 104–5,
136

special interests 124, 259
speech motor functions 135
speed assessment 103
splitting 24
sports 138, 139
staff
assessment 230–1, 233–6
knee-jerk reactions 231–2
professionalism 13, 14, 17,
37–44
Stälhardske, M. 292
Stallard, Paul 338, 377
steering the will of others 79–80
Sterling, M. 100
stochastic noise 113
story telling 159
stress
challenging behaviour 203,
204, 209
cognition 181, 183
communication 153, 155,
172
energy 173–9, 176–7
penalty marking 217
powerlessness 353
sensory processing issues 125,
126, 127
time perception 178–9
toolbox 277–8, 282
visual aids 292, 293, 294,
295–9
structure 43, 220, 223
Studio III™ 377
subtext 160, 161, 163, 168
supervision 25, 59–62
surroundings 283–4
surveys 195, 225–7
swimming 109, 139
synaesthesia 115, 119–21

Table Topics 330
tactile-auditory synaesthesia 120
tactile perception 109–11, 282
Taekwondo 138
tagging places 359, 363
Tai Chi 138, 139
Talk About Autism 375
task boxes 299, 300
taste 115–16, 121
TEACCH 40, 197, 295,
299–300
teachers 17, 33, 40–1, 50–1,
57, 95
team sports 139, 141
teenage behaviour 29, 30, 87,
89, 93, 288, 289, 344,
345
teeth 79, 131, 362
telephones 87, 200, 296, 353,
361–2
temper 149, 201
temperature perception 110–11,
315–17

theory of mind
    challenging behaviour 193,
        206, 207, 259–64
    communication 155, 164
    development perspective
        145–6, 148
    diagnostic criteria 189
    energy and stress 175, 176–7
thermometers 315–17
thirst 118
thought–feeling–action 337–40
thought-voice 121
threatening behaviour 58, 193,
    200, 243, 264–6
thresholds 318–20
tics 113, 187, 228
time model 312
time perception 41, 77, 178–9,
    240, 290, 292, 295–9,
    361–3
Time Timer 240
Tipper, Michael 215, 216
tips, tricks and gadgets 359–63
    alarm clocks 362
    belt bag 361
    brushing teeth and hygiene
        362
    key finders 362
    learning to shop 359–60
    smart phones and apps 361–2
    structure in the fridge 361
toileting 78, 150, 199–200,
    262–4
toolbox 275–363
    adjustments 280–2
    assessments and analyses 220
    conversation as a tool 318–35
    information as a tool 283–91
    introduction to the tools 276–9
    methods and approaches
        354–8
    reward systems 214
    self-knowledge and self-
        esteem 336–53
    tips, tricks and gadgets
        359–63
    visual aids 292–317
touch 109–11
Tourettes Action 376
Tourette's syndrome 113, 187,
    261
transference 24
transitions 299, 318–20
triad of impairments 88, 144,
    186, 189
Triple Stories software 310,
    338, 377
trust 45, 50, 52, 85, 223, 343
truth telling 157, 194–7, 341
turn-taking 139, 140, 318, 329,
    331, 333
Twain, Mark 25
Tyrer, Peter 375

United Response 77

values 44, 46
van Manen, Max 40–1, 50,
    51, 57
verbal expression 152, 154, 226
verbiage 264–6
vibration 113, 247
violent behaviour 90, 202,
    266–7, 269–70, 271
vision 55, 56
Visser, Coert 376
visual aids 292–317
    choices and ability to form
        mental images 292–4
    clothes-by-temperature-
        thermometer 315–17
    communication 154–5,
        162–3
    escape routes 314–15
    executive functions 183
    five-point scale 313
    good aids that no one uses 93
    informed choices 294–5
    nag-free information 310–12
    social stories and comic strip
        conversations 300–10
    stress, overview and time
        295–9
    TEACCH 299–300
    time model 312
visual perception 102–8
    detail orientation 107
    light sensitivity 105–7
    prosopagnosia 107–8
    sense of direction 104
    spatial relationships 104–5
Vitamin D 106, 228
vocal tics 113
voice-hearing 114–15, 121
voice notes 261–2
voice recognition 108
vomiting 115
voting rights 77

walking 130, 131, 138, 162,
    198
Waltz, Mitzi 14–15
washing 27–8, 78, 134
Waters, Geraldine 123, 124
Watling, Renee 123, 124
web resources 374
weighted blankets 267
Wennberg, I. 99
whiplash 100
white noise 113
Wilkner, Pamela 289
will 46
Wiltshire, Steven 107
Winterbourne View scandal 68
withdrawal of benefits 217, 261,
    262, 346

working memory 181, 183–4,
    359
World Health Organization 189
written information 138, 226,
    308, 311, 359

younger children 333–5